Since the day of Walter the Penniless
no such gathering was ever seen. . . .
Nothing so picturesque, few things so
terrible have happened in our time.

Spectator (London), April 28, 1894

I think this movement is the most
dangerous this country has seen since
the Civil War. . . . Intimidation of
Congress by the presence of a body of
armed men is rebellion pure and simple,
and should be stamped out just as the
great Rebellion was in 1861.

Thomas Byrnes (superintendent of
New York City police) in the *North
American Review* 451 (June 1894)

The Coxey movement died out as
rapidly as it started and within the year
it is already a half forgotten episode.
It is almost impossible to realize now
the intensity of feeling it evoked,
or the grave apprehensions that
permeated the entire country as to the
extent it would reach and what it
portended. It had no precedent in this
country and it is not probable its like
will ever be seen again. It was as unique
in its character as a stray comet that
flashes athwart the sky and is gone—
unheralded, incomprehensible and
evanescent.

from the *Second Annual Report of
the Bureau of Agriculture, Labor and
Industry of Montana, 1894* (Helena:
State Publishing Company, 1894)

CARLOS A. SCHWANTES

COXEY'S ARMY

An American Odyssey

University of Idaho Press

Moscow, Idaho

1994

Published in the
United States of America

98 97 96 95 94   1 2 3 4 5

LIBRARY OF CONGRESS CATALOGING
IN PUBLICATION DATA

Schwantes, Carlos A., 1945-

Coxey's army: an American odyssey /
Carlos A. Schwantes.
    p.   cm.
Originally published: Lincoln :
University of Nebraska Press, 1985.
Includes bibliographical references
and index.

ISBN 0-89301-174-6
1. Working class —United States —
History. 2. Unemployed —United
States —History. 3. Coxey, Jacob
Sechler, 1854-1951.   I. Title.
HD8072.S354. 1994
331.13'7973—DC20   94-29020

COVER ILLUSTRATION: Library of
    Congress
COVER DESIGN: Joanne Poon

For My Sons, Benjamin and Matthew

CONTENTS

List of Illustrations, viii

Preface, ix

Prologue: America's First National Crusade against Unemployment, 1

1 Chicago and the Birth of the Commonweal, 23

2 Wheels in My Head: The Making of a Reform Crusade, 34

3 Marching with Coxey's Army, 49

4 Big Savage: One More Mountain to Climb, 60

5 Maryland, My Maryland, 71

6 Fry's Californians: Taming the Octopus, 83

7 San Francisco Overland, 98

8 Kelley's Dilemma: The Rail Barons and Women in the Ranks, 113

9 Jack London and the Road East, 133

10 Hogan's Wild West Show, 149

11 May Day, 166

12 Coxeyism East and West, 186

13 Coxey's Western Boatmen, 209

14 Soldiers of Misfortune, 222

15 The Rivals; Or, Gambling on Jumbo, 231

16 The Disinherited, 246

17 Coxeyism in Perspective, 261

Notes, 281

Index, 311

ILLUSTRATIONS

xiv Jacob Sechler Coxey

5 Carl Browne

8 Map: Routes of the Armies
of the Commonweal

38 An example of Carl
Browne's "artwork"

54 Coxey's army—
early days on the road

76 Carl Browne with Coxey's
army on the Chesapeake
and Ohio Canal

88 Lewis C. Fry

107 Charles T. Kelley

117 Kelley's arrival at the
transfer, Council Bluffs,
Iowa

126 Kelley's "angels"—Miss
Hooten and Miss Harper

135 Jack London in Kelley's
army encampment

170 Carl Browne with Coxey's
army near Washington, D.C.

171 "Weary tramps"—
Coxey's army in camp

192 Kelley's "navy" on
the Des Moines River at
Ottumwa, Iowa

233 Jumbo Cantwell

272 "We demand nothing
but Justice"—Kelley's
army in Iowa

This is the story of pilgrims' protest. In the depression year of 1894 there arose suddenly out of the ranks of America's unemployed a grass-roots reform movement known popularly as Coxey's army. For six or seven weeks it captured the attention of the nation. Other protesters had marched on local institutions of government—as in Bacon's Rebellion in Virginia (1676) and Shays's Rebellion in Massachusetts (1786–87)—but never on the nation's capital, unless Robert E. Lee's Army of Northern Virginia so qualified. Indeed, in the minds of many observers, the Coxey movement did reawaken unpleasant memories of Civil War strife, for not since the days of Lincoln had security about the White House and on Capitol Hill been so strict.

Long before Coxey's legions reached Pennsylvania Avenue, the press had turned their odyssey into the biggest story since the Civil War, or so some journalists immodestly claimed. In the ability of the press to sustain widespread public interest in the day-to-day doings of the unemployed, in its creation of personae like the "Great Unknown," and in its broad hints of impending violence (not to mention titillating stories of love and sex), it seemed to be practicing for the journalistic frenzy that four years later riveted the nation's attention on alleged Spanish atrocities in Cuba and helped precipitate a war. It was not yet dyed-in-the-wool yellow journalism, but coverage of the Coxey movement occasionally showed a yellowish tinge.

The Coxey movement, then, is a chapter in this history of journalism. It is also a chapter in the history of American reform, particularly the history of the Populist revolt and of the formative years of organized labor. It is a reminder, too, that the modern welfare state had roots in popular protests. In the West, where most of the several thousand marchers originated, Coxey's army was seen as confirmation of an observation made a few months earlier by history professor Frederick Jackson Turner that the frontier and the personal opportunity it connoted were now past.

Even when the Coxey movement ended, its memory remained part of the growing-up experience of boys and girls for the next generation or two: in countless homes, children grimy from play were admonished by their parents to clean up or they'd look like something from Coxey's army. On occasion boys and girls reenacted a version of cops and robbers in which youthful "Coxeyites" stole wagons and were pursued by "federal marshals." Without realizing it, perhaps, both parents and children were perpetrating a widespread but erroneous notion that Coxey's army was merely an agglomeration of dirty, thieving tramps. Today, except for a sentence or two in introductory college history texts, the Coxey crusade has faded from public consciousness, although its call for public-works jobs anticipated a crucial element of the New Deal programs of the 1930s and was repeated by both Democrats and Republicans in response to the hard times of the early 1980s.

The historian could examine this movement from any of several perspectives. I've elected to follow a narrative style of presentation, if only to be true to the sense of foreboding that the Coxey legions created in the nation. But I have also organized each chapter to focus on a particular aspect of America's first national crusade against unemployment—such as how the jobless survived before the creation of the modern welfare state or how the common folk of the Gilded Age perceived railroad power and that of corporations in general. The march itself serves as a dramatic vehicle by which to conduct readers on a journey through the mainstream of American life in the 1890s, as well as into some of its bizarre and now-forgotten byways.

This book, like all books, represents something of a personal odyssey. Often during the course of research and writing, my thoughts turned to that day in the summer of 1964 when my first paying job ended unexpectedly in a mass layoff. I was one of the fortunate ones,

I suppose: while my earnings were to have paid college tuition that fall, many of my fellow warehousemen had families to feed, bills to pay, and no alternative careers. I'll never forget the look of concern on their faces. Things could have been worse, of course, had not a modest social safety net cushioned their rapid descent into the ranks of the unemployed. I was bitter, nonetheless, at having experienced a form of economic callousness that I had never before encountered in my middle-class world; I learned firsthand that a job, no matter how menial, entailed something more than money. The loss of that job represented a form of humiliation that I did not want to repeat—or to forget—or to have my children experience.

Although this book centers on an event that occurred long before I was born, I still feel a certain kinship with the Coxeyites that transcends the seventy-year gap between 1894 and 1964. And in recalling their journey, I hope to share with my children a bit of the practical education in economics that for me began two decades ago in a warehouse in Indianapolis. For this reason I dedicate the book to Benjamin and Matthew.

During my research I had the opportunity to visit many parts of the United States and to use the resources of several repositories of history. My thanks go to the staffs of the Colorado Historical Society, Denver Public Library, Huntington Library, Idaho Historical Society, Iowa State Historical Department, Indiana State Library, Indianapolis Public Library, Library of Congress, Nebraska State Historical Society, Ohio Historical Society, Oregon Historical Society, Washington State Library, and the libraries of Whitman College and the Universities of California–Berkeley, Nebraska–Lincoln, Oregon, Idaho, and Washington.

Although I was able to travel to those places in person, I visited many others only through letters of inquiry and the medium of interlibrary loan. I am grateful for their assistance, too. Through countless interlibrary loans, Lee Johnston of the Walla Walla College Library helped me obtain the newspapers that form the backbone of this study. Paying the cost of renting or photocopying such materials was the Walla Walla College Faculty Grants Committee.

The National Endowment for the Humanities made it possible for me to spend a year in Seattle at the University of Washington. History department chairman Wilton B. Fowler kindly extended to me the privileges of a visiting scholar, and Richard C. Berner, head of the university's archives, provided a secluded yet congenial place to work in the Suzzallo Library. While at the University of Washington I was fortunate to be able to draw on the expertise of a number of fine scholars: Alfred Runte, William J. Rorabaugh, Thomas Pressly, Vernon Carstensen, and Robert E. Burke of the Department of History, and Joseph Butwin of the Department of English.

To Bob Burke I owe a special debt. He read and commented on the rough draft of each chapter, offering the insights of a master of American history and of California and the West in particular. As a frequent lunchtime companion, he served as a sounding board for my ideas and helped me untangle numerous problems of organization. He provided needed words of encouragement and on occasion a much-appreciated ticket to the opera or symphony; he even re-awakened in me a long-dormant interest in stamp collecting. That contemplative hobby, along with an understanding wife, two young sons who loved to explore the many attractions of the Seattle area, and friends at the Green Lake Church, helped a workaholic to keep his research and writing in proper perspective.

For a variety of reasons I'm also beholden to Jonathan Dembo and Howard Droker, two free-lance historians living in Seattle; W. Thomas White of the James Jerome Hill Reference Library in St. Paul; Carol Zabilski of the *Pacific Northwest Quarterly*; and Professors Richard Maxwell Brown of the University of Oregon, Sidney Fine of the University of Michigan, and Robert A. Henderson, former chairman of the Department of History at Walla Walla College.

The editors of the *Annals of Iowa*, *Arizona and the West*, *Idaho Yesterdays*, and *Pacific Northwest Quarterly* kindly gave me permission to use portions of my previously published articles.

Finally, I alone am responsible for any errors that appear on these pages.

COXEY'S ARMY

Washington might defend
herself against Coxey's army
by sending the United States
Senate out to meet it. Whichever side got licked the country
would be the gainer.

Louisville Courier-Journal,
March 24, 1894

America's First National Crusade against Unemployment

By noon an estimated thirty thousand men, women, and children are waiting elbow to elbow under the canvas awnings and shade trees along both sides of Pennsylvania Avenue. They nearly cover parts of Capitol Hill. Normally only the inauguration of a president attracts so many onlookers, but this is no inauguration: Grover Cleveland occupies the White House, his term not yet half completed. This Tuesday—May 1, 1894—belongs to Jacob Sechler Coxey and his army, a protest as unprecedented in the history of the United States as the massive unemployment that gives it life and purpose.[1]

Coxey's name is on everyone's lips, first as a murmur and then as a shout as his carriage pulls into view. Behind him march the four hundred tatterdemalion veterans of the Commonweal of Christ, the advance guard of America's first national crusade against unemployment, a "petition in boots" that hopes to pressure Congress into financing a program of public works to employ the jobless until the economy regains its health.

Some call Coxey a revolutionary; others say he is a crank. Slight of build, clean-shaven except for a light brown mustache, wearing wire-rimmed glasses and a dark gray business suit, he looks more like a harmless middle-aged professor than the wild man that newspaper cartoonists typically draw to represent cranks. Occasionally he rises and bows to the crowd. His flashing blue eyes betray a sense of humor.

For the past six weeks Americans have read numerous accounts about Coxey, his army of unemployed, and the imitators he has inspired. The daily press often carries the story on page one, and rare is the four-page country weekly that does not print at least some news of the Commonweal. In fact, since the end of the Civil War in 1865 perhaps only the disputed election of 1876 has generated more intense newspaper coverage. Readers have pondered, laughed at, or worried about the Coxey movement a great deal. Some regard it as a national joke, only slightly less humorous than Congress and certainly less expensive. They wonder whether it draws its inspiration from Phineas T. Barnum or from the Communards who gained control of Paris in 1871. Who are the marchers? Who is Coxey? And what does it all mean?

In fact, much about the Coxey movement defies conventional logic; and that, together with the hard times that began in mid-1893, helps to account for the seemingly insatiable popular interest in its progress. Coxey himself is a wealthy man, owner of a sandstone quarry in Ohio along with three ranches and several dozen blooded race horses. Most of the horses in the procession today are his. For Acolyte, a stallion, he reportedly paid $40,000, enough money in the 1890s to hire eighty laborers for a year. Coxey is reputed to be worth a quarter of a million dollars. In Gilded Age America people of his wealth usually do not associate with unemployed workmen.

When in late March the thinly clad Commonwealers tramped out of Coxey's hometown of Massillon, Ohio (near Cleveland), in a snowstorm, it seemed impossible that they would survive to parade through the streets of Washington. Could they live off the land for more than four hundred miles? Not since William Tecumseh Sherman and his Union soldiers marched three hundred miles across Georgia thirty years before had anything like it been attempted. But when marchers crossed the Appalachian Mountains and descended into the valley of the Potomac, disbelief and derision turned to amazement and alarm. No one knew how large or dangerous the Commonweal might become by the time it reached Capitol Hill.

Turning from Fourteenth Street onto Pennsylvania Avenue, marchers glimpse the White House off to their right. Except for the extra guards, life there appears normal. A routine cabinet meeting is reportedly in progress. Outwardly the president is calm, stolid as the Rock of Gibraltar, to which the heavy-set Grover Cleveland bears a slight resemblance. But those around him are clearly nervous. They scan the minute-by-minute dispatches forwarded by special agents shadowing the procession. Guarding the president is the largest detail of secret service agents, District of Columbia police, and watchdogs assembled since Civil War days. Special telephone lines have been run to call in police reserves if necessary. Throughout the city two hundred extra policemen are on duty, and detectives from several large cities of the Northeast quietly mingle with spectators.

Many of the president's men fear that Coxey's army will attract violent individuals, possibly not as marchers but certainly as sympathizers. Within living memory, men of this description have assassinated two presidents; and just six months ago another gunned down the popular mayor of Chicago. During the winter a "Jack the Ripper" had slipped into the White House, slashed the curtains in the Green Room, and stabbed his knife through several elegant sofas and chairs. All this, combined with the many threatening letters the president has received of late, lies behind the effort to "crank-proof" the White House. "The air seems to breed cranks and the demon of destruction is abroad in the land," frets the *Chicago Herald*.[2]

Among the many reporters accompanying the marchers is young Ray Stannard Baker of the *Chicago Record*. This is his first big assignment. He arrived in Massillon on March 15, accompanied the Commonweal from Ohio to Washington, and wrote enough copy about it to make a medium-sized book. Before the aspiring journalist dropped out of the University of Michigan Law School, he had met Cleveland during a trip through Ann Arbor in 1892. To Baker the president was a "great slow-moving hulk of a man, ponderous in what he said, but with something about him, some inherent power, that impressed me more profoundly than any other speaker I had ever heard up to that time."[3]

As the Commonwealers move slowly down Pennsylvania Avenue, spectators who have waited peaceably for hours rush out to greet them. Some seem so determined to climb into the carriage with their hero that journalists form a cordon of special guards to keep off intruders. Occasionally the sympathizers nearly block the broad thoroughfare, until a vanguard of twenty-five mounted policemen pushes them aside.

The procession takes half an hour to pass. At its head and acting as an escort are members of the Public Comfort Committee of Washington, D.C.—local sympathizers, the most prominent of whom is the petite suffragist Annie Diggs, who rides in a carriage with her husband and two small daughters. Just yesterday Diggs and many others tried to persuade the leaders to call off the march "to prevent possible bloodshed and save Mr. Coxey's life." District police have forbidden Coxey to speak from the Capitol steps as he promises to do. And it is an open secret that backing the police is the muscle of the United States military, held in readiness out of sight. The test of wills will climax in a few minutes, and no one can predict the result.

Behind the Diggs carriage comes the "Goddess of Peace," Mamie Coxey, a willowy seventeen-year-old girl of such striking beauty that a spontaneous cheer greets her unexpected appearance. She rides a white Arabian, one of her father's. On her head is a red, white, and blue liberty cap to which are attached silver letters spelling "peace." From beneath the cap, iridescent auburn hair cascades onto her shoulders and pure white riding habit. With a small parasol she shields her delicate face, which flushes with excitement when the crowd cheers her by name. Her slender fingers, clad in white kid gloves, toy nervously with the reins.

Riding behind the goddess on the magnificent gray Percheron stallion named Courier comes a man who looks much like Buffalo Bill. He wears a large white sombrero tilted rakishly over his right eye and has hair that reaches to his shoulders. Buttons fashioned from silver dollars decorate his fringed buckskin jacket. This is Carl Browne, the Californian who is chief marshal of the Commonweal. Though Coxey gave his name to the movement and uses it to publicize his program of building roads to help the jobless, Browne conceived the march. Likewise, the Goddess of Peace and the marchers' many bizarre banners and slogans are products of his inspiration. Coxey had known nothing about his daughter's being in the parade until she surprised him in Washington yesterday. Some fear that the mysterious Californian has cast a hypnotic spell over Coxey, who boarded him at his Massillon home last winter.

Browne is a natural showman, and this is his greatest performance.

Carl Browne. From Henry Vincent, *The Story of the Commonweal* (Chicago, 1894).

But today his mind is only partly on the crowd and his men. His thoughts keep coming back to the vision of loveliness just ahead. He will later write, "I thought she was the most beautiful (and do so now) sight I ever beheld." Though Mamie Coxey is thirty years his junior, Browne is in love with her. He dares not tell a soul, especially her protective father, at least not yet.[4]

To all appearances Browne is a vain, insensitive man. Whether peddling his ideas on religion and various political nostrums or painting the outlandish panoramas he calls art, he is a caricature of the Gilded Age promoter, a figure who might have sprung from the imagination of Mark Twain. "There's millions in it," says a Twain character; there's publicity in it, adds Browne. But Browne has an introspective side that few know. The death of his wife three years earlier shattered him emotionally and helped kindle his fanatical devotion to the idea of reincarnation. Concealed under his bandanna he wears a necklace of amber beads, a final gift from his wife.

Following Browne is another member of the Coxey family, the leader's eighteen-year-old son, Jesse. Riding a handsome stallion, he wears a coat of Union blue and pants of Confederate gray, symbolizing the joining of North and South in the Commonweal.

Two black trotters pull the carriage bearing Coxey, his wife, and their two-month-old son, Legal Tender—"Leeg" for short. Father chose the odd name, a reflection of his obsession with monetary reform. When the crowd cheers the mother, she blushes demurely and occasionally holds up her peacefully sleeping infant. The second Mrs. Coxey is an attractive woman, hazel-eyed, her black hair worn in a braid; today she wears a tailor-made tan gown. "Coxey! Coxey!" The roar continues for the length of Pennsylvania Avenue.

Next come the troops, mostly veterans of the long journey from Massillon. They march along smartly in uniforms that defy description: dilapidated shoes yellow with the dust of country roads, threadbare shirts and jackets, and battered but functional hats that shield their faces from the noonday sun. In place of a sword each man carries a long oaken stave of peace bearing a white flag with the slogan "Peace on earth, good will toward men, but death to interest on bonds."

Road-weary wagons decorated with gaudy specimens of Browne's artwork creak along at intervals between the various groups of men. A Commonweal band of six pieces, mostly bass drums and cymbals, pounds out a rendition of "Marching through Georgia." Banners set forth words of inspiration that flow from the mind of Marshal Browne. One reads: "Co-operation, the cerebellum of the Commonweal," and another, "The medulla oblongata and all other parts of the reincarnated Christ in the whole people." The juxtaposition of mysticism with the call for jobs makes sense to Browne and certainly helps to attract the eye of the press, but it also brings forth guffaws and derisive words from the skeptics who refuse to accept the Commonweal as a legitimate reform movement.

The skirl of a bagpipe heralds the passing of a small Philadelphia contingent headed by Christopher Columbus Jones, a wizened pump-maker who sports a suit of shiny broadcloth and an oversized stove-pipe hat to mock the money barons. The old man rides at the head of his troops in a hansom cab. The Philadelphians bring their own Goddess of Peace, Virginia La Valette, a plump, red-cheeked maiden of eighteen who is draped in an American flag.

As the Coxey carriage passes the National Hotel, it halts briefly while Mrs. Coxey hands her sleeping infant to a nursemaid. If trouble erupts on Capitol Hill, the mother wants to be prepared.

The Senate convenes at noon and remains in session for twelve minutes; members adjourn as custom dictates when they receive news of the unexpected death of a colleague, Francis Stockbridge of Michigan. Members of the House have spent the morning discussing bills pertaining to the protection of birds and game in Yellowstone Park and the accounting offices of the Treasury Department. Congressmen want to remain in session until after the Commonweal arrives to avoid creating the impression that they adjourned early out of fear. Nonetheless, extra guards are on duty in the building, and heavy pine gates, such as are used to control inauguration crowds, have been erected on each side of the main rotunda. Sergeant-at-Arms Snow of the House has taken special precautions to protect the cash locker that contains the pay of congressmen: last night guards slept beside the huge safe.

At the other end of Pennsylvania Avenue more dispatches reach the White House: "House reports there is large crowd all about the Capitol but everything quiet." "Coxey army just reached Peace Monument and going up hill to B Street and Delaware." After weeks of protest and posturing, Coxey's army halts in the shadow of the Capitol. Lawmen nearly surround the building, and more are hidden inside. If he still expects to deliver his speech from the Capitol steps, Coxey must somehow push through the sea of blue-jacketed officers.

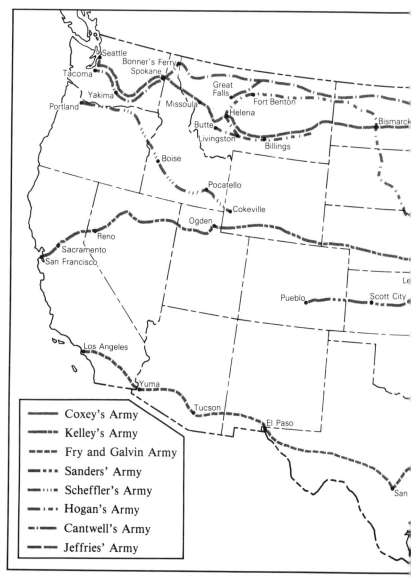

Map: Routes of the armies of the Commonweal

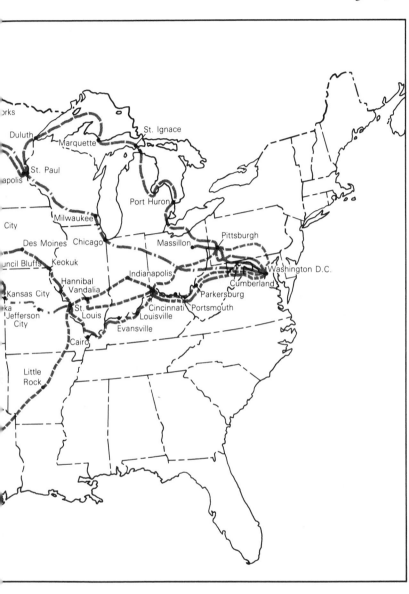

orks

Duluth

Marquette

St. Ignace

St. Paul

apolis

Port Huron

City

Milwaukee

Des Moines Chicago

Massillon

Pittsburgh

uncil Bluffs Keokuk

Indianapolis

Washington D.C.

Hannibal

Cumberland

Kansas City Vandalia

Parkersburg

ka

St.

Cincinnati Portsmouth

Jefferson Louis

Louisville

City

Evansville

Cairo

Little
Rock

But will he? Will club-wielding policemen beat back the Ohioan and his followers in an effort to discourage others still on the road? The nation holds its breath and waits.[5]

An important question that no one could answer that May Day was how many troops Coxey actually commanded. Not even Coxey knew, for the crusade had produced such a sudden and spontaneous outpouring of support that he had no way to keep track of all the local divisions and regiments that claimed to be part of his grand army. One newspaper counted thirteen contingents numbering more than five thousand troops still on the road, and that guess was probably as good as any. Of equal worry to opponents of the movement were the unknown thousands who joined Coxey in spirit, who fed and sheltered the men along the way, who turned out with brass bands and banners to cheer them on or to intimidate federal marshals and other lawmen attempting to halt their progress. Especially for the numerous marchers from the Far West, the support of sympathizers was crucial. Too poor to charter passenger coaches to take them to Capitol Hill, some three thousand miles distant, crusaders stole rides east on railway cars and walked only when ditched by unsympathetic lawmen. Occasionally they stole the trains themselves. Their struggles across the high mountain passes and deserts of the West made Coxey's journey from Massillon seem almost like a Sunday School outing by comparison.[6]

This was a war—a curious one to be sure, but a war nonetheless. Newspapermen who covered the protest called themselves "war correspondents" and addressed Coxey as "General," although he objected to the military title. Federal authorities dispatched U.S. Army troops on several occasions and confined captured Coxeyites in hastily constructed prisoner-of-war camps. The battle line ran nowhere in particular, sometimes through the rolling hills of western Pennsylvania and sometimes through the plains of Kansas.

For a few days the battle line followed the crest of the Cascade Mountains in remote Washington, a state that contributed more recruits per capita than any other, and federal authorities wanted to keep them there. At the two-mile-long Stampede Pass tunnel, where driving winter winds piled the snow nearly thirty feet high, marchers found federal marshals blocking the west portal. Lawmen gave the pilgrims the cruel choice of scaling the pass high above the railway line or returning home. Though ill-fed, lightly clad, and without snowshoes, most defied the odds and struggled over, courting pneumonia all the way. Driving them on was a passionate desire to join the great protest on Capitol Hill. Ahead lay an uncertain future, but one of hope; behind lay the assured misery of joblessness and hand-to-mouth existence. Veterans in other Coxey regiments were attracted to the movement by similar circumstances, and on the road to Capitol Hill they would battle obstacles no less formidable than the white hell of Stampede Pass.[7]

At times the Coxey protest was so varied and complex that it resembled a twenty-ring circus with half a dozen side shows. In addition to Coxey's band, which captured the most national and international attention, large armies converged on the nation's capital from the major cities of the West—Los Angeles, San Francisco, Portland, Tacoma, Seattle, Salt Lake City, and Denver—and not just one contingent from each city but two or three from Los Angeles and Denver. Armies formed in Houston, Saint Louis, Chicago, Boston, Omaha, Lincoln, and dozens of smaller places like Reno, Butte, Fargo, and Walla Walla.

A Polish Coxey's army organized in Chicago and marched through America's industrial heartland.[8] Two contingents were led by women. Another was headed by a lawyer, Edward J. Jeffries, who later became a judge in Detroit, where his son served as mayor.

If every news item, government document, and photograph relating to the Coxey movement at both the local and national levels could be gathered in one place, the collection would fill a small library and reveal details of a protest that no contemporary could possibly have seen in its entirety. The crusade passed through three phases, and only during the first, from mid-March until early May, could one easily follow its progress by reading one or two good metropolitan dailies.

During the second phase, which lasted until mid-June, activity centered in the West, where numerous incidents of train stealing by the armies of unemployed continued to capture front-page headlines. National wire services carried so little other news of the movement, though, that Coxey and his lieutenants in Washington had no idea of what was happening west of the Mississippi. And neither did President Cleveland. After mid-June, the press in cities like Cincinnati, Wheeling, and Buffalo carried news of the arrival of marchers from the West, but unless a person scanned dozens of regional journals he could not hope to formulate even a sketchy picture of the Coxey movement in its final phase.

From the beginning, most newspapers tended to belittle the Commonweal as nothing more than a collection of tramps; but the sheer volume of press coverage contradicted that simplistic view. Americans would not walk around the corner to see tramps. They preferred to "vag" them—to sentence the vagrant to the local workhouse where he could spend thirty days breaking stones, chopping wood, and learning the value of the American work ethic. Before the advent of the Commonweal, armies of tramps rode trains across the West and seldom received much attention.

On one level the Coxey movement was engaging melodrama, complete with heroes like the swashbuckling John Sherman Sanders and his men, who stole a train in Colorado and dashed across the prairies in a locomotive chase that appealed to anyone who had ever read a dime novel. In Montana, Coxeyites built rafts and sailed down the Missouri River in a great American adventure straight from the pages of *Huckleberry Finn*. Perhaps even Jack London's tales of struggle for survival owed something to Coxey: London accompanied a California army halfway across the continent.[9]

No one did more to foster the press's melodramatic treatment of the movement than the outrageous Carl Browne. But it would be a mistake to treat him as a simple charlatan. A sometime journalist, Browne recognized that the movement's bizarre trappings attracted the attention of a jaded press and excited more publicity than any reformer could ever dream of purchasing. Even Samuel Gompers, the founder and longtime head of the American Federation of Labor, who had only caustic words for "reformers" who used the American worker, called Browne "a big-hearted lover of men, a dreamer and an idealist."[10]

Often obscured by the emphasis on melodrama was the fact that Browne, Coxey, and other guiding spirits of the movement managed to illuminate the economic ills besetting America in the late nineteenth century as few had done before. During those years the nation experienced a disturbing and poorly understood transformation from a rural-agrarian to an urban-industrial economy. One result was a roller-coaster business cycle. Hard times in the 1870s had been accompanied by a series of major railway strikes and urban disturbances. During a less severe slump in the mid-1880s, anti-Chinese riots had erupted on the Pacific Slope. In 1893, with the worst downturn yet, normally confident and optimistic Americans shuddered at the thought of what the future might bring. Already during the fall and winter of 1893/94, the ominous cry "Bread or Blood" had been heard in several of the nation's cities, and the rise of Coxeyism suggested that worse was yet to come.[11]

The season of economic despair began in mid-1893, when panic on Wall Street signaled the start of a depression that would last four years. Within six months nearly five hundred banks and sixteen thousand businesses had failed. Only two of the five western transcontinental railroads remained solvent. No matter what the industry, people fortunate enough to retain jobs frequently saw their wages cut by one-fifth—or even by one-half. Every month thousands more involuntarily joined the ranks of the army of unemployed, although no one could be sure of the exact number: the federal government did not keep such statistics, and neither did many states. What statistics were available were crude and not always meaningful. One report estimated that on January 1, 1894, 25 percent of the breadwinners of Montana and Utah were without work; 50,000 were jobless in California. In Chicago that figure was close to 100,000, and in New York City it fell somewhere between 100,000 and 200,000, depending on who was guessing. Making matters worse was the fact that the jobless often had dependents who constituted an even larger portion of the destitute; an estimated 7,000 unemployed San Franciscans, for example, had 20,000 dependents. Atlanta had 3,000 out of work with 15,000 dependents, while for Philadelphia the figures were 62,500 jobless and 187,000 dependents.[12]

The grim statistics caused the head of the New York Central Railroad, Chauncy M. Depew, to comment: "I have been through all the panics of the last thirty years, but I have never seen one in which the distress was so widespread and reached so many people who previously had not been affected as this Panic of 1893." And what advice did he offer the jobless? Join Coxey's army, commit suicide, or "cheerfully and courageously do the best you can and not cry."[13]

The press added a human dimension to the unemployment statistics. Journalists told of hopeless, penniless old men wandering the streets of Saint Paul, of men in the prime of life without jobs in the timber country of Wisconsin and Oregon. In the Iron Range near Lake Superior even the largest mines had closed. The stillness in towns like Ironwood and Hurley was deathlike. With forty inches of snow on the ground outside and temperatures hovering near eight below zero, people huddled around fires; some had neither food nor clothing for their children. In some cases only the kindly merchants who fed the miners and their families loosened the grip of starvation.

In Denver, a relief camp opened in River Front Park using tents provided by the state militia, but it attracted so many indigents from all over the West that it was forced to close for lack of facilities. For a time the railroads of Denver allowed the jobless to ride east on freight trains, but the number of freeloaders grew so great that the companies cancelled the offer and begged authorities for protection.

The annual convention of casket manufacturers reported that business was off because of the depression, and one member tried to make light of the situation by quipping that times were so bad that the sick could not afford to call a doctor and thus improved their chances for recovery. But unemployment was no joke. The blow was psychological as well as economic.[14]

"Last cent gone," a thirty-two-year-old widow living in Chicago penned in her diary for November 10. "Children went to work without their breakfast. Gave them car fare and a nickel each for lunch and promised them a royal dinner when they got home. . . . This awful struggle is wearing me out. I cannot sleep and my face is beginning to look haggard." Newspapers carried stories of people in similar circumstances who committed suicide rather than steal food.[15]

There was simply no escaping the sights and sounds of hard times. Iowa schoolmarms were occasionally surprised by a band of homeless wanderers who had broken into the classroom for a night's shelter. And whether the railroads approved or not, passenger trains on the western lines were overrun with freeloaders clinging to any place a human hand could grip. Frequently half as many people rode outside the cars as within. Some perched on the roof and braved the hail of cinders blown back from the locomotive, while others crouched under the cars on the trucks, suspended only inches from the whirling and dangerous axles. Many such passengers were well-dressed men on their way to the cities of the East where they believed—erroneously—that work would be easier to find than in the sparsely settled Rocky Mountain country. Husbands promised to send money back to support their wives and children in Denver or Cripple Creek, but some families would never be reunited.

In cities of the East, the jobless congregated outside newspaper offices every morning trying to be the first to scan the "help-wanted" ads. Sometimes they also participated in public protest meetings and signed petitions to be forwarded to Congress, probably the most ineffective thing an unemployed person could have done in 1893.[16]

It was not simply that congressmen were insensitive to the plight of the jobless. Most were charitable men, but they nonetheless reflected the survival-of-the fittest ethic that then prevailed in America. When asked what the government could do to help, the nation's leaders typically answered, "Nothing." They argued that "economic laws are a part of the machinery of the universe as much as the laws of gravitation." Unemployment was a natural phenomenon like an earthquake or cyclone, a product of forces beyond human control. Government tinkering with economic laws could only make things worse. "Laissez-faire," said one apologist for the philosophy of governmental inaction, "has its drawbacks, but it means, on the whole, wealth, vigor, resource, and capacity for recuperation."[17]

Each bout of economic depression in the nineteenth century yielded its crop of platitudes about the need for the jobless to bear their suffering and privation with patience. Beyond their limited personal resources, the only help they might receive came from private charity and local relief programs. Occasionally small-town merchants extended credit and a helping hand to the jobless, and saloon keepers allowed homeless men to bed down on the sawdust in an out-of-the-way corner of the bar—"Hotel de Drunk," they called it. Saloonmen were generous with their food, too, although hard times threatened to end the time-honored custom of the free lunch with a five-cent beer.

Private charity took a bewildering variety of forms. The *New York World* gave away more than a million loaves of bread, and the rival

New York Herald distributed thousands of dollars worth of clothing. A Tacoma philanthropist, A. V. Fawcett, served Christmas dinner to a thousand children who ranged in age from two to fifteen. They consumed 75 turkeys, 500 pies, 200 pounds of cakes, 300 loaves of bread, 500 pounds of potatoes, 5 cases of corn, and 50 pounds of coffee.[18]

A cheap and efficient method of relief favored by both private and municipal charities was the soup kitchen. Great caldrons filled with donated meat and vegetables provided mulligan stew to all comers. In some locales an able-bodied man might first be required to earn his meal by chopping firewood, which was then distributed to heat the homes of the poor. For a single meal, a man often had to chop a sixth of a cord of wood, working all the while on an empty stomach. Destitute women were occasionally assigned jobs in a municipal laundry.

Cities also established free employment bureaus and funded public-works projects like digging ditches for sewer lines. In this way Seattle employed 600 diggers, 200 to a shift, for 15 days. In Chicago men in tailor-made suits stood in line for pick-and-shovel jobs that paid 15 cents an hour. When snow blanketed the city in December, Chicago hired 20,000 shovelers for a few hours to clear its streets. Occasionally a community attempted to systematize the welter of overlapping and ineffective public and private programs, but in some places the poverty was so overwhelming and the confusion so great that officials were reduced almost to throwing loaves of bread at the unemployed.[19]

Surrounded by an ocean of misery, the affluent sought to insulate themselves from the human dimensions of hard times. In almost mocking disregard for the true plight of the impoverished, hard-times parties and masquerade balls became the fad. A hostess gave a prize such as a sack of flour to the guest who dressed as the most forlorn specimen of poverty or a broom to the most deplorable example of shabby gentility.

In Chicago a lavish charity ball—the highlight of the city's social calendar—took place in January 1894. "It was the night for the poor," recorded the *Chicago Herald*, "a gala, dazzling, blinding spectacle for the rich." The money it raised would buy bandages for the injured and food baskets for the hungry. Many of the city's foremost citizens were present: Robert T. Lincoln (the well-to-do son of the president), Mrs. Potter Palmer, the Philip Armours, George M. Pullman, and Marshall Field. The ball was a visual feast, a maze of color and beauty, of silken gowns trimmed in ermine and diamonds, and corsages of red roses. While the affluent danced away a frigid night, the poor huddled outside, their scantily clad bodies pierced by sharp winds sweeping off ice-covered Lake Michigan. Such contradictory scenes typified the times that gave rise to the Coxey crusade.[20]

The depression of the 1890s, no less than earlier depressions, thrust into prominence a host of protest writers and orators and a colorful assortment of reform movements; but none had the captivating qualities of Jacob Coxey's crusade against unemployment. Even its enemies admitted that Coxeyism represented a significant grass-roots educational force. It sparked a public debate on the past and future course of American history such as had seldom occurred before.

Observers did not have to study or understand Coxey's public-works program in order to see that its enthusiastic reception in many quarters, particularly the West, was a symptom of serious social or economic malaise in the United States. Traditionalists, for example, saw Coxeyism as proof that a pernicious paternalism had undermined basic American values: "Men have been taught to rely upon legislation rather than upon themselves." To other observers the prevalence of roving armies in the West confirmed that the classic American frontier had indeed disappeared by 1890. Scarcely nine months before Coxey launched his march, a young history professor, Frederick Jackson Turner, gave a public address in which he spoke of "democracy born of free land" and the end of the frontier. No longer would a series of frontiers "furnish a new field of opportunity, a gate of escape from the bondage of the past." From the assertions of Turner and others a person might easily conclude that America was used up. Certainly the rise of Coxeyism made the historian's gloomy pronouncements seem almost prophetic. The fact that Canada, with millions of acres of fertile land still available almost for the asking, was spared the trauma of roving armies of indigents seemingly confirmed the correctness of the popular and long-standing environmental approach to America's unemployment problem.[21]

For many of its supporters, Coxeyism represented a cry of distress, a grass-roots outpouring of rage directed not just against the 1890s depression but against all the changes that had disinherited the nation's common people. During the three decades that followed the Civil War, rapid industrialization and its consequences had profoundly altered the lives of the nation's producers—farmers and industrial workers alike. When confronted by the corporate combinations and nationwide marketing arrangements that increasingly dominated life in America (the "rings" and "trusts" of popular rhetoric), producers experienced a disturbing sense of powerlessness. They feared for the future of political egalitarianism and economic opportunity. And lending scholarly credence to their worst nightmares were conservative spokesmen like William Graham Sumner, who described the thirty-year growth of industry in the United States as leading to "its all pervasive control over human life." Unlike the disinherited, though, Sumner and other apologists for laissez-faire pleaded for Americans to accept the new social and economic relationships.[22]

Farmers, particularly those in the newly settled parts of the West, struggled with falling crop prices and mounting debts that in their eyes were the products of a national market controlled by financial conspirators in the East. These westerners wanted the price inflation that the "free and unlimited coinage" of silver money would bring, but the eastern moneylenders who supposedly controlled Congress denied them this by maintaining the nation's commitment to the gold standard. Silver versus gold, debtors versus creditors, West versus East: all were different ways of describing one of the chief struggles that animated American politics in the 1890s. At the same time, an increasing number of workers found themselves in the employment of others—a condition of dependency that became increasingly common after the Civil War.

The great depression of the 1890s exposed the dangers inherent in wage work, a system that many in the post–Civil War generation had yet to accept as legitimate. "There is something wrong when such a large number of people are thrown up like driftwood on the shore, out of place, out of use," worried the *Cleveland Plain Dealer*. "Wage slavery" was a term frequently used to describe the worker's condition of disinheritance, and it held an especially bitter connotation for

Americans who had vivid memories of emancipating the black slaves. In an article on the Coxey movement, James B. Weaver, a Civil War general and Populist presidential candidate, lamented, "The poor African slave found a welcome in Canada where neither master nor bloodhound could molest him. But the wage-slave of to-day cannot look to the North Star to guide him to freedom. All the nations of the earth have federated to cut off his retreat and hold him to his hopeless task. The few own the earth and dictate the terms upon which the multitude may live upon it." [23]

The words of General Weaver suggest that Americans did not have to listen to revolutionary socialists or study ponderous volumes of European political and economic theorizing to encounter bitter indictments of the prevailing order. The editorial pages of respected dailies like the *Plain Dealer* complained that "For years, the rich have been growing richer and the poor poorer. For years the legislation of this country has been in favor of privileged classes." Similar sentiments were voiced by dozens of other papers that could hardly be called radical, and by President Cleveland in his 1888 message to Congress, which denounced the "communism of combined wealth and capital." [24]

The San Francisco cynic Ambrose Bierce railed at what he called a "pickpocket civilization," while the author of a poem called "The Disinherited" presented the problem as a series of contradictions:

> They bake, but others have eaten;
> They burn, but others are warm;
> They build, but their heads are unsheltered,
> Are bare to the pitiless storm.
>
> They till, but the crop goes from them;
> They reap, but their "Harvest Home"
> Means to them that their product is stolen;
> They brew, but they taste but the foam.

Some producers joined protests like the Knights of Labor, the Alliance movement, and the Populist party. In their meetings, which at times resembled religious revivals, they sang about their fears and hopes in anthems such as "Hurrah for the Toiler," "All Hail the Power of Laboring Men," and "Justice for the Farmer." Each of these, which appeared in *The Alliance Songster* of 1891, had as its theme the past glory, present misery, and future redemption of disinherited American producers.[25]

Richard Olney, President Cleveland's attorney general and future secretary of state, eloquently summarized the complaint of the disinherited when he observed that they felt "a sense of wrong—a conviction that they do not have fair play—that society by its very constitution necessarily works injustice and inequality, favoring a few with not only abundance, but with a superfluity of blessings, while excluding the great majority not merely from the luxuries, but almost from the decent comforts of life." The disinherited, it could be added, were not necessarily part of a deep-seated culture of poverty. Most aspired to middle-class status. They were angry but not necessarily alienated, a description especially fitting Coxey's army.[26]

People who believed themselves disinherited saw in the Coxey crusade an agency for their redemption; and members of similar agencies—the Populist party and organized labor—provided the movement its primary institutional support, especially in the region west of the Mississippi. There the popular crusade might have served as inspiration for L. Frank Baum's *The Wizard of Oz*, published six years later. Though Baum denied that his book was anything other than a story for children, it could easily serve as an allegory about a troubled America in the 1890s.

In Baum's tale, Dorothy's home is lifted from its Kansas foundations by a cyclone, and when it returns to earth some distance away it crushes the wicked witch of the East. On Dorothy the witch's silver shoes possess magical powers, much like the "free silver" that westerners in Coxey's day believed would release them from bondage to the gold standard and the money barons of Wall Street (the wicked witch of the East?). Following the yellow brick (gold?) road on her way to see the Wizard of Oz, whom she hopes can send her home to Kansas, Dorothy meets a scarecrow who wants some brains (the debt-encumbered American farmer?) and a tin woodsman rusted and immobilized for nearly a year by an unexpected rain (the economic depression of the 1890s?). The woodsman wants a heart. He was once human, but the wicked witch of the East enchanted his ax: it often slipped and cut off parts of his body that then had to be refashioned from tin. The result was that in time he became a machine lacking any vestige of its human past. Together the little troop undertakes a crusade, each member seeking something from the wizard.[27]

The breadwinner who depended on others for wages was as helpless in a severe depression as a tin woodsman in a sudden downpour. But unlike the tin woodsman, the unemployed worker still had to eat. During the fall and winter of 1893 the time was ripe for any crusade that portrayed Uncle Sam—Congress or President Cleveland—as a wizard, who by inaugurating a program of public-works jobs would free the American worker frozen into idleness by hard times.

The last generation, prophesied a West Coast newspaper, had to deal with the problem of slavery; the present will deal with the labor problem. "We have established man's right to life and liberty, now we will establish his right to the products of his labor." In that battle Jacob S. Coxey and his army of protest proposed to take the lead: "What I am after," said the Ohioan, summarizing his movement for the press, "is to try to put this country in a condition so that no man who wants work shall be obliged to remain idle. I have a family myself and I don't want my own sons to ever starve for want of work."[28]

CHAPTER 1

Chicago asked in 1893 for the
first time the question whether
the American people knew
where they were driving.

The Education of Henry Adams,
An Autobiography

Chicago and the Birth of the Commonweal

Eighteen ninety-three was Chicago's year in the sun: the World's Columbian Exposition that opened there in May to celebrate four centuries of American achievement served as a coming-of-age party for
the brawny, youthful metropolis by Lake Michigan. At least 27 million people attended, more than had come to any earlier world's fair.
"Sell the cook stove if necessary and come. You *must* see this fair,"
Hamlin Garland wrote to his parents on their Dakota farm. Until
the exposition closed in October, Chicago was the meeting place of
America's past and future, where replicas of Columbus's three caravels
vied for attention with the transformers and dynamos of General
Electric and Westinghouse. It was also where the accomplishments of
industrial civilization stood in greatest contrast to its failures. Surrounding the White City of the exposition were filth and squalor,
disease-ridden slums, and air heavy with stench.

Not all the excitement in Chicago was confined to the exhibition
halls, where visitors could view a map of the United States in pickles
or a Krupp cannon weighing 130 tons, or to the Midway Plaisance,
where the sinuous and much-talked-about Little Egypt danced the
hootchy-kootchy. Chicago was equally alive with ideas. Churchmen
and academics gathered for international congresses. And there were
the lunatics—at least that is how Chicago's popular and expansive

mayor Carter Henry Harrison phrased it when he welcomed the six hundred delegates to the Bimetallic League convention (the "silver congress") that opened in Central Music Hall in August.[1]

With a twinkle of humor in his dark eyes, the burly but handsome mayor observed: "Some of you may be rather wild. It is said you are lunatics—silver lunatics. I look down upon you and say I am rather glad to welcome such lunatics as you." After noting that the world called Luther, Columbus, Franklin, and Morse lunatics, Harrison said of the delegates, "My friends there may be crazy men here . . . [but] your aim is to strike the shackles from the limbs of the masses." The monetary reformers reveled in the mayor's welcoming remarks and thereafter for the next three days publicly addressed one another as "fellow lunatics" or "cranks."

It was one of the few things they joked about. For the most part, this was a terribly earnest gathering. Delegates traveled to Chicago from all parts of the United States, but westerners predominated—farmers and metal miners in particular. Two hundred fifty delegates arrived from Colorado alone. Among the many politicians in attendance were William Jennings Bryan, the "sod-house" congressman from Nebraska who filled the Music Hall with his oratorical magic; Representative Francis G. Newlands of Nevada; and Idaho's three-man congressional delegation, unanimously in favor of free and unlimited coinage of silver.

Delegates listened intently to Colorado's Populist governor Davis Waite—old, bent, and feeble, his voice barely audible—mercilessly flay the "money power." In a repeat of a controversial threat he had made earlier in Denver, he warned, "For it is better, infinitely better, rather than that our national liberties should be destroyed by the tyranny that is oppressing humanity all over the world, that we should wade through the seas of blood—yea, blood to the horses' bridles." As he ended his speech, delegates cried, "Hit 'em again, governor!" "Strike from the shoulder!"

In speech after speech delegates declared war on England, on Wall Street, and on the East—all the forces they perceived as tormenting honest and long-suffering westerners. Bedlam threatened as dozens of delegates promoted their favorite resolutions from the floor, argued with one another, or threw their straw hats into the air to show support for a particular measure. But one thing everyone agreed on was the need for Congress to get more money into circulation. This, they argued, would make it easier to borrow the capital necessary to develop the West and thereby create prosperity and jobs, particularly in the silver industry so crucial to the economy of several western states. Conservative voices like the *Chicago Tribune* had long been skeptical of the claims of the silverites, arguing that what they really wanted was an inflationary dollar to swindle city workers. Better stick with gold, the only honest money.

Presiding over a raucus discussion of the platform was the "Minnesota Don Quixote," Ignatius Donnelly, his round and cherubic likeness belying the fact that not long before he had written a novel so graphic in its prediction of America's collapse in a bloody war between the haves and have-nots that one publisher rejected it with the hope that it would never "see the light." *Caesar's Column* nonetheless appeared in 1889 and sold thousands of copies.[2]

It was at the silver congress that the odd friendship between Jacob S. Coxey and Carl Browne had its chance origin. After a heated dispute between Browne and Donnelly over a section of the platform, Coxey walked over to congratulate the Californian. Browne was grateful for any support: "I felt immediately drawn toward Mr. Coxey, and among all the men I had met he impressed me the most." Coxey was similarly impressed by Browne and invited him home to Massillon to discuss further a public-works idea the Ohioan had been incubating since 1891.

Except for being "fellow lunatics," the two men were studies in contrast. The shy and retiring Coxey scarcely uttered a word publicly at the silver congress. But the tall and powerfully built Browne created an immediate sensation when he appeared on the floor in his Buffalo Bill suit. To all who would listen he declared, "Coming, as I do, from the western frontier, I wear the garb of the frontiersman, and not that of the patent medicine fakir, as some weak minded persons may think—educated, as such are, that 'clothes make the man.'" He later claimed that a San Francisco business paper, the *City Argus*, which commissioned him to attend the Columbian Exposition as its artist and correspondent, had provided the Buffalo Bill suit so he could join an exhibit labeled the "wild and woolly West." In fact,

Browne had a short memory, for several years earlier he had lectured on the streets of Los Angeles in his frontier garb and was not above wearing it to sell patent medicines.[3]

Within three months after the silver congress adjourned, the United States Congress met in special session to repeal the Sherman Silver Purchase Act of 1890, a measure that conservatives like President Cleveland and eastern businessmen believed had helped trigger the depression by destroying confidence in the economy. In effect, Congress ended mandatory purchases of the white metal by the federal government, placed the United States solidly on the gold standard favored by creditors (bondholders), and further angered producers in the West and South who believed that "tight money" undermined their economic well-being. The losers could now sing with even greater conviction a chorus from one of the era's many anthems of protest:

> Yankee Doodle, banks and bonds,
> Yankee Doodle Dandy;
> Bounce the banks and burn the bonds;
> Oh! Yankee Doodle Dandy.

For all its sound and fury, the Chicago gathering was significant mainly for introducing Coxey and Browne to one another. Coxey returned home to Massillon; Browne remained in Chicago for several more months to agitate among the city's growing army of unemployed. During that time the idea of a great protest march by the nation's unemployed took shape in his fertile mind.[4]

Each day during the summer of 1893 railroads brought thousands of visitors to Chicago's Columbian Exposition. The majority came to stare at its exhibits, but for some it offered hope of temporary work. Most of the job-seekers ended up penniless, however, living in the city's flophouses and jails—not as prisoners but as economic refugees in search of a warm place to sleep when the frosts of autumn chilled Chicago's nights.

Almost every freight train steaming in from the West added to the city's jobless population. The newcomers were sometimes well dressed and looked like bankers, though they arrived in cattle cars. "They are not tramps," a Santa Fe conductor observed of the hard-rock miners and farm boys. "I will take my chances on hauling them free." People called the new class of passengers "deadheads" to distinguish them from ordinary tramps. While an occasional struggle for survival erupted among the destitute, mutual help was more common. When a group of 125 deadheads on a Rock Island passenger train traveling from Iowa to Chicago learned that two of their number were newlyweds, they passed a hat and purchased tickets so that the young couple could ride inside the coach. Scandinavians, Poles, and Czechs among the deadheads were certain to find a helping hand among fellow countrymen in Chicago's ethnic neighborhoods.[5]

Abandoning the halls of the University of Michigan Law School for the streets of Chicago, Ray Stannard Baker observed firsthand the perils that awaited farm boys fresh from the prairies who sought jobs in the big city. "What I found in Chicago, or seemed to find, was a cheapening of human beings. . . . But in Chicago the man seemed lost. I myself felt lost. One became part of a crowd; there was no anxious family looking on, no real neighbors." Baker wrote of the city's hurrying people, crowded streets, clanging streetcars, the ragged men dashing into gutters to pick up cigar butts, the biting, distinctive odors of the stockyards, and the Chicago River—the dirty, wicked, but always fascinating city.

Baker observed a parade of Chicago's unemployed in which a man carried a placard that read:

BLACK SLAVES OF 1863
WHITE SLAVES OF 1893

"I knew that my father had no realization of such conditions—and had never had. He and all our family, for two hundred and fifty years, had been pioneers. If anyone was discontented in one neighborhood or found it hard to make a living, all he had to do was to load his belongings into an ox-cart and go west, and there was plenty of free land, free water—a free sky."[6]

The protest that Baker observed was one of several in Chicago that summer. In mid-August a crowd of five thousand unemployed assembled at the Columbus statue in Lake Front Park, just east of Michigan Avenue. They picked up free copies of radical literature and listened to impassioned speeches. The choice of the Columbus statue was of symbolic importance. "Like him," declared one speaker, "we are on a voyage of discovery, and hope to find this afternoon some remedy for the evil conditions of labor that makes so large a gathering of the unemployed in Chicago." Orations were in German and Polish as well as English, but an overriding theme was clear no matter what tongue was spoken: "Work! Work! Bread! Bread!"

Drawing up a manifesto that included the phrases "We believe we have been reduced to our present state by a few schemers who have misled us as a people through our representatives" and "We believe wage slavery more degrading than bond slavery ever was," the protesters resolved to march to city hall. There they would demand that Mayor Harrison provide them public-works jobs.

The almost daily demonstrations at the Columbus statue resembled a three-ring circus, with English speakers on the west side and Polish and German on the east, while a short distance away a lone figure clad in a Buffalo Bill suit lectured on the money question. One afternoon four hundred jobless men staged a spontaneous march through downtown streets and around city hall, carrying cardboard signs scribbled "We Want Work."

Police declined to interfere with the paraders unless they became violent, although the likelihood of trouble increased as participants in the "voyage of discovery" charted an increasingly dangerous course. One afternoon, after listening to the usual voices of protest, the jobless fell in behind a brass band and marched six to eight abreast to city hall. Near their destination a mail truck attempted to drive through their ranks, but protesters grabbed the horses' reins and brought the vehicle to a halt. When policemen tried to clear a passage, fighting erupted; officers wielding billy clubs chased after hundreds of protesters who fled into city hall to escape the melee. Before the fifteen-minute battle ended, nearly a thousand lawmen had collected in and around the building.

Carter Harrison, who was having his gray beard trimmed in a nearby barbershop, rushed outside to survey the trouble. Perhaps because he had been mayor during the bloody Haymarket Riot eight years earlier, the brief outburst recalled unpleasant memories and prompted him to act quickly. In any case, an alarmed Harrison summarily banned any further parades.

"Not at any time?" questioned the chief of police.

"Not at any time. And watch these meetings. Keep your officers at the Lake Front and allow no disturbance. Break up any meeting that may become disorderly."

Accompanied by an army of policemen, the jobless straggled back to Lake Front Park. Just as their protest meeting reconvened, someone shouted, "Here comes the mayor!" The irrepressible Harrison took the podium to calm the troubled waters with the oil of his rhetoric: "I sympathize with the honest laborer, but I despise the professional labor disturber. . . . You must have patience. The Eternal Jehovah took six days to make the world, and you cannot remedy all the ills of your situation in twenty-four hours." Harrison promised that city officials would do all they could for the jobless. When the mayor ended his talk, listeners gave him three cheers.

On the afternoon of August 30 an estimated twenty-five thousand people gathered for the greatest protest meeting yet. They covered parts of Lake Front Park and the grounds of the Art Institute nearby, where a labor congress was in session. In addition to the local speakers, well-known national figures like Samuel Gompers and land reformer Henry George were on hand to address sections of the enormous crowd. They spoke simultaneously from the several wagons that served as podiums. During the course of his oration the head of the American Federation of Labor advanced the intriguing idea of a temporary federal-works program: "Why does not the state improve the country roads?"

Carl Browne, as usual, staged a side show of his own—an illustrated lecture that lasted from 2 until 7 P.M.

The enormous size of the latest protest caused a worried Mayor Harrison to extend his ban to include all demonstrations in Lake Front Park. The summer's protests had not been without effect, for they prompted city officials and businessmen to take a closer look at the problems of the unemployed, to systematize the haphazard system of relief, and even to provide some menial jobs. But it was not enough. Before the end of the year many a jobless worker's meager savings ran out. All over Chicago people grew desperate.[7]

Owners of coal yards complained about the lack of police protection to stop the poor from pilfering fuel for heat. And December winds blowing off the lake sent thousands more looking for shelter. A common cry heard on the streets was, "Please, mister. I ain't got no place to sleep tonight. Can't you spare me a dime?" For ten or fifteen cents he could get a bed for a night in a filthy lodging house. For five cents he could sit all night in a cellar. But even that was too expensive for some. At the Harrison Street police station homeless men packed the hallways and cells every night. The station house stank and was often so crowded that half the men were forced to stand, but at least it was warm. In the morning the jailer gave each man a steaming cup of coffee and a chunk of bread—a day's rations for many. The scene was repeated at other station houses. Unemployed women were less visible, but many of them too found shelter in police stations or the Young Women's Christian Association.[8]

More than a thousand men and boys found refuge inside Chicago's city hall. Shortly after five each evening they filled its corridors and stairwells. Each arrival took a single sheet from a pile of newspapers and placed it on the flagstone floor as bedding. Ray Stannard Baker happened to visit the building one evening and upon opening the door was overwhelmed by the rush of fetid air. "I stopped just inside the doorway. Dante in his Inferno never bettered the sight I saw there." The sleepers were laid out like corpses, their heads to the wall, their feet touching in the middle of the hall. Shoes and brass cuspidors served as pillows, though a fortunate few used their overcoats. Everyone tried to avoid the puddles of slush tracked in by the latecomers. Some of the sleepers had families in other cities and a few months earlier had worked at the Columbian Exposition.[9]

On the evening of October 28, Chicago prepared for a gala celebration to be held two days later to mark the closing of the Columbian Exposition. The fair had been a great success, one of many in the career of Carter Harrison. But that evening as Harrison dined at home, a stranger knocked at the door and demanded to see him. In the darkened hall, Patrick Eugene Prendergast, a disappointed officeseeker, accosted Harrison and fired three shots. The mayor died fifteen minutes later. Was Prendergast a madman, a crank, or a lunatic? For stunned Chicagoans the distinction was unimportant: their planned celebration turned into a rite of mourning. Demolition of the great White City began a few days later, and wood that once sheltered the wonders of the industrial world was now given away to warm the destitute.[10]

Who could give meaning to such twists of fate? Or to the great contradiction haunting late nineteenth-century America: why progress was so clearly juxtaposed with poverty? People wondered how long the contradiction could remain unresolved before the apocalypse imagined in Ignatius Donnelly's *Caesar's Column* became a frightening reality.[11]

Cataclysm was a popular topic of discussion in the 1890s. The reviews and magazines teemed with pessimistic articles. Their common foreboding was that rapid economic change during the past three decades had led America into an unfamiliar thicket called the "labor problem," where old certainties like equality, self-reliance, and personal freedom seemed inadequate guides. In Chicago, as elsewhere, the learned and the not-so-learned pondered the ominous signs of the times, but seldom in more opulent surroundings than when members of the city's Sunset Club met in late December to discuss unemployment. Following a lavish dinner, they settled back in the overstuffed chairs of their gilt-edged banquet hall to sip coffee and listen to presentations by Jane Addams, Florence Kelley, W. T. Stead, and others.

Stead, an English minister and writer who was soon to publish a stunning exposé of the city's vice problem—*If Christ Came to Chicago*—made perhaps the deepest impression. He proposed a simple solution for the 100,000 men and women out of work: "Employ them! Give them work as if they were your blood relations. . . . I think if I was an eastern potentate and brought my janissaries to the door of this hall and then compelled you to change clothes with the starving poor, living for a week as they have to live, hunger as they have to hunger, you would raise all the money wanted to lift them from the depths." [12]

For Carl Browne the two months that followed the silver congress had been an exhilarating time of agitation and thought. With a facility for juxtaposing ideas in a manner as startling as his appearance in downtown Chicago in a frontier costume, he lectured day after day on the money question.

"The best thing the sand lot end of the Lake Front produced last night was Carl Browne's proposed revolution," observed a *Tribune* reporter. On one occasion he called for the city's unemployed to assemble on October 14 at the Administration Building of the World's

Fair and there form a provisional government. He advised them to come unarmed and carry a small United States flag and a white banner with the words, "Peace on Earth, Good Will to Men." Browne believed that no Pinkerton thugs would dare fire upon the people, and thus a provisional government could be established "free from English dictation."

Browne typically lectured from atop a barrel placed beside a wagon that displayed his panoramic history of the money question. During the course of his lengthy presentations he let down a series of canvas panels (fourteen in all), each illustrated with his lurid renditions of bankers, Wall Street, and the "old vampire" gold. Rattling along at a lively rate, he offered free silver as his solution to unemployment. "How will free silver help us to get work?" hecklers invariably shot back. "Carl Browne is voluble, but he is more amusing than convincing," said the *Chicago Herald*.[13]

After a month more of agitation, Browne finally accepted Coxey's invitation to visit Massillon; there the two reformers talked into the night about various solutions, especially Coxey's pet proposal to have Congress appropriate $500 million to put the unemployed to work building roads. On December 7, 1893, they issued *Bulletin no. 1* of the Good Roads Association and sent the full text of Coxey's proposal to Congressman Thomas Geary from Browne's home district, who introduced it in the House, and to William A. Peffer, who did likewise in the Senate.

Browne returned to Chicago in mid-December to lobby for Coxey's plan at the annual convention of the American Federation of Labor. He had an important ally in John McBride, delegate from Massillon and an old friend of Coxey, who formally introduced the measure. With little debate, the 142 delegates unanimously approved it.

Although the American Federation of Labor was at this time weak and struggling, its endorsement gave Coxey and Browne a psychological boost. But of immeasurably greater importance in the history of the Commonweal march was the site of the labor federation's Chicago convention—the council chamber in city hall. The corridors jammed with sleepers that reminded Ray Stannard Baker of Dante's inferno also shocked Samuel Gompers, who had to pick his way over their bodies to attend one of the evening sessions. "It was a scene that burned into my mind." That same scene disturbed Browne and more than anything else was responsible for the "petition in boots." When Browne took ideas and slogans that had been collecting in his mind for months and even years and combined them with Coxey's public-works proposal, the result was the Commonweal of Christ.[14]

During the previous summer's agitation on the lakefront he had seen how noisy speeches and marches to city hall had forced Mayor Harrison and Chicago's leading businessmen to address some of the problems of the unemployed. He now hoped that a march on Washington to promote Coxey's jobs plan would prompt an even more effective response from the federal government, an incredibly optimistic belief considering that the government had never before shouldered any responsibility for the jobless. But if he could attract a few thousand indigents into the ranks of the Commonweal, he was certain to arouse the interest of a nation haunted by fears of cataclysm.

When Browne sent Coxey a telegram from Chicago proposing the march, the Ohioan invited him back to discuss further the startling scheme. Shortly after New Year's Day 1894 he returned to Massillon, optimistic that Coxey would pay for publicizing the march.

But Coxey opposed the plan, worried that thousands of destitute people would descend on his farm and warning Browne that "he could not afford to feed all the hungry men in the country." After hours and days of discussion Browne changed Coxey's mind, and on January 31 they issued *Bulletin no. 2* of the Good Roads Association. It contained a petition for readers to sign and return, a petition to be presented to Congress by the jobless themselves on May 1. Browne wanted the march to originate in Chicago, where he would be assured many recruits, but Coxey insisted that it must begin in Massillon. Since the Ohioan was paying the bills, Browne yielded.[15]

CHAPTER 2

Coxey is a most amusing
crank, and is having lots of
excitement and work
out of his army.

Duluth News-Tribune,
quoted in *Public Opinion* 16
(March 22, 1894)

Wheels in My Head: The Making of a Reform Crusade

Jacob S. Coxey had all the attributes of a successful businessman,
which indeed he was; but in the eyes of many people his obsession
with monetary reform branded him a crank—perhaps all the more so
because he challenged the laissez-faire economic system under which
he prospered. It did not appear to make any sense.

Eight miles northeast of Massillon was Coxey's 160-acre ranch.
Many of his 125 blooded horses were pastured there. He also owned a
ranch near Lexington, Kentucky, and another near Guthrie, Oklahoma. Horses, though, were primarily a hobby. The real source of
Coxey's wealth was an unglamorous but lucrative sandstone quarry
four miles north of Massillon overlooking the yellow Tuscarawas
River. The two railway lines that paralleled the river near the Coxey
home each ran a spur into the 15-acre quarry. The large and rambling
white frame residence was surrounded by a grove of mulberry, catalpa,
and willow trees. Behind it stood a large barn, a blacksmith shop,
workmen's cottages, and a mill for crushing sandstone into fine silica
sand. In many respects Coxey operated an ideal workshop in this
garden-like setting. He was a generous employer who never missed a
payday and had never experienced a strike by his fifty workmen.[1]

Coxey was thirty-nine years old when planning for the great
crusade began, and he enjoyed the excellent health and youthful

vigor of a man half his age. In fact, at that time he had not yet reached the midpoint of his exceptionally long life—one that spanned the administrations of nineteen presidents from Franklin Pierce to Harry S. Truman, a total of ninety-seven years.

The secret of his longevity? Once he concocted and sold an elixir called "Cox-e-lax" that promised to cure everything from constipation to dizziness and gallstones. On another occasion he revealed to reporters that he never wasted his energies resisting temptation, and during the years that preceded the march the most irresistible temptation for Coxey was often a sleek racehorse. He further did not object to "a little harmless flirtation" when his wife was not around. Intensely interested in public life, Coxey ran for more offices as the candidate of more parties than he could remember. But only once did he win a significant victory: in 1931, when he was in his mid-seventies, Coxey was elected mayor of his beloved Massillon. No one thing in his life, however, really accounted for his longevity or his peculiar interest in monetary reform.

Coxey was born on Easter Sunday, April 16, 1854, in Selinsgrove, Pennsylvania, a pleasant tree-shaded hamlet on the Susquehanna River about forty miles north of Harrisburg. Six years later his family moved twenty miles farther north to Danville, in Montour County. Danville too was situated on the west bank of the broad but shallow Susquehanna, but unlike orderly and pious Selinsgrove, it pulsed with the energy of the industrial revolution.

Coxey's father worked in an iron-rolling mill. Young Jake attended public school for eight years and then, at age of sixteen, took a summer job as a water boy in the mill where his father worked. During the winter months he helped on a farm. A bright lad, he advanced quickly from water boy to machine oiler to boiler tender. By the time he left the mill at the age of twenty-four, he had become a stationary engineer like his father.

An uncle living near Harrisburg launched Jake's career in business when he invited his nephew to join his scrap-metal firm. Three years later, in May 1881, Jake made a trip to Massillon to purchase an abandoned blast furnace for scrap. He liked the Ohio community and returned the following month to buy a farm and a small, unprofitable sandstone quarry. Erecting a crushing mill, Coxey produced a special type of sand needed by the steel, glass, and pottery industries, which were then enjoying boom times. He proved to be an excellent salesman, and soon his white sand was in great demand in Pittsburgh and the Ohio Valley. The young businessman's prosperity seemed assured. Coxey used part of his rapidly accumulating fortune to indulge his passion for racehorses. Beginning in 1887, his racing colors appeared on tracks from coast to coast. But his love of the sport—not a particularly respectable one in the eyes of pious Americans, including his wife Carrie—was no doubt a prime reason that their fourteen-year marriage broke up in 1888. They had four children. Two years later he married Henrietta Jones, who was more accepting of his foibles. At the time of the march they had two children, the youngest being the newborn Legal Tender.

Even as he had acquired wealth, Coxey had not neglected the world of ideas. As a young man he spent countless hours reading and thinking about the money question, arguing endlessly with his fellow workers about politics, interest rates, paper money, and bank credit. He brought the same searching mind to questions of religion. In 1893 the former Episcopalian had not attended church for years, but not because he was indifferent: "I felt within a craving and a longing on the subject of religion which the churches seemed entirely unable to satisfy. There were many undefined beliefs in my mind which I was unable to concentrate into any concrete form, and when Carl Browne explained to me his theories of reincarnation, I knew in a flash that it was what I had been searching for."[2]

The bond between these two men was far more complex than a shared interest in monetary reform. So strong was Browne's influence over Coxey that some of the Ohioan's friends and relatives worried that his new associate possessed occult powers. Browne did little to calm their fears when he explained the relationship with such statements as "We are equal, Brother Coxey and I. He represents the state and I the church." Or "Brother Coxey has plenty of this world's goods and he is obeying the Savior's injunction to 'sell all that he hath and give to the poor.' It shows how thoroughly he believes in the work."

People called him a crank, acknowledged Coxey. "[They] assert that I have wheels in my head and am crazy; some even go so far as to advance the theory that I am in a hypnotic state; the work of my assistant, Carl Browne, and am acting under the powerful influence of this so-called agitator in my road scheme." But he brushed aside their criticism, adding, "It doesn't hurt me to be called a lunatic." What the Californian did supply was the metaphysical insight that Coxey craved to give meaning to his life. Browne was a theosophist, a member of a mystical faith that attained some prominence in southern California; and although his understanding of its teachings seemed at times disjointed and incomplete, he converted Coxey to its main tenet: reincarnation.[3]

When in early January 1894 Coxey announced that he had had a dream in which he was presented an easy way for Congress to finance his good roads program, skeptics were amused. "When Mr. Coxey had completely swallowed this idea [reincarnation]," chuckled Ray Stannard Baker, who was among the unbelievers, "he began to have marvelous dreams. On New Year's morning he woke up with his scheme of non-interest bearing bonds completely formulated. He claimed to have dreamed it, and there are those who are cruel enough to believe that he certainly must have had an unusually bad nightmare." Detractors regarded non-interest-bearing bonds and reincarnation as belonging in the same category as bottled moonbeams to restore lost youth. Despite the bizarre side of his program, Coxey essentially proposed to prime the nation's economic pump, to use public-works jobs to get the "20,000,000" mouths in workers' households "eating the farmers' products" and thus benefiting all producers.

The first part of Coxey's program, that of better roads, originated on a dark and rainy night in December 1891, or so he claimed. Driving home from Massillon, bucking and lurching through an endless series of ruts and mudholes, Coxey keenly realized the need for good roads. He further realized that only the federal government had the resources to construct such a system. The Good Roads Bill, which combined Coxey's highway proposal, his fiat-money ideas, and his desire to help the unemployed, was introduced in Congress in 1892. It got nowhere. In early 1894 he added his non-interest-bearing bond proposal, a complicated scheme that would provide federal loans enabling local governments to construct schools, courthouses, libraries, museums, and other public buildings in addition to streets and highways. To Coxey's two ideas, Browne added the march on Washington.[4]

Five years older than Coxey, Carl Browne was born in Springfield, Illinois, in 1849. His father served in both the War with Mexico and

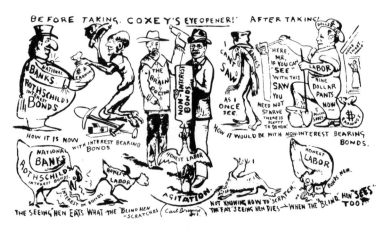

An example of Carl Browne's "artwork." Courtesy Library of Congress.

the Civil War, but the only battle Browne ever fought was that for survival. He was by turns a printer, painter, sculptor, farmer, cattle rancher, journalist, cartoonist, and politician, according to his own humble admission. On occasion he even dispensed patent medicines, as in 1896 when he advertised "Carl's California Cure" made by "Carl Browne, man's mightiest microbe master."

The microbe master was also an orator of note, though not so much for what he said or how he said it but for sheer stamina on the stump. In 1892, when he toured Nebraska on behalf of Populist candidates, he once lectured for three hours above a raging windstorm. The same heroic quality characterized his artwork: "As an artist Carl Browne belongs to a distinct school. In fact," conceded one critic, "he constitutes the entire school." But Browne was not without formal training, as he was quick to note, for as a young man he had apprenticed with a carriage- and housepainter. That experience probably accounted for his love of oversized paintings and the bright and garish colors that adorned his circus wagons.

In 1869, when he was working as a sign painter in western Iowa, he visited a friend in Omaha. On the spur of the moment the two set out to pursue their California dreams. Browne desired more than anything else to paint a gargantuan panorama of Yosemite. This he later exhibited up and down the Pacific Coast, such panoramas being a popular form of folk art in the nineteenth century.

Among Browne's many boasts was that he had been in more jails than any other living agitator for labor's cause. The artist-as-agitator phase of his career first attracted public attention in San Francisco in the late 1870s when he drew cartoons lampooning the city's wealthy for a radical newspaper, the *Open Letter*. His handiwork caught the attention of Denis Kearney, leader of the "Chinese Must Go" crusade, who made Browne his private secretary. In 1878 they crossed the continent together to take the cause of Chinese exclusion to Boston's workmen in historic Faneuil Hall and to enlighten President Rutherford B. Hayes during an interview at the White House. Some people called Browne the brains of the Kearney movement.

In a remarkable gesture that foreshadowed Coxey's confrontation in Washington sixteen years later, Kearney proposed to deliver a protest speech from the steps of the Capitol; despite police objections, he succeeded. Browne diverted the attention of the lawmen long enough for Kearney to begin his address, and with a crowd of Washington workmen listening intently, the officers declined to interfere. In the early 1890s, in another episode that anticipated the Commonweal, Browne proposed to march "a host of congenial tramps" to the California capitol in Sacramento and intimidate "some of the boodling lawmakers." But the ragged army never materialized.

Browne more than once delivered an oration dressed as a silver knight or as Daniel Boone or Davy Crockett. He stumbled into serious trouble, however, when he insisted on holding street-corner protests in Los Angeles dressed in a heavy overcoat, corduroy pantaloons, top boots, and a skull cap. Publicity-sensitive city officials interpreted his garb as libeling their much-advertised ideal climate and had him committed briefly to the state hospital at Napa, or so claimed one of Pulitzer's correspondents.

A shadowy but nonetheless important figure in Browne's life was the woman he married in 1872, Alice Courier, the daughter of a sea captain. Little is known about their relationship except that they met in California and lived for a time in Berkeley. In the early 1890s Alice suddenly exhibited the frightening signs of severe mental illness. Her relatives, except for her mother, urged that she be committed to an asylum. The grief-stricken husband refused. For a year he remained almost constantly at his wife's bedside in their mountain retreat in Napa County and attempted to nurse her back to health. But in December 1892 she caught pneumonia and died. "Just before death came to my wife, as I was sitting by her side, I realized with the quickness of a flash of lightning that within me was reincarnated a portion of the soul of Jesus Christ. I knew at the same time that I was absorbing into my soul the soul of my dying wife." After that unusual experience, metaphysical language and symbolism became an integral part of Browne's reform schemes.[5]

In Massillon the preparations for the "petition in boots" went forward only fitfully at first. The date set for the beginning of the crusade was Easter Sunday, March 25. But Coxey, who like his second wife was still skeptical about the scheme, left most of the initial organizing to his chief lieutenant, houseguest, and spiritual confidant. The Californian was a prolific writer and promulgated so many manifestos that Coxey worried about the cost of having them all printed. *Bulletin no. 3* of the Good Roads Association contained a map of the proposed route, notices of meetings to be held en route, and designs for badges. Another bulletin issued in late March contained Browne's orders to the troops and several anthems composed especially for the crusade.[6]

When the weather warmed enough to permit Browne to work outside, he turned his attention to the panorama wagon that he insisted must accompany the procession. He loved it like his own child, though to the uninitiated it resembled a junk dealer's outfit. All day he worked, buckskin coat off, sleeves rolled up, the precious necklace of amber beads adorning his tan throat. He also fashioned dozens of Commonweal banners to be carried in the procession. At its head was to be a huge oil painting of Christ, which bore a suspiciously close likeness to Browne, or "Humble Carl," as he now preferred to style himself.

Popular interest in the Commonweal was almost nonexistent until early March, when it suddenly attracted the attention of the nation's press. It was Coxey's good fortune that the Massillon *Independent* had a lively young reporter who saw in the bizarre crusade an opportunity to get plenty of space and recognition for himself in the big city dailies. This young man's dispatches over the wires of the Associated Press began to familiarize newspaper readers everywhere with the name of Coxey. By mid-March many of the country's best-known daily papers had sent reporters of their own to cover the developing curiosity.

The more news that the press carried about the Commonweal, the more people and mail poured into Massillon. A few of the letters contained threats, but the majority offered support of one kind or another. Many people sent poetry and checks. Coxey had to hire a secretary to correspond with all the people interested in organizing similar protests in other parts of the United States. One letter-writer claimed to represent 500,000 people who would be with Coxey in Washington on May 1. Others promised 1,500 recruits from Pittsburgh, 68 from Fort Wayne, 200 from Spring Valley, Ohio, 1,000 from Wabash, Indiana, 1,200 from Chicago, and 1,000 from Woonsocket, South Dakota—a remarkable feat for a village of less than 1,000 inhabitants. H. B. Clark of Chicago requested permission to join the march with 150 baseball players and raise money for it by offering an ongoing tournament in towns along the way. Also from Chicago was a letter from Patrick Eugene Prendergast, soon to hang for the murder of Carter Harrison. He expressed regrets that under the present circumstances he could not join the Commonweal.

Each day's flood of mail caused Coxey to view the march with considerably more optimism than at first. "The success of my undertaking is assured. I shall camp on the Capitol steps at Washington with 500,000 men." A few days later, however, he sounded a somewhat more ambiguous note: "This movement will either mark the second coming of Christ or be a total failure." Coxey's neighbors were not necessarily pleased when their community made headlines. Many only shook their heads in wonder. They could not understand why one of the wealthiest and shrewdest men in the county wanted to head such a dubious enterprise.

Except for his grown son and daughter and his second wife, Coxey's family shared the neighbors' concern. "Browne is a deep dyed villain, and he is working for Coxey's money and nothing more," fumed the leader's first wife, who held the second mortgage on his sandstone quarry. "The idea of bringing the name of the Savior into this movement and displaying banners inscribed with His name and decorated with His picture is an outrage. Browne is to blame for all this, and he is a wretch, but Coxey is sincere."

Coxey's father, who lived in Philadelphia, so opposed the march that he refused to talk to reporters, although he would describe his offspring as a "stiff-necked, cranky, pig-headed sort of a son." A sister, the wife of a prominent Pennsylvania businessman, called Jake an embarrassment to the whole family, adding, "but he always was a headstrong boy, and when he made up his mind to do something he did it."

Massillon was not a difficult town to reach. Located in the valley of the Tuscorawas River nine miles west of Canton, it was the meeting place of three railway lines, the most important of which was the New York–to–Chicago mainline of the Pennsylvania. Each day the freights passing through Massillon dropped off new recruits for Coxey's Commonweal. And each day the telegraph wires leading out of town pulsed with millions of dots and dashes that, when translated into newspaper stories, introduced a nation to the unemployed barbers, cooks, miners, and laborers that were the main actors in the drama. During the next several weeks they became as familiar to Americans as soap opera characters in the age of radio and television.

Among Coxey's motley cast was a sawed-off Irishman with a black eye, Abraham Lincoln Jenkins, whose claim to fame was that he had recently won a wager by eating four pounds of cheese at a sitting. Browne thought a man of his ability would make a valuable addition to the ranks. Ruddy-faced William Iler, a two-year veteran of the United States Army and a steamboat man, volunteered to serve as commissary officer. He was assigned instead to drive Browne's panorama wagon, and to millions of readers he became "Weary Bill" because he always looked tired. Iler claimed that Browne converted him to the cause during the summer of demonstrations in Chicago's Lake Front Park. Offering his talents as bandmaster was John J. Thayer of Canton's Grand Army Band. As bugler, Browne appointed J. E. "Windy" Oliver, another United States Army veteran. "He is the Gabriel trumpet to be blown on Easter Sunday making the bankers and boodlers think the world has come to an end," boasted the Californian. Also on hand was Oklahoma Sam, a tall, muscular young cowboy from Coxey's Guthrie ranch. A Chicago journalist, Henry Vincent, served as the movement's official historian.[7]

Claiming to represent Native Americans was Honoré Jaxon, clad in the costume of the Métis and carrying only a blanket, a hatchet, and a few cooking utensils. Though born in a buffalo camp on the Great Plains of the United States, he eventually migrated north of the border and was educated at the University of Toronto. He had participated in an Indian rebellion in western Canada and had been captured. His scorn of reservation life caused him to become a lecturer on the oppression of Indians and industrial workers and an ally of Coxey's crusade. A brawny black recruit from West Virginia, Jasper Johnson, served as the army's standard-bearer.[8]

Not lost in the colorful assemblage was its flamboyant originator, who started coming into Massillon each day dressed in different costume, much to the delight of small boys and reporters. He remained busy issuing manifestos, writing songs, and refurbishing his panoramic history of the money question. Each of the three-by-six-foot canvas panels was a maze of bright unblended reds, yellows, and greens. "As an outburst in art," observed one journalistic critic, "it is as awful as it is unique. Browne has to explain it or one wouldn't know whether it referred to national banks or the Orkney Islands." One of the more obvious caricatures was that of Shylock the moneylender, whom Browne portrayed as a huge octopus with his tentacles wrapped around America. He planned to use this and other gaudy illustrations in lectures along the way.

The most bizarre example of Browne's promotional genius was his creation of the "Great Unknown," a mystery man introduced to a large crowd in Massillon's public square on the night of March 19. The handsome stranger was about thirty-five years old, slim and erect—like a former military man. He wore a yachting cap, but the most notable elements of his attire were the expensive-looking double-breasted blue overcoat and the patent-leather boots. He sported a light, neatly trimmed mustache, spoke with a slight accent, and walked with a cane and a noticeable limp, the result, some thought, of a battlefield injury.

Illuminated by the flickering light of gasoline flares, the Unknown spoke to the crowd about poverty in Chicago before the infamous Haymarket Riot of 1886. Because he occasionally punctuated his graphic presentation with calls for the poor to rise up and lay the rich low, one reporter described the speech as bloodcurdling and anarchistic. "It is Fielden of Chicago," someone shouted and the crowd burst into applause, mistakenly thinking that the stranger was one of the martyrs unjustly convicted in the Haymarket affair. The speaker raised his arms to silence his hearers.

"I am the Great Unknown and the Great Unknown I must remain." For the sake of convenience he took the name Louis Smith, but to all he was a source of endless speculation and a major reason for the rising tide of public interest in the crusade. Everyone thought there was something familiar about the Unknown but could not say what. Browne appointed him assistant marshal. Accompanying the Unknown was Nero, a large collie.

The one thing that Coxey and Browne initially did not do was to call their protest an "army." That label was affixed to it by the press, which also called Coxey "General," though the Ohioan protested that his only title was president of the Coxey Good Roads Association. "Neither Marshal Browne nor I have any more rights than the poorest soldier," Coxey explained. The newspaper terminology stuck nonetheless, much to the disgust of Browne, who hated the implied association between armies and bloodshed and the Commonweal of Christ. He proposed to organize the men into cantons and communes, terminology that raised instead the specter of the French Revolution from which it was borrowed. Equally disconcerting to conservatives was his choice of May 1—International Labor Day—as the date for the rendezvous of the jobless on Capitol Hill.[9]

Army or not, some form of discipline had to be imposed on the recruits collecting in Massillon, and Browne's assistant marshal proved a natural for the task. The Unknown drilled the men frequently and quietly introduced the military system that Browne so despised.[10]

The color and excitement that the Commonweal brought to Massillon reminded people of the Oklahoma land rush a few years earlier. Folk from the surrounding countryside journeyed to town just to see the show. Whenever Carl Browne appeared in public he was immediately surrounded by eager reporters: "Carl is a friend to the reporter. He gives them all the news," gushed one. Some observers were appalled by events in Massillon, however, and called on Ohio governor and future president William McKinley to suppress the movement. McKinley, however, maintained a discreet silence, at least until the marchers were safely out of the state.[11]

Easter Sunday dawned cold and blustery. From the camp on the

Tuscarawas River the sound of a bugle called Commonwealers to breakfast, which consisted of coffee, bread, and pieces of meat that they roasted over campfires. At eight the Unknown summoned the men into line and drilled them for nearly an hour. Then Browne delivered a short sermon. Small boys hoping to see their hero, Oklahoma Sam, darted in and out of the crowd that was gathering on Massillon's main street; perhaps as many as ten thousand people waited to see what would happen next.[12]

The promised crusade got under way at half past eleven, when the Unknown cried in a voice that could be heard for half a mile, "Everybody march!" As the Commonweal moved through the streets of Massillon, it resembled nothing so much as an old-time country circus. At its head was Jasper Johnson, carrying the Stars and Stripes, and trotting at his heels was Bunker Hill, a mongrel bulldog and unofficial mascot. Next came the seven-man Commonweal band led by J. J. Thayer, and then Carl Browne riding the magnificent milk-white stallion Courier. In honor of the occasion he had added a delicate white lace necktie to his buckskin garb. He looked pale and nervous. Riding a blooded mare, the Great Unknown dashed here and there issuing orders and trying to keep the marchers in line and their spirits up. He distributed badges and exhorted Commonwealers to stand firm and not mind the occasional scoffing and jeering of those on the sidelines.

As Coxey rode by in a phaeton driven by a black coachman, he occasionally bowed to onlookers and called out to his friends. In another open carriage were Mrs. Coxey, her three-week-old son, and her sister. They would accompany the Commonweal to the edge of town. The troops came next, waving aloft some thirty or forty banners that displayed Browne's peculiar artwork and cryptic slogans. The colorful procession contained something for everyone, noted Ray Stannard Baker: "There were beggers in rags and tags, agitators, patent-medicine men, Negroes, tramps, cranks, Carl Browne, cowboys, cattle-punchers and last but not least, Honoré J. Jaxon, professional half-breed Indian." Easter chimes pealed in the background.

For all the excitement, only 122 crusaders marched with Coxey out of Massillon, and of those an unknown number were undercover officers sent by the chief of police of Pittsburgh to join the ranks, watch the movement, and get acquainted with the marchers. Most significant for the future of the Commonweal, however, was its unofficial honor guard of 44 journalists, a number greater than had covered many major party conventions.

Gamblers offered 2–1 odds that the marchers would never reach Pittsburgh; according to one report, Coxey's life insurance policy had been revoked because company officials feared he might soon meet a violent end. In any case, the hint of trouble to come only added to the suspense and sold more papers.[13]

People who now dismissed the Commonweal as a bubble that had burst because so few recruits set out with Coxey missed its true significance. Members of Coxey's band were, in the words of the perceptive Englishman W. T. Stead, the "sandwich men" of poverty, those who by calling attention to themselves advertised a larger cause. During the hard times of 1893 newspaper readers had grown weary of discussions of what to do with tramps and the jobless. "It seemed almost impossible," said Stead, "to contrive any device by which this grim and worn-out topic could be served up in good salable newspaper articles." But Coxey and Browne found a way, compelling the newspapers of the continent to devote from one to six columns daily to reporting the Commonweal—that is to say, to echoing the clamor of work for the workless.[14]

What Coxey and Browne essentially did was to create an unemployment adventure story that the press found irresistible. With characters sufficiently colorful and the perils of the journey sufficiently great, curiosity alone drew to the drama readers who cared little or nothing about complex economic issues or what it all portended. Whether by accident or design, the originator of the Commonweal applied to social protest a few of the lessons he had learned in art. From the experience of exhibiting his gargantuan panoramas, the Californian knew that no matter how bad a work of art might be, if it were sufficiently outrageous it would elicit comment and attract wider attention.

And what could be more outrageous than mixing together serious and widespread concern about unemployment, the theories of reincarnation and non-interest-bearing bonds, the name and likeness of Jesus Christ, the Great Unknown, a silica sand seer worth a quarter million dollars, the Buffalo Bill of Napa County (or Napa State Hospital), and dozens of mystical slogans and drawings? All that were needed to round out the phantasmagoria were violence—the theft of a train, perhaps—and sex, and those would be supplied soon enough. Surely in Carl Browne's version of hell, to be ignored was a far greater torment than to be derided or criticized.

Newspapers made the most of the inherent ambiguity of the drama. And certainly part of the suspense lay not simply in speculating whether the Commonwealers would make it to Capitol Hill or what they would do once they got there, but whether a clear meaning for America would finally emerge from the discordant elements. Each day's press coverage was similar to peeling off one layer of an onion only to find yet another. What would removal of the final layer reveal? Perhaps nothing, proving correct those people who treated the Commonweal as lighthearted entertainment, the product of a nation's innate love of adventure, or as "fresh evidence of the elasticity of the American spirit."[15]

The decades of the late nineteenth and early twentieth centuries constituted the golden age of the crank in America, and Coxey and Browne were only two members of that eccentric fraternity. Why at that time so many people should be labeled cranks and should have attracted so much attention is no great mystery: those years were what one historian has aptly described as a "shake-up period," an era of dramatic and unusually rapid economic change that undermined prevailing norms, institutions, and patterns of behavior. At the same time, vast new areas of knowledge had not yet been professionalized and systematized in the colleges and universities; in fact, the ivy-covered bastions of conservatism and elitism would likely terminate a professor for advocating such heresy as the government ownership of railroads. The result for the common person was an extraordinarily freewheeling type of economic and intellectual democracy, unchecked by past restraints and as yet unchanneled by new laws and institutions.[16]

Neither the barons of industry nor the self-appointed microbe masters feared the restraining hand of the federal government. Congress did not create the first national regulatory agency until 1887 (the Interstate Commerce Commission) and did not follow that with the Food and Drug Administration until 1906. The golden age of the crank was thus the best of all worlds for the stock manipulator, backyard inventor, patent-medicine fakir, and amateur political economist.[17]

If an inventor succeeded in producing something the world considered practical (and thereby valuable), he might advance in status from tinkerer or crank to wizard or genius. Until the Wright brothers got off the ground at Kitty Hawk, they were no different from the other eccentrics who proposed to build a flying machine. Before he died on the eve of World War I, Carl Browne took up the challenge of building an improved flying machine. Had he succeeded, society would certainly have treated his other eccentricities more charitably. During the golden age of the crank, in short, a person might easily shift from concocting patent medicines to building improved airplanes and social and financial theories.[18]

A crank in its most literal manifestation is a handle to activate a piece of machinery. Who could tell whether one of the eccentrics whom society labeled cranks in the 1890s might succeed in activating the social machinery that would resolve the contradiction between progress and poverty? And which of the cranks would devote his entire life seeking to activate a perpetual-motion machine? In either case, newspapers duly reported the activities of each.

CHAPTER 3

It is not the part of wisdom to treat the crazy propaganda of Coxey merely as a joke."

Ohio State Journal,
April 13, 1894

Marching with Coxey's Army

On Easter Sunday the Commonwealers marched nine miles in a sharp, frigid wind, snow, and sleet to Canton (population 26,189). More pilgrims joined the ranks along the way, but out of a total of two hundred marchers fewer than a dozen had overcoats and gloves. Despite the inclement weather, spectators lined both sides of the rolling and rutted road and followed in overcrowded cars of the parallel Massillon and Canton Electric Railway. At Reedurban the column halted for a quick lunch of canned salmon sandwiches.[1]

When they reached Canton about four o'clock that afternoon, several thousand more spectators cheered them on. They marched past the home of Governor William McKinley and hastened to pitch camp in a vacant woodlot adjoining the local workhouse. Tormenting them all the while was a freezing wind and blowing snow. Stark County provided a supper of ham and eggs, and sympathizers donated dry straw for bedding.

Going into a camp for the night, the Commonwealers typically formed a circle in true western fashion: the chief marshal would advance to the center, followed by the color-bearer, who planted his flag. Pickets took their stations at the perimeter. Other men prepared supper or pitched the tents. The Commonweal owned two tents, a round one about sixteen feet in diameter that sheltered many but not all the men, and a square one decorated with Browne's artwork that served as headquarters. Coxey and Browne usually slept in a local hotel or rooming house rather than in camp with their men, a curiously elitist practice that bred resentment among the troops and no end of criticism by the press.

Along the country roads and in the little towns of northern Ohio, the Commonweal always created a sensation. People lined the fence rows and street corners to see in person the characters about whom they had read so much. The pulse quickened as the American flag swung into view, held proudly aloft by Jasper Johnson, faithful Bunker Hill at his side. Invariably bringing up the rear were Weary Bill and the famous panorama wagon.

In between, popular interest centered on Coxey, the Unknown, and then the magnificent stallions, an order of status that bruised Browne's enormous ego and in time made him jealous of the mysterious stranger he had helped to create. The curious wanted to see if they could place the handsome and well-dressed mystery man. "The Great Unknown is being identified regularly about five times a day by people who are sure they know what they are talking about," reported Ray Stannard Baker. To some he was a German major, an Austrian captain, a Colorado militia officer, an anarchist, or an actor. He appeared well read and possibly was a man of wealth.

This much was certain: the Unknown was a fine horseman and a natural leader. Though he had a bluff and brisk way of ordering the marchers about, his influence over them was complete. Unlike Coxey and Browne, the Unknown shared all the hardships of the trail, including the camp's crude sleeping facilities. "Why that man could arm us with Winchesters and make a real army out of us," said one marcher. "We would shoot anyone he ordered us to." The Unknown's favorite admonition to each man, however, was to keep up his personal appearance while on the road.

New recruits straggled in each day. Usually the person enrolling them was Dr. "Cyclone" Kirkland of Pittsburgh, a short, shriveled man about sixty years old who practiced medicine and whatever else struck his fancy. In addition to recruiting officer, he served as the army's physician and unofficial astrologer. The stars, he reported to Browne's delight, told him this was to be the greatest movement the world had ever seen. As for his name, he claimed to be the reincarnation of an Indian chief named Cyclone.

Kirkland's watery blue eyes were forever discerning signs in the heavens that augured well for the march. One night he awoke the entire camp to see a most wonderful sign, an enormous stellar wheel. "No one but he could see it," complained the reporter for the *Post-Dispatch*. "Others have wheels in their heads."

At Alliance, Cyclone in his role as recruiting officer signed up a typical recruit:

"What is your name?" asked Kirkland, who was nearly blind.

"Peter Miesner."

"Peter, Peter—that's a good name; you've heard of Peter the Great and Peter the Apostle. You may sometime be Peter the Great. Try. 'Some men are born great, some achieve greatness, while others have greatness thrust upon them.' Unborn children may yet rise up to call you blessed. What is your occupation?"

"A miner."

"I see. You labor in the bowels of the earth. Be faithful and you shall receive your reward. Credit where credit is due. *Sic semper tyrannis.* Never call a man by a nickname. Step aside and be good. You belong to the greatest army on earth."

Although each day's march followed a predictable routine—bugle at seven, washtime before breakfast, rations distributed to each man for the meals later in the day—creative reporters (some of whom secretly slipped into the ranks as recruits) invariably found something new to whet readers' interest in the ongoing saga of Coxey's argonauts. To speculation about the identity of the Unknown they added a spicy new mystery: who was the veiled lady who arrived in Alliance from Chicago? Rumor had it that she was a very attractive brunette, about thirty years old, who would serve as a goddess of peace. But why did she wear that heavy black crepe veil? A chambermaid revealed to reporters that the mystery woman had a black eye that she claimed was the result of a child's accidentally striking her with a piece of furniture. By the maid's reckoning, however, the child must have been a giant.

Reporters suspected that the veiled lady was married to the Unknown, who had once said of his wife, "She will not join the army.

I would not have her in the march for $1,000 a day." Had he given her the black eye in a fit of rage? Whoever she was, Browne wanted nothing to do with her. Afraid that the presence of a woman would spark damaging press speculation about immorality in the ranks, he ordered the veiled lady to travel well ahead of the men.

One day, as Ray Stannard Baker happened to walk around the corner of a tent, he spied the Unknown alone. The mystery man, unaware that he was being observed, burst into a fit of laughter from which he recovered almost instantly. Was he feeling the tension of command or merely laughing at himself and the whole spectacle? Without providing an answer, Baker dutifully forwarded his observation to the *Record* and thus contributed further to the growing interest in the Unknown, the Veiled Lady, and other members of the Commonweal.

While the sensationalism undeniably generated much interest in the Commonweal, Browne never forgot that its main purpose was to educate people along the way in financial matters. A night seldom passed that the professor in buckskin did not conduct an impromptu reform lyceum for any locals who turned out to study the petition in boots (and sometimes bring it donations of crackers, pies, or bacon). Using a long stick to point to his artwork, Browne patiently explained its symbolic meaning and inevitably launched into a vigorous attack on the existing economic order. He was a forceful speaker, but not a humorous one.

On most Sundays, Browne, sometimes aided by Coxey, conducted a special religious service in his inimitable style. He mounted the panorama wagon and in a smooth but ungrammatical tongue proceeded to put his listeners in a relaxed mood by relating a few parables before launching into a strange and wondrous monologue laced with bits of prophecy, politics, finance, and reincarnation. The rank and file Commonwealers apparently viewed Browne's religious views with considerable skepticism, as something to be tolerated. "Their minds are apparently too full of economic questions," claimed one cynic.

Whatever the marchers' doubts about reincarnation, there was no dispute about one matter: liquor in the camp. Browne showed absolutely no toleration for public drunkenness. And indeed the Commonweal was a model of Spartan rigor. Coxey's army was remarkably free not only of drunks but also of female camp followers and thieves. The well-fed chickens that strutted outside the large red barns dotting the northern Ohio countryside were often the subject of wistful remarks, but no Commonwealer undertook to steal one. "Every crime that is committed within thirty miles of our line of march will be laid at the doors of the army," Coxey warned. "People are doing their best to throw discredit on our work."

Marching east from Canton, the Commonweal followed a route roughly paralleling the tracks of the Pennsylvania Railroad through Louisville, Alliance, and the Quaker settlement of Salem, in slavery days a center on the underground railroad. The folk there gave the pilgrims an especially warm reception. In other communities they were met by residents bearing hot coffee and sandwiches. As a rule, the Commonwealers fared well in any locale that contained members of the Populist party or organized labor.

It was hard not to feel some compassion for the woebegone soldiers of misfortune who plodded through the seemingly bottomless mud and slush of northeastern Ohio. Again and again the wagons bogged down and the marchers had to be called back to free them. At Garfield some boys collected bushels of snowballs to pelt the Coxeyites, but the pilgrims' appearance was so forlorn that the would-be tormenters allowed them to pass unmolested. The Commonweal covered an average of about three miles in an hour, or a total of fifteen to twenty miles a day. Before long, the men's feet hurt and their enthusiasm flickered, especially when Coxey left for a few days on a business trip. Some newspapers claimed that he had abandoned the crusade. In an attempt to boost the men's spirits, Cyclone Kirkland organized a glee club.

The last day of March found the Commonwealers trudging across a bleak and rolling landscape dotted by coal mines and an occasional oil derrick. As they neared the Pennsylvania border, they wondered whether their interstate movement would attract the attention of federal authorities. Rumors circulated that legions of militiamen blocked the way ahead. But their fears proved groundless. Not a deputy was in sight when they entered Pennsylvania. In fact, scarcely was there any sign of a border dividing the dandelion-studded hill.

Next morning the people of the picturesque and fertile Beaver Valley gave the Commonweal its most impressive reception to date. It

Coxey's army—early days on the road. Courtesy Library of Congress.

was Sunday, and thirty thousand spectators turned out all along the valley to cheer the marchers on. They also contributed nearly five tons of provisions. Coxey was elated by the warm welcome, which contrasted favorably with frosty receptions in a few towns earlier. The triumphal march through the Beaver Valley was an auspicious way for the Commonweal to begin its second week on the road.

At Economy, a quaint old Rappite town, the Commonweal reached the Ohio River; and as the pilgrims continued down the broad valley, they noticed the unmistakable signs of a new season. The air was balmier now, and the hills that lined the river wore the yellow-green mantle of new spring growth. Ahead lay Pittsburgh and adjacent Allegheny City, Pennsylvania's second- and third-largest cities. In fact, their combined population of 345,000 was larger than that of any other urban area through which the Commonweal would pass—including Washington, D.C. In many respects they formed a single city (as indeed they became a few years later), one built on a foundation of iron and steel, glass, and oil. Some sixty iron and steel mills, sixty glass works, and sixty oil refineries covered the cities by day with a dense pall of smoke and illuminated them by night with the fiery glow of blast furnaces and foundries.

When the pilgrims arrived on April 3, the two communities were Coxey's for the asking, much to the dismay of the police department of Allegheny City. The marchers had to pass through that area first and planned to camp there for the night. At the last minute, lawmen forced Commonwealers to detour around Allegheny City's large working-class neighborhoods, known to support Coxey's cause. But the rerouting failed to dampen popular enthusiasm, and residents of Pittsburgh and Allegheny City lined the new route in unprecedented numbers.

All morning the newsboys shouted nothing but "Coxey! Coxey! Coxey!" Clerks whispered "Coxey" to one another in the half-deserted department stores. Public-school students were dismissed so they could see the procession. Onlookers standing forty deep cheered wildly as Coxey passed by, and their presence snarled traffic.

Not since the troops had returned to Pittsburgh from the Civil War had the area been the scene of such enthusiasm. Telegraph lines carried little else but Coxey news; his face stared out from every newspaper sold on the street. Bakers worked the word "Coxey" into the icing of cookies served at lunch stands. Red, white, and blue badges with "Coxey" in gold letters fluttered from several thousand lapels. Leading the procession were two policemen, followed by four detectives and four hundred members of the Pittsburgh Iron Molders' Union, each man carrying a ceremonial walking stick. Next came a hundred bicyclists, all shouting for Coxey and his program of good roads. They were followed by companies of pattern makers, boiler-makers, bakers, and other labor organizations, each man wearing the badge of his union. A uniformed band of forty pieces passed by, play-ing a special Coxey's march; and everywhere small boys and "Kodak fiends" added to the excitement and confusion.

Carl Browne rode along on Courier and occasionally tipped his sombrero to the crowd. As usual there were Jasper Johnson, Old Glory, the yellow mongrel Bunker Hill, Dr. Cyclone, banners, and the rank-and-file Commonwealers, now numbering two hundred fifty. Coxey rode in a phaeton beside his black coachman. A reporter noted that the leader had a dab of black soot on his nose. The press missed nothing.

By the time Coxey's Commonweal reached Pittsburgh it was clear that, aside from the popular press, the two institutions doing most to sustain the industrial army movement were the Populist party and union labor. The labor press, reflecting the sympathies of workers in Pittsburgh and most other communities outside New England and the South, overwhelmingly championed the cause, treating the petition in boots as representing America's economic underdogs. Yet labor's support was not without some reservation, as a fiery debate within the Baltimore Federation of Labor revealed. When that body voted to endorse the Commonweal, dissenters protested that they had endorsed only the principle of free speech. "Who are these people?" complained one union man. "Coxey is a horse speculator and 'Unknown Smith' and Carl Browne are patent medicine men or fakirs."

"We are opposed to picking up a lot of darn infernal tramps who are living on the public," emphasized a cigar maker. But another member retorted that Coxeyites were "as good workmen as could be found." What was probably the prevailing belief among organized workers was expressed by a union man in Terre Haute: "They may be wrong. They say their scheme is only an experiment. If it succeeds, every laboring man will be benefited."[2]

Populists, who seemed congenitally disposed to aid the underdog, overwhelmingly supported the Coxey crusade, although some would have preferred to see the men remain at home and "march on the ballot box" instead. A common belief maintained that Coxeyism had its origins in the Populist party and that the party was exploiting the movement for its own selfish ends: "The Coxeyites are populists of the lowest grade, mobilized, so to speak, for active service. All populists look to Washington for aid or relief, but the Coxeyites start for Washington in person," fumed the *Nation*. Actually, in all but a few Coxey contingents, Democrats and Republicans vastly outnumbered Populists, although several march leaders maintained close ties to the Populist party and at least one (Edward J. Jeffries of the Seattle contingent) was a ranking state party official.[3]

Another notable feature of the Coxey movement was how few members it recruited from the South or Northeast. Of the several thousand soldiers who took to the road, fewer than three hundred were *not* members of western or midwestern armies. Except for very small contingents that arose briefly in Houston and the steel-making center of Birmingham, Coxey had no imitators in Dixie. The reason was not that the South lacked industry and thus unemployment. By 1894 several industrial centers had arisen there, and joblessness was a problem in Atlanta and Richmond no less than it was in Boston and Providence.

In fact, New England, one of the most heavily industrialized sections of the United States, contributed so few marchers to Coxey's cause that a wealthy patron could have sent them all to Washington in three or four railway coaches. The same was true for Coxeyites from New York and Pennsylvania.[4] Christopher Columbus Jones recruited fewer than one hundred men from Philadelphia, a city with a population of more than a million in 1890, or about ten times that of Montana and only slightly less than California, two states that gave birth to large and multiple industrial armies. Clearly, the population of a community or region, numbers of idle factories, or tallies of jobless men were by themselves poor predictors of the popularity and strength of the Coxey movement.[5]

What, then, helped account for the movement's greater popularity on the sunset side of the continent? Foremost, westerners saw in Coxeyism something more than a crusade for jobs; it served as a vehicle for voicing a host of regional desires and grievances. The westerner need not be an unemployed wageworker to support a proposal for a federal irrigation program, a key plank in the platform of every West Coast contingent. "There is nothing anarchist or unreasonable about this objective," said the *Los Angeles Times* in response to a California army's irrigation proposal. Moreover, many a westerner voiced the same approval of some Coxeyites' call for federal aid to put the ailing Rocky Mountain silver industry back on its feet.

More than in any other region, wageworkers in the West were familiar with seasonal employment and the boom-and-bust cycles that characterized its major industries, and were consequently no strangers to a migratory way of life. For the young and restless types who came west seeking adventure, the Coxey movement offered a special appeal, a chance to see new country, or simply a chance to return to homes in the East. "These people have not taken root in the country. They have not acquired homesteads; they have put no money in the savings bank, or if they have it has been drawn to meet the pressure of hard times," observed the *San Francisco Bulletin* of local Coxeyites. For many seekers, the depression of the 1890s disproved the popular equation of the West with opportunity, and that disappointment heightened their interest in Coxey's protest.[6]

Imagine how a discontented iron worker in Pittsburgh or a struggling farmer in Michigan in the 1880s might have reacted to the many promotional brochures that had presented the new West as paradise on earth, where wages were good, strikes and lockouts unknown, and crops immune to failure. It was a considerable deviation from the truth, but who outside the region would know that? Even if the salesmanship sometimes appeared ludicrous, and even if no one could be certain how many people it enticed west, the message conveyed a decade before by the deluge of pamphlets, handbills, and broadsides had been plain: in their collective attempt to equate the West with opportunity, the promoters had hammered home the message that both wageworkers and farmers would be better off living there. Perhaps the wageworker might even acquire the means to become a farmer and thus achieve his emancipation from "wage slavery." The ideal was to gain personal independence, and life and labor in the West had clearly seemed to offer that opportunity. The pamphleteers had been mythmakers, purveyors of a dream of boundless new opportunities, a dream that won the West.[7]

Perhaps because they expected so much in coming west, residents of the western states were quick to complain about injustices, real or imagined. Squeezed by reality and hard times, debt-encumbered westerners resented the economic power of their eastern creditors. They were unhappy about railroad rates, which they complained were too high, and about railroad power in general. An important vehicle for expressing western resentments was the Populist party, which had its primary following in the South and West and did much to cultivate the belief that the thousands of unemployed men walking the streets of Denver, Seattle, and elsewhere were the victims of financial conspiracies hatched on Wall Street or in London. In 1893, several prominent Populists of the West went so far as to call for a conference to discuss the region's commercial secession from the East. People spoke of a new sectionalism and described the West as a "simmering, seething cauldron of discontent." From that witches' brew of discontent emerged the large industrial armies that Coxey's example inspired.[8]

CHAPTER 4

Coxey's men are going to Washington hoping to get what is left after the sugar trust and the other monopolists are given all they ask."

St. Louis Post-Dispatch, April 22, 1894

Big Savage: One More Mountain to Climb

Coxey's men scarcely had time to reflect on their triumphal entry into greater Pittsburgh before they stumbled into a morass of trouble. That night, while Coxey spoke to a gathering of nearly seven thousand people, his army found itself under virtual house arrest in Allegheny City.[1]

Only after they had filed into a local baseball park and pitched camp did they realize their predicament. Nervous Allegheny City police, leaping on the Commonweal "as though it were a dangerous snake," sealed every entrance to the camp. The night air was cold and raw, and the pilgrims were obliged to sleep on bare ground without even a handful of straw for bedding. To make matters worse, a steady drizzle nearly extinguished their campfires, and high winds billowed out the canvas of the large round tent and badly ripped it. Police refused to allow anyone to leave the park to get the needles and thread necessary to make repairs.

When in desperation twenty-eight Coxeyites escaped to seek warmer quarters, police arrested them for vagrancy, and a judge hastily sentenced the lot to the local workhouse for thirty days. This discouraging fate further dampened the spirits of the Commonwealers and made many of them ready to surrender and head home. They probably would have but for the Unknown, who by working house-to-house outside the camp had stirred up sympathy for the prisoners by asking the question: "Hasn't a quiet and orderly American citizen the right to personal liberty?" Allegheny City officials, meanwhile, concluded that they really did not want the expense of providing for the prisoners. As a result, after a day of confinement and enforced rest, Commonwealers were escorted by policemen to the city limits. The chief of police of Allegheny City was not done with Coxey and his army, though; he sent a letter to his counterpart in Washington, D.C., describing the visitors in derogatory terms and helping set the stage for a future confrontation on Capitol Hill.

A fife and drum corps and an army of trade unionists escorted Coxey's men through Pittsburgh and across the Monongahela River. Merchants in south Pittsburgh were exceedingly generous, adding to the army's commissary 100 pounds of bologna, 200 pounds of beef, 5 sacks of flour, and a dozen bushels of vegetables. The shouts of hundreds of workers and the screeching whistles of locomotives and steamboats cheered the marchers on as they wound along the river. While on the road, the Commonwealers were soaked by the first storm they had encountered outside camp—but not a man defected from the ranks. As they neared Homestead early that afternoon, local workers fired salutes with rifles and a small cannon. A banner at the edge of town read, "Homestead Believes in Coxey's Good Roads Bill."

Homestead had not been on Browne's original itinerary, but even before the Commonwealers left Massillon a committee of steelworkers laid plans to have them detour through it. Just two years earlier, Homestead had been the site of a bloody battle between union men and three hundred Pinkerton hirelings of the steel king Andrew Carnegie. Although workers won a celebrated fight with the Pinkertons, who were brought upriver by barge, they ultimately lost the war. Now they saw Coxey as a champion of labor.[2]

For the next several days, Coxey's men tramped south through the smoke-begrimed valley of the Monongahela on yellow clay roads made sticky by rain, winding up and down the scarred and barren hills that bordered the river. These were by far the worst roads yet encountered, and at times they slowed the Commonweal to a crawl.[3]

In the industrial towns of the Monongahela Valley, the Commonweal gained some new recruits—mostly Slavs and Czechs who spoke very little English but were enthusiastic supporters of the crusade. Before this addition the pilgrims had been, in Ray Stannard Baker's words, all "Americans and Negroes." Some of the original Commonwealers were not happy with the newcomers, but Coxey and Browne welcomed them with open arms. Also joining was Alexander "Cheeky" Childs, rumored to be a nephew of Andrew Carnegie, and Donald Fitch, a highland bagpiper and stonecutter, whose favorite tune was "After the Ball," which he rung with great effort from his reluctant instrument. He admitted he knew "varra leetle" about Coxey's bills, but believed that Coxey was a "gran' mon."

Despite Coxey and Browne's compassion toward the East European recruits, the crusade as a whole remained very ambiguous on matters of race and ethnicity, voicing lofty ideals but also harboring the prejudices of the larger society in which it operated. In the 1890s, hostility to blacks and immigrants from southern and eastern Europe was on the rise in the United States. On the West Coast, most Coxeyites reflected the region's extreme hostility toward Chinese immigrants. Nonetheless, in a community as spontaneous and eclectic as an industrial army, it is perhaps remarkable that as much harmony prevailed as did in matters of race and ethnicity, most notably between whites and blacks. Compared to the American Federation of Labor and Eugene Debs's newly formed American Railway Union, both of which contained many members openly hostile to Chinese and blacks, Coxey's ranks remained remarkably open to all comers.[4]

After a week of toiling up Pennsylvania's Monongahela Valley, the footsore Commonwealers reached Brownsville and the historic National Road, which had seen better days but was still an excellent highway in this area. Its hard-packed clay surface made the march easy. All along the pike farmers turned out to cheer, and Fitch the bagpiper treated them to "After the Ball." The Commonwealers were spectators, too; they noted that farmers in the area lived in log buildings with stone chimneys on the outside and split shingle roofs. When the National Road wound along a ridge, the men saw the Allegheny Mountains blue and misty in the distance. Few knew anything about how they would cross them, but soon they learned more than they ever wanted to know.

Even as the Commonweal seemed to surmount all obstacles on its journey from Pittsburgh to Uniontown, a town of narrow and rambling streets at the foot of the Alleghenies, internal friction increased by the day. At Homestead the Unknown formally instituted a military system of organization. Browne overruled him, issuing a special order prohibiting military titles. Even so, the newspapers continued to call Coxey "General" and further irritated the Californian when they treated the Unknown as his equal. More trouble erupted in Uniontown when four familiar figures, now known as the "Pittsburgh dime museum freaks," tried to rejoin the ranks.

From the beginning Browne had taken an exceedingly dim view of the often-voiced assertion that his men were freaks. So when Cyclone Kirkland, Weary Iler, Jasper Johnson, and Bunker Hill had succumbed to temptation in Pittsburgh and agreed to appear for a week in a Coxey exhibit at a local dime museum, Browne excommunicated them all. Now they had returned and asked to be reinstated to the ranks. Fellow marchers cheered their return and supported their request. The Unknown, in charge of the camp, let it be known that he, too, favored reinstatement but would defer to his superiors. A special officers' meeting turned them down.

The Cyclone was furious and sputtered, "Dark clouds are tumbling in the east. The blood of Mars is dripping on Coxey. The war is on. Is it a cyclone or is it a misguided hand? We shall see." He threatened to organize a group named Counterwheel, which would admit women as members. With their aid, he prophesied, his group would become a dangerous rival to Coxey's. In fact, the Cyclone was all bluster, for little more was seen of the Pittsburgh prophet or his fellow museum freaks.

While the Commonweal camped in Uniontown, two other events of significance occurred. For the first time, the troop failed to maintain Browne's published schedule. A terrible rain, snow, and windstorm forced the army to remain in the dance pavilion at Mountain View Park another day. Equally significant, or so some claimed, "the humble theosophist" unexpectedly molted. When he appeared on stage in a local opera house clad in a new broadcloth double-breasted suit, stand-up collar, and a derby that perched uncomfortably on his head, his men were stunned into silence. They finally cheered, but lamented one, "It didn't seem natural."

The mountains lay just ahead, and the army was—in Browne's words—on the "threshold of cataclysm." A Pittsburgh paper explained: "Today it has finished the last march through the land of plenty, and tomorrow it plunges into the mountains and the land of moonshine." In that sparsely settled country there was scant chance of a handout. Hardtack, bacon, and coffee would likely be the army's only fare until it reached Cumberland, Maryland, five days beyond.[5]

The second morning in Uniontown dawned with the promise of no better weather than the day before. The Unknown wanted to remain in camp yet another day, but Browne feared that the men would never reach the Capitol by May Day, and ordered them to prepare for the march. They ate a breakfast of coffee, bread, and crackers; and spirits were high despite the inclement weather. "I would be willing to wade rivers and live on hardtack alone," claimed one member, "if I could see Mr. Coxey's bills pass." He might have felt differently by evening, for even Browne was to admit that the day's climb was one of the most trying ordeals of the whole journey.

Commonwealers tramped out of Uniontown in a steady drizzle, past rows of smoking coke ovens and workers' shanties. The pieces of burlap that some marchers tied around their shoes to keep their feet warm and dry proved of little use in ankle-deep mud. And as the thinly clad men wound higher up the steep and rocky western slope of Chestnut Ridge, rain changed to snow. Time and again the commissary wagons bogged down during the six-mile climb and had to be pushed by squads of sweating, grunting men wet to the skin. Cowboy crusaders used their lariats to assist the tired and worn-out horses through the foot-deep snow.

Along the way the Commonweal passed stagehouses and inns now deserted. Before railroads had eclipsed the National Road in the 1850s, the inns' carpeted dining rooms and egalitarian barrooms had rung with the laughter of teamsters and travelers. Once this had been the nation's main highway between east and west; settlers, soldiers, merchants, and presidents passed along on foot, on horseback, and in vehicles of every description, from Conestoga wagons to fast-flying stagecoaches that covered the 130 miles from Cumberland to Wheeling in twenty-four hours. Damp snow now festooned the tangled bushes of laurel and raspberry with a garland of ermine.

As darkness fell, the marchers were forced to camp in an abandoned colonial mansion that stood back from the road on a wind-swept knoll. A large hole yawned in the roof, but the Commonwealers soon drove out the cold with a roaring blaze in the capacious stone fireplace. They stuffed their shabby coats and hats into broken window sashes. Outside, the snow continued to fall and shutters creaked ominously in the wind. The inhabitants of this region consisted mainly of rabbits, crows, and bears that lived in the stunted oaks and laurel bushes that stretched for miles in all directions.

This was a primitive and isolated land, bypassed by the railroads and thus by the mainstream of American history since the Civil War. News of the march terrified the scattered residents of the backcountry, who prepared for trouble by loading their rifles with bear shot. The Scotch-Irish mountaineers hardly read newspapers; but they knew the stories old-timers told of guerilla bands that terrorized the area after the Civil War, and they wanted no repeat of their pillage.[6]

Each day's march through this country brought new troubles. Some of the marchers located some whiskey bottles that they had stashed away for an emergency and proceeded to drink themselves into a stupor. A Pittsburgh newspaper identified the Unknown as a Pinkerton spy. He denied it, but that rumor continued to haunt him. Browne was so afraid that drunken mountaineers would shoot up the camp that he could scarcely sleep at night. His men saw him occasionally examining loads in the two long-barreled sixshooters that he now carried. The Californian grew peevish and overbearing, and men reduced to a diet of hardtack, sowbelly, and black coffee found him hard to take. They grumbled louder than ever. Browne's mind buzzed with rumors of a plot to have the Unknown succeed him somewhere in the mountain country on the strength of a bogus telegram from Coxey, who was absent on another of his many business trips.

A dwindling number of Commonwealers continued to plod along the National Road through the wild backcountry, up ridges and down into hollows and past tumbledown villages. Donald Fitch played so insistently on his bagpipe that the sufferers begged him to cease. Sullen mountaineers wearing long scraggly beards, threadbare pants, and shoes patched with rags occasionally gathered alongside the road to watch.

On a bridge of three graceful stone arches the Commonweal crossed the Youghiogheny River into Somerset County—the heart of Pennsylvania's moonshine country. Browne expected trouble when he spied the sheriff and a posse of six deputies waiting just ahead. But they were there only to preserve the peace between the Coxeyites and the moonshine-making mountaineers. At every crossroad more deputies stood guard. Many county residents barricaded their doors in expectation of violence, but the Commonweal passed through without incident. A day later it reached a white obelisk with letters painted in black, "Maryland State Line." Browne ordered a halt. Bandmaster Thayer began to trill "Maryland, My Maryland" on his coronet. The bass drummer couldn't follow, but a mule nearby brayed along in a lighthearted and festive manner, or so reported Ray Stannard Baker.

The men gave three cheers for Maryland and three more for Pennsylvania. The road ahead was muddy, but at least the snow was gone. Glad to be out of the land of moonshine, Browne became his ebullient self once again. He promised the Commonwealers that the road ahead would be "sunshiny and downhill," but when the locals heard that they only shook their heads in disbelief. They knew that one more range of the Alleghenies blocked the way, and that obstacle bore the ominous name of Big Savage Mountain. Though it actually was named for an early surveyor, John Savage, its double meaning became abundantly clear to the men who struggled toward its summit.

It was a steep thirteen-mile climb. As the men trudged along the National Road in ankle-deep mud, a brisk head wind sapped their strength and morale. Fewer than 140 argonauts now remained in the ranks. Browne gave up his usual stallion so that it could pull a stalled wagon, replacing a horse that had dropped dead on an earlier climb. The big Californian rode instead on a shaggy cow pony and looked ridiculous. Frequently he stopped the column so he might lecture a knot of onlookers on the money question, delays the sweating troops considered unnecessary and increasingly intolerable. Once he halted the column and ordered three cheers for something, the men cared not what. All they saw was a log cabin, a cat sleeping on the doorstep, and four lanky mountaineers lounging beside the road.

Just before they reached the 2,850-foot summit, the Unknown, who had been doing most of the work of keeping the column moving and the men's spirits up, became hungry and rode back to the commissary wagon for a heel of bread and a bit of cheese. Browne spied him and rode over.

"What are you thinking of, Marshal Smith? I should think you would know better than to eat food before a crowd of hungry men. Don't let me see such a thing again." The Unknown did not respond to the Californian but chewed each bite with a firmly set jaw.

A short distance ahead Browne spied a group of onlookers and ordered the Commonweal to halt while he delivered another of his grandiloquent greetings. The men grumbled aloud. The Unknown, still smarting from Browne's sharp rebuke, galloped forward. Leaning forward toward Browne, he erupted, "See here, Browne, you fat-faced fake, this is my bark today; next time I'll bite. Just you get it through your head that if you ever try to make another grandstand play around me I'll make a punching-bag out of your face." He grabbed Browne by the collar and continued, "Confound you. I found you on your uppers in Chicago. I picked you out of the mud. I've the greatest mind to pull you out and and show you up before the men right now."

Browne rode ahead in silence, then, coming to another group of rustics, lapsed into his old ways. "Commonweal, halt!" From back in the ranks came the youthful voice of Jesse Coxey: "Commonweal, forward march!" The men had been complaining to the lad about Browne, and in his father's absence he now moved to undercut the Californian.

Browne's eyes bulged with rage. Again he ordered, "Commonweal, halt!"

"Forward march!" shouted the Unknown. The two leaders glared at one another. The Unknown suddenly wheeled around to face the men: "Men of the Commonweal, you and I have roughed it together. We have fought it out with the winter weather from the Ohio to the Alleghenies and we have won. You know how I have been with you, working for your comfort while others were enjoying their ease and you were tired, hungry, wet, and cold. It is for you to say, men, who shall command you. I have nothing more to offer. Will you have Smith, who has brought order out of chaos and made the army what it is, or will you follow this leather-coated polecat?"

There was a moment of dead silence. Then a man at the front of the column threw his hat in the air and shouted, "Hurrah for Smith!" The rest of the army picked up the cry. "Smith! Smith! Give us the Unknown! We don't want that leather-coated freak anyhow. You're the man. Hurrah for Smith! We want Smith! We want to turn down that greasy old humbug." Not a voice was raised for Browne. The Unknown waved his hand to silence the uproar. "If you say Smith is to command you, then Smith will command you." Galloping to the head of the column, he cried, "Obey only my commands and those of Jesse Coxey. Now, Commonweal, attention! Forward!"

Browne bellowed out in rage: "Commonweal, halt! Men this is mutiny. What do you fellows mean by taking up with this hireling Pinkerton? This man has been written up as one and I believe it. He's a Pinkerton."

The marchers jeered and the Unknown snapped, "That is a falsehood spoken by a coward, and not one of our people will believe it."

Browne shot back, "You may lead these men astray if you wish, but I control the commissary wagons and I shall not proceed." The Unknown coolly detailed a force of men to take charge of the commissary and left Browne in possession only of his rickety panorama wagon. As the column headed for Frostburg, Browne commandeered Coxey's empty phaeton and started off at a furious pace, vowing that he would swear out warrants for the arrest of both the Unknown and Jesse Coxey. A short while later, the Commonweal overtook its deposed leader sitting forlornly beside the road. One of Coxey's expensive horses had dropped exhausted in its tracks. Smith generously returned the shaggy cow pony to Browne, who took it and without a word sped off to telegraph news of the mutiny to Coxey.[7]

When Browne received no immediate reply from Coxey, he was clearly worried. The Commonwealers, meanwhile, camped in Frostburg under the command of their new marshal, who became more confident with each passing minute. The next morning, just at sunrise, the pilgrims spied a lone carriage tearing furiously down a distant mountain road. As it drew nearer, they recognized Coxey and cheered wildly. Their leader's face was pale and his clothes spattered with the mud of the road from Cumberland, over which he had raced since midnight.

The deposed marshal was first to greet him. After talking briefly with Browne, the Unknown, and his son, who told him that the Californian was a scoundrel and a crook, Coxey mounted a soapbox near the center of the big room in the Frostburg Opera House, where the army had spent the night. Speaking to his followers for a few moments, he called all those in favor of the Unknown to rise. One hundred fifty-eight did—all but four members of the Commonweal. The Unknown was visibly exultant. Browne's complexion changed from white to bright red, and he bit his lip in anger. But no one was prepared for the surprise Coxey next sprang.

"I cast 154 votes for Brother Browne," said the leader in a calm voice, "and I further order that Mr. Smith, the Unknown, be forever expelled from the army."

Coxey called for the marchers to ratify his decision. All meekly voted in favor of Smith's expulsion.

"Then it is settled," replied Coxey. "Mr. Smith goes to join some museum aggregation, if he likes."

The men murmured, "Jesse Coxey must go too; he was as much to blame as Smith."

"All right, if Jesse was wrong he will have to go too."

The Unknown walked across the street to a vacant lot where several marchers had collected around a campfire and mounted a stack of lumber. "I have been deposed," he shouted, "by a patent-medicine shark; a greasy-coated hypocrite; a seeker for personal advancement. When Browne was driven from the lake front last fall by Mayor Harrison, I befriended him, got him a place to speak and this is the way he repays me." The Unknown and Browne nearly came to blows before Coxey appeared on the scene: "Smith, get out of this camp or I'll have you arrested inside of five minutes." Vowing vengeance, the Unknown hired a carriage; he and a handful of followers, most notably Jesse Coxey and "Cheeky" Childs, drove ahead to Cumberland.

Coxey's support of Browne in the face of overwhelming opposition by the men strengthened the suspicions of those who believed Browne exercised a hypnotic influence over the wealthy businessman. Coxey's explanation, however, was simple, if undiplomatic: "Smith had nothing to do with the creation of this movement. Browne and I did it and I paid for it. Our names are on the bills, not Smith's. Suppose the men did want him. What of it? Who are they to tell what they will have and what not? We propose to run the Commonweal— Browne and me—and if any upstart objects, why, he can get out of the bandwagon." In the egalitarian armies of the Far West, such autocratic blustering would have cost a general his command; but the truth was that no other contingent had a financial angel like Coxey. A few days later the Ohioan made his loyalty to Browne even clearer: when a reporter asked him how the army got along without him during his frequent absences, he replied, "Oh, I'm not necessary. Browne is in charge."[8]

For the Commonwealers, with Big Savage Mountain and the Alleghenies behind them and their leadership differences apparently patched up, the future looked brighter than at any time since they had left Massillon. They basked in the sunshine and warm breezes of a Maryland spring. And as they tramped toward Washington, their ranks filled once again.

CHAPTER 5

Commonweal Comrades—we have "crossed the Alps" of our journey, where the ice and snows met our legion; not with "the cold hand of death," thanks to unceasing care, and we are now in the sunny Italy of "Maryland, My Maryland."

Carl Browne to Commonwealers

Maryland, My Maryland

To the men who braved Big Savage Mountain, the Potomac Valley was paradise. They were south of the Mason-Dixon line now, in the land of "we 'uns and you 'uns." At Frostburg they named their camp after the southern general Robert E. Lee, and evening campfire talk turned to such curious subjects as, "Did the Marylanders talk like the Negroes, or the Negroes like Marylanders?" [1]

The morning march from Frostburg was easy, mostly downgrade through rolling countryside under a brilliant blue sky. When the troops caught their first glimpse of the Potomac River, they burst into spontaneous cheers. Browne whooped along with his men and swung his sombrero around and around, like a cowboy who had reached Dodge City after several hard months with the herd. The column halted again shortly before reaching the state's second largest city, Cumberland (population 12,729). It was Coxey's kind of place, a community of workshops and factories where the "labor question" meant more than an academic debate. Marchers unfurled their banners, tuned up their musical instruments, and put on an impressive show for the numerous onlookers who lined the dusty road. The Commonwealers camped in a baseball park at the outskirts of the city, and a large and sympathetic crowd paid a small admission fee to see the pilgrims and hear the usual speeches.

Reporters crowded into the headquarters tent to question Coxey and Browne about the Unknown. They were seeking spicy tidbits to enliven their dispatches. Both Commonwealers answered question after question, until at last Browne stretched out on a cot and pulled a blanket over his head and Coxey stepped outside.

Coxey was despondent about the recent problems with his much-beloved but troublesome son. He lamented at length to reporters about the difficulty of raising the boy. Two years earlier, Jesse had run away to Baltimore and shipped out for the African coast, though a few months later he returned home repentant. The father then sent him off to school, but the restless youth soon dropped out.

This time, however, Jesse really did not have any interest in continuing a rebellion against his father. In fact, the Unknown's contingent never amounted to much, and within twenty-four hours the prodigal son returned with the words, "Say, dad, give me a quarter. I am dying for a smoke." Making the quarter a half-dollar, the indulgent father reinstated Jesse as a regular member of the Commonweal.

Browne, secure in his command once again, was in a generous and expansive mood when over dinner in the Cumberland Hotel he finally revealed the true identity of the Great Unknown. "Smith, the Unknown, was all right until the newspapers began to praise him and then he lost his head. I don't want to accuse him. I always feel magnanimous toward the fallen. I was even willing to play powder monkey to Smith for awhile in order to preserve the peace, but before long he became unbearable. The bad reincarnation in his nature got the best of him."

The Unknown was actually A. P. B. Bozarro, revealed Browne, a patent-medicine man, trance medium, and wizardo supreme of an organization called the American Patriots, which Bozarro himself had founded. Wearing an Indian costume and hair that swept his shoulders, Bozarro had sold his elixirs from a tent on Peoria Street on Chicago's west side. He had befriended Browne when Carter Harrison halted further agitation by the jobless in Lake Front Park, and the two outcasts became partners of a sort. The sage of Calistoga, California, lectured on the tariff and labor questions and drew large crowds to purchase Bozarro's blood purifier, which the maker guaranteed would cure anything from sluggish blood to cancer. The medicine man also lectured on "bironical tubes" and "manatomy."

Bozarro occasionally appeared in a flashy cowboy outfit decorated with beads "to attract the female eye" and claimed to be a "native son of the golden west." (Browne said he was from no farther west than the bluegrass region of Kentucky and that his true family name was Howard.)

When Browne began organizing the Commonweal, he realized that he needed someone to relieve him of day-to-day details and immediately remembered his old friend in Chicago. Bozarro came to Massillon overflowing with enthusiasm for the cause, but "looking so tough, ragged, and disreputable I was ashamed to introduce him to Coxey," recalled Browne. Bozarro begged the Californian for a chance to begin life anew, so together they arranged to cut his hair short, get him a new suit of clothes, and give him a new identity. In this way the wizardo supreme underwent a quiet transformation to become the Great Unknown, "a great advertising card," in Browne's words, and assistant marshal of the Commonweal. One day Bozarro almost spoiled his new identity by slipping into nearby Canton and becoming involved in a brawl with a hotel waiter. The whole matter was hushed up.[2]

On the road from Massillon, Coxey was so pleased with Bozarro's work that he sent home for a beautiful stallion so that his assistant marshal might make a good appearance. The former patent-medicine fakir charmed everyone except Browne, who increasingly brooded about the figure he had created. But that was all in the past now. When Browne returned from the Cumberland Hotel to the headquarters tent, he assumed a cross-legged position and gloated over his recent triumph. "Nothing can hurt us now. We have been attacked within and without, and we have been uniformly victorious."

The local electric railway made such a profit hauling sightseers to the ballpark that it invited the pilgrims to remain in camp another day, sweetening its request with a gift of $100. Men exhausted by their arduous trek over the Alleghenies needed little persuasion. The horses, too, were fatigued and footsore, and the wagons and tents were desperately in need of repair. Only a few crumbs of hardtack remained in the commissary.

The generous folk of Cumberland soon remedied the food problem, and marchers spent the extra day visiting with townspeople and refurbishing their equipment. They even found time for a friendly game of baseball. When they were not answering more questions from the press, Coxey and Browne used the day to perfect their plans for a grand rendezvous of the armies of protest on the outskirts of Washington.

With the mystery of the Unknown (and of the veiled lady, his wife) dispelled, and the Commonweal drawing closer to the nation's capital, people wanted to know more about its leaders. Reporters covering the march were "wearing down a good deal of gray matter trying to unravel Browne," noted a correspondent for the *Washington Star*. "One gives up in despair with the remark: 'He is a creature too inscrutable even for the guess of a hardened reporter.'" To those who called Browne a buffoon and a fool, the *Star*'s man responded that the Californian was a natural leader, "far from lacking in brains or ability." Another correspondent added this caveat: "Coxey is popular. Browne is feared rather than liked." [3]

In his exceptionally skillful manipulation of public opinion, Browne proved his worth. Before the Commonweal reached a community, the Californian usually had searched out tidbits of regional lore and history and added these to his public addresses, much to the delight of the locals. He carefully selected the name of each night's camp to ensure a maximum of goodwill. The name "Camp Thackeray," for example, assigned to the bivouac in Cumberland, was chosen to honor the English author William Makepeace Thackeray, whose novel *The Virginians* Browne thought to be popular in the Potomac Valley.

Especially in his most outrageous moments—his Sunday reincarnation services—Browne continued to generate the newspaper publicity so necessary to sustaining the movement. The Unknown had been a godsend to reporters, and with him gone, the press now focused more closely on reincarnation and the "wonderful psychological influence" that Browne apparently exercised over Coxey. It was far easier to hold public interest by exploiting the personal side of the movement than by attempting to explain the mysteries of the money question.

A reporter asked Coxey: "It is said that Carl Browne believes himself a reincarnation of Christ. Do you share his belief?"

"Yes, I do in part. I believe that every man has something of Christ in him, even the most lowly."

"Who do you think you are?"

"I think I am Andrew Jackson. I don't say that I'm carrying around the whole of his spirit, but I'm sure I've a part of it."

That he possessed the spirit of Old Hickory was a notion planted by Browne; and Coxey, noted the press, "seems pleased with the idea and does not combat it."[4]

The press emphasis on the bizarre bothered a Pittsburgh reform paper, the *National Labor Tribune*, which believed that Coxey's good ideas relating to unemployment were being subjected to ridicule "due to his blunder in having admitted the side-show business of Carl Browne. Browne outraged the religious elements of the population and is regarded as a laughing-stock by those not given to religion." But, argued another, the Commonweal without Browne "would be like the play of 'Hamlet' with Hamlet left out."[5]

It was six o'clock in the morning, April 17, and the sun had just crested the rugged mountains east of Cumberland when the bugler shrieked reveille. As the men prepared to resume their journey, Browne appeared bright and fresh in a new striped linen shirt with a broad sailor collar, which he sported especially for the coming voyage. As they marched through Cumberland, the Commonwealers' morale was as high as the sun overhead. Awnings were down on the sunny side of the quaint and twisting streets, and it seemed as though the whole town had gathered under them to cheer for the petition in boots as it wound its way down to the docks of the Chesapeake and Ohio Canal.

Just below Cumberland lay a network of artificial lakes filled with canal boats, many of them abandoned and in all stages of deterioration. Out-of-work families were living in some of their cramped cabins. The Chesapeake and Ohio Canal, like the National Road, had seen better days. Arriving at the wharf, which was nothing more than a narrow strip of land between the canal and the Potomac River, Commonwealers immediately began the work of embarcation.[6]

Wagons had to be taken apart and stacked, and eighteen nervous thoroughbreds had to be coaxed slowly up the gangplank into the

Carl Browne with Coxey's army on the Chesapeake
and Ohio Canal. Courtesy Library of Congress.

hold of an old boat, the *A. Greenless*. Thousands of townspeople
stood for hours in the broiling sun to watch the loading process.
Browne silently surveyed the scene with an almost angelic smile. Just
as the noon factory whistles blew, he moved to the prow of the
flagship *Benjamin Vaughn*. Assuming a suitably nautical pose beneath
his portrait of Christ, he gave the orders to shove off.

Their voyage down the historic waterway had not been part of
Browne's original plan. Canal boatmen were not even sure what fare
to charge for the unusual cargo, but they finally agreed to haul the
men and their baggage the eighty-four miles to Williamsport for
fifty-two cents a ton—the usual rate for perishable goods. The price
was quite a bargain, for even at the speed of plodding mules the canal
ride saved several days of marching through rugged country and enabled the Commonwealers to make up time lost in the Alleghenies.

As the boats passed the South Cumberland glass works and a steel
and tin plate factory, workmen came outside as a group and cheered
lustily. On the poop deck Browne gave orders in a deep voice to the
mules, but they paid him no attention. Behind the two boatloads of

Commonwealers came a third vessel, the *Mertonville*, which had been rechristened by its occupants the *Flying Demon*. Although this boat was not officially a part of Coxey's fleet, its new name and occupants were of considerable significance to it. A few weeks earlier, as the Commonweal plodded through the snows and mud of northern Ohio, Browne had lost his temper after reading newspaper accounts of the troubled journey and had lashed out at reporters, blasting them as "argus-eyed demons of hell." The name stuck, becoming the press's private joke.[7]

The reporters covering the march organized a fraternity—the AEDH—led by archdemon Austin Beach of the *Pittsburgh Times*, and made honorary members of the Western Union telegraphers who accompanied them. Soon even Browne found pleasure in the humorous twist the journalists had given his epithet. When the Coxey flotilla sailed from the Cumberland waterfront and passed the still-moored *Flying Demon*, he called out, "I salute the argus-eyed demons of hell." The reporters were cleaning and loading their craft. It had previously hauled coal, and though the journalists were not an exceptionally fastidious lot, they hated to appear more disreputable than the Coxeyites.[8]

At each lock, thousands of curious Marylanders and West Virginians gathered to watch the flotilla pass. And all day, as trains rumbled by on nearby tracks, engineers saluted with their whistles and passengers crowded to the open windows of the coaches and vigorously waved their hats and handkerchiefs. Commonwealers spent the day admiring some of the most beautiful mountain scenery the American continent had to offer.

At nightfall Coxey's boats entered the locks across the Potomac from Green Spring, West Virginia; overhead a few stars dotted a steel-blue sky. The moon rising over the Maryland hills silvered the ripples of the river, which here looked much like a dashing mountain stream. All around were the sounds of a warm spring night; a congregation of frogs in a nearby swamp held high carnival, while a whippoorwill called from the sycamores that stretched their white arms over the river.

The boats passed Paw Paw, Maryland, at midnight and entered a long tunnel bored through a solid mountain of rock. Many of the voyagers sat up and called to one another, listening like children to the strange echoes their voices made. All night the mules plodded softly along the earthen towpath.

After pausing near Bell's Lock for a breakfast of bacon, bread, coffee, and hardtack, the men sailed forth again, passing Turkey Foot Bend and the village of Great Cacapon. The balmy air filled Browne with inspiration. Standing on the prow, where he tried to speak knowledgeably of the booms, spars, gunwales, and binnacles of the battered boat that was his flagship, he reflected on the day long past when Cleopatra floated the Nile on her perfumed barge to meet her Antony.

Coxey sat behind him, dictating business letters to a male secretary who was ticking away at a typewriter. Glee club members clapped hands and tapped heels as they sang old southern favorites. Other men stretched out on the decks like cats, soaking up the sun and breathing in the fragrance of wildflowers dotting the Maryland countryside. Off to one side the clear waters of the Potomac splashed over a series of boulders.

Later in the day, Browne arranged a special treat for the Commonwealers. To all who marched with him across the Alleghenies, he issued a special certificate praising their "heroic conduct in crossing the Cumberland mountains in the face of snow and ice and despite police persecution and dissension breeders." What Browne soon discovered, however, was that the dissension-breeders had not been left behind. The wizardo supreme—alias the Unknown—and a handful of followers were traveling ahead of the Commonweal, posing as its advance guard and collecting donations intended for Coxey's men. Livid with rage, Browne wired ahead for their arrest.

As the flotilla passed through the historic Civil War country west of Harper's Ferry, Captain Barger of the *Flying Demon* shared a dark foreboding with the reporters. "I used to hear about John Brown before the war, and how he stirred up the people on the slave question," recalled the old Confederate soldier. "I 'low that Coxey is doing just the same thing. Everything is going wrong—Congress, the President, and the millionaires—and there has got to be a war and lots of bloodshed before any change can come. I reckon Coxey's army will bring on great change and it will be right bloody." Ray Stannard Baker thought the old man's fear made good copy, and so did his editor, who ran it in the *Chicago Record*. It was the kind of incident that kept readers from losing interest in what might happen next.

After the arduous crossing of the Alleghenies, no group derived more pleasure from the voyage down the canal than the fourteen reporters, four telegraphers, and one lineman on the *Flying Demon*. Before leaving Cumberland, they had loaded into the old barge six cases of bottled beer, two kegs of beer, and four gallons of whiskey in stone jars. They also rented two extra mules, so that they might keep up with the Commonweal even when they stopped periodically to file their stories.

In addition to Barger, the regular skipper, the demons had an admiral of their own, complete with paper hat and tin horn. When the *Flying Demon* cast off from Cumberland, he ordered all hands below for a drink. Every fifteen minutes he blew his horn and ordered everyone below for another drink. Soon the demons were singing, dancing, and drunk. They even had their own song composed by demon W. P. Babcock of the *New York World*:

> Demons come from all the states,
> Brought together by the fates,
> Yet they are the best of mates
> For all are blooming reprobates—
> Ta Ra Ra Boom De Ay
> The demon's life is gay
> Until the first of May.
> Ta Ra Ra Boom De Ay.

Near-pandemonium reigned when one demon pulled out a pistol and began target practice. The journalists also played practical jokes on one another. In the dead of night one of the merry pranksters let loose with wild shrieks of "Fire! Murder! Help! Save the Mules! Run for your lives! The hoboes are upon us!" Whether the perpetrator was dumped overboard for a midnight swim is not known. Leaving Hancock, the men of the *Flying Demon* raised a red flag on which they had painted "Demons of Hell" in blue letters. Coxey was not amused, for from a distance it looked like the banner of socialism. He insisted that they take it down.[9]

Similarly unimpressed with the high jinks of the demons was a reporter from a small reform paper, the *American Nonconformist*, who rode with the Coxeyites. "These are the chaps," he complained of his fellow journalists, "who are writing a history of Coxey's movement in the daily papers for 65,000,000 of Americans to read." They were not careful to file accurate stories, he added.[10]

Accurate or not, the press carried the name of Coxey from coast to coast and beyond. More than three dozen American reporters and one each from papers in London and Paris covered Coxey's preparation for the march from Massillon. "Never in the annals of insurrection has so small a company of soldiers been accompanied by such a phalanx of recording angels," mused W. T. Stead of Coxey's 125 men. Another person added that Coxey "achieved more of a national reputation on a smaller amount of capital than any man I know of."[11]

Although the number of recording angels dwindled after that first day on the road, a hard core of twelve reporters remained with the army all the way to Cumberland, where their ranks increased once again. Each night they sent out dispatches detailing the crusaders' progress—sometimes as many as 100,000 words—to all corners of the nation. Most of the journalists were in their early twenties and had been selected for the assignment by editors who believed they could endure the rigors of the road better than older hands. Paid by the column inch, they quickly developed a knack for turning every smudge of dirt on Coxey's nose into salable news.

Baker's editor on the *Chicago Record* was like most in that he encouraged this practice. "We can stand plenty of matter now," he wired his cub reporter in late March. He carefully instructed Baker on how to portray the leaders: "Don't put Browne too much in evidence as the hero of the plot is Coxey, though he seems to be rather a puppet in Browne's hands." His editor further advised him to interview recuits and write hard-luck stories, to treat the people with humor "but not with ridicule," and "send plenty of gossip."[12]

The *Chicago Tribune* ran a cartoon portraying Coxey, the San Francisco general Charles T. Kelley, and other protest leaders around the country as hot-air balloons kept aloft by a stream of "newspaper notoriety." The *Kansas City Star* editorialized that "whatever Coxey and Kelley and their so-called armies of Industrialists may become or do, they must give credit to the newspapers. If it were not for the press which has exploited their mad performances, they would never have been heard of, and when the press tires of them they will sink back to the obscurity to which they belong."[13] At the moment, though, there seemed to be little danger of their slipping back into obscurity. Some journalists believed that because the times were so dull, the press needed the Coxey movement as much as the Coxeyites needed the press.

The power of the press was nowhere better illustrated than in the downfall of the Unknown. Several Chicago correspondents had recognized Bozarro from the beginning but had humored him and helped to fashion the identity of the Unknown for "the reason solely that it excited interest and made the story more readable and interesting." After Browne exposed his rival, reporters had no further interest in the Unknown, though he literally begged for their attention. In the eyes of the press Bozarro was now nothing more than a pathetic hanger-on.

In the drama of getting out the news, the unsung heroes were the telegraphers whose dots and dashes flashed the stories across the wires. E. P. Bishop supervised the telegraph corps. He was an experienced man, having been responsible for getting on the wires some of the sensational news events of the late nineteenth century, most notably the Johnstown Flood and the Homestead Strike. To transmit the reporters' copy, a lineman would shinny up a pole, cut a wire, and splice in a special portable telegraph key. Four telegraphers working out of sheds or at times in an open field converted the written word into electrical impulses. Reporters could occasionally be seen sprawled full length on the hard ground scribbling out copy as fast as it could be sent.[14]

Traveling along the Chesapeake and Ohio Canal as night fell, the *Flying Demon* docked at a point near Green Spring, West Virginia. It was time for reporters to file their stories. But Green Spring, which consisted of nothing more than two houses and a railroad station, lay on the opposite side of the Potomac. When the reporters and telegraphers hunted up a ferryman to take them across to the depot where they could send out their dispatches, they were greeted with "I knowed you was coming, but taint no use going over."

"How's that?"

"I was up to the telegraph station an hour or two ago, when the man got the message saying you fellows was acoming and wanted him to telegraph something like 150,000 words."

"Well, what did he do?"

"He went to bed, cap'n, and told me to tell you'se all he was dying." [15]

Two days after leaving Cumberland, Coxey's troops ended their voyage at Williamsport. It was six o'clock in the morning when the flotilla docked, but despite the early hour and to Coxey's surprise and delight, six charming girls waited to welcome him. He shook their hands, and Browne insisted that each girl have a badge of honorary membership. The Californian used the occasion to speak for a solid hour on the virtues of American women, and a crowd of onlookers besieged the Commonwealers with questions.

The Coxeyites pitched camp just east of Williamsport on a bar of land that divided the canal from the Potomac River. There they set about performing their many chores, and a shoemaker and a tailor kept busy until dark making repairs. Two Commonwealers were drummed out of the ranks for being pickpockets, and "Tootling" Charley the bugler was booted out for being drunk. Said Browne, who showed no mercy toward tipplers in the army, "You can do no more blasting on the bugle for us, and the quicker you take yourself away the better." A suddenly repentant Charley flung both arms around the Californian and begged to stay, but Browne refused to reconsider.

The Californian was infuriated to learn that his old nemeses Bozarro and Childs had bested him once again. They had come this way only hours earlier, collected $30 intended for the Commonweal, and spent it on themselves. Now they were headed for Hagerstown to work the same fraud.

This was "Camp California." As always, Browne chose the name for a purpose, in this case to bestow special recognition on the state that had contributed so many recruits to West Coast branches of the Commonweal. Those armies—and indeed they were *armies*, for the aggressive western generals did not shy away from military terminology—were now getting almost as much publicity as Coxey's band.

CHAPTER 6

A tramp has no friends and he is
the prey of every little policeman
who can get at him, but as long
as I am governor no man will be
deprived of his liberty because he
is ragged and hungry.

Texas Governor James Stephen
Hogg, 1894

Fry's Californians: Taming the Octopus

Something about the Coxey movement struck Americans as quintes-
sentially Californian. Perhaps it was its character: utopian, seemingly
out of plumb, even whimsical. Perhaps it was Carl Browne. It was
a shame, lamented the *Sacramento Record-Union*, that one of the
crusade's "chief schemers" could still call the Golden State his home.
In the eyes of the newspaper, Carl Browne was a "precious fraud and
dabster" and the Coxey march was "impractical, wild-eyed and mis-
leading." The *Los Angeles Times* was no less harsh: "We know nothing
out here of Mr. Coxey, but the fact that he has chosen as his lieutenant
such a buffoon, blackmailer and renegade as Carl Browne, of degraded
lineage, is sufficient to stamp the whole enterprise as one which is not
entitled to a moment's serious or respectful consideration."[1]

But Browne was hardly the only Californian worthy of such acidu-
lous comment. Even in the golden age of cranks, California was
home to more than its share of colorful characters, some of whom
made even Carl Browne look conventional. Pursuing a far more outrageous course than Browne was "General" Stephen Maybell of San
Francisco's Heaven at Hand army, which antedated the Coxey movement by several months. "It is part of our religion to seize the government of the United States and reform it," Maybell harangued listeners at his nightly rallies. "It is my intention to march straight

to Washington and demand a government for the people and by the people. If we don't get it we will eject Congress and behead Cleveland." Maybell's lack of success was proof that wild language alone was insufficient to launch an "on to Washington" crusade.[2]

For the several thousand jobless who suffered through the winter of 1893/94 in California, the state had lost all its glitter. Many were eager to join any crusade that set its face toward Washington, if only to get out of California. Most preferred Coxey and Browne over the bloodthirsty Maybell. Their main dilemma was not one of leadership but how to get across the continent, or even across the miles of undulating desert that formed the state's eastern boundary.

Coxey's base at Massillon was by comparison within a stone's throw of his objective. More miles separated Los Angeles and the District of Columbia, for example, than had been covered by Napoleon on his ill-fated march from Paris to Moscow. It was, in fact, a far greater distance from any point on the Pacific Slope to the nation's capital than that traveled by medieval Europe's crusaders to the Holy Land. If the unemployed of California wished to join Coxey on Capitol Hill on May Day, they had no choice but to ride the rails, a hike overland being simply out of the question. The railroads of the West thus played a key role in the history of the Coxey movement.[3]

W. T. Stead, the ubiquitous English journalist, offered some comparative perspective on the power of western railroads. "No one who has not been in America," he explained in 1894, "can adequately realize the extent to which civilization is an affair of railroads. Railways in England were conveniences of communication. In the United States, especially in the Western States, they were necessaries of existence."[4]

So marvelous was the transforming power of the nation's railroad builders that they inspired the Reverend Lyman Abbott to write, "The steel rail he lays is an enchanter's wand, and where it enters[,] a community of homes and a long line of villages spring up as if by magic, and a ceaseless chime of church and schoolhouse bells ring in the advent of a blessed civilization." Others marveled at railroad power but feared it was the crushing strength of a giant octopus, a term Californians used to describe the Southern Pacific Railroad monopoly. In no other state did a single corporation so dominate the economy or so corrupt political life. The Southern Pacific was California's single largest landowner and its largest employer of labor. The rail system was the longest in the nation, with its main line extending more than three thousand miles from Portland in the Pacific Northwest to New Orleans on the Gulf of Mexico.[5]

Nowhere was the power of the steel rail more visible than in southern California in the late 1880s. For years the Southern Pacific had dominated overland transportation to the region, but in 1886 that changed with completion of the Santa Fe Railroad. The advent of competition sparked a rate war that drove prices so low that on March 6, 1887, the price of a coach seat on the Santa Fe from Kansas City to southern California dropped to the sum of $1. Before competition the same ticket would have cost $125.

Low passenger rates helped precipitate an avalanche of prospective ✓ settlers, and the great southern California land boom was on. In response to railroad and chamber of commerce blandishments, thousands of clerks and laborers came west seeking a better life. So, too, did real estate promoters or "boomers"—men of smooth talk and ingratiating manners who made gullible fools of otherwise intelligent people. People sometimes waited in line for days to get the first choice of lots in a new town or subdivision, often attracted by nothing more substantial than brass bands, free lunches, and circus performances. The true humbugs used even more dubious means to sell little plots in the desert and coastal swamps to the "greenhorns": they hung oranges on the shaggy arms of Joshua trees and sold the desert wastes as citrus groves.

Between January 1887 and July 1889, more than sixty new towns were laid out in southern California. Los Angeles, which had fewer than twelve thousand citizens in 1880, grew to more than fifty thousand by 1890. The boom collapsed in 1888, only to take off again a few months later. For the skilled and unskilled workers who came west to claim southern California's golden opportunities, the rapid growth meant jobs.[6]

The depression of 1893 changed everything. All over the West, out-of-work men who desired to return to their homes in the East or even to look for a job elsewhere found railroad passenger rates substantially higher than when they had ridden out only a few years earlier. Officials of the city of San Francisco, the Southern Pacific system, and the Salvation Army quietly worked out a plan to transport the unemployed of the Bay area to the far ends of the railroad at Portland, El Paso, and Ogden. With a population of fifteen thousand, Ogden was especially incensed that California, with more than a million people, got rid of her unemployed in that manner.

Many jobless westerners simply climbed aboard outbound freight trains without receiving support from anyone. Even as Southern Pacific freights hauled California's jobless east to El Paso, they passed westbound trains filled with unemployed men from San Antonio and El Paso expecting to find better times in California. This spectacle caused the *Los Angeles Times* to fear a return to the mendicancy of the Middle Ages, when bands of the destitute roamed the European countryside.[7]

In Los Angeles in early March 1894, spokesmen for several hundred jobless men who had spent the past winter camped in an empty warehouse requested that the city council persuade Southern Pacific or Santa Fe officials to transport their industrial army to Washington. Spokesmen for the unemployed were polite, although quartermaster J. O'Brien, a Civil War veteran, threatened violence when he blurted out, "Some people say the railroads will not take us. If they do not, I am sorry to say, we will take the railroads. In the name of God, gentlemen, help us get away." Without enthusiasm the council agreed to petition the railroads for help.[8]

While the railroads deliberated, the unemployed paraded through Los Angeles streets under their "On to Washington" banner. This legion had originated after one of Browne's numerous manifestos found its way into the hands of an old California associate, Lewis C. Fry. He urged the city's unemployed to organize for their mutual protection and benefit, and together they met to write an elaborate constitution and elect Fry their general. Their demands, as stated in the constitution, made no mention of Coxey's road-building scheme, and their use of military titles and organizational patterns was at variance with Browne's instructions. This was an outfit independent of Coxey but desirous of joining forces with him at the Capitol.

On letterhead consisting of a dove, an olive branch, and a gold bug (considerably better-drawn than Browne's renditions), Fry's men issued a call to the unemployed in some eighty communities throughout the West. Their purpose was not to gain additional recruits for

Fry but rather to encourage the formation of similar contingents in other parts of the region.[9]

Reporters sensed a good story and asked Fry for more details of his crusade. When he replied that his pilgrimage would take twenty days, the press response was, "How are you going to live on the road?"

"Why, I'm going ahead of the army and will hold meetings in all of the large towns. I shall ask the citizens to feed us and the unemployed to join us." Fry imagined he would be leading a million men by the time he reached Washington. When reporters asked what they would do if the government attempted to block their progress, Fry replied, "Lay down as prisoners of war and demand that the government provide for us."[10]

Fry's estimate of twenty days on the road was far off the mark unless his army obtained a train, and that the railroads refused to provide. Fearful that Fry's men might attempt to steal one, the Santa Fe dispatched its chief detective, J. Frank Burns, to shadow the army. The press too wanted further information about the obscure man who proposed to lead a million petitioners to the steps of Congress.

Fry was a tall, powerfully built man in his late forties. Dark, deep-set eyes highlighted a face that was smooth-shaven except for a small mustache. Deep wrinkles creased his forehead, and his hair thinned noticeably in places. Around his neck he sported a blue scarf and on his lapel a small American flag. Most of the time he wore a slouch hat and overcoat. His speech was occasionally coarse and ungrammatical but always effective: "If the government has a right to make us die in time of war," he once told his troops "we have the right to demand from her the right to live in time of peace."

Unlike Coxey or Browne, Fry was a workman, not a showman or businessman. Born in Iowa, he had moved to California at the age of seven. During his adult years he had worked at various times as a mechanic in the Southern Pacific's shops in El Paso, Los Angeles, and elsewhere. Once when a reporter asked him where he was educated, Fry replied with a wry smile, "I got my education with other kids in the street reading circus bills." When Fry sided with fellow workers against the railroad in a labor dispute, he lost his job and was blacklisted as a troublemaker. With a wife and four children to support, he became an itinerant labor reformer, falling in with Carl Browne in the early 1890s when the sage of Calistoga proposed to lead a march

Lewis C. Fry. From Henry Vincent, *The Story of the Commonweal* (Chicago, 1894).

by the jobless on the state's capitol. The Coxey movement thus seemed tailor-made for a man of Fry's background.[11]

Fry's growing ranks made Los Angeles policemen uneasy, and they actively sought to discourage recruitment. On one occasion they arrested eleven of Fry's men and charged them with vagrancy for begging on the street; a judge gave them twenty-four hours to leave town. When Fry and his men picked up rumors of a secret city council conclave that was discussing ways to force the army to disband, they immediately set out for Washington without the hoped-for train.[12]

The Los Angeles contingent, nearly five hundred members strong and led by a fife and drum band, started east on the morning of March 16, almost two weeks before Coxey left Massillon. Commanding the troop was J. L. Gould, Fry having traveled ahead by regular coach to Tucson, five hundred miles distant. The general had once worked in the Southern Pacific shops there and expected no trouble obtaining provisions from old friends. Meanwhile, his men tramped in a steady rain to the village of Monrovia at the foot of the San Gabriel Mountains, where they camped for the night. The next day's trek over sandy roads was no more pleasant than the first. Their commissary, never well-stocked, was so bare that the crusaders would have starved but for the oranges they appropriated from the groves that lined the road near Pomona. At Colton, a railroad junction sixty miles east of Los Angeles, the San Bernardino County sheriff gave the pilgrims hardtack biscuits, salt meat, and beans in exchange for their promise to hop the next freight for Yuma.

An American flag flew over their dusty and windswept camp. To the northeast of Colton towered the snowcapped summits of the San Bernardino Mountains. To the east was San Gorgonio pass, 2,560 feet high, after which the Southern Pacific line descended into a wilderness of sand, yucca, and cacti. In that desolate country—some of the driest in the United States—they could not expect to walk any distance and survive. Unless they wished to disband in Colton and risk the wrath of the sheriff by reneging on their promise, Fry's men had no choice but to "capture" a train. Crewmen protested but made no attempt to dislodge the freeloaders when they boarded a freight for Yuma. Beyond Indio, an oasis of palms, the railway descended into the Salton Basin, more than two hundred fifty feet below sea level. Here strong crosswinds blasted the sides of the cars with sand and tormented any pilgrim who rode outside.

They crossed the Colorado River near Yuma, then followed the ancient and sunburned valley of the Gila. Giant saguaros forty feet tall stretched their spiny arms upward toward a sky turquoise by day and iridescent with starlight by night. The dry air of the Sonoran Desert desiccated the men and after sunset nearly froze them. Several

times the railroad bounced some of the freeloaders off and forced
them to walk. Some men grew frightened and returned to Yuma,
but the majority continued toward Tucson, the Arizona Territory's
largest town with a population of five thousand.

The train reached the quaint old town of one-story adobe brick
buildings just at daybreak. A large crowd of spectators was on hand
to see the cars roll to a stop, their tops covered with the forms of
poorly clad, dusty men. The visitors climbed down the handholds
slowly; they were stiff from a cold night in the desert and hungry, not
having eaten since leaving Colton thirty-eight hours earlier.

Fry's men formed a makeshift camp and permitted no one to enter
or leave without permission. Fry had done his advance work well, for
Tucson residents were generous with their food. Soon each company's cook was hard at work filling the morning air with the aroma
of breakfast. After the meal the cooks rested and the bakers went to
work. Other men did their washing, while some played cards or read.
All seemed to have at least a modest education, and several claimed to
be out-of-work journalists. At five o'clock that evening the crusaders
boarded another freight and headed east into the gathering night.
Throughout their stay in Tucson they had been well behaved. Now
they would make the 300-mile journey to El Paso.

The railway line took them over Dragoon Summit, past Cochise,
and over the Continental Divide in New Mexico. Distant mountains
were castles with towers, domes, arches, and minarets. This countryside was stunning—a land of cloudless sky and amber sunsets, of
grayish-brown plains tufted with blue-gray sagebrush, of white sands
and towering yucca—but it was also dangerous. Said one captain, "I
told Fry it made my nerves a little shaky to think of starvation out
there."

El Paso was in an uproar as the army headed across Arizona and
New Mexico toward Texas. Many of its ten thousand citizens imagined that all sorts of terrible things would happen when the indigents arrived, and the mayor took no chances. No sooner had Fry
reached town on March 21 to make advance arrangements than he
was jailed for vagrancy. His Honor also issued a stern warning to the
town's citizens: "The so-called industrial army, numbering between
900 and 1,000 men, will reach El Paso tonight. These men have plundered and robbed the people in their line of march. It is now neces-

sary that the citizens of El Paso all prepare for the protection of their property and their families."

El Paso officials called for every able-bodied male to assemble at five that evening "to serve the city to prevent the invasion of this horde." Citizens rushed out to buy guns and ammunition to protect their families. Confirming their worst fears was word from the Southern Pacific office that Tucson was being looted and burned by hunger-crazed men.

The panic-stricken mayor wired Austin, begging governor James Stephen Hogg for protection and urging that he petition the War Department to place the Fort Bliss garrison at the disposal of the state. But scarcely had his message sped to the Texas capital than the telegraph clicked out word from the mayor of Tucson that the visitors had been well disciplined. El Pasoans greeted that dispatch with cheers. Then came word from Governor Hogg that Texas could handle the matter without federal assistance. Hogg blandly added, "Doubtless the railroad that brings the men into Texas will carry them through the state on their mission to interview Congress."

An immense crowd collected at El Paso's courthouse. Chairman Juan S. Hart, editor of the *Times*, was hard-pressed to preserve order amidst all the excitement. His plea was that the pilgrims be treated in a humane manner, and in the end his argument carried the day. Citizens started a subscription to buy food instead of guns and bullets.

Fry's army reached El Paso the next evening. Meeting the ten-boxcar train at the depot were more than a thousand people, including the citizens' committee and the police. General Fry was there, too, a local court having overturned his drumhead conviction for vagrancy. The pilgrims marched in companies to city hall. Some were sick from drinking alkali water in the desert, but the feast prepared by El Pasoans seemed compensation enough. At city hall, the citizens' committee had readied a bubbling pot of beans and plenty of bacon, bread, and coffee. After allowing the visitors to bivouac that night on city hall grounds, where citizens provided wood for campfires, El Paso officials ordered Fry and his men to move on. Back to the Southern Pacific yards they went, and Fry headed southeast to San Antonio by coach, expecting that his men would soon follow.

But in El Paso something was wrong. No freights steamed through the Southern Pacific yards that afternoon, and none came the next day. Fry's men grew restless and uneasy. Finally on Easter Sunday, March 25, just about the hour that Coxey's band departed Massillon, someone spotted an eastbound Southern Pacific freight lumbering through the yards, and the men clambered aboard, unaware that they were falling for a clever trap set by the railroad. The Southern Pacific was about to strike a blow against all the freeloaders who had beset it in increasing numbers since the depression had begun.

When reporters asked Superintendent W. G. Van Vleck what the railroad could do about the problem of deadheads, he replied: "What can we do? We are powerless to do anything but protest. Law is impotent. We have appealed to the constituted authorities and when Gov. Hogg is called upon he says he will not interfere to give us protection and by his official acts upholds these organized bodies in unlawfully and illegally taking possession of the valuable property of railroads and interfering with the running of trains." [13]

Scarcely a day had passed since October without Southern Pacific freights in Texas being practically overrun by a band of men demanding free transportation. Some had pilfered goods from the freight cars. And now there was the Fry army. For railroaders like Van Vleck, that was the last straw. If Hogg, who had made a career out of baiting the Southern Pacific, would not act, the company would take matters into its own hands. Fry's men, of course, knew nothing about the railroad's trap. Their train chugged uneventfully across the Chihuahuan Desert of west Texas until it reached Finlay, seventy miles east of El Paso and still more than five hundred miles west of San Antonio. Here the train suddenly swung onto a siding, the cars uncoupled from the locomotive, and the men were left stranded.

Finlay consisted of a telegraph station and a handful of Mexican families. Surrounding it was a desert of prickly pear cacti and dagger-sharp lechuguilla and a variety of animals, including prairie dogs, coyotes, tarantulas, and rattlesnakes. To the southeast was the Big Bend country of the Rio Grande, so unknown that another six years would pass before a party from the United States Geological Survey would undertake the first scientific expedition through its gorges.

The Southern Pacific could scarcely have picked a more forsaken place to strand the freeloaders. But as an extra precaution, the railroad ordered its crews not to haul Fry's men out. In fact, they stopped running eastbound freights through Finlay. The Southern Pacific persuaded a judge at Marfa to issue an injunction forbidding the men to interfere with the contents of the cars (mostly citrus fruit from California) and order out a company of Texas Rangers to enforce his edict. Fry's men would either starve or steal the fruit and be arrested.[14]

Texas newspapers and the national wire services quickly headlined the drama of men left to suffer and die in the desert. "They have been camped on a desert of sand and cacti for three days without food, and some of them are so weak they cannot stand. Many of them are mere boys," fumed Pulitzer's *St. Louis Post-Dispatch*. The press appealed to emotion by running stories of the indigents huddled together trying to escape the cold of the desert night and the stinging blasts of sandstorms. While Fry's pilgrims survived on a diet of flour and cactus roots boiled in a battered coal-oil can, stony-hearted rail barons waited for them to starve, or at least that was the impression conveyed by the newspapers.

With all of Texas in an uproar, Governor Hogg blasted the railroad. Outraged by its tactics, he threatened that if the Southern Pacific succeeded in starving the army to death he would make the railroad suffer if it cost him his last dollar on earth. Never did he alter his conviction that the company had brought the indigents into Texas and was responsible for hauling them out. When Hogg learned that Texas Rangers armed with Winchester rifles were guarding railroad property, he exploded. In an angry telegram to John Hughes, the commander of Company D, he asked, "By what authority are you in the service of the Southern Pacific company, guarding their trains at Finlay and preventing the removal of the starving men at this point? You are hereby commanded to remove your force from Finlay and to interfere in no manner whatever unless either side resorts to arms."

Hughes complained that the Southern Pacific had gotten his men to Finlay under false pretense, and added, "I find Gen. Fry a very reasonable and pleasant man, and he is very desirous that no violence be done [to] any of his men." Hughes and his Texas Rangers retreated to Sierra Blanca, a village about twenty miles east. Fry's men straggled behind on foot, occasionally helped by maintenance crews who defied company orders by transporting some men by handcar. The Southern Pacific won itself no friends when it objected to the crusaders' use of company water in tanks along the dry, dusty route. At Sierra Blanca, Fry's army made a meal out of a single scraggy cow that someone had donated. Some of the men were so famished after their fifty-four-hour ordeal that they could not keep the beef on their stomachs.

The adverse publicity and Hogg's verbal blasts seemed not to trouble the Southern Pacific. With considerable aplomb, Julius Kruttschnitt, vice-president and general manager of the Southern Pacific subsidiary that linked El Paso with San Antonio, informed reporters, "We are beset by a mob of nearly a thousand men. They boarded our train and compelled the crews to take them to El Paso." He steadfastly denied that the railroad had taken the law into its own hands. "It is a mystery to me," continued Kruttschnitt, "how in the world some people persist in calling these men 'confederates' and express sympathy for them as an army of unemployed men. The great majority of these men are professional tramps."

When asked if the Southern Pacific would haul the men out of Sierra Blanca if ordered to do so by the governor, Kruttschnitt smiled benignly, "Well, I hardly think that there is any law to compel us to transport people who refuse to pay their fare. Of course, if there is, we will obey its mandate." Kruttschnitt, for what it was worth, was at least more flexible than general superintendent J. R. Wentworth of the Frisco, a Santa Fe affiliate in the Southwest, who stated bluntly: "Tramps can take possession of trains but they cannot run them. There is no power on earth to compel us to operate our road if we do not want to."

Of Governor Hogg the *Dallas Morning News* observed, he "was born in a storm and has been in one ever since." First elected to state-wide office in 1886 at age thirty-five and becoming in 1890 the first native Texan elected governor, Hogg pictured himself a champion of the people against "soulless corporations." Earthy in speech, this lawyer and son of a Confederate brigadier general could hold a Texas crowd spellbound for hours while he blasted away at railroads and capitalists in general. His stormy battles with the Southern Pacific endeared him to the common people, and by his defense of a starving army of unemployed men he gained further stature as a David battling Goliath. "Food, not fines," promised Hogg, "will be the treatment of the law-loving, law-abiding element in this state when men commit no greater crime than traveling as tramps for lack of work."

After Kruttschnitt's defense of the Southern Pacific, Hogg fired back, "You can truthfully say that neither the cormorant nor the Commune can disgrace Texas while I am governor. When a railroad company hauls tramps or unemployed penniless men into this state it cannot dump them into a barren desert and murder them by torture and starvation without atoning for it, if there be any virtue in our machinery of justice. Nor will I allow them to be shot down on Texas soil by any armed force whatever, no matter how much the Southern Pacific or other enemies of the state may howl about the Commune."

Kruttschnitt coolly responded to Hogg's blasts by saying that the governor was misinformed. The railroad had not willingly carried the men into the state, and they could only blame themselves for being stranded in the desert. "Let me tell you," shot back Hogg, "if the Southern Pacific had taken out and left a lot of cattle or hogs in that barren place, where they would have starved to death, I would hold the road responsible. It seems very strange to me that these men would have sidetracked themselves in a place where they could get nothing to eat, and yet it is charged that they misplaced a switch in order to commit this suicidal act."

While the war of words between Hogg and the Southern Pacific continued, the situation at Sierra Blanca grew worse by the hour. Finally sensing that he and the railroad had lost the battle, Kruttschnitt wired Hogg with an offer to carry the men back to El Paso, but emphasized, "This is purely gratuitous, without the slightest recognition of any legal or other obligation resting upon us in these premises or any lawful right or power on your part to require and enforce it."

Now it was the El Pasoans' turn to worry. They quickly raised a purse to pay the Southern Pacific to take Fry's men in the opposite direction—southeast to San Antonio. The railroad complained that the sum was too small but in the end agreed to accept this face-saving measure. When the rescue train steamed into Sierra Blanca, Fry's men wept with joy. They had been trapped in the desert for more than five days, and during that time the five hundred men had eaten only two scrawny old cows and five hundred pounds of flour. The pilgrims piled aboard the seven coaches and three baggage cars, only too glad to escape west Texas.

Many citizens of San Antonio were no happier than those of El Paso to have Fry's army pay them a visit. "It looks like San Antonio will have an elephant on her hands when the army arrives," protested the *Express*. "As one good turn deserves another it has been suggested that a train be chartered by the people of this city, and the entire force, including Gen. Fry, be sent back to the good people of El Paso."[15]

Released from their desert prison, Fry's men expected to remain in San Antonio for the next several days recuperating from their ordeal. Fry, in fact, wanted to remain in Texas until weather in the North grew warmer. Though it was nearly midnight when the special train reached San Antonio, a large crowd was on hand to greet the pilgrims; but to everyone's surprise, the cars were switched immediately to the tracks of the International and Great Northern Railroad and hurried north. The army picked up forty new recruits in San Antonio, but veterans of the desert ordeal were not happy: "We have been through the hardships and now they come to eat of the rations."

A few hours later the train paused in Austin, where Fry's men wanted to march to the governor's mansion to thank Hogg. The governor's aide, Captain Harry Owens, met them at the depot instead. Fry shook his hand and asked that his men be allowed to see the governor.

"You mustn't do it," responded Owens. "He's treated you well and you mustn't abuse his kindness."

Fry then requested to see the governor by himself, but Owens again politely refused. Said Fry, "You tell the governor we heartily appreciate his kindness and will not forget it."[16]

After a thirty-minute layover in Austin to stretch their legs, the men continued north by train to Longview, where they were fed by sympathizers and transferred to other cars for Saint Louis. There Fry expected to remain only a short time before continuing by train to Washington. The general was wrong; his cross-continent adventure had only begun. But his army's next major difficulty, that of being stranded on the banks of the White River in Indianapolis in late April, would not attract even a fraction of the press coverage that attended its ordeal in Texas.[17]

As for Governor Hogg, his act of kindness placed him in a familiar location—in the center of a storm. The *Dallas Morning News* chastised him for "threatening an ordinary railroad official like an old-time overseer threatened the Negro on the plantation. . . . The slop and froth of communist declamation in which the governor has regaled himself for a week should certainly conclude at once." On the other hand, the Central Industrial Council of Dallas, a labor organization, adopted a resolution endorsing Hogg and condemning the Southern Pacific; and the *Rocky Mountain News* of Denver, a Populist-leaning paper, said of the Texas governor that his humane action "merits the approval of all people who lay claim to civilized impulses." [18] In the eyes of Fry and his men, Hogg was a hero. He was the man who tamed the Southern Pacific octopus. Fry told a group of onlookers in Texarkana, "Say, you fellows have a great governor in Texas. He believes starving workingmen have got some rights." One of Fry's lieutenants, Ben Lewis, promised that after the march on Washington he would return to Texas to see Hogg. "He's a four time winner."

Hogg, though, had no desire to see Ben Lewis or any other person connected with the Commonweal. In truth, he had no real sympathy with the movement. "I acted as I did for humanity's sake alone and the sober second thought of the people will approve my action." [19]

In an open letter to Texas Coxeyites, Hogg was even more blunt. "Of all the chimerical schemes, unpatriotic steps or foolish freaks into which American citizens have ever been allured, this 'National Tramp' is the most pitiable and inexcusable." And Hogg later approved when a sheriff broke up a Houston army that tried to steal aboard a Santa Fe freight near Bellville. His primary desire in helping Fry's men across Texas was to pass them through the state as quickly as possible.[20]

The *Galveston News* wondered where the governor's logic would lead and imagined a troubled aftermath. "Governor after governor demands that the railroads shall pass them on and on—around the world. Nor will they stop at a single circumnavigation. Round and round they must go from land to land throughout the endless ages of eternity." [21]

As for Hogg's adversary Julius Kruttschnitt, his handling of the Fry episode only enhanced his standing with superiors at Southern Pacific headquarters in San Francisco. Eventually he advanced to become chairman of the sprawling rail and land empire. Meanwhile, in early April 1894 the Southern Pacific prepared to apply whatever lessons it had learned in Texas to an even larger army of indigents making its way east from the San Francisco Bay area.

CHAPTER 7

If Utah was an independent power and California was another, there would be ample cause for Utah to declare war upon California for conspiring with the Southern Pacific to send their hoard of destitute men in upon this soil.

Salt Lake Tribune, April 9, 1894

San Francisco Overland

Fry's soldiers of misfortune were only the first of many out-of-work Californians to attempt the trek east. The odds were long that any of them would ever reach Capitol Hill. The man left in charge of the industrial army's barracks in Los Angeles was Colonel Arthur Vinette, a French Canadian by birth and a carpenter by trade. Organizing a second division of approximately two hundred men, many of them married, he set forth for Washington in early April, following the same general route as Fry. But before Vinette's men had a chance to get stranded in the desert, they met trouble as they boarded a freight train at Colton. Lawmen used a fire hose to drive them off the cars until sympathizers slashed the hose with knives and axes. A heavily armed posse arrived a short time later from nearby San Bernardino to clear the train. The freeloaders, soaked to the skin, were detained briefly, and Vinette ultimately spent almost a month in jail. That broke the spirit of the second division, although Vinette and a few followers eventually made a pilgrimage without fanfare to the nation's capital.[1]

Industrial army organizers in California's largest city, San Francisco, were more fortunate. Even as Fry's men struggled to survive in the Texas desert and as Coxey's marched through the slush of northern Ohio, the streets of San Francisco rang with exhortations for the unemployed to join the great crusade to Washington. Promoters staged rallies at Furniture Workers' Hall and published a Coxeyite sheet called the *Appeal*.

Heading the San Francisco division was a thin, wiry man with stiff, bushy hair and a prominent black mustache: George Baker, a common laborer. Because his inspiration came more from Fry than from Coxey, the thirty-six-year-old Baker had no reservations about military trappings. He decorated his threadbare jacket with epaulets and a piece of coarse ribbon signifying a badge. Baker held the rank of colonel, and William Parsonage served as chaplain. Several older members who were veterans of the Civil War advised their comrades on military matters. By the end of March, the San Francisco army had 1,500 men on its rolls, making it the largest of all the Coxey contingents.

As in Los Angeles, the marchers requested that city officials find them railroad transportation, not an unreasonable plea considering that other out-of-work Californians had already been transported free (or nearly so) to distant ends of the Southern Pacific. But this time the railroad offered only a prohibitively expensive rate of one cent per person per mile. The city by the Golden Gate was no stranger to agitation, having weathered the Kearneyite protests some fifteen years earlier; but it was eager to unload its industrial army onto another community, and none was more handy than its less flamboyant relative across the bay—Oakland, the Brooklyn of San Francisco. Mayor L. R. Ellert had no trouble obtaining funds to buy the men ferry passage one way.

On Tuesday, April 3, the day of Coxey's triumph in the Pittsburgh area and of Fry's arrival in Saint Louis, Colonel Baker and six hundred followers marched down Market Street to embark for Oakland. Among the crusaders were many who owned only the clothes on their backs, some of them having been out of work for as long as eight months. Their officers were conspicuous in their secondhand uniforms. One regiment carried a large American flag, while others held aloft banners reading "We are Hungry and Discouraged" and "Melican Man Must Go," a not-so-subtle reference to the "Chinese Must Go" slogan of the Kearneyites. Missing were the metaphysical slogans of Coxey's group.[2]

The San Francisco army had much to learn if it ever expected to reach Washington, starting with American geography. When its spokesmen first approached Mayor Ellert for help, they estimated that the army would need a few hundred dollars and a wagonload or two of provisions to see it through to Washington. When the army reached Oakland, it had no advance guard to smooth the way. Its leaders would either learn that a cross-continent journey required more planning than that, or all would perish from starvation.

Oakland authorities furnished the men food and lodging in the cavernous Mills Tabernacle but remained angry about having to sustain the unemployed of San Francisco, which had a population six times as great as their city's. In a tart letter to Mayor Ellert, Oakland Mayor George C. Pardee protested the imposition. Pardee was quite willing to aid the jobless, but only those of Oakland. And the nation at large shared his localistic view. In fact, in its presentation of the jobless problem as a national concern and not simply a local one, the Coxey movement made its most significant departure from traditional American thinking. "These men," observed economist Thorstein Veblen, who did not sympathize with the crusade, "disregard the fact of local units and local relations with a facility that bespeaks their complete emancipation from the traditions of local self-government." When the Southern Pacific, which was in a far more accommodating mood after its troubles with Fry's army, offered to haul the men out of Oakland for a few hundred dollars, Pardee "snapped at the offer like a hungry trout rising to a particularly delicious fly."[3]

On their third evening in town, the marchers were waiting at the depot when a special train of six boxcars rolled to a stop. Hardly had they started to climb aboard before their youthful new commander-in-chief, Charles T. Kelley, protested that the accommodations were not fit for hogs, that the railroad had promised to furnish them passenger coaches. When he put the matter to a vote, the men overwhelmingly elected to return to the Mills Tabernacle.

A furious Mayor Pardee telegraphed Governor Henry H. Markham for militiamen, mobilized his entire police force, and swore in two hundred special deputies. At two o'clock the next morning, while the pilgrims slept peaceably in the tabernacle, a general fire alarm sounded, summoning additional men to the building. A force of twelve hundred men armed with pistols, Winchesters, and heavy clubs surrounded the tabernacle, and the sheriff presented the dazed and uncomprehending sleepers an ultimatum to leave Oakland within two hours. The men wanted Kelley's advice, but police had already dragged him off to jail. His followers refused to budge until he was released, and this the city reluctantly did an hour later. Kelley returned to the tabernacle an instant hero. Though he had eclipsed Colonel Baker under somewhat mysterious circumstances, nobody henceforth successfully challenged Kelley's leadership.

The night was chilly, and wisps of fog floated above the darkened streets as six to seven hundred crusaders again assembled at the depot. Colonel Baker would accompany the troops east this morning, Kelley promising to catch up a few days later after he organized additional companies in the Bay area. This time the troops accepted passage on the special train of seven freight cars that steamed out of Oakland just as the gray dawn of April 6 broke over the hills east of the bay. By noon it had reached Sacramento, where residents furnished lunch. There Kelley's army picked up three hundred additional recruits and provisions enough for five days. Enlarged to seventeen boxcars, the special headed east again that afternoon.[4]

In truth, not all the pilgrims were headed for Capitol Hill to join Coxey. Many simply wanted to get home. Many of those who joined Kelley's ranks believed erroneously that when they reached the land east of the Mississippi River they would fare better.

The train steamed past numerous orchards and vineyards east of Sacramento and headed up the west slope of the Sierra Nevadas, through timbered snowsheds near the seven-thousand-foot summit, then descended rapidly along the Truckee River into the Nevada desert country. Near the busy little town of Reno they added more recruits to their ranks and more cars to their train, so that by the time they reached Ogden, more than a thousand men were packed tight into twenty-seven boxcars and cattle cars. Many of the new men had been metal miners, but now they looked to Congress for work.

The lengthy crossing of the alkaline and sagebrush plains of the Great Basin Desert was uneventful, except for the shivers and chills the thinly clad Californians suffered as they rode through the frosty night in unheated cars. Train crews observed that the Kelleyites were a well-behaved lot and doubted that they had a single weapon among them. Only the pilgrims' habit of jumping off the cars at every stop to stretch their legs annoyed the railroaders.

This practice led to tragedy near Corinne, north of Utah's Great Salt Lake, where the special train was sidetracked to let two sections of a westbound express pass. One of those who jumped off was an unemployed waiter, Gus Holmquist, a quiet Swede. He crossed the tracks and stooped beside a pond to wash the grime of the road off his face. As soon as the first section of the passenger train roared by, he started back across the tracks to his car. With water and soap still in his eyes, Holmquist was blind to the locomotive of the second section bearing down on him. Comrades yelled, but even if he heard their cries it was too late to jump aside. The impact hurled Holmquist several hundred feet into the air; he died instantly of a broken neck, and the Coxey crusade had suffered its first casualty.

On his body comrades found a letter from the wife and four children who were awaiting him in Boston. Carrying his broken body to one of the boxcars, they draped it with an American flag. Everyone gathered around with heads bowed, more aware than ever of the perils of the road.[5]

The special train clanked to a halt in the countryside seven miles northwest of Ogden on Sunday afternoon, April 8. The Southern Pacific connected with the Union Pacific at Ogden, and the California road had not yet completed arrangements for the crusaders to continue to Omaha. After a delay of several hours, an ultimatum arrived from the Union Pacific: it refused to carry the men for less than full fare. The Rio Grande Western, the other line that ran east from Ogden, offered the same terms: nearly $40,000 to take the men to Denver, far more than either the Kelleyites or the Territory of Utah could pay.

The Union Pacific and the Rio Grande Western were simply playing stubborn. Everyone knew that railroads could offer reduced rates if they desired. At about the same time, the Santa Fe had offered a group of Chicago hotelmen traveling to Denver a special rate of $3.13 each—by sleeping car! That was a "cheaper rate than any in the history of railroading, where any charge at all is made," observed the *Rocky Mountain News*.[6]

In Utah, as in Texas and most other western states and territories before the crusade ended, the petition in boots triggered conflict between the railroads and federal authorities on one side and local officials and citizens on the other. The western railroads, aided by federal courts, had earlier broken the back of state attempts to reform the industry through the Granger laws. But popular resentment of railroad power and practices remained very much alive in communities west of the Mississippi River and needed only a visitation by Coxeyites to burst into the open. The result was that when the Coxey movement ended, the railroads, backed by the federal government, had established even greater domination over small-town America. That outcome was not entirely foreseeable, however, during the early weeks of the crusade, when the western lines were still groping for legal and political solutions.

Railway executives and business leaders in general would have liked nothing better than for public officials in the West to take a firm stand against the Coxey movement, particularly when its more desperate and daring members began to steal the trains themselves. "There never was a body of men who so richly deserve extreme punishment," fumed the *Commercial and Financial Chronicle*. The *Railroad Gazette* likewise wrung its hands. "We have chronicled from week to week some of the incidents of that aspect of Coxeyism which consists in forcibly seizing and running railroad trains. Was such a spectacle ever seen before in any country? Could such a spectacle be seen now in any other country calling itself civilized?" The *Railroad Gazette* partly blamed the railroads themselves for the problem: "They have weakly failed to demand protection from municipal and county officers until folks think they have no right to it."[7]

In fact, the railroads were simply reaping the harvest of their past and present acts of arrogance and occasional folly, acts that were plainly visible in an age that had yet to discover the magical arts of public relations. It was certainly no accident that their problems were greatest in those parts of the West where they held the most power. The reason was obvious: not only were their passenger, freight, and express services often the sole links to the outside world, but their ratemaking authority gave them the ability to prosper some of the region's newly established communities and blight others. In short, railroads dominated the lives of townspeople in the West to a degree unthinkable after the coming of the automobile and publicly financed highways, and many citizens resented it. Thus the drama unfolding in Ogden, like that in west Texas, revealed yet another aspect of one of the most troubling relationships of the age: corporate versus individual power.

For the second time in two weeks, the Southern Pacific found itself in an impossible situation. In Utah, though, the railroad could pose as one of humanity's benefactors. It was an amazing but clumsy charade, for through it all the leaders of the lumbering rail giant showed themselves to be as contemptuous of constituted authority in Utah as they themselves had been in Texas. Utah's governor, Caleb West, initiated the standoff between the territory and the Southern Pacific when he served notice on company officers that Utah law prohibited the railway from bringing indigents into the territory.[8]

Ignoring both the law and West's threats, the Southern Pacific held the Kelleyites west of town for several hours and then pulled them into the Ogden yards. The sight of men huddled together like cattle evoked a sympathetic response from onlookers. "It was an exceedingly pitiful sight," observed the *Salt Lake Tribune*, which had bitterly opposed the move in the first place. "Men, pale, cold, without covering or blankets, and wan, with hollow, sunken eyes, hunger and destitution pictured on their faces, looked out of the sides of the common cattle cars." But when they climbed out to pitch camp, they found themselves surrounded by five motley companies of territorial militiamen armed with shotguns, rifles, and muskets of every imaginable make. An artillery company brought along a vicious-looking Gatling gun that it conspicuously planted in front of city hall. On orders of Governor West, the Kelleyites were confined to the railroad yards under virtual house arrest.

From atop parked freight cars thousands of onlookers had gathered to watch the spectacle. To them, West's sending out a military force complete with a machine gun to face the defenseless Kelleyites was nothing less than a farce. Other Utahans, however—those more distant from the scene of confrontation—applauded West's show of force; and leading newspapers reflected the deep division of opinion among the territory's residents. The paper most supportive of the Kelleyites was the *Standard* of Ogden, published in an industrial center populated by a large number of railroad workers. It called the Kelleyites "our brothers" and appealed to townspeople to help them reach Washington, where perhaps the object lesson of a "hungry starving multitude" would chasten Congress and "bring a blessing to the nation."

The courts, too, jumped into the fight, and soon the telegraph lines that linked Ogden with Southern Pacific headquarters in San Francisco hummed with advice, threats, and counterthreats. The United States District Court enjoined the railroad from bringing indigents into Utah. The response of Southern Pacific general superintendent J. A. Fillmore was to term his company's action "a humane act that had to be performed, regardless of the law. Those unfortunate men wanted to go on toward their homes, and we helped them. If the law wants to punish us for that, I guess we can stand it."

C. F. Crocker, the railroad's first vice-president, later elaborated on the railroad's reasons for bringing the Kelleyites into Utah. "It seems to me the company did right; that it did a good thing for the men as well as all concerned. We had to make a low rate to get them out of Oakland or submit to the power of numbers and haul them for nothing. The railroad is naturally open for whatever business is offered."

Believing now that it had public opinion and the Interstate Commerce Act on its side, the Southern Pacific stepped up its pressure on Governor West by refusing to take the men back to California for less than full fare. That amounted to about $35 a head, or approximately $35,000. The railroad had received $600 to haul them from Oakland to Utah.

Poor Caleb West. The territory could pay $40,000 to send the Kelleyites on to Denver, $35,000 to haul them back to California, or accept the expense of housing and feeding them in Ogden. A one-time soldier in the Confederate Army, West had battled Yankees; but just now corporate power seemed a far more formidable threat. His Kentucky blood at a boil, the governor lashed out at the railroad for refusing to obey the court injunction. He brought forth only a suitably condescending reply from the railroad's president, the magisterial Collis P. Huntington, who along with Leland Stanford and other members of the Big Four had built the western portion of America's first transcontinental railroad three decades earlier. Calling West's demand for removal a mistake, he noted, "We have taken these men east in the course of business, hoping that the condition of the industrial army, so called, would be bettered thereby, as they can't get work here and hope to better their condition by getting something to do on their arrival in the east, where there is a large field for employment." Huntington emphasized that the railroad would not haul the men back for less than the regular rate.

In response to further blasts from West, Huntington wired back a second and even more unctuous reply: "It was in a kindly spirit that we took them, and we believe now, after careful consideration of the subject, that your people will do what they can to help them on to their destination. . . . As a matter of common humanity we all should do something to help them on their way."

President Huntington forwarded $100 to help the Kelleyites. "Oh, it wasn't much," the parsimonious "philanthropist" explained to reporters. "It won't hurt me any and it won't help them much. I intended it more as moral support. Sometimes moral support is better than money-giving." A $100 contribution from the Rio Grande Western and miscellaneous gifts from Ogden sympathizers raised a purse of nearly $600 to feed the pilgrims. With each passing hour the stranded Kelleyites evoked more pity and less hostility from Utahans, and Governor West, a Grover Cleveland appointee, found himself denounced by the local press as an agent of the "Washington Junta."

With the territorial governor and the railroad hopelessly deadlocked, the judiciary stepped up its effort to force an end to the dispute. On April 9 the court reaffirmed the injunction issued the day before in the name of the people of the territory of Utah, the city of Ogden, and the county of Weber. But the Southern Pacific remained unintimidated, and with extraordinary bravado it now ordered the Kelleyites to vacate its cars or pay a daily rental fee of $3 for each. This charge was to be paid by the parties who detained them there with an injunction, namely the state, city, and county. "This aggressive action of the company was somewhat of a bombshell and it appears the plot was thickening," fretted the *Salt Lake Tribune*. The ploy frightened the city of Ogden into withdrawing its support for the injunction and caused an increasing number of Utahans to criticize their governor for provoking a stalemate that cost the taxpayers more each day.

The plot took still another twist when the commander of the in-

Charles T. Kelley. From Henry Vincent, *The Story of the Commonweal* (Chicago, 1894).

dustrial army, General Kelley, arrived from California on the morning of April 10. When he stepped from the train a loud cry went up as a thousand voices chanted "Kelley! Kelley! Kelley!" The crusaders shook his hand, hugged him, and hailed him as the messiah who would deliver them from the hands of Caleb West and lead them out of the modern land of Zion.

Governor West paid the general a visit, and at West's request Kelley asked his followers whether they wanted to go back to California. "On to Washington" was their unanimous response.

"Do you understand what it means to go ahead?" their leader asked.

"Yes, Yes," they came back with one voice.

"Are you prepared to undertake the suffering and privation which you are sure to undergo?"

"Yes, Yes."

There was spontaneous applause, and the men gave three cheers for Kelley, his wife at home in California, Colonel Baker, and the good people of Ogden. And cheers too for Colorado's Populist governor Davis Waite, whom they regarded as a supporter.

Kelley, working diligently to get his men to Denver, learned of a Colorado law that fined a carrier $200 for each pauper it brought into the state. "Can our army stop a day or two in Colorado without being resisted by force of arms?" he wired Governor Waite.

"Any citizen of the United States has the right of passage through Colorado," responded Waite. Speaking to a Denver audience about Coxeyites a few days later, the governor added, "Their cause is just and they should be aided instead of hindered. Were I called upon to order out the militia against them, I probably would do so, but it would be only as a commissary department."[9]

The final chapter of the confrontation between state and railroad began the day after Kelley's arrival. Federal District Court Judge James A. Miner announced his decision after listening to hours of testimony, including a statement by the Southern Pacific's local superintendent, S. W. Knapp, that he would obey the court order only if the railroad willed it. Complained Miner: "This is one of the most difficult decisions I have ever been called upon to make. . . . There are no precedents. . . . The court is obliged to travel over a road which has never been traveled before to my knowledge." He then amended the earlier injunction and now permitted territorial officers to use force to eject the Kelleyites.

West was elated. He called the decision "a great victory" and talked of running the train to the Nevada line under military authority if the railroad failed to comply. The governor, however, never got his chance. The citizens of Ogden were tired of his blustering and the military furor he had created. The city's workmen adopted a resolution condemning West's use of the militia and staged a grand parade to show their support for the stranded Kelleyites. Among the banners they waved aloft were "Spike Your Gatling Guns" and "Men are not Cattle."

It was Judge Miner's decision that brought Ogden's growing hostility toward West to the surface and precipitated a heated discussion between Mayor Charles M. Brough and the governor. Finally, after fifteen minutes of fruitless arguing, Brough called to his staff, "Come on."

"Where are you going?"

"Going down to march that industrial army out of town. We have stood this damned monkey business long enough. Salt Lake has run this thing up to date. Now Ogden will take a hand."

"Going to start them on their way east?"

"Why, hell, yes."

A few minutes later the mayor entered the Kelley camp and called the leaders together.

"Boys, you have said that you were going to Washington if you had to walk. Now, we are going to take you at your word. Get your men in line and follow me."

"How about the militia?"

"Never mind the militia. You follow me. You'll march east from Ogden to the Wyoming line. The citizens of Ogden have taken up a subscription to buy food, clothing and blankets and these will follow in wagons. Fall in."

In less than forty-five minutes the men were ready, although as they eyed the lofty Wasatch Range ahead they really did not relish the idea of walking. Mayor Brough and other city officials took their places at the head of the column; the Kelleyites fell in behind in companies with flags and banners flying, one of which read, "Favors for corporations, but none for Hungry Men—C. W. West."

With a wave of his cane, the mayor signaled the start of the procession, and Kelleyites marched quietly out of "Camp Andersonville," where for the past three days they had baked in the sun. They tramped along the main street, where several thousand equally quiet onlookers had gathered; and as they passed city hall they gazed curiously at West's infamous Gatling gun. The mayor led the column to the edge of town, where he bade the visitors good-bye.

Nine wagonloads of provisions caught up with Kelley's men at Uintah, a siding on the Union Pacific eight miles east of Ogden. The crusaders camped here but remained uneasy, fearing that West and his militiamen would appear to head them back to California. But the governor was a helpless and defeated man. Collis P. Huntington offered a last ingratiating word: "It seems very cruel that those poor men should have been marched from Ogden to Uintah. They ought to have been carried by rail." The rail baron proved a better prophet than he realized.

A few hours after Kelley and his men halted at Uintah, a Union Pacific freight rumbled into the siding to allow a passenger train by. It seemed more than coincidental that the sidetracked train consisted of twenty-seven empty boxcars, and that assistant superintendent Garret O'Neil happened to be aboard, and that the crewmen made little effort to keep the Kelleyites from loading themselves and their provisions into the cars. Once they were aboard, O'Neil ordered the conductor to collect their fares. Passing along the side of the cars, he called out politely:

"Tickets, please, Gentlemen."

"We never pay anything on the cars," a voice came back.

"Then get off the train," responded the conductor disingenuously as he slid the doors shut with the men inside. O'Neil gave orders to proceed and wired headquarters in Omaha that Kelley's army had captured the train. The whole affair appeared to be an elaborate charade to allow the Union Pacific to avoid charges that it brought indigents into a state in violation of the law.[10]

Governor John E. Osborne of Wyoming promised to make no attempt to interfere with the men during their presence in the state if they did not violate the law. And with approval from Omaha, Union Pacific men hurried the special along to avoid delaying any regular trains on the railroad's main line. The pilgrims assumed they were headed for Denver, but even the railroad was not sure where they were going. Superintendent W. A. Deuel telegraphed General Manager E. Dickinson and asked what he should do if Kelley's army stopped in Cheyenne and insisted on going to Denver. Dickinson replied that he should do nothing, that Kelley had so many men in his ranks that they could easily overpower Union Pacific employees and go anywhere he wanted simply by commandeering its trains.[11]

In Cheyenne a large crowd gathered at the Union Pacific's imposing Romanesque station, hoping to learn when the pilgrims from the coast would arrive. After a wait of several hours, during which a good portion of the city's twelve thousand citizens collected to greet Kelley's men, the smoke of the special train appeared on the horizon. As it came closer, onlookers noticed that the sides and tops of its cars were embroidered with a fringe of humanity, and from every open door men waved flags and banners. As befitted a general of such an army, Kelley rode in a private car of sorts: a yellow caboose bobbing along at the rear.

Much to everyone's surprise, the special did not stop. It steamed rapidly through the Wyoming capital on tracks that headed east to Omaha instead of switching south toward Denver. Citizens waved hats and handkerchiefs as the crusaders rolled by, and cheers were exchanged. Just beyond the east edge of town the train halted briefly to collect a ton of beef donated by the people of Cheyenne, and the crusaders sent up a cheer that could be heard a mile away.

Kelley was disappointed that the railroad had not routed the special by way of Denver, but he gladly settled for Omaha, five hundred miles farther east. "I had hoped to call upon Governor Waite and personally thank him for his expression of sympathy, but it will be impossible for me to do so. We must hurry on to Washington as rapidly as possible while we have the opportunity."[12]

All along the Union Pacific main line that bisected Nebraska from east to west, crowds turned out to greet the Kelley special. At each stop or when the train ran slowly, "Frenchy," a bulky soldier of swarthy complexion, took his place at the front of the engine and waved a huge American flag. He was impressively attired in an old band uniform.

When the train paused just outside Grand Island, 1,000 loaves of bread, 50 dozen boiled eggs, 100 pounds of bologna, 200 pounds of cheese, bacon, 50 pounds of coffee, 10 cases of crackers, 6 cases of canned pork and beans, and 100 pounds of boneless ham were waiting for the men. Kelley thanked the citizens and delivered an impromptu speech detailing the reasons for the army's pilgrimage. When the train reached Fremont at half past four Sunday morning, April 15, nearly 150 residents waited beside the tracks in the early morning mist. They were part of a vigil that had begun the previous afternoon. The local "war" correspondent was there to write up the story for the town newspaper. Kelley's army was big excitement in these parts.

Aside from not being routed through Denver, just about the only disappointment that Kelley and his men experienced as they traveled the thousand miles from Ogden to Omaha occurred at North Platte, Nebraska, where they just missed receiving three steers that Buffalo Bill Cody had sent to the station from his ranch nearby. Kelley lamented the loss, adding that he had four butchers in his ranks. But he scarcely had time to reflect on Cody's act of kindness. As the train rolled toward the end of the Union Pacific line, the facile mind of the citizen-general had to race ever faster merely to comprehend the range of problems that crowded in upon him.[13]

CHAPTER 8

The more opposition they meet, the stronger they become. The laboring classes all over the country are in sympathy with them.

E. St. John, General Manager of the Chicago, Rock Island and Pacific Railway on Kelley's Army

Kelley's Dilemma: The Rail Barons and Women in the Ranks

Bolting out of the Far West on their special train, Charles T. Kelley and his thousand men headed straight for Iowa. Had they been invaders from Mars, state officials would have been no less certain how best to prepare for their arrival.

Saturday, April 14, was a day of rapidly mounting tension. In Des Moines, Governor Frank D. Jackson pondered the telegrams he had received from nervous officials of the Chicago and North-Western Railway, begging him to use the state militia to bar Kelley's men from Iowa. Jackson, a lawyer and a Republican party hack who had been inaugurated governor only three months earlier, knew that there was no precedent for such action; but neither was there any precedent for Kelley's army. He knew also that time was running out.

At that moment the special train was steaming across central Nebraska and in a matter of hours would cross the Missouri River bridge into Council Bluffs, where the Union Pacific line ended. There the problem of transporting Kelley's men would be thrust into the reluctant hands of four midwestern lines that connected to Chicago and points east. It was a situation similar to the one encountered in Ogden.

The Chicago and North-Western took the initiative by announcing that it would do anything to keep the army of unemployed off its trains. The railroad's attorney, Nat M. Hubbard, threatened that the line would even shut down for ten days rather than transport the Kelleyites. His solution was to keep them out of Iowa entirely by using state troops to block the bridges that linked Council Bluffs with Omaha.[1]

A very concerned Governor Jackson finally agreed to dispatch seven companies of state militia—about four hundred men—to Council Bluffs. Then he headed west to the potential trouble site on a special train provided by the Chicago and North-Western. Jackson found Council Bluffs alive with rumors of impending trouble. He spent his first few hours in Council Bluffs in a secret conference with local law enforcement officers and railroad managers, passing around law books and studying them late into the night. Iowa's chief executive should also have studied the newspapers to learn what his counterpart in Utah had done wrong, for the railroads were leading him into a similar confrontation. The companies would not hesitate to sacrifice Jackson to protect their interests.

Chicago and North-Western officials repeated their demands that the Kelleyites be barred from the state, but Sheriff John T. Hazen of Pottawattamie County—which like Ogden and Weber County in Utah was the home of many railroad workers—and the Iowa attorney general would not agree. In the end, the governor ordered militiamen simply to keep the peace and prevent Kelley's men from scattering once they reached Council Bluffs. The meeting adjourned around midnight, and all parties wondered what the morning light would bring.[2]

At about half past nine the next morning the Kelley train rumbled slowly across the Missouri River bridge and clanked to a halt at the Union Pacific transfer station. Iowa's militiamen were waiting for them in battle array. But neither the sight of the troops nor the low morning fog dampened the holiday mood of the pilgrims from the West Coast. Twenty-six boxcars were festooned with red, white, and blue bunting, American flags, and a large banner that read, "Government Employment for the Unemployed." There arose a loud and sustained cheer, and faces weary and grimy from long days on the road smiled at the swelling crowd of sympathizers that pushed among the soldiers. "The Union Pacific has been very good to us," smiled Kelley, summarizing his journey from Ogden.

Sheriff Hazen climbed into the car, introduced himself to Kelley, and asked, "What is your intention; what do you propose to do?" "Our position has been a peculiar one," answered the general. "Since we left Ogden we have hardly had time to map out a plan. We hardly know just what we want ourselves. We want to rest a time at least, if we can get the privilege. The men have been cooped up in the cars. It would do them lots of good to get stretched out." Hazen had no objection.

Jumping down onto the cinders, the travelers hurriedly washed up before enjoying a hearty Sunday breakfast topped off with a thousand pies donated by the Omaha mercantile firm of Brandeis and Sons. The railway yards were soon packed with an estimated thirty to forty thousand people. By foot, carriage, and streetcar they came, at least twenty thousand from Omaha alone. They donated carloads of bread and other food, bedding, and $1,000 in cash.[3]

After breakfast the Kelleyites fashioned makeshift barbers' chairs from railroad ties and old pails and relished the luxury of haircuts and shaves. Some lounged around reading the papers, while others regaled visitors with tales of their cross-country odyssey. The center of attention, though, was Charles T. Kelley, the self-styled general who led the army of misfortune.

Those who expected to see a burly, pugnacious roustabout from San Francisco's Barbary Coast were probably surprised when they spotted him. He looked and acted more like a mild-mannered captain in the Salvation Army. A diminutive man, thirty-two years old with blue eyes and a small black mustache, Kelley wore a uniform consisting of a short overcoat and a middy cap. His voice was soft but firm, and he exhorted rather than commanded his men. "Oh, Company K," he might say to a company that was marching along smartly, "that's right good. God bless you." To another company his exhortation might be, "Keep straight ahead; we'll get there. Victory is ours."

His revivalistic style prompted newspaper stories that he was indeed a former Salvationist and that his wife was one, too. Kelley denied that allegation, as well as the claim by an Omaha paper that he had abandoned his wife and infant daughter in California. In fact, he had been working as a typographer for the *San Francisco Chronicle* when a delegation asked him to lead their army to Washington; and,

Kelley claimed, his wife encouraged him to go. As for the story circulated by an Omaha paper that he was "Cigarette" Kelley, a tough character, prizefighter, and gambler who once frequented Nebraska and Wyoming, he joked that if his wife read that story "she would apply for a divorce." One thing was clear, though: General Kelley was a natural leader and a fluent speaker.[4]

When Kelley got up to address the Sunday afternoon crowd, everyone listened attentively as he explained his program, which was not entirely the same as Coxey's road-building scheme. The Kelleyites believed that if Congress would put the jobless to work for three years digging irrigation ditches in the arid West, "the people [would] be on their feet once more." This proposal would provide both jobs and productive lands for any workers who wished to take up farming. "Talk about hard times," Kelley continued, "this is the richest country in the world and there is no reason why a single individual should beg for bread." Referring to Governor Jackson's calling out the Iowa militiamen, the man from California assured his listeners, "We have a mission to perform, which is to secure legislation and not to steal and plunder." The crowd cheered wildly at the conclusion of Kelley's presentation.

Through a series of speeches and newspaper interviews, Kelley provided an extremely curious public with additional details about himself, the purpose of his march, and his overland adventure. He revealed that he was a native of Connecticut, had run away from home at a young age, sold newspapers on the streets of Chicago, learned the printing trade, and worked at various times in Saint Louis, Kansas City, and San Francisco. He was a member of the International Typographical Union.[5]

During their Sunday in Council Bluffs, Kelley's men demonstrated to the skeptics that they were indeed an army and not an agglomeration of tramps. Each member carried a blue cardboard membership card that he had to show before retiring for the night and wore an insignia consisting of a small American flag pinned to his lapel. When he joined up, he signed an obligation to uphold the law, had his name, occupation, and body measurements recorded, and received a serial number—just as if he had joined the regular army. Kelley's army was organized around two divisions and fourteen com-

Kelley's arrival at the transfer, Council Bluffs, Iowa. From Henry
Vincent, *The Story of the Commonweal* (Chicago, 1894).

panies, run by a staff of colonels, captains, sergeants, and aides besides the general himself.

Chaplain William Parsonage conducted regular religious services,
and three pharmacists and a hospital steward cared for the sick. The
camp hospital was well supplied with blankets and medicine. Kelley's

army, in short, presented quite a contrast to Browne's reincarnation services and Cyclone Kirkland's ad hoc doctoring. In addition, a central commissary collected all donated food and and distributed it to each company, which was responsible for its preparation.

Kelley opened a recruiting station in Council Bluffs and inducted several new members, but he abruptly suspended enlistment when he learned that an Omaha judge had promised freedom to any petty convicts who would leave town with Kelley's army. The general refused to accept such men, saying that he was already taking care of too many people: "It is giving me gray hairs." About a dozen men accepted the judge's offer, but others refused. One black prisoner spoke for many when he said he would rather remain in jail all summer than march to Washington to be shot and killed.

In Council Bluffs and Omaha, though, the only killing was with kindness. As in Ogden, Kelley and his men rapidly won people's hearts by their good behavior and simple appeals to basic human emotions. Visitors and newspaper reporters were impressed by the army's Sunday prayer meeting. Dressed in their tattered garments and gathered around campfires, hundreds of men raised their voices in hymns and prayers—something conspicuously missing from the religious services of Browne, who did not believe in prayer. The singing of Methodist gospel hymns, duly recorded in the next day's papers, reached an audience far larger than the one that worshipped in Council Bluffs' darkened railway yards; and it evoked widespread support for the visitors.

Except for the Union Pacific, which allowed the Kelleyites to remain in its boxcars one more night, the railroads steadily lost favor in the eyes of the public. All day Sunday, while Kelley and his men made friends with the local populace, railway officials huddled in conference with Governor Jackson and remained stubbornly opposed to transporting the crusaders further east. At one point, Kelley was invited to the meeting and questioned closely by railroad attorneys. Proving himself a more articulate antagonist than they expected, he carefully explained his arid lands program but added, with tears in his eyes, that his men demanded nothing. And the railroads gave nothing. They voted unanimously to refuse to carry his men for less than full fare. Kelley, who had expected to remain in Council Bluffs less than a day, replied, "I don't know what course we shall take.

I shall have to think it over." Though Kelley had failed to budge the railroad officials, he did impress Governor Jackson with his sincerity. The Iowa chief executive redoubled his efforts to find transportation for the Kelleyites across the state.

On Monday afternoon, when it became obvious that they would be remaining in Council Bluffs longer than expected, Kelley and his men accepted the offer of a campsite on the chautauqua grounds three miles across town. There the Kelleyites and militiamen mingled together on friendly terms, setting up camp. Because the Kelleyites expected to leave the chautauqua grounds in a few hours, they did not mind bedding down without shelter under a clear sky. But during the night a spring storm blew in and soaked them. A few managed to fashion huts of sticks, and Kelley made the rounds by lantern to keep his men's spirits up. Coming across one of the brush huts he called to its inhabitants:

"You're pretty snug in there aren't you?"

"Oh, yes. All we need is a pianner."

At the chautauqua campsite, rain was not the only problem. The army was almost out of food. Consuming $600 worth of food a day, the Kelleyites had nearly used up the contributions they had received on Sunday. And as the rain continued, the men grumbled ever louder about their lack of shelter. The camp hospital was soon full.

While his men spent the day gathering twigs and limbs for shelter and fire, Kelley began to think about the unthinkable: crossing Iowa on foot. Studying a map to calculate how long it would take his army to reach Davenport, three hundred miles away, at the rate of fifteen miles a day, Kelley concluded that an overland walk was impossible; the towns through which his men would have to travel were too small to feed them. The railroads remained their only hope, but railroad executives refused to relent. Fortunately, a steady stream of sympathetic citizens visited the chautauqua grounds and brought donations of food and clothing. And across the river in Omaha, the merchant Emil Brandeis and Mayor George P. Bemis, a popular friend of workers, solicited aid from businessmen.

After spending another miserable night in the rain and hail, the Kelleyites awoke Wednesday morning to the sight of a stout German woman driving up with a wagonload of comforters and loaves of homemade bread. Soon, additional wagons arrived with meat and

more bread. The best sight of all, though, was the departing militiamen. Governor Jackson sent them home in a move that Kelleyites in-
correctly interpreted as a prelude to the arrival of a train to "capture."

Actually, the governor's decision was not part of any well-conceived
plan. He readily confessed that he was dealing with a problem like
nothing that had ever happened before, a problem that he called
a novel expression of discontent. More than anything else, it was
the mounting furor provoked by stubborn railroad executives that
prompted him to recall the militiamen. Although railroad leaders
were the primary targets of public wrath, Jackson was stung by bitter
criticism that he had showed himself to be a lackey of the rail barons
when he called out the militia at their request.

Early in the week Jackson had defended his use of militiamen by
asking, "If the railroads persist in refusing transportation to these
men, will Kelley's men adhere to his peaceful policy?" But with popular indignation reaching dangerous levels in Omaha and Council
Bluffs, the governor took a more conciliatory line: "I feel the keenest
sympathy for these men. What the final outcome will be I cannot say,
but I feel confident now that the problem will resolve itself." Jackson
reportedly sought to charter a boat to take Kelley's men downriver to
Kansas City; at the same time, he hoped to stall other western armies
before they reached the state by threatening to arrest Union Pacific
general manager E. Dickinson for having brought Kelley's paupers
into Iowa in violation of state law. But if Jackson imagined that his
maneuvers would calm public opinion, he failed to take into account
spokesmen like Judge Hubbard of the North-Western.

Every time Hubbard opened his mouth he not only increased local support for the Kelleyites but also made a violent confrontation
more likely. He readily admitted that he had influenced the governor
to call out the state militia. Furthermore, blustered Hubbard, "If
these tramps and bums try to capture one of our trains, there will be
trouble." He warned that "should they gain possession of a train by
hook or crook, or by the sympathy of our trainmen, we will ditch the
train if it destroys every car and hurts alot of men." Hubbard maintained that "this movement must be stopped now and right here, and
I don't think the people show good judgment in feeding these people.
There is too much false sympathy for these men." Bluntly declaring
that "our road was not built for charitable purposes," Hubbard did

not hesitate to suggest that the Kelleyites should be starved into disbanding.

By contrasting the callousness of men like Hubbard with the plight of the Kelleyites, the daily press evoked a tremendous out-pouring of public sympathy for the crusaders. Organized labor in Omaha and Council Bluffs held indignation meetings to denounce Judge Hubbard and warned him to leave Council Bluffs at once. The judge, unmoved by criticism, threatened that the North-Western would kill Kelleyites to defend the prerogatives of management: "We will steam up a wild engine, open the throttle and send it down to meet the captured train, and let the wreck solve the problem of whether we are obliged to carry these men without remuneration." "Judge Hubbard," remarked one of Kelley's officers, "must be two or three kinds of an ass."

Frustrated by the impasse and fearful that time would run out be-fore his men could rendezvous with their fellow marchers on Capitol Hill on May Day, Kelley ordered his troops to march to the village of Weston, seven miles east of Council Bluffs. Moving out of Camp Chautauqua on Thursday, April 19, the army now numbered four-teen hundred men and formed a column half a mile long. The dirt road led them through rolling countryside that was just beginning to reveal the colors of spring. Morale was high, and though a cold, steady rain turned the road into mud several inches deep, the men marched along singing "We'll Never Turn Back 'Til Our Mission is Finished." Along the way, farm families greeted them with words of welcome and donations of meat and potatoes.

Dragging along in his buggy was Sheriff Hazen, reluctantly carry-ing out a request by the railroads to keep an eye on the procession. "I am in sympathy with these men," protested the lawman. "They are creatures of circumstances." Like a tormenting spirit, a special train carrying railroad officials, including Judge Hubbard, shadowed the procession. Hubbard had just added to the tension by announcing that the North-Western would not carry Kelleyites under any circum-stances, not even for payment of full fare.

While Kelley and his men quietly pitched camp in Weston, popular anger at the railroad's intransigence boiled over in Omaha and Council Bluffs. After the Rock Island twice rejected Governor Jackson's re-quest to transport the men—with Iowa paying the bill—a Council

Bluffs newspaper editorialized that the railroad should be compelled to carry them: "The Rock Island owes something to this state which gave it a rich endowment of fertile land."

Failing that, the sentiment was growing among Kelley's many sympathizers that they should take overt action to batter down the wall created by the railroads. On several occasions Union Pacific shopmen staged conspicuous marches from Omaha to Council Bluffs' chautauqua grounds to bring food and money to Kelley's stranded men. Once they marched with loaves of bread impaled on pikes. Operating employees of the Union Pacific offered to donate their services to any road willing to carry the Kelleyites eastward. Actually, though, Kelley had an engineer and three firemen in his ranks, should he decide to capture and operate a train. And on Friday evening, an enormous crowd of sympathizers roamed the railroad yards of Council Bluffs looking for a train to take to Kelley at Weston.

That morning a thousand people had crowded into Omaha's Knights of Labor hall to pledge themselves to blow whistles and ring bells in the Union Pacific shops, local factories, and churches as a signal for workingmen and women to march together to Council Bluffs. There they would demand for a final time that the railroads carry the crusaders. The workers were motivated by feelings of altruism and sympathy, mixed with a perfectly rational desire for self-preservation: they feared that if Hubbard and others succeeded in starving the army into disbanding, the influx of unemployed men from the Far West would further depress the local job market.

Five hundred Union Pacific shopmen and their families marched on signal to Council Bluffs, where they were joined by hundreds of others, most notably the packinghouse workers of south Omaha, described by one nervous Iowan as "corn-fed Omaha steers." The crowd of workers had swelled to more than eight thousand by the time it confronted the Council Bluffs mayor and various railroad representatives. "Such a scene as that upon the streets of Council Bluffs will probably never be seen but once in a lifetime," observed a local newspaper.[6]

At times Council Bluffs resembled a three-ring circus. In one part of town a delegation of about two hundred women met with North-Western officers, hoping to succeed where men had previously failed. In another location a mass meeting denounced Judge Hubbard.

Elsewhere, a third group telegraphed railroad presidents, urging them to transport Kelley's army out of Weston. All the protesters eventually congregated in a city park to await a response from the rail barons. At about four o'clock the telegraph clicked out a reply: the railroads would provide no train. The crowd responded with a loud hiss and a shout: "We won't wait any longer. Let's get a train."

The women, who had been conspicuous in the day's events, took charge. They led a thousand people to the Milwaukee and Rock Island depots but found them locked and the engines and cars gone. Just then a three-car Union Pacific passenger local rumbled across the bridge from Omaha, and in a moment the crowd swarmed over it. One of the leaders of the Omaha Knights of Labor, a son of the engineer and himself an engineer, swung up into the cab.

"Pop. You are our prisoner."

The old man exploded with a series of expletives but surrendered his seat and climbed down. A dozen women filled the cab and decorated the locomotive with American flags. When the young engineer agreed to run the engine but refused to start it—presuming that he could thus avoid legal responsibility for his action—Edna Harper pulled open the throttle.

After the citizens had attached some freight cars from the yard, the special steamed rapidly along the Rock Island tracks to Weston, its bell ringing and its whistle blowing. The army, surprised in the midst of its evening religious services, sent up a mighty cheer when the train slowed to a stop, and Kelley thanked his sympathizers in a short speech. All the while Harper and two companions, May Cromer and Anna Hooten, stood demurely at his side. When Hooten was urged to address the men, she related the details of the capture but wondered aloud whether she was motivated more by patriotism or foolhardiness. She was afraid she had almost forgotten her womanhood in her desire to do good for the cause. The delighted Kelleyites presented each woman with the badge of the army.

Although he did not admit it at the time, the train-stealing greatly disturbed Kelley. He desperately needed the transportation but did not want his army to abandon its peaceable posture. He knew, too, that the railroads wanted nothing better than to provoke his army into lawless acts that would turn public sentiment and the government against it.

Worried and uncertain about what steps to take next, Kelley suggested to the women that it would be safer to move the men after daylight. And noting that the eleven-car special was too small to carry his troops, he requested that sympathizers return it to Council Bluffs, along with twenty marchers in need of special medical attention. Kelley permitted Harper and Hooten, who were afraid to go back for fear of arrest, to remain temporarily with the army. Though it was nearly midnight when the captured train returned to Council Bluffs, it was met by a crowd of nearly five thousand people, half of whom were workers from Omaha.

If the train capture left Kelley confused, the mass protests and the revolutionary implications of bread impaled on pikes frightened some railroad executives. Protesters were convinced that their actions had had the desired effect when news arrived of a remarkable interview that had appeared in Saturday's *Iowa State Register*. The wall of railroad intransigence seemed about to crumble at last. E. St. John, general manager of the Rock Island, told a *Register* reporter that he had talked with Kelley in Omaha and inspected his men at Weston. He described the troops as "intelligent, determined men. . . . There are no bums among them. . . . Their leader is a man of brains and character and great determination, and he is a religious man, too."

Emphasizing, "I would not be one bit afraid to take them to Chicago," St. John was clearly worried about the revolutionary implications of the march and the mass protests by workers in Omaha and Council Bluffs. The situation, he believed, was "very similar to the French Revolution. It is a terrible thing, and it made me sad to find that there were sixteen hundred respectable, well-meaning men reduced to such desperate straits in this country." Given the dangerous level of social tension in Omaha and Council Bluffs, he criticized the unnecessarily provocative language of Judge Hubbard, saying, "Such brutal utterances drive people mad." He also denounced Hubbard's call for the Iowa militia.

While St. John admitted that for the past several days he had been out of touch with Rock Island president Ransom R. Cable and was not sure what railroad leaders were planning in Chicago, he nonetheless sent Cable word of his willingness to transport Kelley's men. St. John, it soon became apparent, was a lone voice crying in the wilderness, for his president continued to refuse Rock Island help for Kelley.

Railroad leaders in Chicago had apparently formed a blind pool that enabled them to share the risks and costs of blocking the Kelleyites. Whichever railroad was nearest to Kelley's line of march simply quit operating its trains or rerouted them over another line, and all companies shared the resulting expense.[7]

With their hopes dashed yet another time, sympathizers in Omaha and Council Bluffs continued to provide food and moral support for Kelley's men; but they were not certain what else to do. And neither was a discouraged Kelley. His two most pressing dilemmas were how to organize a march across Iowa if a train was not soon forthcoming, and determining the status of women in his ranks.

Saturday was another day of watchful waiting, of rumor and disappointment. The army whiled away the time with oratory and song, often to the soft accompaniment of General Kelley on his banjo. The two women in the ranks, Hooten and Harper, added occasional words of encouragement. And welcome indeed was the news from Mayor Bemis that Omaha was sending additional supplies. From Woodsmen of the World came word that its lodge brothers would welcome Kelleyites everywhere along their journey.[8]

An increasing number of women wanted to join Kelley's army. Before it arrived in Council Bluffs, many women had spent a sleepless night, fearful that Kelleyites would slip in before dawn, raid their homes, and "subject them to indignities." But when the women learned of the orderly demeanor of the sojourners, fear turned to fascination. Some of them skipped Sunday church services in order to view the marchers in person. And their sympathy for the soldiers of misfortune grew with each passing day, becoming most apparent during Friday's capture of a train. When women asked to join his ranks, Kelley good-naturedly refused, saying it was hard enough to manage men without attempting to manage women. Kelley made an exception for Hooten and Harper, though, saying that the spirit of humanity motivated him to provide for the two. He regarded them as mascots, he said, and was fearful that he would incur the wrath of organized labor if he forced them to return home to face arrest.[9]

Although tongues inevitably wagged about the relationship of two attractive women with fourteen hundred men, Kelley sought to protect his army's reputation and that of Hooten and Harper by housing them in a special tent or hotel when possible. And the two

Kelley's "angels"—Miss Hooten and Miss Harper. From Henry
Vincent, *The Story of the Commonweal* (Chicago, 1894).

usually rode in a carriage with the army's official photographer. Similarly, he refused to permit the female reporters covering the march to
remain in camp with the men overnight. The question of women
joining his ranks came up again and again, though, and soon Kelley

must have wondered if he had done the right thing in permitting Hooten and Harper to remain. Even within his own ranks some men objected to their presence, perhaps fearful that insinuations of immorality circulating in the press would reach their wives back on the Pacific Slope.[10]

A traveling salesman from Topeka returned home one day to find that his lonely wife had left to join Coxey's army. Friends suggested that he send letters to General Coxey and Kelley to prevent her enlistment. If the newspaper story was true, the distraught husband had little to fear, for Coxey no more than Kelley wanted women in his ranks.[11]

Coxey had given the question of female recruits some thought when his movement was still in the formative stage but concluded that the Commonweal must not entangle itself with "daughters." If it were an ordinary military campaign, he explained, "we might use our women sympathizers as nurses, but we expect no bloodshed, and under such circumstances a nurse would be an expensive luxury." While Coxey saw women as participants in certain well-defined spheres of activity, Kelley's concern was that observers would imagine the worst about the relationship between women and men in his ranks and that it would cost the movement vital popular support.[12]

Women nonetheless played a variety of notable roles in the Coxey crusade. Most often they served as members of home guard units and women's auxiliaries, patterned after Civil War organizations that women had formed to send the amenities of life to soldiers on the battlefield. The Women's Relief Corps of Denver, for example, which owed its existence to the local Women's Populist Club and the Home Guard, not only cared for wives and children at home but also forwarded clothing and food to crusaders on the road. Without such organizations, the armies of the Pacific Slope probably would not have started east. The commanders of the Seattle and Salt Lake City armies had, like Kelley, left wives and young children in the care of home guards and women's auxiliaries.[13]

The activities of these women's groups were widely advertised. When a contingent of metal miners from Butte formed itself into a navy and sailed down the Missouri River, a reporter asked whether any of the voyagers were married. "Lots of them, and the people of

Montana are supporting their wives and children now," one responded. Anticipating criticism of this arrangement, he added: "But what could the men do if they stayed at home? There was no work for them to do, and there would have been one more person to feed."[14]

Some women resented their husbands joining the crusade. Two women drove to an industrial army camp outside Salt Lake City, broke through the picket lines, and returned with a sheepish man in tow. As angry words were exchanged, one woman ended the argument with a blow to the face of her "liege lord." She exclaimed loudly that she would thrash any man who would desert his wife and children to follow a "will-o'-the-wisp" across the deserts of the West. The case of Mary Cook was different. When her husband marched out of Salt Lake City with the local Coxeyites, she ran out of money to feed herself and her child and forged a check for $10.15. Confronted and humiliated by the bank that detected the forgery, she returned home, swallowed strychnine, and died in terrible convulsions. Had she lived in Salt Lake City, where various support groups were active, instead of in tiny Pleasant Grove, things might have been different.[15]

Home guard and auxiliary units existed in every western city that sent an industrial army east, and in many smaller towns, too. One of the largest of these bodies was the Women's Commonweal Society of Chicago. Probably its most prominent member was Lucy Parsons, wife of the Haymarket riot martyr Albert Parsons. Also notable was Mrs. J. H. Randall, a neatly dressed middle-aged woman who eventually left the organization to go east with her husband, the commander of the main Chicago army. While on the road, the "mother of the regiment," as she was sometimes called, acted as the army's advance guard. It was her task to find the marchers a place to sleep and line up their next meal.[16]

Other organizations helped. The Women's Christian Temperance Union provided assistance in a number of places. In the nation's capital no person or organization did more to rally support for the various armies assembling there than the *Woman's Tribune*, edited by Clara Bewick Colby. The *Tribune*, which also promoted women's rights and Populism, solicited contributions from reform-minded readers all over the United States and distributed these from a comfort station that it established in the District of Columbia. Closely associated with Colby and the *Tribune* was Annie Diggs, who sent messages to governors Lorenzo Lewelling of Kansas and Davis Waite of Colorado and "other good men and women everywhere" urging them to support the Coxey movement.[17]

Not all women who aided the Commonweal were part of any formal organization. Women in Nebraska and Iowa, for example, banded together temporarily to furnish soup, coffee, and sandwiches to Kelley's overlanders. Other "mothers of the Commonweal" acted alone. One of the movement's most notable supporters in the Missouri Valley was Mary G. Jones, who gave speeches and solicited contributions in a number of communities. Unfortunately, the army she sought to help most, a contingent from Denver, disintegrated near Kansas City after its commander took the treasury of $108 and never returned. Later, as a prominent supporter of coal miners in North America, she was known as Mother Jones.[18]

Occasionally, women provided words of encouragement when they were needed most. Mary Hobart, a fire-and-brimstone Populist orator and songwriter, used incendiary language to inspire Seattle and Tacoma troops stranded in Puyallup. Pointing her finger at the deputy marshals standing nearby, she said, "You villains, if you dare to shoot down one of these Commonwealers your names will go down in the black rolls of infamy as long as time shall last." Calling the officers "pinheads," she thundered, "The women have something to say about this. We're getting enlightened too. We're tired of bringing children into the world to be made marks for deputy marshals to shoot at."

When she finished, the cheering of the Commonwealers could be heard blocks away. Hobart seemingly confirmed an observation made earlier by the *San Francisco Examiner* that women associated with the Commonweal "have been more radical than the men." The paper labeled this the "feminine Amazon side" of the movement.[19]

Among the most prominent adornments to Coxey's ranks were various "goddesses" and the "angels," Anna Hooten and Edna Harper of Kelley's contingent. A few other women slipped into the ranks disguised as men. For example, in Pueblo, Colorado, two boyish-looking soldiers, Cyrus and Thomas Gordon, joined the army of Rocky Mountain metal miners led by John Sherman Sanders. No one suspected anything until Topeka, where the group was confined after they had stolen a train. At the "prison camp," tubs were set up and the men of each company were ordered to strip for a bath. The Gordons refused, claiming they had bathed earlier when their train had been sidetracked near Topeka.

One of Sanders' officers voiced his suspicions to United States marshal S. F. Neely, who was also a doctor, and the lawman called in a female physician to examine the Gordons. The two young men turned out to be sisters, Emiline and Lenore. The women explained that they had moved from New York to Colorado with their parents in 1889, that their father and mother had recently died, and now they wanted to return to New York. The female physician took pity on the girls and arranged for them to complete the trip by regular railway coach.[20]

Given that women were excluded from the ranks of the industrial armies, how did Anna Ferry Smith become a commander? Smith joined the movement in April when a second regiment was organized in Oakland to follow Kelley. The would-be leader of the group, John Barker, broke with precedent when he announced his intention to recruit women as well as men. "An attempt is being made to have poor women enlisted in the army and a few have signed the roll," noted the *San Francisco Bulletin*. "The idea is to have women along so that they will create sympathy in the various cities."[21]

Barker reportedly began recruiting the wives of men in Kelley's ranks. "These men have been out of work for months and there is nothing in California left for them to do," the *Omaha Bee* reported. "What few articles they had left were turned over to their wives and children. These things will be converted into cash and the women and children will come next." But things did not work out quite that way. When Barker failed to make good on his rash promise to secure transportation from the Santa Fe, his standing with his followers plummeted, while that of the irrepressible Anna Smith rose. Although very few women joined the regiment, its three hundred male members elected Smith their commander-in-chief and demoted Barker to assistant.

When they sailed up the Sacramento River on a steamboat hired by the city of Oakland, General Smith declared: "I will land my men on the steps of the Capitol at Washington," and added, "I am a San Francisco woman, a woman who has been brought up on this coast, and I'm not afraid of anything, not even hunger. I have a woman's heart and a woman's sympathy, and these lead me to do what I have done for these men, even though it may not be just what a woman is expected to do."

Who was Anna Smith, the stout, middle-aged woman who, with her gold-rimmed spectacles, looked as if she would be more at home in a second grade classroom than on the road with an army of unemployed men? She looked like a worthy country woman, the *San Francisco Examiner* said, who was "ready to sit up all night with a sick friend and courageous enough to tell a young wife that her husband has been drowned trying to swim the river." Smith had lived a many-faceted life. During the Civil War she served as a military nurse in Pennsylvania. After that she moved west to Colorado and California, where she briefly studied law and then found her calling as a lecturer for such reform organizations as the Farmers' Alliance, Bellamy Nationalism, and the Populist party. Her first husband had died, and she had divorced her third about four years before the march.

To a reporter for the *Examiner* she explained why the men had selected her as their leader: "One reason was that I have some local reputation as a speaker and the men want me to speak for them when we get to Washington," she said. Smith also believed that her presence would signify to onlookers that the men were "peaceable and orderly."

The city of Oakland, it turned out, had not bought passage for the army all the way to Sacramento; before they were halfway there, Smith and her followers were forced to disembark and walk. The spectacle of two women marching at the head of three hundred men through California's orchard country, singing the "Marseillaise" to the accompaniment of bagpipe and drums, arrested attention. The *Examiner* called the procession the "most fantastic body" of all the armies that originated in the state. At Walnut Grove, a group of Chinese brought out a very generous donation of rice. Whether they were moved by sympathy or terror, no Caucasian observer seemed to know.

The Smith-Barker army, as the contingent was usually labeled, reached Sacramento. There, friction with another group of Coxeyites who had arrived first caused Smith to turn south through the San Joaquin Valley. Toward the end of May they reached Fresno, where long days on the road caused about a third of the marchers to leave the ranks and the remainder to split into two groups. One of these was a band of a hundred workingmen who wanted to go east to their former homes. The hundred who remained with Smith and Barker seemed content to stay in California, living off one community after another. They came to grief in early June when the Kern County sheriff's department dumped them in the Mojave Desert.

Made desperate by a lack of food and a blinding sandstorm, they put a torpedo on the tracks one night and halted a Santa Fe fruit express, which they promptly commandeered. As they rolled east toward Barstow, a brakeman dropped off and sent out word of the capture. Because the bankrupt railroad was at that time in the hands of a federal court, federal marshals arrested the Coxeyites for violating an injunction to keep off the cars, and a judge in Los Angeles sent them to prison for contempt of court. Anna Smith reappeared later as a spellbinding lecturer for the Socialist Labor Party in California.

The involvement of women in the Coxey movement inevitably played into the hands of those hostile to the crusade. The press seized every opportunity to patronize women sympathizers and portray them as proof that the march was bizarre beyond reason. Nonetheless, their overall contribution to the crusade was vital, a fact that Charles T. Kelley and his army stranded in western Iowa in mid-April appreciated more with each passing day. The immediate role that women played for them was as providers of daily nourishment and moral support. Had women in rural Iowa been unsympathetic, it is unlikely that Kelley's army would have remained intact during its ongoing test of wills with the rail barons.

CHAPTER 9

This movement has attracted the
attention of the country as nothing
else in the way of labor agitation
has ever done, and as nothing else
without violence ever could have
done.

Jacob S. Coxey, *Washington Post*,
April 21, 1894

Jack London and the Road East

Young Jack London finally overtook Kelley's troops in Council Bluffs
after bumming his way by rail from California. Whether the future
best-selling author ever became a card-carrying Kelleyite remains uncertain, but he accompanied the army as far as the Mississippi River
and left a diary account of how the largest contingent of the Coxey
movement struggled across Iowa in the spring of 1894. The hardships
of those days provided him material for later writings. And, in its
own way, the journey proved to be a struggle for survival not unlike
those that London subsequently described in the frozen Klondike.[1]

London was with Kelley's men when they set out for the Iowa
capital on foot on Sunday, April 22. The 180-mile trek overland began
pleasantly enough. Along the way, men and women who were dressed
in their Sunday finest welcomed the Kelleyites with oratory and
tables groaning with a feast. Leaving their plows in the furrows during the best week of spring weather, farmers drove all night to view
the crusaders. Some brought wagonloads of provisions from as far
away as twenty-five miles. Republicans, Democrats, and Populists;
Protestants, Catholics, and Jews; city laborers and tillers of Iowa's
black soil: all demonstrated their support for Kelley's crusaders.[2]

In his tramp diary, London noted the enthusiastic reception at
Neola, where the army spent the night. "It was more like Fourth of

July than a peaceful Sunday in a quiet country town." He described an idyllic scene, an evening spent in song and worship around the campfires, but his sketch ended on a somber note, a portent of the many troubles to come that nearly destroyed the army by pitting soldier against soldier in a brutal struggle for survival: "At 10 o'clock we started to march to a stable in the town which our second lieutenant had procured for us. We were stopped by the pickets, but Col. Baker came along with quite a jag and a woman on his arm & passed us through. He will most likely be court martialed tomorrow."

The news that a ranking officer was publicly drunk and consorting with prostitutes quickly reached Kelley. Ever since they had arrived in Iowa, he and his men had carefully cultivated a reputation for morality and decorum. But if through the folly of an officer like Colonel Baker the army lost its good name, marchers could expect little sympathy or support from the men and women of western Iowa. Without their aid the protest was doomed.

Wasting no time, the normally mild-mannered general literally kicked Baker out of his tent, stripped the cherished epaulets from his shoulders, and with a stern rebuke dismissed him from the army that Baker had helped to start. A hastily convened court-martial sustained Kelley, despite Baker's loud protests that he had not been drunk and was merely escorting visiting women to a hotel because the army had no accommodations for them in its bivouac. He stalked off, complaining that Kelley's command had gone to his head, and wondered aloud if the general had lost his sanity.

The episode might have been dismissed as a mere personality conflict caused by the pressures and disappointments of the past week had not a far more serious dispute erupted, making everyone wonder whether the entire army would not soon disintegrate into warring factions. An ugly disturbance near the village of Walnut brought into the open the growing friction between marchers from San Francisco and those from elsewhere, primarily Sacramento.

When Sacramento men charged that San Franciscans received preferential treatment, urban rivalries flared anew. Everybody was supposed to take turns riding in the limited number of wagons furnished by local farmers, but men driven half mad by aching and blistered feet found it easy to imagine that others rode longer and more often than they. Jack London, nominally attached to a small company

Jack London in Kelley's army encampment. Courtesy Iowa
State Historical Department, State Historical Society.

from Reno, complained: "As usual our company was walking while
the S. F.'s rode. I walked 6 miles to the town of Walnut enduring the
severest of tortures & I arrived in a most horrible condition. I resolved to go no further on foot."

Contributing noticeably to the friction was the popularity of
Colonel George Speed, who exercised greater influence over the Sacramento men than Kelley did. A hatter by trade and a socialist agitator far to the left of Kelley, Speed was an impetuous man who
chafed at Kelly's unwillingness to take bold action. When Kelley disciplined Speed for failing to obey an order, Speed angrily demanded
that Kelley account for several thousand dollars collected by the army
in Council Bluffs before he charged others with disobedience. Each
man's supporters joined in a heated exchange of epithets: "Soup
fiends!" "We want our money!" Citizens watched in alarm as former
comrades menaced one another with sticks and long-blade knives.

The Coxey movement had a way of bringing out the best and
the worst elements of human nature, both along the line and in the

ranks; at Walnut the ideal of brotherhood nearly perished as a result of jealousy. Fortunately, Kelley calmed the men before they shed any blood, and he rebuked both factions for publicly airing the army's dirty linen. A court-martial reduced Speed to the ranks by a vote of 20 to 3, but the disgraced man's friends rallied around, refused to recognize the sentence, and elected him their new general. Two groups of sullen troops proceeded along the road from Walnut to Atlantic. In the lead were Kelley's eight hundred men, followed by Speed's two hundred seceders. Although the weather was perfect as they paralleled the Rock Island line across the undulating blue grass prairies and past the newly planted fields of corn, a perceptible pall hung over the ranks. To Jack London the procession resembled a "grand retreat" by broken men.

A volunteer army that was operated according to the principles of democracy and equality and composed of discontented men—many of whom had met for the first time only a week or two earlier—was a volatile organization. And certainly it was easy enough for the crusaders to complain; when they had left California they never anticipated being stranded in Iowa. Nonetheless, something had to be done to resolve the bickering, and soon. The cross-country march was difficult enough when morale was high, but with men as dispirited as these it was nearly impossible.

By the time the marchers reached Atlantic, the halfway point and largest community between Council Bluffs and Des Moines, the tension between the two factions was so high that many observers feared the crusade would unravel on the spot. Sobered by that prospect, the rival leaders acted through intermediaries to resolve their differences; and in a scene not unlike one of the era's great Dwight L. Moody revival meetings, Kelley, Baker, and Speed met before an overflow crowd of townspeople at the Atlantic Opera House, promising to forgive and forget past differences. To climax their tearful repentance, the trio knelt in prayer. Afterwards they drove to camp to announce their reconciliation.

Morale soared once again. It was a time for singing, dancing, and good fellowship with local residents. A baseball game between the visitors and the Atlantic club ended in an 11 to 4 victory for the home players. Baseball games, like the frequent singing of gospel and patriotic hymns, were apparently calculated to ensure a maximum of goodwill. Kelleyites played ball in several towns along the way, and although they claimed to have professional players in their ranks, the home teams usually won.

Even as Kelley's army resolved its internal differences, the telegraph clicked out word of further trouble ahead: Chicago, where they had hoped to be days earlier, now officially prohibited Kelley's men from entering the city. Chicagoans were alarmed by a rapidly growing contingent of Coxeyites in their midst and did not want to host an additional thousand battle-hardened veterans from the Far West.

Chicago's threat scarcely worried men who had traveled so far and overcome so many obstacles. By the time they left Atlantic, they viewed the road ahead with a curious mixture of optimism and fatalism. And to their delight, they discovered that the squabbling of the past few days had not turned local people against them. Iowans continued to enjoy the show, gathering all along the road to watch the crusaders pass. No circus had greater drawing power. A reporter had the misfortune of being caught in a barber's chair in one village when the army arrived, and neither threats nor bribes could bring the barber back to finish the shave until the last man had marched past. Typically the column tramped along with Kelley at its head, riding on a black thoroughbred Morgan on loan from a sympathizer in Council Bluffs. The men followed rank upon rank in individual companies. Each company had a mascot—most often a rooster, but the Sacramento men had a vicious-looking bulldog.

An advance guard preceded the main body of marchers across Iowa, collecting donations of food, arranging for wagons, and preparing the evening campsite. At Adair, an overnight stop, citizens donated 1,200 loaves of bread, a beef, and 50 pounds of coffee. That was the standard fare, although the town of Anita added an extra touch much appreciated by the sojourners: pretty girls dressed in their Sunday best, who sliced the bread, poured coffee, and ladled out soup.

As nice a gesture as that was, a train ride to Des Moines would have been even more welcome. On they trudged, through a blur of villages like Casey, Menlo, Dexter, and Van Meter, each looking very much like the one before, each being a station stop on the Rock Island and the farmers' link to the wider world. Fighting blisters and fatigue, the Sacramento men grew more restless with every passing mile. They took to walking along the Rock Island track, passing time by counting ties, singing tracklaying chants like "Drill, Ye Tarriers, Drill," and carefully eyeing each passing train.

The hostility between Kelleyites and the railroads reappeared when the Rock Island resumed running its trains along the line of the march. Across the rolling country east of Atlantic, freights lumbered uphill at a crawl; and although Kelley ordered his men not to steal rides, some could not resist temptation. Pinkerton detectives and extra crewmen assigned by the Rock Island to keep freeloaders off its trains sprang from car to car, kicking off the Kelleyites. Several times those who were summarily ditched hurled rocks back at the guards.

Fearful that desperate men might succumb to temptation (or to blisters) and steal a train, Rock Island officials distributed circulars among the crusaders, warning them of the dire consequences that would follow such an illegal act. Kelley believed that the notices were designed to incite his men to violence as a pretext for calling in federal troops, and he advised the company not to worry. But many of his followers were clearly spoiling for a fight with the hated Rock Island, and only respect for Kelley restrained them. Could he keep that respect much longer in the face of rising complaints from footsore and weary men?

Saturday, April 28, found Kelley's army encamped at Stuart, a week's march from Council Bluffs and still forty-one miles short of Des Moines and its promise of relief. All week long, sympathizers in the Iowa capital had collected food and supplies in anticipation of the pilgrims' arrival. Just that morning, in fact, a rumor circulated among the Kelleyites that their Des Moines supporters had obtained a Chicago Great Western train to hurry them east. Buoyed by the prospect of an easier journey ahead, Kelley decided that the time had come to march straight through to Des Moines in one herculean step. Apparently he believed that the feast awaiting his men would keep their grumbling on the road to a minimum.

It was to be a long march that Kelley's men would not soon forget. All the stiff joints and blisters of the past week would pale in significance compared to the trouble that lay just ahead. Newspapermen, unable to find a precedent in American history for the Coxey movement, sometimes compared it to the Israelites' exodus from Egypt.

But before the march from Stuart to Des Moines was over, those given to biblical allusion might have compared the sufferings of the Kelleyites to those of Job and wondered whether anyone with less wisdom than Solomon could have led them.

All day they plodded across the Iowa countryside. The weather was pleasant enough, but each painful step dimmed the vision of the delights that awaited them. In this test of will it was easy to fail. Jack London complained once again: "Walked 11 miles through the town of Dexter to Earlham where we had dinner. My feet are in such bad condition that I am not going any further, unless I can ride. I will go to jail first." London, with his broad smile and ingratiating manner, played upon the sympathies of bystanders, who bought him a rail ticket to the next town. Others were not so fortunate.

Marchers reached Van Meter at dusk. Des Moines was still nineteen miles ahead. The men rested briefly until nine o'clock, when Kelley ordered them to move on. They could barely see the road in the darkness, and those who believed that providence favored their crusade were dismayed when about a mile ahead nature unleashed her full fury against them. A dust storm of apocalyptic proportions blew out of the blackness, and the men stumbled about in confusion, swallowing sand and trying to rub it out of their eyes. Kelley shouted words of encouragement but they were lost in the tempest.

The sky opened, and rain fell in torrents. Flashes of lightning and thunderbolts gave the march the semblance of a true military engagement. Instead of cannonballs, lightning smashed through the limbs of trees. Men from the West Coast, unaccustomed to the violence of a spring storm in the Midwest, were terrified. They broke ranks and raced into a stand of trees for protection—until someone shouted that tall trees would attract the death-dealing lightning. They bolted into the open again and prostrated themselves on the sodden ground.

When the storm abated, they slogged and slid along the muddy road toward Des Moines. Or was it Omaha? In the darkness many had lost their bearings. They stumbled through potholes and occasionally tumbled headlong into ditches filled with waist-deep water. Curses filled the murky night. They cast aside their waterlogged and worthless shoes and tried to protect their feet by wrapping them with their shirts.

Half-naked and with mud matting their hair and filling their eyes, ears, nostrils, and pockets, they broke into small bands. Some made a wrong turn and ended up at the village of Waukee, several miles out of the way. Hungry and exhausted, others simply dropped in their tracks, preferring to await the morning light before struggling on to the Iowa capital.

When Sunday dawned, Kelley was a general without an army. Neither his followers nor the fleet of wagons promised by Des Moines sympathizers materialized. In the Iowa capital, in vivid contrast to the warm welcome to Omaha, city officials and the press were indifferent or even hostile to the crusaders. Prior to their arrival, the *Leader* described the Kelleyites as "an army of tramps and malcontents who are hunting for snow to shovel in summer." Governor Jackson voiced a similar opinion.

Gradually, though, little bands of men appeared on the horizon, and for the next several hours they collected on the city's west side, organizing for a triumphal march through Iowa's largest city. Considering the ordeal of the past night, they were in amazingly good spirits. But even now nature was not done with the unemployed miners, hatters, and printers who would reform the nation's economic system. Halfway through their four-mile march across town, the heavens opened once again, drenching the argonauts and the numerous spectators who lined Grand Avenue. The men finally reached their temporary home, an abandoned stove foundry, and at seven o'clock that evening ate their first real meal in twenty-four hours.

If, after overcoming all the difficulties of the past three weeks, Kelley's men concluded that no new trouble could befall them, they were wrong: in Des Moines they encountered sympathizers who promised more than they delivered or who wanted to exploit the army for their own narrow purposes. Several days before the Kelleyites arrived, when they were the city's chief topic of conversation, General James B. Weaver sensed an opportunity to make political capital out of "Kelley's disinherited army." Weaver, a local leader of the Populist party and the party's presidential standard-bearer two years earlier, convened a meeting of sympathizers and nominated as chairman B. O. Aylesworth, president of Drake University in Des Moines. Aylesworth, a philosopher by profession and an idealist by temperament, readily accepted, calling it an honor. The professor lent respectability to the proceedings, but Weaver was clearly in charge.

Weaver next enlisted the support of organized workers, women's groups, and clergymen. Together they were supposed to collect enough food to feed the army, but scarcely had they begun their task than the odd coalition split apart. Organized labor sensed that it was being used as a tail to a Populist kite and drew back in resentment. Conflict between sympathizers so hampered the collecting of food—despite the glowing reports they sent Kelley—that Des Moines Mayor Isaac L. Hillis stepped in and appealed to citizens to help the marchers as a matter of charity rather than sympathy.

Residents proved surprisingly generous; people from all walks of life donated food and clothing to the visitors. On one occasion, just as Kelley was about to address a large crowd, a beautiful basket of flowers was handed up to him, a gift from the ladies of Des Moines. The Kelleyites curried the favor of the townspeople through their usual games of baseball. Jack London recorded three games, with the Kelleyites winning two, though not by impolitic margins. London's account also recorded one of the army's chief concerns as the hours and days ticked by in Des Moines: "We spent the evening round the fire singing & joking till 11 when we went to bed. It was awful cold. Wednesday was spent in camp. No transportation."

The Chicago Great Western train that sympathizers had supposedly promised turned out to be a mirage. The Kelleyites still had half a continent to cross before they could join forces with Coxey, and all the while their ranks swelled with additional mouths to feed. How long the citizens of Des Moines would continue to supply nearly four thousand free meals a day was a question on everyone's mind. Another question was whether they would ever rendezvous with Coxey's Commonweal.

Even as London and his fellow westerners struggled across Iowa, Coxey's band wound along the country roads of Maryland. From "Camp California," where they camped on the banks of the Chesapeake and Ohio Canal, they hiked inland. This was countryside rich in history. Here Robert E. Lee's troops retreated after the Battle of Gettysburg in July 1863, and nearby was the battlefield at Antietam Creek. Memories of those dark and bloody days flooded back to Civil War veterans in Coxey's ranks. The journey from Williamsport to Hagerstown was short, only six miles, but many of Coxey's veterans struggled along with perceptible limps. Most carried walking sticks carved with the names of towns through which they had passed.[3]

Along the way they came to a tollgate. "Advance that flag," ordered Browne. "Now do you propose to stop the American flag?"

"I ain't got nothing to do with no American flag," replied the toll collector, crossing his two hefty arms so as to display every bulging muscle, "but I want toll for them horses and machines."

Coxey reluctantly handed over a dollar bill and received two cents change.

During the bivouac in Hagerstown, Coxey left on a business trip to New York, and Browne made one of the more memorable purchases of the crusade, an enormous strip of canvas measuring eight feet high and three hundred feet in diameter. Painted on its side in great black letters were the words, "He is Alive!"—a cryptic reference not to reincarnation but to circus days, when the canvas housed a collection of sideshow freaks. The Coxeyites hoped to raise money by enclosing their nightly bivouacs and charging visitors a small admission fee. "Ten cents for gents; ladies free!" Seemingly oblivious to the irony was Browne, who had earlier expelled Cyclone Kirkland and the other hapless Coxeyites who exhibited themselves in a dime museum.

On Sunday, April 22, Brown held "reincarnation services" in Hagerstown. As he had done before countless other audiences, he climbed on the panorama wagon and took his place beside the portrait of Christ. He smiled until the crowd gave him a polite cheer. After reciting a poem called "Mystery of the Whence," he drew a series of pictures that looked like spiders to explain his views of reincarnation. On he droned as camp cooks filled the air with the aroma of Sunday dinner and his followers grew restless. Browne paused to warn that no one would eat until he finished his sermon. Hungry men cast longing eyes toward the great bubbling kettles of stew, but none dared grumble aloud for fear of being drummed out of the ranks before dinner. No worse fate could befall a Coxeyite.

After a three-day pause, the army repacked its gear and headed east toward a notch in the Blue Ridge Mountains, Turner's Gap. They marched along the old National Road once again, and that meant more encounters with the tollkeepers Browne so loathed. Each step took the men that much closer to the village of Boonsboro. The surface of the dirt road was packed hard and smooth, perfect for hiking—almost as perfect as the Maryland air, which was heavily perfumed with the fragrance of spring blossoms. Marchers crossed and recrossed Antietam Creek and paralleled seemingly endless miles of stone fences.

About two miles west of Boonsboro, a solitary figure waited nervously in the middle of the pike. The short, dumpy man held a hand to his bushy eyebrows to shield his eyes from the afternoon sun as he scanned the horizon for the first sign of Coxey's army. He wore a frayed Prince Albert coat and a soiled and shiny vest. His salt-and-pepper beard was long and unkempt, and a wave of thin greasy hair flowed out from under his slouch hat and down onto his shoulders.

Soon he spied a cloud of dust, and then Old Glory fluttered into view. The solitary figure removed his hat. Browne immediately recognized him and ordered the column to halt while he galloped forward.

"Hello, Colonel!" the marshal shouted, his voice filled with excitement.

"Well, well. If it isn't old Carl. How are you, anyway? How's the Commonweal?"

"Boys," announced Browne, turning toward his men, "this is Colonel A. E. Redstone, the man who worked so faithfully for the interests of the Commonweal in Washington." Years before, the two had been partners in protest in California.[4]

Redstone, a patent attorney in Washington and publisher of a small reform paper, bubbled with confidence as he shared the latest news with Browne. "I have been in communication with all the various branches of the Commonweal, and every one of them will join Coxey before the army reaches Washington. Kelley will have 1,800 men, Fry 1,600, Jones 1,000, and there will be a Massachusetts contingent of 6,000." Rattling on like a steam engine out of control, Redstone painted a glowing picture of the preparations under way in Washington: "As the Commonweal passes the city limits it will be met and escorted down Pennsylvania Avenue by 15,000 men, 500 prominent ladies, the local Typographical Unions, the entire force of the Grand Army of the Republic in the City, besides a large number of wheelmen. I wouldn't be surprised to see the army welcomed by a large number of senators and representatives."

Redstone then waved a large packet of letters above his head. These he distributed to the cheering men. With that flourish, he climbed into Coxey's empty carriage for the ride to Boonsboro.

Shortly before reaching Boonsboro, the Commonwealers crested a rise in the road from which they could survey the Maryland countryside and the village below. The afternoon sun glinted across the rooftops and highlighted South Mountain in the hazy distance, part of the Blue Ridge that they would cross tomorrow. A crowd of folks from miles around escorted the visitors into town, and Browne repaid their kindness by giving his illustrated lecture on finance. The troops found enough energy for a game of baseball, a sketch of which soon appeared on the front page of the *Washington Star* under the caption, "A Proof of Patriotism." Presumably the Nervous Nellies in Washington could draw some comfort from that claim.

Meanwhile, Browne picked up two rumors that disturbed him greatly: a company of United States Army cavalrymen waited ahead on South Mountain (presumably to intercept the Commonweal), and George Francis Train waited in Washington to supplant Coxey and Browne. "Ever since the army started," growled Browne, "the Tacoma man has deluged Coxey with postal card advice and has repeatedly offered to come take charge of the army."

Train was no garden-variety crank. By all odds he was the best-known specimen of the golden age of cranks. Like Coxey, Train was a wealthy and successful businessman. He had, in fact, helped finance the Union Pacific Railway through the *Credit Mobilier* and once had owned five thousand lots in Omaha, where his nephew and Coxey sympathizer, George P. Bemis, was mayor. Train modestly took credit for beginning the salmon-canning industry on the Columbia River in the Pacific Northwest and for suggesting that Tacoma serve as the Pacific terminus of the Northern Pacific Railroad.

But that was the sober side of Citizen Train, who apparently acquired the title during his participation in the 1871 Paris Commune. He also set a speed record for circumnavigating the globe, a feat that probably served as a model for Jules Verne's Phileas Fogg in *Around the World in Eighty Days*. He now spent his days conversing with children in an effort, as he explained it, to keep a generation ahead of everyone else.[5]

A reporter for the *Washington Star* overtook the sixty-five-year-old Train as he laid plans to commandeer the Coxey movement. Where Browne was a believer in reincarnation, Train claimed to have something called "the Force" backing him, "a Force so stupendous as to surpass comprehension." He barely paused for breath as an unceasing stream of oratory poured from beneath his silvery mustache. "I tell you the revolution is coming. . . . Charles and Cleveland, Commonwealth and Commonweal, Commons and Congress, Cromwell and Coxey! Look at the C's. Isn't that amazing." Train skipped from thought to thought as lightly as a mountain goat tripping from one rock to another. He bragged that he had learned twenty languages, that he spent his fortune buying peanuts for the children in New York's Union Square. "I am the greatest man alive. I am the best known man in the world. I am the greatest mystery of the age; no one understands me except little children."[6]

Browne understood. Train made him uneasy, fearful perhaps that the man with "the Force" might detract from his own flamboyance; but first he had to deal with the rumored troop of cavalry. Before leaving Boonsboro, the marshal visited a carpenter and then a dry goods store, where he purchased a quantity of muslin and some tacks. He revealed his plans in an elaborate special order: "There is a rumor here that a detachment of United States Cavalry has been ordered to Frederick, so I have made a lot of sticks four feet long and one inch square and on which we will attach small white flags bearing the words, 'Commonweal of Christ. Peace on Earth, Good Will Toward Men.' I ask you to carry them, and if that will not be sufficient to stand them off we will call our friends, the ladies of Maryland, to protect us."

Accompanying a wagonload of the oaken clubs of peace, Commonwealers trudged along the National Road as it wound up the steep sides of South Mountain. The local folks who gathered along the way were unusually excited. Some remembered Civil War battles in the area, and one group of old women asked the Commonwealers: "Is there going to be another war? Are your wagons loaded with rifles and ammunition? Will there be a fight at the county line?" So persistent were the questioners that Coxey's men were thoroughly alarmed by the time they neared the summit.

The crest burst into view as the column swung past the great stone Dahlgren chapel, and just as Browne feared, silhouetted against the sky was a troop of horsemen blocking the road. The sun glistened off their saddles and bridle trappings—and off the two long-barreled six-shooters that each man carried. As the Commonwealers marched toward the horsemen, one of the mystery riders suddenly galloped forward.

"Where is your leader?" he demanded. Because Coxey had not yet returned from his business trip and Browne, who usually rode at the head of the column, was suddenly missing, no one gave the order to halt. The Commonwealers thus said nothing and continued marching. The riders on horseback divided to let the relentless column pass. When Browne at last galloped up, the Commonwealers learned that this force was a posse gathered by the Frederick County sheriff.

"I have summoned my deputies to allay the fears of the people along the road," said the sheriff. Browne was relieved, but the Commonwealers remained on guard.

The column descended into a valley and continued through the quaint hamlet of Middletown. Beyond town, at the bottom of a gully, the Commonwealers halted beside a clear bubbling spring for lunch. They munched their hardtack and bologna in silence, keeping a wary eye on the troop of deputies. (The marchers called them "Pinkertons.") Later that afternoon, as the Commonwealers neared the village of Frederick at the foot of the Blue Ridge Mountains, the pike filled with bicyclers and curious blacks.

Ray Stannard Baker, who was later to write a pioneering study of race relations called *Following the Color Line* (1908), observed that the blacks of Maryland had a warm regard for the Commonweal. "They always come out and stand in a row along the white-washed fences and cheer lustily. There are a number of Negroes in the army and they all know that Coxey and Browne make no distinction between them and their white companions. This fact has made all the Negro population friends."[7]

In Frederick, the spectacle of thirty armed and mounted deputies protecting the public from inoffensive Commonwealers prompted a group of young loafers to poke fun at the lawmen. One annoyed deputy pulled a revolver from his holster and held it up to show that he meant business. But bystanders raised a loud cry of indignation, and the lawman quickly returned the gun to its holster. Two deputies then got into a brawl with one another. Almost immediately, public opinion swung behind the Coxeyites, and county officials found themselves dodging criticism that they should have spent less on wages for special deputies and more on food for the visitors.

Commonwealers set up camp within the confines of their freak-show canvas and during their two-day visit raised nearly $20 from the curious. A patriotic game of baseball between the army nine and a Frederick team ended in a 16 to 10 victory for the locals. After a supper of beef stew, southern-fried ham, bread, and crackers, Browne and Coxey, who had returned from New York, hosted the usual educational hour. Browne used the occasion to deflect press criticism of his artwork, noting that his pictures were for the benefit of the working class and as a consequence were rough and more in keeping with that people. "Had they been for the rich, they would have been painted on silk and perfumed with rosewater."

Coxey related how workingmen were compelled to wander from place to place in search of jobs. He called for them to join his crusade instead. "We might as well starve on the steps of the legislative halls at the Capitol as anywhere else, and the stench arising will help to make them take immediate action in the matter." A reporter observed that when Coxey finished his speech, there were many noddings of heads and nudgings of approval. "The net result is that Coxey leaves a trail of new thought in the minds of many who will recall and possibly pursue it later as Coxey partisans."[8]

For now, though, the ones doing the pursuing were reporters, and Coxey was their quarry. His recent business trip to New York by sleeping car prompted reporters to speculate about the leader's personal fortune. Responded Coxey, "I always travel in a sleeper and stop at good hotels. I can get nothing out of money but pleasure and comfort. J. D. can get no more." (By "J. D." he was no doubt referring to another distinguished Ohioan, John D. Rockefeller.)

Another reporter asked, "Are you a rich man, General?"

"Well some persons say I am."

"But are you?"

"Well, I haven't got more than enough to give me a good bed and plenty to eat. No man can have more than that."[9]

The reporter for a Frederick paper gave the question of Coxey's wealth a peculiar twist: "People find it difficult to believe," he interjected, "that a thoroughly balanced man has enough of Christ in his heart to spend not only of his time but his money in the way you are doing with an unselfish singleness of purpose . . . and people on this account regard you as unbalanced on the subjects you are pressing."

"It matters not to me if I am deemed a crank. I know I'm right. I don't care if I'm ruined financially in this work. I can recover."[10]

While Coxey's men bivouacked in Frederick, Browne received an important telegram from the movement's official historian, Henry Vincent, announcing that a thousand striking iron molders were leaving Chicago by train for a rendezvous with the army just outside Washington. The news was electrifying. Commonwealers cheered wildly and danced in the red glow of their campfires. But even as they celebrated, another telegram arrived. It reported that militiamen had fired on Kelley's men and killed six. Joy immediately turned to rage. Browne motioned toward his stout clubs of peace and growled, "We do not intend to go armed to Washington, but we will be 'peaced.'"[11]

In fact, neither telegram was accurate. Only a handful of iron molders joined forces with the Commonweal, and the bloodshed occurred not in Iowa but in Montana, where a Coxey's-army version of a Wild West show suddenly burst into the nation's headlines.

CHAPTER 10

Where is the governor? Where is the
United States marshal? Where is
the Montana militia? How in the hell
do you expect one Irishman to
stand off the whole of Coxey's army?

Superintendent J. D. Finn of
the Northern Pacific Railway

Hogan's Wild West Show

Ascending the tortuous grade to Montana's Homestake Pass, a 6,356-
foot-high crossing of the Rocky Mountains and the Continental Divide, the stolen train quite possibly set a speed record for the climb.
Three hundred Coxeyites rumbled through the night in six open coal
cars, cold and uncomfortable but exhilarated. Dropping down the
eastern slope of the mountain divide, they clipped along the Northern Pacific tracks at better than forty miles an hour.

At Whitehall, the wild train (a railroad term for any train operating without regular orders) paused at the dispatcher's office for orders—or more precisely, to give them. Crewmen demanded a clear
track ahead. If any train was headed their way, warned one army wit, it
should cover its headlight so the men would not see it. The engineer
signed the dispatcher's log "Grover Cleveland"; leaving Whitehall, he
opened wide the throttle. This train was indeed bound for glory. Or
for a smashup or the open arms of the law.[1]

The breath-stopping odyssey had its origin among the almost five
hundred homeless men, mostly miners, who bedded down each
night in the chairs and on the hard plank floors of Butte's numerous
saloons and gambling dens. Months had passed since they had slept
in a regular bed or eaten a square meal, and their number was growing. They were part of an estimated 20,000 Montanans without

work in December 1893, a sizable portion of the state's 132,000 residents. The primary cause of their joblessness was the collapse of Montana's foremost industry: mining. Nearly one-third of the gold, silver, copper, and lead mined in the United States came from Montana.

In 1894, Montana was in many ways still a wide-open and untamed frontier—although of a peculiar sort, because giant companies dominated its mining industry. During the good years, they reaped enormous profits and employed thousands of wageworkers. The state's mining centers, in fact, could be described as the wageworkers' frontier, places where the intersection between an individualistic frontier heritage and the new industrial order was especially abrupt and violent. This frontier was ripe for a protest against unemployment, and that was especially true in Butte, a smoky city of mines, smelters, and reduction works with a population of 10,732. The "richest mining camp on earth" was the copper heart of Montana's mineral kingdom.[2]

The Butte Miners' Union took the initiative in organizing a Montana contingent of Coxey's army. With 3,500 members, it was the largest labor organization in the state and probably in the entire northwestern corner of the United States. Under its auspices more than two hundred jobless men banded together in early April to form the nucleus of a Montana commune. Recruits poured into Butte from other parts of the state, and leaders expected to pick up several hundred more among the idle miners in the camps of Idaho's panhandle. The number of intelligent-looking, well-dressed men in the ranks surprised many observers. Presiding over the initial meeting of the Montana commune was a short, wiry, thirty-five-year-old unemployed teamster, William Hogan, who had worked at one of the local mines. The men elected him their leader.

By day the Hoganites drilled on an empty lot or paraded through Butte's narrow streets. Floating conspicuously above their heads were two banners. One depicted an enormous silver dollar with the legend above, "Gold at a Premium," and below, "Labor Pauperized." The other banner read, "Free Coinage at 16 to 1." Meanwhile, committees of sympathizers collected supplies for the coming trip to Capitol Hill or appeared before city officials to request rail transportation. Almost nightly there were more mass meetings.

Hogan's army enjoyed enormous support in Butte, because it was all things to all people. To men whose world had collapsed, it offered hope and purpose. As a protest against eastern economic colonization of the West, it evoked sympathy from a broad spectrum of Montanans; and its silver plank appealed as much to the mineral kings as to unemployed miners. And then there were some residents of Butte who would support any movement that promised to rid their city of idle and potentially violent men. The superintendent of the local streetcar company kindly offered Hogan's troops free rides to the south edge of town but regretted that he could take them no further. For transportation beyond the city limits, they were advised to look to the Northern Pacific Railroad.

Like every other transcontinental railroad, the Northern Pacific refused to extend a helping hand to the industrial army movement; as a result, after several days Hogan's restless men found the wait intolerable. With banners and flags flying, they marched from downtown Butte to the Northern Pacific's freight yards. Here they commandeered empty boxcars and pitched camp beside the tracks. What they might do next seemed obvious, but the Northern Pacific simply rerouted its freights around Butte through Helena and demanded that local lawmen clear its yards. Violence was averted on several occasions, but the combination of railroad intransigence and hotheaded orators who stirred the fighting blood of Hoganites and their sympathizers created a dangerously volatile mix.

After superintendent J. D. Finn of the Northern Pacific's Montana Division traveled to Butte in his private car to survey the trouble, he protested to Montana's Republican governor, John E. Rickards, that the Coxeyites had taken over the yards. What should he do? From the state capital at Helena the governor responded: "My understanding of the situation is that your road and property are under the protection of the United States courts. I would advise that you consult with your attorneys. It seems to me that you must look to the courts and local officers for protection before the executive can be called on." Rickards' suggestion that the Northern Pacific turn to the federal courts for help set in motion legal machinery that was to have fateful consequences for Coxeyites throughout the West.[3]

Three major railroads served Butte. In April 1894 a strike had shut down the Great Northern, and hard times had nearly ruined the Northern Pacific and the Union Pacific. Both were now in receivership, and as wards of the court they applied to Montana's federal judge Hiram Knowles for protection. He quickly granted the injunction they sought and directed United States marshal William McDermott to warn Hoganites off Northern Pacific and Union Pacific property in Butte. Anyone who refused to obey could then be summarily arrested for contempt of court and tried by Judge Knowles. If Union Pacific attorneys had thought of this strong-arm legal device earlier, the Kelleyites very likely would never have gotten from Ogden to Council Bluffs.[4]

Popular opinion in Butte stood ready to thwart the marshal. McDermott consequently sent a wire to Washington, asking the United States attorney general for instructions: "Public sympathy strongly in their favor. . . . Am I authorized to employ a great many deputies at large pay? Excitement runs high and I request some positive instruction by wire and will obey to the letter." The marshal received the permission he sought but in the confusion somehow forgot to serve Knowles's injunction.

A delegation of Butte businessmen—who collectively represented some of the most important shippers on the Northern Pacific line— visited superintendent Finn in his private car and forced him to concede that it would be in the city's best interest if the railroad furnished transportation to Hogan's men. Finn agreed to forward that view to his superiors in Saint Paul.

Back came a reply: "I hope it is understood that we do not desire to subject the people of Butte to suffer any inconvenience, but the transportation of these men into Dakota or Minnesota would subject us to a very heavy penalty to say nothing of the risk to railroad property and the personal risks of our trainmen and crews. The question of revenue does not enter into the proposition except as a matter of minor importance." The company refused to quote even a boxcar rate to Saint Paul.[5]

On April 23, rumors of trouble circulated through the streets of Butte. A steady rain and an occasionally violent thunderstorm forced the Hoganites to seek temporary shelter inside the Northern Pacific's roundhouse and sandhouse. McDermott spent the day quietly hiring a motley force of deputies, which he had in place when the railroad ordered a train of boxcars hauled out of Butte, the first Northern Pacific freight to leave town in five days. But then the company managers changed their minds, and the deputies returned uptown to their quarters. An angry crowd followed the hapless posse, shouting such epithets as "Blood suckers!" and "Pimps!"

Word came that the Union Pacific would haul the Hoganites to Omaha for $25 a head, or $10,000 for 400 men. That was too expensive. Influential shippers, including mineral king Marcus Daly, who was sympathetic to organized labor, increased the popular pressure on the Northern Pacific by asking in an open letter what it would cost to ship 500 men to Saint Paul. Back came the railroad's standard response: "If we voluntarily accept them, the road becomes responsible for their safe delivery at destination." These, the Northern Pacific feared, would be followed by a thousand more men from Seattle demanding the same treatment.

That afternoon, Northern Pacific executives demonstrated that they, too, could apply pressure. Butte officials received a warning to remove the Hoganites from railroad property or face the consequences: "In the event of your failure to do so, we shall hold the city liable for any damages we may sustain from the so-called Coxey's army." County commissioners received a similar warning. The game of twisting arms, however, was about to spiral out of control.

The city was already on edge of violence when a meeting at the courthouse that evening brought together three thousand people and several angry speakers. "There is another way of getting to Washington," warned one agitator, "and that is by capturing a train." The audience applauded. "But such a method is unlawful and unjust," he hastened to add, as he disingenuously urged Hoganites to obey the law. Other speakers accused the railroad of stealing the people's landed heritage.[6]

After listening to the words of protest, Hogan and his men marched back to the Northern Pacific yards. They still had no train, but the evening's speaker had planted an idea in their minds: perhaps they should simply commandeer a train. Their situation was desperate, and they knew that without rail transportation they would never reach Capitol Hill by May Day.

Shortly after midnight on the morning of April 24, a band of fifteen figures slipped quietly into the Northern Pacific roundhouse, which unaccountably was guarded only by one man. The raiders were experienced railroaders. They rolled out engine 512, perhaps the most powerful locomotive in the building, and by 1:30 had coupled together a train of six empty coal cars to accommodate the passengers and a boxcar to haul a week's provisions and a few tools. No one raised an alarm, and no one tried to stop them. It seemed almost too good to be true. With three hundred Hoganites aboard, the wild train had soon crossed the backbone of the continent to begin one of the unsung adventures in American history.[7]

At daybreak, just as McDermott's deputies awoke to discover the Hoganites missing, the runaway train rolled to a stop in Bozeman, having completed a ninety-five-mile trip over the Rockies from Butte in just under three hours. During the twenty-five-mile stretch from Logan to Bozeman, they had raced along at nearly a mile a minute. Unless something blocked the way ahead, the federal posse would be hard pressed to capture its quarry.

In Butte the Northern Pacific placed a special train, consisting of an engine and two cabooses, at the disposal of McDermott's assistant, deputy marshal M. J. Hailey, and his lawmen. The eighty deputies would have been as crowded as rush-hour commuters had not fifteen men jumped off at the last moment, declining to participate in what they knew would be a dangerous chase. The posse steamed out of town at six o'clock, about four hours behind the wild train. From the Montana capital Judge Knowles wired Attorney General Richard Olney that Deputy Hailey and his men were in pursuit of the runaways, adding: "A dangerous mob sentiment still prevails at Butte City. Railroad strike, 2,000 miners out of employment, prospect of 2,000 more being placed in condition. May have further trouble there." The Hoganites left behind by the sudden departure of their comrades hastily prepared to follow.

At Bozeman, the engineer who had brought the special from Butte declined to continue any farther and turned the throttle over to a lanky young Irishman, James B. Harmon. Here the Hoganites borrowed a fresh engine (selecting only the best grade of coal from a company stockpile) and traded their drafty coal cars for ten boxcars. While they waited impatiently for the westbound passenger train, which seemed unusually delayed this morning, some of Hogan's men oiled the journal boxes of the cars. Others started campfires to cook a quick breakfast, and a third group loitered about the telegraph office, listening for the latest news. These were seasoned railroaders: between them they possessed many years of experience and nearly a hundred switch keys, curious little resumes of their railroading past.

Superintendent Finn, who was in Livingston—twenty-four miles east of Bozeman—when he received word of the wild train, telegraphed the Northern Pacific attorney in Helena, asking what the government was doing about the theft and adding with a possible twinkle of Gaelic humor, "How in the hell do you expect one Irishman to stand off the whole of Coxey's army?" When a bystander asked Finn if the Hoganites would take the right-of-way through to the end of the road in Saint Paul, he replied laconically, "They have done it so far." The superintendent ordered all regular traffic to clear the track for the wild train.

As the Hoganites loaded aboard their train some three tons of provisions donated by Bozeman sympathizers, distressing news came from the telegraph office: a cave-in had blocked the eastern approach to the Bozeman tunnel, which was located about a dozen miles ahead. The men cursed the report as a railroad trick, but when the *Pacific Mail* didn't arrive, their worst fears seemed to have been confirmed. Some argued that the Northern Pacific had created the cave-in to block their way; but in fact, torrential rains the previous afternoon had loosened a portion of a bank above the track and triggered a slide. Track crews had already started removing the mass when they received word of the wild train and were ordered to cease work. The crusaders could either surrender or do their own track work if they still desired to go east. But surrendering to Hailey's special deputies, whom the Hoganites regarded as the shifty-eyed dregs of Butte, was something no self-respecting man would consider.

The Hogan special left Bozeman at mid-morning and steamed slowly to the nearly mile-long tunnel. There Harmon detached the locomotive and tender and hauled a reconnaissance party of twenty men through to inspect the supposed blockade for themselves. Part of the Lewis and Clark expedition had crossed this mountain on its return journey east in 1806, but Hogan's men had no time to reflect on history; they wanted only to make it. Just beyond the east portal they spotted the cave-in, and it was far worse than they had imagined. The track lay beneath some thirty cubic yards of mud, rock, and timber. And more of the overhanging bank seemed about to collapse at any moment. Engineer Harmon returned for the cars and the rest of the men, so that all might inspect the mess and offer advice on how best to clear it away. They had brought along no shovels or axes, but upon further poking around near the slide they discovered tools that the section gang had hidden. There were fifteen shovels and two very dull axes.

Back in Butte, the Northern Pacific office was overrun with Hogan's well-wishers, who wanted to know how the great adventure was progressing. News of the cave-in was discouraging, but at the tunnel, Hogan's men were confident that they could remove the barrier before Hailey and his posse overtook them. Dividing into relays of fifteen men each, they worked furiously to clear the twenty-five feet of buried track. The slimy, gelatinous clay proved maddeningly difficult to shovel away. Men worked up to their knees in the mass; using the two dull axes, they managed to remove some of the timber buried beneath. But when the tracks were almost clear, the top of the bank crumbled again. Hogan's men attacked the mass anew. The bank gave way a third time. Sweaty relays of men continued shoveling. One hour, then two hours ticked by.

Finally, when still more mud and debris cascaded onto the tracks, it became apparent that only heroic measures or a miracle could save the Hoganites from capture. Engineer Harmon surveyed the problem closely; an experienced hand, he had once worked as an engineer on the Rio Grande and Southern Pacific lines. After warning his comrades to stand clear, he climbed into the cab of his locomotive and, getting up a full head of steam, backed slowly into the tunnel. Then, with bell ringing and whistle shrieking, Harmon's cannonball blasted from the dark portal in a great cloud of smoke and steam.

The locomotive's cowcatcher plowed into the muck, throwing a shower of mud, rock, and shattered timber in every direction. But about halfway through, the engine faltered. Harmon grabbed for a valve and shot a stream of sand under the slipping drive wheels. They bit the rails anew, and the train lurched forward, somehow remaining on the tracks and clearing the ooze just as the bank collapsed again. Three hundred bystanders cheered and climbed aboard, bringing along their newly acquired tools; soon they had left the Belt Mountains in their wake.

At 4:45 that afternoon, the mud-spattered special eased to a stop in Livingston, a town of 2,800 people, many of them employees of the railroad. An immense crowd of well-wishers waited at the station, bringing banners and flags, words of encouragement, and still more provisions. The army's spokesman, William Cunningham, a forty-year-old Irishman and a former president of the Butte Miners' Union, climbed atop the first boxcar and treated spectators to a flourish of oratory. Meanwhile, Hogan's men appropriated four more cars and a fresh engine. As they uncoupled the old locomotive, engineer Harmon affectionately patted her grimy side rods: "She's a hard looking machine, but she's a dandy."

Superintendent Finn, always remaining one jump ahead of the Hoganites, wired Billings, asking the sheriff to call out every able-bodied man in Yellowstone County to stop the runaways. But the undersheriff, thinking the telegram was a joke, wired back, "All of our ablebodied men are busy selling real estate. Stop Coxey's army at Livingston." Finn ordered his men to dynamite a bluff in order to block the tracks ahead. Sharp-eared Hoganites overheard the news on the telegraph and prepared to dig through once more. They were in a confident, even invincible mood as they steamed east from Livingston. From the rear car someone hung a large banner reading, "Do they miss us at home?"

The wild train roared through Big Timber at dusk. Sparks occasionally flew from the screaming flanges as they rounded a curve, and the rapidly whirling side rods of the locomotive blurred into a broad sheet of steel. At times the wheels seemed to hit only the high spots on the rails.

The wild train paused only briefly while Hoganites inspected the cave-in caused by Finn's crewmen. Compared to the slide at Bozeman tunnel, it was an insignificant obstacle, easily cleared away. And when they were past it, they carefully piled the rocks back, hoping to slow the deputies now rapidly gaining on them. At the Bozeman tunnel earlier that afternoon, the Northern Pacific had met Hailey and his lawmen with another train on the far side of the barricade; they lost almost no time there.

And Finn was ahead busily creating more obstacles to surmount. At Billings, eighty miles east of Livingston, he ordered his crews to spike the switches in the railway yards so that they led only onto side-tracks, and to blow out the switch lamps. Finn hoped that in the dark these tricks would confuse and derail the overconfident argonauts.

Caught in a shrinking gap between Finn and Hailey, the odds length-ened that the Hoganites would ever escape Montana, much less reach Washington. But they seemed unconcerned as they sped through the night. From Livingston to Glendive, some 340 miles away, the rail-way line followed the Yellowstone Valley and the historic route tra-versed by William Clark and his Corps of Discovery in 1806.

Atop the rear car the Hoganites posted a lookout, who peered into the blackness for any sign of Hailey and his posse. Then, about one o'clock on the morning of April 25, the wild train suddenly and unexpectedly lurched to a halt. The fast run had required so much steam that the water supply had run dangerously low; now the en-gine crew feared that they hardly had enough to reach the next tank. Detaching the cars, they ran the locomotive and tender ahead to search for water; as luck would have it, they found a tank only a mile ahead.

But when they lowered the downspout to fill the tender, scarcely a drop ran out. Finn's crew had been there first and deliberately drained it dry. Just then, one of Hogan's men shouted with joy: he had spied a pool of water in a marshy area ahead. Forming a bucket brigade, they quickly drained it. They found more puddles. Soon the locomotive returned for the boxcars, but it still had only a tiny sup-ply of water. The crewmen knew that the hours of the wild train were numbered unless they could find a tank that Finn had somehow over-looked. To conserve precious water, the Hogan special crawled along slowly now.

Barely were they rolling again before the rear lookout cried out. Everyone turned to see the headlight of a locomotive roaring around a curve about a mile behind. Hogan spied a bridge just ahead and ordered engineer Harmon to position the last car in the middle of the span. If they had to make a stand, that was as good a place as any—steep embankments on the bridge approach made it difficult to capture the train from the rear, and the cold and swiftly flowing Yellowstone made attack from any other direction impossible.

The trainload of marshals halted in the cut. From the bridge Hogan's silent men saw dozens of dark figures armed with rifles and revolvers silhouetted clearly in the headlight of the pursuit loco-motive. Cautiously the deputies marched forward in a narrow col-umn, only to halt in confusion when they saw how Hogan had positioned the runaway train on the bridge. Marshal Hailey stepped forward and ordered the Hoganites to back their train off the bridge and surrender, or his men would open fire.

The deputies shouldered their Springfield rifles and aimed them at the train. Just then, a band of Hoganites stepped into the beam of light as it played on the rear boxcar. They waved the United States flag and the banner of the Butte Miners' Union and dared Hailey's men to shoot.

The special deputies hesitated. Most of them had been recruited only hours earlier from the pool halls and gambling dens of Butte. If word got out that they had fired on unemployed miners armed only with Old Glory and the emblem of the most powerful union in the region, they would be marked men. After moments that seemed like hours, Hailey's men lowered their weapons and retreated to their train. The valley of the Yellowstone rang with the thunderous yells of the victors as they piled back into their boxcars and steamed east once again. Though the wild train barely crawled along, the lawmen made no attempt to overtake it; instead, they followed behind at a discreet distance, uncertain what to do next. The overconfident Hoganites believed they had frightened the deputies into leaving them alone.

Shortly before eleven the next morning, Hogan and his men rolled to a stop in Billings. As in Bozeman and Livingston, a flag-waving, cheering crowd was on hand to greet them. The entire village of fifteen hundred people, in fact, seemed to have turned out to demonstrate its support or pity for the ragged pilgrims. The mayor of Billings presided at a banquet that townspeople had prepared in their honor, and Cunningham responded with one of his flowery orations. Everyone enjoyed the holiday mood, so much that nobody seemed to notice or care when the train carrying Hailey and his deputies eased to a stop just beyond the west edge of town. Carefully blending in with the crowd of well-wishers, the lawmen made their way toward the runaway train.

Two of the deputies suddenly sprang into the locomotive cab and pulled their revolvers on Hogan. "Shoot and be damned," he reportedly cried. In the pandemonium that they sparked, the poorly trained deputies lost their heads and opened fire on the mingling crowd of Hoganites and townspeople. The gunfire immediately dropped two citizens of Billings. Charles Hardy fell to the ground, clutching his chest; he died almost instantly from the bullet that tore through his lung. Several other people were wounded.[8]

Enraged citizens picked up bricks, coupling pins, pieces of iron, dirt clods, stones—anything they could lay their hands on—and pelted the deputies, some of whom seemed too stunned to resist when townspeople grabbed the rifles out of their hands. Most of Hailey's men turned and ran for their lives, though the local sheriff and his deputies immediately caught and arrested ten of them. Others dashed for the safety of the Northern Pacific roundhouse, where a hooting and jeering crowd surrounded the building for nearly an hour. The federal lawmen trapped inside begged the Northern Pacific to take them anywhere out of Billings—anywhere, that is, except Butte, where they feared an even more unpleasant reception.

Butte, a rough-and-tumble place even in the best of times, was in an uproar, too. People crowded around newspaper bulletin boards to read the latest dispatches from the battlefront and filled the streets with wild talk about how they would punish the federal deputies. That night, Hogan's sympathizers staged a mass protest meeting at the courthouse, vigorously denouncing the attack on their friends by "an armed band of mercenaries composed of the scum of humanity."

While Hailey's men cowered in the Billings roundhouse, the populace readied another train for the Hoganites. When someone discovered that Finn's men had emptied the water tanks, they rang an alarm bringing out a company of firemen, who used their pumper and hose to fill the locomotive's empty tender. The Hoganites departed Billings at about one o'clock that afternoon, buoyed by the town's support.

When they had gone and calm returned to Billings, Hailey's deputies crept quietly from the roundhouse to their train. It steamed only slowly out of town, for the federal lawmen were in no hurry to continue the pursuit. Unintentionally they left one member of their posse hidden in a sandbin near the roundhouse; though badly beaten, he was afraid to emerge for fear that citizens would lynch him. And they might have, for as the *Billings Weekly Gazette* observed, the wonder is that the town did not arise "*en masse* and crucify every slinking cur of a deputy implicated in the outrage."

The *Gazette* spoke for many Montanans in Butte, too, when it described the federal deputies as "the scum of the great mining camp, mercenary ruffians who would assassinate their brothers if there was a dollar in it, and each of these hobos was decorated with a deputy marshal's badge, armed with rifles and revolvers and the authority of the United States to arrest these inoffensive workmen." In a similar vein, the *Butte Bystander*, a Populist paper, editorialized, "Marshal McDermott has been severely criticized for selecting his deputy marshals Tuesday afternoon from the lowest and most worthless class in the city, but it must be remembered that decent men, or reputable citizens, would go to jail sooner than accept such commissions; and this perhaps accounts for the fact that this gang of deputies selected by him, was composed almost entirely of pimps, prize fighters, rounders, ex-convicts, professional beats, and general all-around worthless characters."[9]

As the wild train made its way east from Billings, J. D. Finn and his men remained ahead of it, continuing to drain the railroad's water tanks. But this time the Hoganites were prepared. Among the carload of tools they had picked up in Billings was a long hose, which they now used as a siphon, occasionally refilling their tender from the creeks that flowed under the track. They were prepared for a long and hard journey.

When the eastern press picked up news of the chase, it turned the Billings confrontation into a holocaust:

> Blood Flows From Coxeyism
> Montana Allies Defend Their
> Train from Marshals
> Battle Between Law and Anarchy

That headline appeared in the *New York Times*. The accounts carried by eastern newspapers were rife with errors. According to one Associated Press bulletin, Marshal McDermott bravely ordered the Hoganites in Billings to surrender, an amazing feat considering that he was 150 miles away at the time. Although such reports were garbled and unnecessarily inflammatory, they helped set the stage for intervention by the United States Army.[10]

Pleas for help poured into the White House. Governor Rickards, who knew that the federal deputies were not eager to tangle with Coxeyites and that many of the state's militiamen were openly sympathetic to the unemployed, wired President Cleveland: "Impossible for state militia to overtake them. As governor of Montana, I hereby request that you have federal troops at Ft. Keogh intercept, take into custody, arrest and hold the Coxeyites subject to orders of the United States court issuing writs referred to." [11]

An emergency conference brought together Cleveland, Olney, and General J. M. Schofield, commanding general of the United States Army. Schofield had been on his way to Philadelphia to speak at a Union League banquet honoring Ulysses S. Grant's birthday when events in Montana overtook him. Although Schofield was unenthusiastic about calling out federal troops, preferring to let local authorities handle the matter, the outcome of the meeting was certain. Almost to a man, the cabinet officers of Cleveland's second administration shared the president's conservative, probusiness point of view. In 1893, secretary of war Daniel S. Lamont was the director of no fewer than fifteen corporations, including the Contintental National Bank of New York. The one westerner in the cabinet was the secretary of agriculture, J. Sterling Morton of Nebraska, who had battled agrarian reformers for twenty years as an attorney for the Chicago, Burlington, and Quincy.

No cabinet member did more to shape the policy of the Cleveland administration toward Coxeyites than Attorney General Olney. For two decades he had been one of Boston's leading railroad and corporation lawyers. He had served as a director and counsel to the Boston and Maine Railroad since 1884 and of the Boston-dominated Burlington since 1889. And as attorney general he continued to serve the railroads as much as his public duties allowed. (As the chief legal officer of the United States, he earned $8,000 a year and at the same time received $10,000 a year for services rendered to the Burlington.) Said the *San Francisco Call*, "Not much is expected of Attorney General Olney in his official capacity. Since he has been attorney general he has not shown any disposition to quarrel with the corporations he formerly served and which, so far as the public knows, he still continues to serve." [12]

Olney's prorailroad point of view prevailed during the White House conference. When it ended, General Schofield ordered Colonel J. H. Page at Fort Keogh, on the plains of eastern Montana near Miles City, to halt the advance of the Hoganites. "There is no concealing the anxiety," worried the *New York Times*, "as to the outcome of the meeting between Col. Page's troops and the 500 miners, who are known to be desperate characters."[13]

At ten that evening Hogan's troops arrived at Forsyth, about one hundred miles from Billings and forty-five miles short of Miles City. Finn's crews had prepared for them in the usual fashion, spiking the switches open and rendering every locomotive in the roundhouse inoperable. Undaunted, the argonauts fired up a fresh locomotive. Using a hose to carry steam from their Billings engine, they created a draft that sped up the fire-building process; meanwhile, a company of fifty rough-looking miners intimidated the roundhouse foreman into finding them a throttle to replace one that Finn's men had removed. Two hours ticked by.

Finn continued ahead to Miles City, where he loaded five hundred infantrymen from Fort Keogh aboard a special train for a hurried trip back to Forsyth. Uncle Sam's troops, carrying well-filled knapsacks, cartridge boxes, and rifles tipped with glistening bayonets, assembled in Forsyth so quietly that they took the crusaders completely by surprise. Not a shot was fired. After 340 miles the chase was over. (By contrast, the great locomotive chase of the Civil War covered less than 90 miles.)

At the depot, where Colonel Page had established his headquarters, there was much posturing in the grand military style. His troops quickly rounded up their quarry—except for Hogan. The problem was that the captors had no idea what the illustrious commander looked like. Actually he stood nearby and winked to his men to keep quiet. After watching the show of force for several minutes, he called to a messenger boy to take him to Colonel Page. The Wild West show was almost over.

The Hoganites viewed the professional soldiers with respect, in contrast to the contempt and scorn they reserved for the inept federal deputies. But their old nemeses arrived a short while later to share in the glory of the capture. Then two passenger trains pulled in, and off jumped another hundred Hoganites who had bummed their way from Butte. They willingly joined their companions in custody.

News of the capture angered people in Butte, and Hogan gained many additional sympathizers. Some people firmly believed that the Northern Pacific had staged the whole affair to lure the naive crusaders into the hands of federal authorities. "It looks as if the men were deliberately led into a trap," observed one prominent business-man. Trap or not, there were also those who did not want the pris-oners returned to volatile Butte. When a group of businessmen asked the railroad not to return Hogan and his men, a company spokesman responded, "Please say to our friends in Butte that judging from our lack of success in detaining the army in Butte, I don't feel there is any chance of our being able to return them to that point nor do I desire to do so."

No one knew what to do with so many prisoners. While Northern Pacific attorneys and Judge Knowles spent a full day in conference, United States troops, federal deputies, and Montana militiamen stood guard over the men in Forsyth. Knowles wanted to return only the ringleaders to Helena for trial and release the others, but railroad attorneys in New York protested that the whole lot must be tried. Olney agreed and proposed to President Cleveland that two com-panies of soldiers be retained to guard the Hoganites. But where in Montana could so many people be confined?

Few Montanans, in fact, desired to see the whole army imprisoned. When Knowles reluctantly ordered all the prisoners returned to Helena, the influential *Anaconda Standard* protested, "It appears that his disposition of the men is in accordance with the instructions of Northern Pacific attorneys in New York, who, living within easy reach of the Tombs, and Blackwell's Island and Sing Sing, evidently have a very high opinion of Helena's prison facilities." A few days later the *Standard* added, "It is admitted that it will be impossible to find a jury in Montana to convict these men whose only crime has been to help themselves to boxcars." There was no federal law mak-ing train-stealing a crime, but they could be held for contempt of court. And in contempt proceedings no jury was necessary. Railroads in receivership could thus short-circuit popular sympathy for the Coxeyites.[14]

Until the trial began, the only major problem remaining was that of the federal deputies. They begged the soldiers to protect them on the return trip through Billings to Butte. "Seventy-five armed men," observed the *Helena Independent*, "were never more struck with ter-ror than these deputies are." As for Colonel Page's infantrymen, they spent the day after the capture sitting in the shade, munching on pea-nuts and dates and "wondering if Congress will brevet them for gallantry in the peanut war as they call it." The soldiers disliked having to break up Hogan's army and were filled with scorn about the way the railroad and the federal government obtained their services.[15]

No one knew at first whether Hogan's Wild West show in Montana would damage the entire Coxey movement. Many feared the worst. When Kelley shared the news with his followers during their tramp across western Iowa, someone cried out, "First blood of the revolution!" Ever the moderate, Kelley responded with a frown and a lament that "this is the worst blow we have had. We will now be regarded as lawless men, we, who have broken no laws. But we will march to Washington through thousands of regulars and tens of thousands of the militia. Not by physical force, men, but by law and through favorable public opinion." Kelley warned that if it became necessary to commit a single illegal act to reach their goal, he would return home to his "Bess and the babe."[16]

Coxey, who was in Frederick, Maryland, tried to place the episode in the best possible light. "I earnestly regret it if there has been any trouble in the West," he told reporters. "Of course, those men had no legal right to take possession of that train, but questions of ethics do not carry much force with hungry men, and these men are starving for lack of employment. Violence, I want to say, has no part in our program." Added Browne, "Them fellows ain't under our charge and of course they can't hold us legally responsible. . . . I don't believe it's going to hurt the movement. The people of the West ain't been ground down under the heel of the money power till they have had all the fight took out of them."[17]

Browne was right on all counts. Fortunately for the Coxeyites, the Montana episode did not turn a noticeable number of people against them; but it did make authorities in the District of Columbia more apprehensive.

CHAPTER 11

The Lord knows what is best to
do with them but I don't.

Senator John N. Camden on the
Coxeyites, in the *St. Louis Post-
Dispatch*, April 29, 1894

May Day

On the morning of April 26, Coxey and his men marched out of
Frederick to begin the last leg of their five-week pilgrimage. Washington lay only fifty miles and four days' march away. The weather
was warm and sunny, and though a sheriff's posse of ten men rode
along behind the column, the marchers were confident of reaching
their goal. That night they set up camp near Hyattstown and charged
visitors the usual dime admission.[1]

Just outside their "He is Alive!" canvas wall, an uninvited gang of
swindlers set up shell games to fleece the rustics. A prominent farmer
lost five dollars in the crooked games, and another lost ten. Coxey
and Browne drove off the thieves with the sheriff's aid, but other
peddlers remained to sell pictures of Coxey, badges, poems, and
books. As the crusaders neared Washington, camp followers became
increasingly numerous and troublesome, and the two leaders dared
not relax their puritanical discipline.

The "Coxey puzzle" dominated conversation in Washington after
the crusaders reached Cumberland. Rumor mills worked overtime,
fed by news of Browne's potentially lethal clubs of peace and reports
of violence in Billings and Council Bluffs. People passed along word
that troops from Fort Myer had been sent into the Maryland countryside to intercept and kill a few Coxeyites in order to deter the rest.

Though the rumor proved untrue, it scared even Browne. To outward appearances, President Cleveland and Attorney General Olney were unconcerned about Coxey's army. Within the administration, however, there was considerable apprehension. Olney professed to see the protest as the first symptom of the impending revolution that he sometimes mentioned in his public addresses. The Montana bloodshed caused General Schofield to worry, "There is no telling to what proportions the movement may swell."

The Secret Service quietly dispatched two agents to Williamsport, Maryland, to join Coxey's ranks in disguise. "I am getting in good condition for tramping and never tire with my brogans on," special agent J. W. Cribbs wired his superiors in Washington. He got along well enough with the crusaders to be called their buddy.

Special agent S. A. Donnella reported that he saw no disposition on the part of the marchers to violate the law. But when Coxey left the ranks briefly to make a business trip to New York and Washington, Secret Service agents shadowed him, anyway. Based on their reports, Secret Service chief William P. Hazen reported to his superior, treasury secretary John G. Carlisle, that Coxey met with no known anarchists during his trip.[2]

As the army drew near the capital, special concern focused on protecting the Treasury Building, which was situated along the line of the proposed march. "The Treasury," observed the *Chicago Record*, "is of course the most sensitive point of danger because its dilapidated vaults, which should have been rebuilt years ago, are loaded with coin and bullion." In Springfield, Massachusetts, Major William H. Rexford, storekeeper at the United States arsenal, received an order to rush 65 carbines and 100 rifles to Washington to be used by treasury personnel. At the Springfield arsenal, another 250,000 rifles were available to be shipped at a moment's notice.

"We do not regard the invasion of Coxey's army as a joke," fretted one treasury department official. He worried that if the marchers failed to achieve their objectives on Capitol Hill, someone would cry, "Here is the United States Treasury filled with money, while our families are starving." Every clerk was supposed to render military duty if necessary, and special weapons were cached all over the building. The vaults were temporarily closed to the public, and police allowed entrance to the building through one door only.[3]

Major W. C. Moore and officers of the district police spent hours preparing for a confrontation with the crusaders; during one strategy session in mid-April, someone attached a sign outside their door:

> Fe, Fi, Fo, Fight
> We smell the blood of a Coxeyite

District officials were relieved to learn that the United States Army troops stationed at the Washington Barracks and Fort Myer were to be held in a state of readiness when May Day arrived, and backing them were another two thousand soldiers who could be brought to the capital from East Coast cities if needed. The tempo of life at the Arlington Barracks, the Navy Yard, and the Marine Barracks picked up noticeably as the Coxeyites drew near. There was an unusual amount of parading and gun cleaning, sailors exercising with pistols and broadswords, and marines loading and shooting rapid-fire weapons.[4]

During Coxey's last business trip to New York, reporters questioned him about police preparations under way in the capital.

"But the police may interfere with you," observed one journalist during the course of an interview.

"That's nonsense," responded Coxey, who had not yet secured official permission to speak from the Capitol steps. "The police can't do it. We're going to camp right on our own property. The idea of prohibiting men who own property from going upon it. I claim that the Capitol steps are a part of my property." But the police took a dim view of unauthorized public presentations; two days before Coxey's army reached Washington, Citizen Train ran afoul of the law when he gave a lecture without a license. He hastily returned to the safety of New York, abandoning all plans to take over the Commonweal.

A few days later, when Coxey learned that an 1882 act of Congress prohibited demonstrations on the Capitol grounds, he turned to a reporter for the *Washington Star* and said, "We will keep off the grass around the Capitol. Of course, I appreciate as well as anyone else the fact that the preservation of the grass around the Capitol is of more importance than saving thousands from starvation." The saber rattling reminded many people of Civil War days. The parallel was inescapable, and it heightened fears in Washington.[5]

Then there were those like New York's police superintendent Thomas Byrnes, who proposed that Congress pass a law to stop the movement. Congress, however, was no more certain what to do in late April than it had been in mid-March, when the crusaders were still collecting in Ohio. In March the chairman of the Senate Committee on Education and Labor, the Reverend James H. Kyle, had predicted that fifty thousand Coxeyites would be in Washington on May 1. "And I, for one, believe that if tramps and vagabonds can be kept out of the procession and a respectable lot of men gathered together, as I think will be the case, the demonstration will have a wholesome effect."

But the Populist senators William V. Allen of Nebraska and William A. Peffer of Kansas initially protested against the public tendency to link Coxey with their party. Said Allen, the movement "[is] absurd and useless. It is the work of a man who, if not a knave, is crazy, and who does not represent any of the principles of our party." Peffer concurred, although the two lawmakers later came to view the crusade in a much more favorable light. Peffer even introduced Coxey's good roads bill into the Senate.[6]

While congressmen deliberated and sailors rattled their broadswords on the banks of the Potomac, Coxey's marchers drew ever closer. Near Rockville, less than twenty miles from Washington, Browne noticed a curious band standing by the pike. Each of the fifteen men wore a shiny badge that read, "The Unknown's Contingent of Coxey's Army. Friendship, Cooperation, and Peace. We favor all law that will bring peace on earth and good will to mankind." The wizardo supreme ordered his troop to give three cheers for Browne, Coxey, and the Commonweal.

But Browne remained unmoved, except to give the Unknown's contingent a long look of scorn. "I thought that the 'Unknown,' alias Smith, alias Dr. Bozarro, patent-medicine vendor, had stopped serving the wicked reincarnation within him, but I see he is still dogging our footsteps," the Californian sneered to a nearby reporter. "His so-called army is made up of men whom we have discharged for drunkenness, thieving, and begging. As soon as we reach Rockville we shall ask Smith and his men to leave our grounds."

"What if they refuse to go?" a reporter asked.

Carl Browne with Coxey's army near Washington,
D.C. Courtesy Library of Congress.

Browne simply motioned toward his clubs of peace.

Not long after the "He is Alive!" wall was in place, the not-so-Great Unknown breached it. "Are we to be admitted as brothers in the Commonweal?" he asked.

"Not much, you ain't," growled Oklahoma Sam, armed with a baseball bat.

"Don't you dare to step over that line," bellowed Browne, adding loud cries of "Traitor! Pinkerton! Put him out!" Bozarro and his men beat a hasty retreat.

Even as Browne ejected his old foe, he welcomed with open arms Christopher Columbus Jones and fifty followers, who had completed a trouble-filled journey from Philadelphia through unsympathetic territory. They brought along a pitiful little commissary wagon not much bigger than a baby buggy.

After an overnight stop in Rockville, during which rain and high winds collapsed a tent and capsized Browne's beloved panorama wagon, the Coxeyites set their faces toward the District of Columbia for the last time. Though the storm had turned the Rockville Pike into a quagmire of red clay that stuck to everything, a band of 150 bicyclists bravely escorted them past the well-wishers who lined the way. On they trudged, through the villages of Kensington, Bethesda, and aristocratic Chevy Chase.

At the district boundary, the marchers came to Brightwood Riding

"Weary tramps"—Coxey's army in camp. Courtesy Library of Congress.

Park, which was to be their home for the next two days. It was 1:15 on the afternoon of April 29. After thirty-five days and a hike of more than four hundred miles in the snow, mud, and spring sun, fording streams and climbing mountains, the greatest march of the nineteenth century, as Coxey labeled it, was nearly over.

The Commonweal had found it nearly impossible to secure a camp-site in the nation's capital. For a time it looked as if the men would be able to use an empty lot in posh Woodley Park, almost adjacent to the summer home of Grover Cleveland. Much to the relief of Washington high society, Coxey obtained Brightwood Riding Park instead when its owner, who bore a grudge against the police for their supposed graft, rented the grounds to the Commonweal for two days for a dollar. Located about seven miles from Capitol Hill, the ten-acre park looked very much like a county fairground. Camp "Thaddeus Stevens" took shape inside its half-mile oval track as pilgrims erected their immense "He is Alive!" canvas and stationed a private at the gate to solicit contributions from the approximately eight thousand Sunday sightseers who arrived to inspect Coxey's rough, weary, dirty specimens of humanity.[7]

Curious spectators treated men who looked like ordinary tramps as if they were freaks or museum curiosities and peppered them with dozens of questions: Was it pleasanter to walk or ride in a canal boat? What sort of man was Coxey? They gawked at the ragged tents and Browne's mud-spattered panorama wagon, at strange legends and signs about good roads and reincarnation, at the battered tin pans and dishes that hung from half a dozen wagons, at the Coxeyite who munched a big chunk of bread, and at those who stretched on the ground with coats pulled over their heads. Fashionably dressed ladies compared notes on the appearance of the men "with no apparent realization of the fact that the subjects of their comments were human beings who could hear and understand them."

All day Sunday a seemingly endless procession of Washingtonians great and humble made their way to the park, creating a cloud of dust that hung heavy over Seventh and Fourteenth Streets. The pretentious carriages of senators and congressmen bowled along past plodding old freight wagons filled with black families. Here and there a monocled foreign dignitary rode along on a horse with a close-cropped tail, and bicyclers darted in and out of the tally-ho coaches, omnibuses, and rigs of every description. Pedestrians lined both sides of the roadway. Twenty times more people wanted aboard the streetcars than the cars could possibly carry. At the park entrance, enterprising blacks and whites sold gingerbread cookies and other treats. And the shell artists had returned to fleece the suckers. Such a spectacle had seldom been seen in the capital since the Civil War.

Among those who made the trip to Brightwood Park were Mrs. Coxey and little Legal Tender; J. Sterling Morton, Cleveland's secretary of agriculture; and the Populist senators Peffer and Allen. Conspicuous with his long gray beard was Senator Joseph Dolph of Oregon. Over there were Senators Charles F. Manderson, William Frye, and Richard Coke, as well as Congressman Constantine B. Kilgore. There was Iowa's dapper young Republican congressman, Jonathan Dolliver, the entire Mexican legation, and two members of the Chinese legation, resplendent in their satin robes and long braided queues. The Japanese minister and his wife were among the sightseers, as were representatives from the legations of Great Britain, France, and Italy.

About two hours after the Commonweal entered Brightwood Park, a trumpet sounded. It was time for Browne's usual Sunday reincarnation service. The Californian, who had shed his buckskin outfit for a more conventional black cutaway jacket, mounted the panorama wagon. After the army's choir had finished its version of "Hold the Fort," he launched into an illustrated sermon on the book of Revelations, looking most intently into the upturned faces of the nation's lawmakers in the large crowd that had gathered around him. In his inimitable way, Browne interwove prophecy and finance, Saint John and the sugar trust, before concluding with the words, "We are here like Grant before Richmond, and intend to fight it out on this line if it takes all summer and all winter."

When Browne finished, Coxey scrambled atop the wagon. "Three cheers for Coxey," someone in the crowd shouted. The ebullient Ohioan bowed and smiled, talking bareheaded for half an hour in the afternoon sun. His subject was the greatest march of the nineteenth century, and he predicted that his bills would pass Congress within two weeks. "This revolutionary spirit of '76 is making the money-lenders tremble now. Congress takes two years to vote on anything if left to itself. Twenty-millions of people are hungry and cannot wait two years to eat."

After the crowds left that night, Browne caused quite a stir in camp by announcing that he intended to take a Turkish bath. Coxey praised the move, and the leader and Browne left camp together to spend the night in the posh National Hotel downtown.

The following morning, the men of the Commonweal awoke from a bad night's sleep on damp ground to find an empty commissary and no breakfast. They sent a wagon into town for food, but by ten o'clock, when it had not yet returned with breakfast, their mood grew stormy. Starvation within sight of the Capitol dome was hard to take, and the men complained bitterly about Coxey and Browne. "They are downtown sleeping at the best hotel," one snarled, "and eating as good meals as the millionaires. The bills are paid with the money made exhibiting us to the public. All this time we are cooped up like so many criminals without anything to eat."

By eleven o'clock, when neither their leaders nor their breakfast had arrived, the murmurings of discontent grew still louder. "This is the worst we have had yet; a good many of the men believe that the leaders have shook us. The feeling is very hostile toward Browne."

"Yes," added another, "they are all downtown drunk and feasting, and leaving us here to starve."

Some men's thoughts turned to the deposed Bozarro. "Unknown always slept with us. . . . He never laid down until we had turned in. One stormy night in the mountains, when the wind was blowing hard, Unknown didn't go to bed until he had seen that every man was comfortable."

When noon came and went and still there was not so much as a stale crust of bread to eat, a few hotheads talked of lynching Browne when he arrived, if he arrived at all. Someone brought a large bundle of newspapers into camp, and for a time the pilgrims forgot their gnawing stomachs to savor instead the latest news of their march or, if a person was lucky, tidings from back home. A Commonwealer from Toledo fairly danced when a copy of the *Blade* fell his way. Hungry though he was, the news was still important. All over camp, men gathered in little knots to learn the latest about Kelley in Iowa, Fry in Indiana, and the several other western contingents.

Finally, at about three o'clock that afternoon, Browne made his entrance, wisely riding on a wagonload of bread. The sight of food had a generally calming effect, and the men listened as Browne told of his fruitless search for a new campsite. "We don't know where we will stay tomorrow night. Perhaps we're going to camp in the Capitol grounds. We're going to carry this thing through to the end. Haven't we done everything I said we would?"

"All except having a hundred thousand to form the parade," one hostile voice shot back.

"I didn't say we'd have a hundred thousand men in line," retorted Browne. "I said there would be a hundred thousand people with us in Washington." Even that figure was a considerable exaggeration, unless Browne counted people who were with the marchers in spirit if not in body.

Coxey and Browne spent the final day of April tending to last-minute preparations. Coxey arose early and went to breakfast in his hotel. Autograph seekers besieged him, but he treated each one kindly. Browne appeared, clean from his Turkish bath, and strutted about the lobby, his massive frame and odd clothing marking him clearly. He was ready to sign a few autographs too, if anyone would only ask him.

The Californian had a little surprise for Coxey. Unbeknownst to the leader, Browne had dispatched Jesse to Massillon on a special mission to bring Coxey's seventeen-year-old daughter back to serve as the Goddess of Peace. Her mother (Coxey's first wife) would not hear of the plan; but while Jesse bade his mother a long farewell, Mamie packed her clothes and slipped out a back entrance. The brother and sister rendezvoused at the depot and headed for Washington by express train. Reported one newspaper, "[Mrs. Coxey] is almost wild and will resort to legal means to secure her daughter."

Browne presented the lovely girl to her father, who could not believe his eyes. While Coxey spent a busy day on Capitol Hill and the Commonwealers waited in vain for their breakfast, Browne remained constantly at Mamie's side. They first visited a dressmaker, who fitted the girl with a white riding habit and blue liberty cap. The couple then strolled to a photographer's gallery, where they had a dozen pictures taken together.

Coxey went to the office of police commissioner Moore to get permission to speak from the Capitol steps. After the Ohioan exchanged greetings with Moore and two other commissioners, the lawman leaned forward and looked Coxey in the eye. "Then it is your idea to make a speech from the east front of the Capitol?"

"Yes."

"You can't do that," Moore and two other officials responded in unison. "The law prohibits it."

"Is there any law against making a speech on the streets?"

"Yes, the law prohibits that, too."

"Well," retorted Coxey, becoming annoyed, "that's what we propose to attempt. It's a Constitutional right."

Moore snapped that he would not grant Coxey a permit to speak in public, because Coxey intended to violate the law.

"I claim it under the Constitution." The words burst from the Ohioan's lips like rifle shots.

When told that only the presiding officer of the Senate or the speaker of the house could suspend the law, Coxey set out to find Vice-President Adlai Stevenson or Speaker Charles F. Crisp. At the Capitol, Coxey caused quite a commotion. Clerks, pages, and everyone else who could get away wanted to see him, and he signed another two hundred autographs. But when Speaker Crisp declined his request, Coxey told reporters, "The chief representative of the Democratic party in Congress has refused to grant these rights to the American people." As for Vice-President Stevenson, Coxey never could locate him. Thoroughly frustrated by the Washington runaround, the Ohioan retreated to Brightwood Park to check on his men.

That evening the newsboys on downtown streets called out, "Extra! Extra! Bloodshed expected tomorrow! U. S. troops may be called out to prevent the Coxey army from marching to the Capitol!"

When the sun rose in a cloudless sky on the morning of May 1, the marchers took that as a good omen, but not as good as the hearty breakfast of eggs, bread, and coffee that atoned for the commissary problems the day before. As for the unresolved issue of speaking from the Capitol steps, Browne warned city officials and congressmen, "The Constitution is superior to any of your local technical laws, and it gives the citizens the right of public meeting and free speech and petition. If the wording does not mean this we will find out what it does mean."[8]

Browne distributed a club of peace to each of his men. Removing his hat, he addressed them solemnly: "The greatest ordeal of the march is at hand; the eyes of the world are on you and you must conduct yourselves accordingly." For the next hour he drilled them, barking out orders to "Carry peace!" and "Shoulder peace!" With the little white flags pointed upward at an angle behind their heads, the men stood ready for their long-awaited arrival on Capitol Hill.

Colonel Redstone arrived with a contingent of organized workers. They carried a large banner reading, "Washington Workmen Welcome the Commonweal. More Money and Less Misery. For the Coxey Bills, and Death to Interest on Bonds." Forty blue-jacketed policemen rode up, too. Browne was uncertain whether they were there to escort the troops or to arrest him. The evening before, he had found a large official-looking envelope in his tent. It contained a blunt message from the sergeant of the local police detail: "You are hereby warned that you and all your command will be arrested if you attempt to march to the Capitol from the Brightwood Park tomorrow."

Just before ten o'clock, the leader arrived in his black phaeton, Mrs. Coxey and little Legal Tender at his side. The marchers applauded wildly. A few moments later Mamie rode up on a prancing white stallion, and Browne took his place just behind her, eyeing the line of march carefully. At 10:15 the Californian bellowed: "Attention Commonweal. Forward march!"

The Goddess of Peace headed the procession onto the dusty road that led downtown. The great white Capitol dome was visible in the distance. Marching down Fourteenth Street at a funeral's pace, they passed the Chinese legation. The whole of the emperor's household stood at the windows to watch, waving parasols and fans at the marchers. The Commonwealers passed the colonnaded Treasury Building, where they observed policemen and soldiers standing guard; then they turned onto Pennsylvania Avenue. From here they saw their goal close at hand for the first time, its alabaster columns and gleaming dome framed by the immense crowd that lined both sides of the thoroughfare.

As clocks struck one, Coxey's troop had made its way up the gentle rise of Capitol Hill and halted just beyond the B Street entrance to the House of Representatives. Waiting for them were an estimated twenty thousand spectators. Three to four hundred policemen blocked access to the building—one for nearly every Coxeyite on the march—and more officers waited just inside.

"Attention, Commonweal, Halt!" Browne's booming voice rose above the noise of the restless onlookers. Dismounting, he escorted Mamie Coxey to the shade of a maple at the curb. "You won't be afraid to stay here, will you?" The girl shook her head.

The marshal handed a set of sealed orders to his officers, then pushed through the crowd to Coxey. "This is the east front," he murmured low. "Are you ready?" Coxey nodded. Rising in his carriage, he stooped to kiss his wife in a display of affection that brought cheer after cheer from the onlookers. Browne handed his sombrero to Mrs. Coxey. Her husband looked pale as he jumped to the ground.

A mounted policeman blocked Browne's way. "You can't pass here with that flag."

"Why can't I pass?" questioned Browne, who was holding one of the staves of peace. Before the officer could answer, an onlooker cried, "Jump over the wall!" In a moment Coxey and Browne had cleared the low stone wall and disappeared into the crowd. Small trees, bushes, and flower beds were flattened by the onslaught of mounted officers in pursuit. Christopher Columbus Jones of the Philadelphia contingent hopped around trying to join his colleagues but was quickly collared by the police. They jammed the old man's tall hat down over his eyes and led him away to a patrol wagon.

Browne in his Buffalo Bill suit was an easy target. And that was his plan: to decoy the officers while Coxey made his way unseen through the crowd to the steps where presidents since James Monroe had been inaugurated. On this site of new beginnings Coxey planned to deliver his long-promised speech offering a cure for unemployment. Browne led officers on a wild chase through the shrubbery before a dozen of them finally tackled him at the southeast corner of the building. "I am an American citizen. I stand on my Constitutional rights," he bellowed.

Browne spun around suddenly, first right and then left; surprised policemen whirled off into the crowd. An officer jumped him from behind while others beat him on the head and face. They tore his shirt from the neck to the trousers and ripped from his neck the memento of his deceased wife, its amber beads scattering in all directions.

As policemen wrestled Browne into a nearby patrol wagon, bystanders attempted to come to his rescue. Grabbing the bridles of the officers' horses, they forced the animals into the low wall and spilled the riders violently to the ground. At this, the police lost their heads. They charged into the crowd, beating everyone within range; mounted officers rode down men, women, and children. People dropped to their knees, dazed by repeated blows from billy clubs.

While all eyes were on Browne and the riot surrounding him, Coxey reached the front steps and climbed halfway up before onlookers spotted him. A great shout went up. Coxey paused for a moment to catch his breath, turned toward the sea of upturned faces, and tipped his hat. He turned to continue his climb, but two officers blocked his way.

"What do you want to do here?" one asked, posing the question on everyone's mind.

"I wish to make an address," Coxey responded in an emotion-choked voice.

"But you can't do that."

"Then can I read a protest?" The Ohioan drew a typewritten manuscript from his pocket and proceeded to unfold it. But before he could open his mouth, officers pushed him firmly backwards down the steps. Coxey tossed the document to a nearby reporter, saying, "That is for the press." His message—essentially a Populist appeal for better treatment of "the poor and oppressed"—would appear later in several newspapers and the *Congressional Record*.

Bystanders watched as officers escorted Coxey to his carriage. Someone in the crowd shouted his name, and others joined in, louder and louder until every man, woman, and child was shouting "Coxey!" Police charged into the crowd to disperse it, causing people to fall over one another in a desperate effort to get out of range. The tatterdemalion army remained quiet and orderly at the center of the tempest.

As Coxey climbed into his carriage, voices cried from the sidelines, "Speech! Speech!" He rose instinctively to oblige them, but his words were lost in the tumult. With a wave of his hand, he signaled his troops to move on. The drummer beat out the step, and the Commonweal marched quietly to a new campsite about a mile away. The whole affair at the Capitol had lasted less than fifteen minutes.

Washington was relieved that the confrontation was not more serious. In Cleveland, May Day demonstrations by the unemployed ended in a bloody riot, and there was trouble also in London and Berlin. That black men and women were so often on the receiving end of the billy clubs was no accident. They were among Coxey's most avid supporters. Just the day before, chief of police W. G. Moore told reporters, "There is a colored population numbering 85,000 in this city, fully half of whom are unemployed and many of whom are vicious. We could not, of course, afford to permit any demonstration which would arouse them. Hence the thoroughness of our preparations." Black businessmen protested this slander, labeling it "the demagogic cry of a war of races," but authorities were in no mood to listen.[9]

Also incensed by police violence was the genial and handsome Ohio congressman, Tom Johnson of Cleveland. He and his colleagues watched the brutal spectacle from the best vantage point on Capitol Hill: the windows and portico of the House wing. The following morning Johnson took the floor to call for an investigation of whether the police had used unnecessary force, "whether unoffending citizens were cruelly beaten, and whether the dignity of this House has been violated." That Congress had no better reception for a peaceful delegation of unemployed men than to meet them with the upraised clubs of police, complained Johnson, who disclaimed any sympathy for Coxey, "is a disgrace. It is politically a blunder, and morally a crime; and it cannot but stir up feelings of bitterness which a proper course would have allayed."

Almost the whole House opposed Johnson's proposal. Congressmen were no more interested in investigating alleged police brutality than in using federal power to do something about the more subtle economic and psychological brutality visited on the nation's jobless by the depression.[10]

Following their confrontation on Capitol Hill, the Commonwealers pitched camp on a vacant lot at First and L Streets, near the mouth of an abandoned canal. Two of their leaders were gone, and gone too was the pilgrims' enthusiasm.

After the riot, policemen took prisoners Browne and Jones to the Fifth Precinct station. Surrounded by eight lawmen, the man in buckskin sulkily submitted to a search that turned up a few soiled pieces of paper, 79 cents in cash, and a .22 pistol, the spring broken and the chamber empty. After a judge set bond for the two men at $500 each, they were lodged in adjoining cells. From behind bars Browne called out to reporters, "Say, ask Coxey to come down and get me out of this, will you?"[11]

As if by a miracle, two angels stepped forward to put up bail for Browne: Elizabeth A. Haines, proprietor of a dry goods store in Washington, and Emily Edson Briggs, one of the major landowners on Capitol Hill (and the first woman admitted to the White House as a press correspondent). Briggs put up bond as an act of compassion, not sympathy, she emphasized. The Californian was nonetheless grateful; and upon reaching camp after having had dinner with Briggs, he ordered the site named "Briggs-Haines" in honor of "that class of citizens who are taxed without representation in legislation contrary to the Constitution of the United States."

In the eyes of his men, Browne was now a genuine hero for perhaps the first time since the march began. The murmurings of the day before were forgotten as they hoisted the big Californian upon their shoulders. From all over the United States, expressions of sympathy and gifts of food poured in, including three hundred pies. The ladies of Little Rock sent a beautiful new banner. Observed Samuel Gompers, with whom Coxey visited immediately after the ill-fated rendezvous on Capitol Hill, "Clubbing may subdue Coxey or Browne, but it will not drive thought out of the people's minds. A club will subdue one man, but it will recruit one hundred for the cause it represents."[12]

The Coxeyites' new campsite was a dismal plot of ground, a former dumping site for manure and garbage. Public health officers worried that humans living in such a mess might easily spread typhoid germs or some other dread disease, and they threatened to close the site. Adversity, though, was no stranger to the Commonwealers; and soon they were busily making their new camp habitable. They raised their canvas wall and with pitchforks and shovels scooped up the garbage and manure. They piled the bricks carefully in an orderly pile, put in rye straw for bedding, and had soon miraculously transformed the camp. Their flurry of activity shattered the convictions of those who believed that Coxeyites would not work.[13]

On the morning after the Capitol Hill riot, Coxey and Browne joined Jones in police court. Coxey had come as a witness for the other two; but soon after the Ohioan entered the room, Judge Thomas F. Miller peered over the bench and solemnly announced, "I have been informed that a man named Jacob S. Coxey is in the court." The judge went on to state that after some investigation the evening before, he had decided to secure a warrant for Coxey's arrest. "I have made out a warrant, but if he is willing to submit I do not care to have it served upon him."

"I am ready," Coxey spoke up promptly.

All three defendants were charged with violating the act of July 1, 1882, that regulated the use of the Capitol grounds. Specifically, they had injured the shrubs and turf and carried banners in the form of the inconspicuous insignias that each man wore on his lapel. All pleaded not guilty. The arrest of the trio on such trivial charges subjected Washington authorities and Congress (which controlled the city government) to much scornful criticism and evoked still more sympathy for the Commonwealers.[14]

While the Commonwealers busied themselves in camp with games of baseball and vaudeville shows, the trial occupied their leaders' time. It dragged on for three days. Several Populist congressmen volunteered their services as defense attorneys, and Browne was delighted to discover among the "argus-eyed demons of hell" several who were willing to speak in his behalf. An Alexandria reporter testified that policemen had driven citizens onto the grass before the army arrived; he was certain that Coxey had not trod on the grass. On cross-examination he stated that there were several thousand people cheering when Coxey reached the Capitol.

"Disorderly, were they not?" interjected the prosecutor.

"Oh, no," returned the reporter. "They had a right to cheer. They were American citizens."

The defense raised the question of the constitutionality of the 1882 law, citing First Amendment guarantees of freedom of speech and assembly, but it was overruled by Judge Miller, who fancied himself an expert on constitutional law. Summing up his case for the jury, the prosecutor pointed scornfully toward Browne. "That man, a working man? A man who looks as though he never did a day's work in his life! Save the word! A fakir, a charlatan and a mountebank who dresses up in ridiculous garments and exhibits himself to the curious multitudes at 10 cents a head!"

Turning to Coxey, he continued in the same vein. "The other man a laboring man! A wealthy man, who owns a stock farm and stone quarries, who admits that he has received all the money contributions for the movement bearing his name, and has never made an accounting."

On the afternoon of May 8, after deliberating less than two hours, the jury returned to the courtroom. Coxey, visiting with his wife and daughter Mamie, took his place with Browne and Jones at the bar. The verdict was guilty: all were guilty of carrying banners, and Coxey and Browne were guilty, in addition, of trampling Uncle Sam's grass. Posting bond, a surprised, bitter, and visibly shaken Coxey left the courtroom on the arm of his wife. When he returned to camp, he mounted a wagon and addressed his followers. "This country is like a big bunch of straw, and all that is necessary to start it into a roaring blaze is the torch. Do you dream that in court today the torch was applied?"

The *Omaha World-Herald*, which voiced sentiments found in other papers throughout the country, observed: "Every detail of the proceedings was stamped with the effort on the part of the prosecutor to make a mountain out of a mole hill. The crime: Carrying banners on the Capitol grounds! Trespassing on the Grass! Great Caesar. If the several kinds of fools who are managing the anti-Coxey crusade at the national capital were in the employ of Coxey they could not do him better service than they are doing him today." [15]

On May 21, Coxey, Browne, and Jones returned to court for sentencing. Judge Miller asked if they had anything to say. Congressman Thomas Jefferson Hudson of Kansas, who had helped to defend the trio, arose and delivered a bitter statement: "You know and I know that he [pointing to Coxey] was not arrested and convicted because he stepped on the grass, but because he carried a political banner in opposition to the political ideas of those who are powerful in the administration of this government. They have demanded the conviction of these men." Judge Miller hotly denied Hudson's assertion.

After Coxey delivered a rambling protest, Miller responded: "You have your head so full of your schemes that you think anything that stands in your way is wrong." The judge then referred to Coxey's "absolute folly" and denounced him as a "dreamer." "I do not know of any case where the court would be more justified in passing the maximum sentence," said Miller before he sentenced each defendant to jail for twenty days. Officers led the trio away in handcuffs, although a dozen white and black prisoners going to the workhouse with them wore no such restraints.[16]

For many observers, the fate of Coxey and his movement after May Day was of little importance. "Coxey has played his trump card and lost the trick and the game," observed the *Indianapolis Journal*. "The moral force of the movement is spent, and hereafter nothing that Coxey may say or do will excite any public interest."[17]

On May 2 Ray Stannard Baker received a telegram from his editor at the *Record*: "Drop Coxey tonight. Report in Chicago Monday noon." As he headed west, the young journalist penned a note to his father. "I bade a joyful farewell to Coxey's army. I was terribly tired of the whole infernal business. I wrote in all about 75,000 words, a big book, on the subject and I didn't have much more to say."[18]

Even as he jotted down those words, though, Coxeyism was gaining strength in the Far West. The region that gave rise to the armies of Kelley and others continued to send forth reinforcements after May 1. More regiments headed east from California, and armies numbering in the hundreds collected in the Pacific Northwest and the Rocky Mountain states. For the next several weeks the real story of the Coxey movement was that of the western armies—headstrong, aggressive, occasionally violent, and buoyed by the support of many sympathizers throughout the region. As the armies of Fry, Kelley, and Hogan had already illustrated, the industrial army movement in the West took on a dimension all its own.

Said Carl Browne, summing up the Coxey movement after May Day, "It is the 1st of May with us till we have that meeting on the steps of the Capitol. The Washington police have shown themselves pretty expert in clubbing heads, but they will have to get more practice on Western heads before they can stop this crowd." [19]

CHAPTER 12

Coxeyism may indeed be said to be
the creature of the Pacific Coast. . . .
The armies recruited in the Eastern
States were contemptible. There were
three score pilgrims from Boston
and even fewer from Philadelphia.

W. T. Stead,
"Coxeyism: A Character Sketch"

Coxeyism East and West

Carl Browne's belief that the fate of the Coxey movement rested with
westerners was less an assertion of regional pride than a simple statement of fact attested to by newspaper tallies of the movement's membership. This was the first nationwide crusade against unemployment,
in the sense that it attracted attention and at least some following in
all parts of the country. It was primarily in the West, though, that it
attained its greatest strength and significance.[1]

Still on the road on May 1 were Fry's three hundred men—predominantly Californians—bogged down in Indianapolis after a harrowing march overland from Saint Louis. Often they had been unable to travel more than five miles a day in the raw, wet weather that
turned midwestern roads into quagmires. Bickering broke out, and
in central Illinois the more impetuous soldiers, constituting about
half of Fry's army, seceded under Colonel Thomas Galvin and vowed
to take a train instead of walk. In this fashion they leapfrogged Fry's
plodders and were now in Wheeling, West Virginia, having crossed
eastern Ohio in railway coaches chartered by the trade unions of
Columbus.

At about the same hour that Coxey made his unsuccessful assault
on Capitol Hill, an army of 450 reinforcements under the command

of Dr. J. H. Randall—dentist, labor organizer, and Civil War veteran—left Chicago. In the Montana capital of Helena, train pirate William Hogan and 400 followers remained under guard at the county fairgrounds awaiting trial for contempt of court.

More than five hundred recruits were camped in Portland, Oregon, on May Day. And in the village of Puyallup, Washington, at the foot of the Cascade Mountains, Seattle and Tacoma armies with a combined strength of nearly a thousand awaited transportation. The most prominent member of this contingent was the Tacoma general, Frank T. "Jumbo" Cantwell, a handsome, barrel-chested saloon bouncer, professional gambler, and frontier original. "We are going to Washington," affirmed Cantwell. "We are not going to plead much longer with these railroads. We will be like Christ. When they smite us on one cheek we'll turn the other, and then we'll smash 'em back one."[2]

The twenty-five-year-old Cantwell was extremely popular with his men, and on one occasion he raised more than a hundred dollars for the cause by sparring six rounds with a man reputed to be the cousin of heavyweight boxing champion "Gentleman Jim" Corbett. Jumbo was a natural showman, like Browne, and his antics were a godsend to reporters who sought to sensationalize the movement. So too was his tall and "divinely blond" wife, Carlotta: "Mrs. Cantwell never appears on the street that her beauty and quiet manners do not attract notice. She usually wears black and her somber attire makes a striking contrast to her fair face and hair." Carlotta was also wealthy, having inherited a fortune from her late husband, Harry Morgan, lord of Tacoma vice and Jumbo's onetime employer. Her ears and fingers sparkled with diamonds. During the course of the Coxey movement, Carlotta rose above her unsavory past to become one of the truly remarkable leaders of the crusade.[3]

Largest of the armies still on the road on May 1 was Kelley's, with eleven hundred men still stranded in Des Moines. Kelley was clearly exasperated with Coxey and his officers for having forced a premature confrontation without waiting for the others. Labeling Coxey's own contingent "only a little squad of Eastern men," he lashed out at Browne, who had scheduled the May Day rendezvous, calling him a "conceited ass." Kelley contrasted the generous support that west-

erners gave the movement with the general indifference shown by easterners, a fact that now caused him to view his army as Coxey's "only hope."[4]

As days passed with no prospect of a train, both the Kelleyites and their Des Moines sympathizers showed increasing frustration. The novelty of feeding the army was gone, and some wished the protesters had never come. Certainly they did not care to board the visitors much longer. "That was the terrifying factor in the situation," recalled Jack London. "We were bound for Washington, and Des Moines would have had to float municipal bonds to pay all our railroad fares, even at special rates, and if we remained much longer, she'd have to float bonds anyway to feed us."

The depressed Kelleyites found fault with their Populist hosts, particularly General Weaver, whose presence they believed discouraged businessmen from aiding their cause. A growing number of troops reported sick: at one time twenty-three were in the hospital. Drake University president B. O. Aylesworth used the delay to learn more about the marchers, and his students conducted a statistical survey that provided the most complete picture of any contingent of Coxey's army.[5] "I am sure they would work if they could," the professor assured listeners after visiting Kelley's men. "They carried books and magazines, one even reading Latin during the hours of camping. I heard one man swear; but no other vulgarity." Drake faculty and trustees, however, did not share their president's interest in contemporary sociology, and he nearly lost his job as a consequence.[6]

Even as Aylesworth edged out of the limelight, another man elbowed his way in. He was James R. Sovereign, a Des Moines resident, labor publisher, and grand master workman of the Knights of Labor. A decade earlier the Knights had constituted the largest and most prominent labor organization in America, but events during the intervening years had reduced the order to a shadow of its former self. Sovereign, like Weaver, sensed a personal opportunity in Kelley's army.

Rushing back from a conference in Chicago, he immediately grabbed headlines with a series of blustering statements. Clinging pathetically to the illusion of power, Sovereign threatened that unless Iowa's railroads provided transportation for the Kelleyites, he would call a massive sympathy strike by members of the Knights of Labor

and Eugene Debs's new American Railway Union. He claimed that Debs had promised him, "Whenever you want us, speak the word. We will be with you in any fight." But when the Des Moines local of the American Railway Union protested to Debs, he quickly wired back, "Pay no attention to the report. It is false." He added, "For God's sake keep the union out of politics and private quarrels."

The situation looked hopeless. The railroads removed their locomotives from Des Moines to frustrate any capture attempt; Kelley warned that his men would starve before they walked on; and members of organized labor, who had generously shared their food with the Kelleyites, feared that the army would disband and seek their jobs, too. Then someone had a brilliant idea. Why not convert the army into a navy and float lazily out of town on the Des Moines River? There would be no stolen trains and no blistered feet.

A veteran canoeist called the proposal impractical. Not only was the distance to the Mississippi more than two hundred miles, but the Des Moines was shallow, filled with sandbars and hidden snags, and obstructed in several places by low dams. Furthermore, the few towns that lined the river could scarcely feed all the Kelleyites. Kelley himself greeted the idea with a derisive laugh, although after a bit of reflection he accepted the proposal. A short test run by some of his sympathizers suggested that small boats could make the trip, and besides, Kelley dared not remain in Des Moines a day longer. As his army swelled to 1,345 members, rations dwindled and the campsite became unsanitary.

On Saturday, May 5, after assembling his men in the abandoned stoveworks that served as home, Kelley admitted that there was no possibility of a train. He asked how many were willing to hike east. No one uttered a sound. Would they then be willing to travel by boat to Wheeling, West Virginia, only three hundred miles from their destination? Shouts of approval filled the air, and the crusaders eagerly awaited a chance to build their flotilla.

The next morning Commodore Kelley established his navy yard at the junction of the Des Moines and Raccoon Rivers, near the site of old Fort Des Moines. Local residents donated money to purchase the necessary materials, and with the help of the carpenters' union, the Kelleyites commenced nailing together the first of more than one

hundred boats. Sovereign, dressed in a Prince Albert coat and sporting a pencil behind his ear and a ruler in his hand, acted as master shipbuilder. Weaver moved among the crews offering free advice.

Fifteen thousand Sunday visitors lined the river banks to watch a spectacle that reminded them of the small boys in *Tom Sawyer*. Also watching discreetly were Rock Island officials, concerned that at several locations their railway lines ran within hailing distance of the river. Kelley, who worked the crowd like an old-time evangelist, raised nearly $300.

The first boat was launched at four o'clock that afternoon. Anna Hooten, who along with Edna Harper had remained with the marchers since the train-stealing episode in Council Bluffs, christened it the *Omaha*. After a brief shakedown cruise, the commodore pronounced the craft satisfactory in every way. But Kelley proved a poor judge of things nautical, for in practice the scows took in so much water that two crewmen had to bail constantly to keep each one afloat. The commander, however, was understandably eager to get his flotilla underway.

By Sunday evening his men had built fifty boats, and a new crew working by the light of bonfires continued through the night. Each craft was eighteen feet long, six feet wide, and one foot deep. When fully loaded with thirteen men, it drew about six inches of water. Made of rough planks caulked with oakum and tar, most of the boats contained lockers for seating and storage facilities. Rough boards served as paddles. The crafts bore names like *Des Moines*, *Ottumwa*, *Queen Isabella*, *General Weaver*, and *Tale of Woe*, and were decorated with American flags and buntings. Kelley, ever mindful of his need for good public relations, assigned one boat to the press.

Launch day was Wednesday, May 9, ten days after the Kelleyites had arrived in Des Moines. Everything seemed perfect for the start of the next phase of the great adventure. The sun shone brightly, and the muddy river ran full with rain that had fallen during the past several days in northern Iowa. Des Moines businesses closed for the occasion. People in a holiday mood lined the banks and asked one another in loud voices, "Which one is Kelley?" They also craned their necks to see the "engine heroines," Hooten and Harper.

Heavy wagons lumbered to the launch site all morning, bringing donations of bread, beef, vegetables, and coffee. Kelley periodically harangued the crowd by reading telegrams of support. This elicited loud cheers from the onlookers. They also cheered the launching of each scow. Kelley's sailors were to have collected a short distance downstream, but in true Tom Sawyer fashion they began racing one another, having too much fun to obey orders. Disappearing from view, they could be heard lustily singing, "We'll hang old Grover on a sour apple tree." Kelley did not shove off until two o'clock, by which time his navy was hopelessly scattered.

In all, 140 boats sailed from Des Moines, carrying nine hundred men. An estimated five hundred women boarded the scows for brief rides. They were supposed to disembark a short distance downstream, but some fifty apparently had no intention of returning.

When Kelley caught up with his navy at the village of Runnells, the first night's port, he found that hunger had made the sailors discontented and surly. They complained about Kelley's lack of leadership during their first day on the river and his spending too much time with "them women," Hooten and Harper. The commissary boat arrived with Kelley, and when the grumblers had eaten they once again became docile. But observers continued to predict future trouble unless Kelley rid his contingent of all women. While Kelley assisted law enforcement officers in capturing runaways from Des Moines and even disbanded a company for refusing to compel a woman to leave, he clung steadfastly to the notion that Hooten and Harper were entitled to special protection because they had risked their reputations and had broken the law attempting to capture a train for his men. As noble as the policy was, it intensified jealousy among his followers. During the trip downriver, Kelley made every effort to ensure that morality prevailed: at night Hooten and Harper slept in a special tent guarded from a discreet distance by three men. Kelley also reminded people that he was bunking with his wife's brother, the treasurer of the army: "Do you think he would stand actions such as have been charged to me? There were some women that got among the men, who are not all saints, at Des Moines, but I soon had them arrested and sent back." The two "angels" remained an attraction second only to the commodore himself.

Next to the jealousy caused by the presence of Hooten and Harper, Kelley's most serious problem was food. Most townspeople along the Des Moines River were generous. But inhabitants of the hamlets of

Kelley's "navy" on the Des Moines River at Ottumwa, Iowa. Courtesy
Iowa State Historical Department, State Historical Society.

Dunreath and Red Rock refused even to sell anything to the navy.
Kelley warned a deputy sheriff that if he could not purchase food, his
men would take it by force. The deputy advised citizens to change
their minds, pointing out that there were enough Kelleyites to capture both villages. Also troubling Kelley were the foragers and pro-
miscuous beggars in his ranks. Jack London and a group of Sacramento men got ahead of the main flotilla, feasted on donations
meant for the entire navy, and left little for the unfortunates who followed. When Kelley tried to discipline the malefactors, the Sacramento men complained loudly about what they called his failure of
leadership. "We ardently believed," London later recalled, "that the
grub was to the man who got there first, the pale Vienna [coffee
made with milk] to the strong."

The cruise through Iowa lasted ten days. "In motion, the army
might be described as a tatterdemalion *Carnival de Venice*," wrote
one onlooker. Each boat was festooned with banners, flags, and
spring wildflowers; their sunburned crews resembled Italian gon-
doliers. So many Iowans lined the riverbanks to watch the odd
flotilla that London protested in his tramp diary that "we would have
to go for miles to find a secluded spot in which to bathe, or make

our toilet." If the navy traveled after dark, farmers built bonfires so as not to miss the passing show. A special glee club boat followed Kelley's flagship and serenaded onlookers with such popular favorites as "After the Ball" and "Daisy, Daisy," often with special Kelleyite lyrics added. And a reporter for the *Burlington Hawk-Eye* took note of an especially curious feature of Kelley's contingent. In an age noted for its racial prejudice, "There are several darkies in the army and they fraternize on a footing of equality with their white companions."

Kelleyites were just as interested in Iowa as Iowans were in them. They commented favorably on the lush rolling farmland through which they floated and were especially curious about how farmers planted corn. In all probability, they would have passed downriver without incident, had it not been for the Rock Island officials who shadowed them "like a hawk hovering over a brood of chickens." Anticipating trouble, the railroad ultimately caused it. The Rock Island infiltrated Kelley's navy with detectives and placed hundreds of armed employees—erroneously thought by Jack London and others to be Pinkertons—at crucial points. One of the most heavily guarded places was Eldon, a village where the Rock Island's Chicago–to–Kansas City main line crossed the Des Moines River. At that site nearly a hundred special deputies, mostly company employees, waited with ax handles and other weapons to prevent the Kelleyites from landing.

As a lead boat floated past, townspeople motioned it over to receive provisions. But the Rock Island guards would not permit it near the shore and hurled stones at the Kelleyites, reportedly breaking the ribs of one and knocking another unconscious. Camped about two miles below town, Kelley's men would have liked nothing better than to punish the railroad that had harassed them ever since Council Bluffs. Jack London, who arrived at the campsite ahead of the main flotilla, described the mood: "Two of the detectives were arrested but the R. R. officials instantly bailed them out. By nine o'clock the boats came in all in a lump, & they were all greatly excited. If any Pinkertons are captured Woe unto them for the men are getting desperate."

Early the next morning, a few of the sailors crossed to the other bank, where twenty-five guards refused them permission to land. In an instant, every boat was filled with excited Kelleyites coming to the aid of their comrades. Some literally ran across the river at a ford, never stopping to pull off their shoes or socks or to roll up their pants. Most of the guards bolted for town. A Des Moines reporter, speaking tongue-in-cheek, quipped that one guard, a fat engineer, traveled so fast that he completed "the quickest run ever made in the Des Moines valley." Two guards who remained were surrounded and disarmed. Kelley once again intervened to avoid bloodshed. Law officers arrested two Kelleyites but released them a short while later. The people of Eldon were so incensed by the Rock Island's disturbing their peace that they forced the company to apologize. Its employees, nonetheless, continued to shadow the navy all the way to Keokuk, where the Des Moines River joined the Mississippi, but they incited no further trouble.

On May 21, after an extended stop near Keokuk, where the men received mail, supplies, and nearly 10,000 visitors, the Kelleyites finally left Iowa. It had been a very long five weeks since they had arrived in Council Bluffs. Their early optimism was gone, and the way ahead looked no easier. At Quincy, Illinois, a short distance from Keokuk and Kelley's boyhood home for ten years, the commodore addressed a large and friendly crowd, promising to reach Washington "in spite of hell," if he lived that long. That was a big if. The Mississippi River was no sluggish, shallow stream. In places its massive current boiled up above the surface as if flexing its muscles, or swirled around in gigantic whirlpools. Such perils could easily send the scows of Kelley's navy to the bottom. At Keokuk they lashed their crafts together to form one great barge and got a tug to assist them, but no one could be sure that the odd vessels would survive as far as Saint Louis, much less make the trip up the Ohio River to Wheeling.[7]

Jack London, for one, had had enough. At Hannibal he wrote in his diary, "We went supperless to bed. Am going to pull out in the morning. I can't stand starvation." The next day he left for Chicago, bumming his way by rail.

London was overpessimistic, for when Kelley's navy reached Saint Louis in late May, it still excited much popular interest and support. "Barnum never drew a greater throng," observed a *Post-Dispatch* reporter of the 12,000 visitors who turned out to view the spectacle on the levee. "The show isn't much in the way of a pageant. There are no roaring lions, no monster elephants, no hippopotamus, no dashing riders, no daring gymnasts. It hasn't a single novel feature, unless an army of worn out, tattered men may be considered novel." But leading a volunteer army of 1,200 men nearly 3,000 miles unaided except for freewill contributions along the way was indeed a remarkable and novel feat, as any military person could testify. "This man Kelley is a genius, among the most illustrious men of history," gushed one journalist.[8] Kelley was a skilled general, but like every successful Coxeyite he got by with help from his friends, most notably organized labor and the Populist party. In Saint Louis the Trades and Labor Council (a citywide federation of labor), the Knights of Labor, and the German Arbeiter Verbund combined forces to aid the Kelleyites. At a mass meeting that they sponsored, Kelley described the journey overland and his arid-lands program. A delegation of the city's prominent labor leaders frequently nodded their heads in approval.[9] When the California general left Saint Louis a few days later, he needed all the support he could muster. But as Louis Fry had discovered two months earlier, the Coxey movement excited far less enthusiasm in the East than in the Far West.

The distinguishing badge of the western Coxeyite was the stolen train; including the minor incidents, they tallied more than fifty. So frequently did they occur during May 1894 that when Commonwealers commandeered a train in the mountains west of Missoula, one newspaper ran the item under a simple headline: "The Same Old Story." Few Montanans had any trouble guessing what that meant.[10]

The episodes of piracy were difficult to number, because there was no agreement on what constituted an act of train theft. Newspapers sometimes confused stealing rides on the cars with commandeering the trains themselves. One reason why most such episodes occurred in the Far West was that Coxey's imitators there had no practical alternative to the railroad if they expected to reach Capitol Hill anytime soon. Another and perhaps even more important reason was that their many well-wishers—both common people and governors like those in Oregon, Kansas, and Colorado—did little to prevent the train thievery, even if they did not openly encourage it. And even governors who disapproved of the movement, like Montana's John Rickards, had worked out no plan for dealing with this unusual form of lawlessness. Some states had no militia whatever; others had inadequate forces. Perhaps if the thieves had been Indians, foreign invaders, or frontier desperadoes, or if they had stolen horses and wagons instead of locomotives, public officers would have found their duty clear. But elected officials at all levels understood the great popular sympathy that the train thieves evoked and were reluctant to act hastily, if at all.[11]

Looking at events from an eastern perspective, the *Nation* was incensed: "Trains have been stolen by organized mobs, and the same public that called for vengeance upon the Jesse James gang and other express robbers, has weakly said of these industrial train robbers, 'Poor fellows, they are out of work and must do something.'"

Even westerners were not really of one mind on the issue. "It is a simple question of law or anarchism," fumed a journal from the state of Washington. But a Populist newspaper from the same state retorted, "It is hard to make the masses believe that any wrong has been committed by a human being in attempting to get a free ride in a box car, when this same public has watched so-called railroad kings steal entire railroads and read in the monopolistic press such men designated as 'Napoleons of finance,' etc." A person did not have to be a Populist to agree.[12]

Hogan's much-publicized Wild West show in Montana inspired two similar incidents on April 28 at opposite ends of the country. The manner in which the governors of Ohio and Oregon handled each episode confirmed for many the contrast between East and West, between reliable and conservative Republicans and wild-eyed and irresponsible Populists.

The Ohio trouble originated with the two hundred men who had earlier seceded from Fry's ranks near Vandalia, Illinois. Marching south to the Baltimore and Ohio line, they stole rides to Cincinnati and beyond without incident. But when the railroad sidetracked the freight they were riding near Mount Sterling, Ohio, the freeloaders refused to abandon the cars. The company rejected Colonel Galvin's offer of $15 to take them on to Columbus; and when the men ignored several entreaties to leave, the railroad persuaded Governor William McKinley to dispatch the Ohio National Guard. Soon a trainload of one hundred fifty militiamen pulled into Mount Sterling from Columbus; bringing up the rear was a flatcar bearing two Gatling guns.

With those ominous weapons, soldiers could easily have raked the "captured" freight from locomotive to caboose.

Facing bayonets and two Gatling guns, the Galvinites—who possessed nothing more lethal than sticks and pocketknives—needed little encouragement to leave the cars. An elderly pilgrim quipped to a comrade, "When the officer in the name of the state asked us to leave I had respect for the great state of Ohio and got off."

"Yes," responded a brawny Irish lad. "Did you see those Gatling guns pointed at us? Well, I had too much respect for them to stay any longer." The people of Mount Sterling raised the $45 fare required to haul Galvin's army to Columbus, and the Ohio episode ended with a whimper. McKinley kept the respect of the state's business and labor leaders, and newspapers all over the country praised his resoluteness.[13]

A considerably more complex saga of train piracy unfolded near Portland. The local contingent of Coxey's army was led by S. L. Scheffler, a short, thickset, dark-complexioned man. The four ex-soldiers who served as drillmasters imposed military discipline on the troops.

Those who imagined that Scheffler's men were mostly jobless loggers were no doubt surprised to learn that among the 500 troops were 14 watchmakers and jewelers, 37 clerks and bookkeepers, 40 machinists, 12 engineers, 7 tailors, 6 bakers, 11 professional cooks, 25 professional waiters, 3 bookbinders, and 13 former shopkeepers. Scheffler himself was a jobless stonemason. Their demands were similar to those of other western contingents: primarily the free and unlimited coinage of silver that they believed held the key to prosperity.

Linking Portland, the largest and most important city in the Pacific Northwest, to Omaha and Kansas City was the Union Pacific Railway, which by late April had already earned an advanced degree in Coxey studies. Recent experience with Kelley's men made it apprehensive about Scheffler's growing numbers. A company official in Oregon warned his superiors that Portland was doing nothing for the men camped near its freight yards, and "they are a hungry mob. What action shall I take?" The advice from headquarters was to call on United States marshals and invoke the aid of the courts.[14]

Blocked by an injunction and despairing of ever getting a free ride out of Portland, Scheffler marched his army twenty miles east to

Troutdale, a village at the foot of the Cascade Mountains, where he hoped it might be easier to secure rail transportation. The townspeople did their best to accommodate the visitors, but a local meat company, fearing a raid by five hundred half-starved vagabonds, wired Sheriff Penumbra Kelly for protection. Kelly in turn requested that Governor Sylvester Pennoyer provide state troops, but Oregon's chief executive curtly refused. It was a civil and not a military matter, he claimed. Scheffler's men, meanwhile, slept in livery stables and barns and talked openly of imitating Hogan's railroaders in Montana.

On Saturday morning, April 28, members of Oregon's industrial army brazenly appropriated the locomotive from a special train that was carrying the Union Pacific's general manager, coupled it to a string of boxcars, and headed east through the serpentine gorge of the Columbia River. Governor Pennoyer, a onetime Democrat now running for the United States Senate as a Populist, refused to lift a finger to recapture the runaways. United States marshal Henry C. Grady stood by in Troutdale, unable to do a thing except wire United States Attorney General Richard Olney for help while he awaited a special train rushed out from Portland.

The Union Pacific cleared the right-of-way for the pirated train as it thundered through the Cascade Mountains and across the arid country of eastern Oregon. Behind, and closing the gap with each passing mile, was Marshal Grady's special. The chase lasted for 120 miles and eight hours, ending only when the runaways slowed for the hamlet of Arlington, where 122 well-armed United States cavalrymen from Fort Walla Walla surprised and overwhelmed them. The surrender was peaceable.[15]

The captives were given water but no food, and by 10:30 that night they were on the move once again. Much to their distress, their jailers took them back to Portland. There, fifty prisoners designated as leaders were taken to the county jail, while the rank and file were confined to a makeshift prison camp in the Union Pacific yards. Thousands of Portlanders brought them food and gifts, and a crowd of 1,500 people gathered opposite the jail to hear to a Populist orator. Someone raised the cry, "Take them from the police," but no one acted on that advice. The noisy crowd then gave three cheers for Governor Pennoyer, a graduate of Harvard Law School, as "one of us."

On the afternoon of April 30, Judge Charles B. Bellinger, a Cleveland appointee, released the prisoners when they apologized for failing to heed his injunction and promised to obey it in the future. The judge then ordered that each man be furnished with supper. Bellinger and the other federal judges who issued blanket injunctions to discourage the Coxeyites from stealing trains were legal pioneers. They had no clear precedent to guide them, and they were not sure where their actions would ultimately lead; but in the short run most Oregonians applauded Bellinger's leniency as the best course.[16]

The night of Bellinger's decision, three thousand men and about a hundred women staged an enormous parade to show their continued support for Scheffler and his men. With brass bands and banners, they marched from the Union Pacific yards through downtown Portland, shouting, "Down with the marshals and up with the Coxeyites!" Over and over they cheered the names of Pennoyer and Bellinger. For conservatives all over the United States, Pennoyer and Governors Davis Waite of Colorado and Lorenzo D. Lewelling of Kansas were symbols of irresponsibility in state government and a prime reason why federal authorities should intervene to crush Coxey's legions in the West.[17]

While Pennoyer continued his senatorial campaign, Portland's Coxeyites resolutely started for Capitol Hill once again. During the first week of May, they quietly slipped out of town in small bands, climbing onto brakebeams and into empty boxcars at night. And because railwaymen ignored their illicit presence, the freeloaders assumed that the Union Pacific had tacitly agreed to help them reach Kansas City. In fact, Bellinger's leniency had surprised the railroad and put it on the defensive, but the Union Pacific also knew something about the decentralized system of American justice. As they rode east, the Coxeyites must soon pass into Idaho, the district of federal judge James H. Beatty; there the railroad would stand firm once again, protected by a new injunction and fresh squads of deputy marshals.[18]

All across southern Idaho the railroad dueled with the Coxeyites. The federal judiciary was allied with the Union Pacific, while a host of sympathizers from small-town Idaho who resented the power of the railroad backed the Coxeyites. Subject to considerable popular pressure, the company reversed itself several times—at one point even ignoring the freeloaders—before it concluded that the time had come for a showdown. The company ordered crews to sidetrack all trains carrying Coxeyites. Several hundred industrials thus found themselves isolated in tiny Montpelier, a railroad division point in the extreme southeastern corner of the state. Trapped in this sagebrush wasteland and fearful of running out of food, Scheffler's men forgot their promise to Judge Bellinger. With the connivance of the townspeople—including a local constable and deputy sheriff—they stole two trains. Those who broke federal law saw no irony in their proud display of Old Glory as they chugged east into Wyoming.

Neither trainload of Coxeyites got any closer to Capitol Hill than Green River, a railroad town in western Wyoming, and they arrived there only as prisoners of Uncle Sam after being surprised and taken captive by federal marshals and soldiers hurried west from Fort Russell, near Cheyenne. After considerable deliberation about what to do with so many troublemakers, federal officials returned them to Boise, five hundred miles west, under heavy guard.

Even as everyone speculated what Judge Beatty would do with the nearly two hundred prisoners, incidents of train piracy multiplied throughout the West. Most were variations on a familiar theme: a bankrupt railroad applied to the federal court for an injunction, Commonwealers defied it (often with the aid of railroad workers and other sympathizers), and a posse of poorly trained deputy United States marshals chased after them, often with assistance from the United States Army.

The farcical struggle with the Coxey bands did nothing to enhance the image of the federal marshals, which in the 1890s was only slightly more impressive than that of the Keystone Cops a generation later. "This Coxey business is a harvest for the marshals," grumbled the *Portland Telegram*. "Under the pretense of guarding railway property they are looting the treasury to the tune of $1000 a day. In all candor this is an absolute waste of the public money, and ought not to be tolerated by the department of justice. In the first place there is no actual danger of the destruction of railway property, and if there was the marshals would be powerless to prevent it." [19]

In a notable incident near Yakima, Washington, federal deputies clashed with members of Jumbo Cantwell's Tacoma army making their way east in small bands. Violence erupted when lawmen attempted to eject the freeloaders from a Northern Pacific freight; two deputies were wounded, one very grievously. Some people blamed the shooting on Cantwell's men, but the marshal, who thought he was on his deathbed, swore that he was shot by a fellow deputy who panicked.[20]

With the federal deputies held in contempt by so many people, Attorney General Olney and various railroad leaders concluded that only firm action by the courts would discourage the train pirates. But by mid-May no one had dared do much more than administer a collective slap on the wrist (as Judge Bellinger had done in Oregon) or send a few ringleaders to jail and free the others (as Judge Knowles had done in Montana).[21]

Another question yet to be answered was what could be done to stop Coxeyites from commandeering trains on those railroads not in the hands of federal courts. The financially sound Southern Pacific, for example, had muddled through confrontations in Texas and Utah; but no clear precedent was established until John Sherman Sanders's army of Rocky Mountain metal miners stole a Missouri Pacific train in Pueblo, Colorado, in mid-May. Steaming east across the plains into Kansas, they ran a gauntlet of ripped-up or blocked track and empty water tanks. At one point they were reduced to laying temporary track and hauling water for their locomotive in dinner pails and tin cups. It was an episode similar to that of Hogan's army in Montana, except that initially no United States marshals dogged Sanders's heels. The still-solvent Missouri Pacific could not claim the protection of the federal courts.

Railroad attorneys sent a message to Kansas Governor Lewelling asking for help in recovering stolen property. Several hours later, Lewelling responded that he had no information that county peace officers had failed and therefore did not believe the situation warranted his calling out the state militia.[22]

It is hard to imagine two states in which Coxeyites could have expected more support than in Colorado and Kansas. Both were hotbeds of Populism, and both had governors sympathetic to Coxeyism. Only a few weeks earlier, Lewelling had described the Coxey movement as "a spontaneous uprising of the people. It is more than a petition, it is an earnest and vigorous protest against the injustice and tyranny of the age." In a famous circular issued the previous fall, Lewelling had ordered county sheriffs not to arrest people in Kansas for vagrancy. The governor noted that he himself had been a tramp in Chicago in 1865.[23]

Another Kansan, Mary Elizabeth Lease, a nationally recognized proponent of Populism, addressed a Coxey rally in Topeka and compared the march to the Crusades. Of the two, though, she believed that the Coxey movement was more important: "The crusades had their inception in mere sentiment; the Coxey movement is a struggle for very existence." Lease went on to blame the old parties for the trouble, adding, "I want to tell you that we've never had a government of the people. At best, we have had but a male oligarchy." Moreover, she asserted that "almost every railroad had stolen from the people represented by the industrial armies, and thieves cannot expect sympathy if the owners recover stolen property."[24]

After failing to receive assistance from Governor Lewelling or the federal court in Denver, Missouri Pacific attorneys pursued an idea that had been floating around in legal circles and was being especially promoted by Attorney General Olney: if Coxeyites blocked passage of the United States mail, they were committing a federal offense, even if the railroad was not in receivership. Thus, even though Sanders and his men were careful to take sidings so as not to delay trains carrying the mail, Missouri Pacific attorneys persuaded a federal judge in Kansas to issue a warrant for their arrest.[25]

At Scott City, Kansas, on the afternoon of May 10, the 220-mile adventure ended abruptly. When they learned that the track had been torn up east of town, Sanders's men surrendered peaceably to a posse of federal marshals. (Trackbuilding had consumed nearly twelve of their twenty-four hours on the road.) Sanders remained confident that his men would ultimately reach Capitol Hill, but he realized that in the present situation the odds were against them. While his men pitched camp on the prairie at the edge of town and enjoyed a supper furnished by local sympathizers, Sanders accepted an invitation from his former adversary, superintendent H. G. Clark, to join Clark for dinner in his private car. Unfortunately, their conversation was not recorded.[26]

Later that evening a train of five coaches arrived to take the prisoners to Topeka. As the train rolled east through the night toward the Kansas capital, the prisoners were all in good spirits. "How far is Topeka from Kansas City?" one of them asked another. When he was told it was less than seventy miles, wild rejoicing filled the coach. "Why, gee whiz," exclaimed one prisoner. "We can walk that in a day, and then if we can't do no better we can float down the old Missouri."

Rolling through the night, the special train reached Topeka the following morning, where an enormous crowd was on hand to greet the prisoners. The men stuck their heads out of the coach windows to talk with their admirers, who included some of the state's officials. Petite Annie Diggs, who had ridden at the head of Coxey's army down Pennsylvania Avenue, was there, too. She stood on tiptoe, and one prisoner nearly fell out a window trying to shake her small hand. Onlookers called Sanders out on the rear platform to have his picture taken. The people of Topeka brought two bushels of cookies, dishpans full of bread, and plugs of chewing tobacco, which they handed through the windows to the prisoners.

The former adjutant general of Kansas, A. A. Artz, informed Sanders that he had a force of sympathizers ready to help if needed. Sanders's response was, "We are not very scared, I can tell you that."

Governor Lewelling provided fifty tents, enabling the visitors to pitch camp in the railway yards. From any angle it was an odd sort of prison. Citizens were allowed inside, and nearly two thousand came to visit or bring donations of food. Everyone was in good humor. "We are very much obliged to Uncle Sam for helping us this far on our journey, providing us with comfortable cars, and keeping us from hunger," Sanders told his many sympathizers. Presumably the prisoners could have escaped easily, but only a few desired to.

No one seemed to know what to do with Sanders's army once it was in custody. A Denver judge who had earlier declined to issue an injunction stopping the men in Colorado stubbornly refused to see how a train of empty coal cars was in any way connected with the United States mail. The *Rocky Mountain News* argued that Sanders and his men had not committed criminal trespass, because they had not removed the train from railroad property. Furthermore, "if mail trains were delayed, it was because the company ditched engines across the track to intercept Sanders and tore up the rails in places for the same purpose. . . . Those who obstructed the mail were the agents of the Missouri Pacific company; and they cannot saddle that offense upon Sanders." Perhaps, joked the Denver paper, the federal statute that made it a crime to walk on the grass could be extended to cover the prairies of Kansas. "If it does, then Sanders' career is ended."[27]

Federal authorities seemed in no hurry to test their new legal theory, for unlike cases of contempt, the question of whether Sanders and company had delayed the mails would be decided by a jury of their Kansas peers. Besides, if any or all of them escaped as individuals or in small groups, it would not bother the United States attorney for Kansas. As he explained to Olney, "My object ever since the arrest has been to disband and disorganize this body of men."[28]

Sanders's troops spent two carefree days in Topeka before lawmen took them further east by train to Leavenworth, on the Missouri River. There a hearing was conducted and a bond of $300 set for Sanders and $250 for each of the 350 men with him. Little else was done. For the next month the prisoners lived on the federal military reservation at Leavenworth, in tents pitched in a glen of shade trees and in old railway cars. The food that Uncle Sam furnished them was that of regular soldiers and not of military prisoners. The atmosphere was relaxed and friendly, as deputy marshals, soldiers, and Coxeyites fraternized with one another. The prisoners' two chief recreations were boxing and fishing. After Sanders was released on his own recognizance, he toured Kansas as a lecturer for the Populist party. He also found time to court the daughter of an official of the Kansas state prison in nearby Lansing, and they were later married.[29]

The case that did more than any other to break the back of the Coxey movement in the trans-Missouri West came to trial in Boise in late May. In it Judge Beatty established a clear precedent for his colleagues in other states to follow. Beatty, who looked upon Coxeyites as "deluded people" and believed that their "wild crusade" must be stopped, had several options open to him as he pondered what to do with Scheffler and his men. He might emulate Judge Bellinger by releasing them on a promise to steal no more rides. This plan had the virtue of keeping expenses down and solving the problem of how to imprison so many men. But Beatty made no secret of his intense disapproval of what Bellinger had done, which he believed was an irresponsible attempt to foist the unemployed of Oregon onto the people of Idaho.

Judge Knowles of Montana had adopted the course of sending the ringleaders to jail and freeing the rank and file, and Beatty might do likewise. Or he might take the radical step of jailing the whole lot; but that was impossible unless he found somewhere large enough to confine so many prisoners, and no such place existed in sparsely populated Idaho. The Union Pacific and Attorney General Olney pressured Beatty to crush the movement by imprisoning all the men.[30]

The trial opened in Boise on May 28. For the next several days, Beatty listened carefully to each Coxeyite's tale of woe. Periodically releasing a few defendants for lack of evidence, he gave every indication that he was being scrupulously fair. The decision that he announced on June 5, however, took supporters of the petition in boots by surprise.

Beatty labeled the movement a conspiracy, meaning that each individual was responsible for anything said or done by anyone else to carry out the objectives of the conspiracy. He admitted that the Coxey movement doubtless contained good men, but during the trial he had seen too many faces "which bore the indelible stamp of the criminal." He thus found every defendant guilty of contempt of court, privates as well as generals.

Beatty then explained how he had solved the problem of confining so many prisoners. He distributed a few leaders among county jails, but most ingenious was his plan to confine the rank and file Coxyites in a special prison that deputy United States marshals were to construct and operate. It would be located in the sagebrush wilderness where the Union Pacific crossed the Snake River from Oregon into Idaho, not far from Farewell Bend, where the old Oregon Trail left the river.

Beatty chose the locale for reasons practical, symbolic, and perhaps even psychological. He registered his disapproval of the actions of his Oregon colleague by sending the prisoners as far west in Idaho and as close to Judge Bellinger's district as possible. He also located the camp where it was most likely to discourage additional Coxeyites from entering Idaho from Oregon. (It was rumored that as many as three thousand industrials planned to start east from Portland after they voted in Oregon's early June election.) Summarizing his plan to Attorney General Olney, Beatty explained, "I get them started *back* instead of *forward* and hope to continue them westward to their place of starting."[31]

On June 12 the prisoners were taken by boxcar to the Snake River confinement, which some called "Camp Despair," and for good reason. Except for the bridge and the railway line that ran across it, the depressing wasteland of sand and sage was devoid of all signs of human habitation. Crushed by the bleakness of confinement and the hopelessness of their cause, many Coxeyites sank into apathy and resignation. Others, burning with resentment, outrage, and a determination to escape, attacked deputies and turned on their former comrades. No one, however, tried to float out on the Snake River, for to the north it plunged through the rugged and forbidding Hells Canyon, the deepest gorge on the North American continent.

Beatty released the Coxeyites in small groups, until on September 1 he freed the last man. The Union Pacific dutifully transported them to Portland, although it later got the federal government to pay for this and other services that the railroad supposedly rendered without charge as its contribution to the "Coxeyite war."[32]

The suppression of Coxey's army in Idaho was only one act in a nationwide drama, but it was an important act. Without question, Judge Beatty's example inspired other courts to follow suit. In Kansas the *Leavenworth Times* took note of what Beatty had done and predicted that Sanders's army, soon to be tried, would also feel the full weight of the law. Indeed, that proved correct, for a jury took less than an hour to find Sanders's men guilty of obstructing the United States mail. The presiding judge sentenced them to pay fines and to serve terms of varying length in county jails throughout the state. Taking a cue from his Idaho colleague, the judge agreed to free them in small groups after they had served eight to eighteen days of their terms. In the words of the state's federal attorney, they were an "utterly broken and demolished band." Sanders proposed to reassemble his army in Saint Louis, but he never did.[33]

Few people other than the Coxeyites and their friends asked

whether they had been given fair trials, particularly in the contempt of court cases. Yet an incident in Utah strongly suggested that the courts had allowed themselves to become tools of the railroads.

The background to the Utah case was familiar enough. Several hundred men formed an army in Salt Lake City under the leadership of a young carpenter, Henry Carter, having been encouraged by newspaper accounts of Kelley's triumphs in Omaha, especially the headline that read, "Had Pies for Breakfast." The way east proved so difficult that on May 13 a portion of Carter's army commandeered a Union Pacific freight near Provo. The train, however, traveled only a short distance before it derailed. Federal marshals arrested the lot for contempt of court. After hearing the case of Carter and several of his followers, Judge S. A. Merritt of the Utah Supreme Court fined the general $100 and sentenced him to five days in jail. Sixteen others received lesser terms.

A week later, a curious document came to light. The *Salt Lake Tribune*, no friend of the Coxey movement, published the incriminating transcript of a telegram sent by a colleague, Judge H. W. Smith, to Merritt before he had heard Carter's case: "It is important that they be found guilty and held for contempt because we have detectives among them, and they intend to carry things with a high hand if their leaders are discharged, and it seems to be the understanding among them that they will disband if their leaders are held."

Merritt wired back to Smith, "I appreciate the situation and concur in your reasoning." When the story broke, Smith denied he had sent the message, but Merritt confirmed that it was genuine. It was a case of "judicial infamy," stormed the Populists, "the most damning evidence yet brought out, showing the corruption of the courts." For some people, though, the quality of justice was less important than the fact that the court took a firm stand against the train pirates.[34]

The wholesale imprisonment of Coxeyites in the West during May and June, far more than the May 1 debacle on the Capitol steps, drained all life from the petition in boots. As long as the crusaders encamped in the nation's capital believed that massive reinforcements would soon arrive from the West, they remained confident of ultimate victory. But men like Judge Beatty blocked and scattered the westerners by a campaign of legal harassment that had overtones of psychological warfare. "The vigorous action taken by the United States courts to arrest and punish the violators of law," summarized the *Report of the Secretary of War*, "and the promptness and intelligence with which troops executed their instructions, soon disintegrated and scattered the fragments of these so-called industrial armies."[35]

CHAPTER 13

I admire the East, but I do not
love it; I love the South, but I do
not admire it; and the West, I
neither love nor admire, though
it entertains me immensely.

Sue Harry Clagett,
"Sectional Traits of Americans,"
West Shore 12 (December 1886)

Coxey's Western Boatmen

Barred from the trains by bayonets and injunctions, and inspired by
the example of Kelley's navy, Coxeyites from Colorado and Montana
unintentionally undertook to write an epilogue to the familiar sagas
of exploration and adventure on the rivers of the West. Their voyages,
if successful, would be far longer and far more dangerous than Kelley's
trip from Des Moines to Saint Louis. The chastened but still determined followers of train pirate James Hogan proposed to boat from
central Montana to western Pennsylvania, only a few hundred miles
from their destination. The nearly four-thousand-mile voyage was
not impossible, but scoffers thought that the miners who fancied
themselves boatmen might just as well plan a trip to Mars. For the
Commonwealers from Denver, the highway to the East would be
the strange and unpredictable Platte, a river that during certain seasons was little more than a braided ribbon of thin mud flowing slug-
gishly around innumerable islands of cottonwoods and willows.

Since mid-1893, the metropolis of Denver had been a powerful
magnet attracting unemployed Colorado silver miners and their
families, as well as the jobless from throughout the West. It therefore
seemed an ideal place to recruit a troop of Commonwealers. But Bert
Hamilton, who initiated the local movement in late March, was
hardly the man to do it. When he appeared at the weekly meeting of

Denver's unemployed and called for volunteers to join his "Free Silver Legion," fifty people expressed an interest. Most potential recruits held back, though, seemingly reluctant to cast their lot with the mild-mannered, earnest young man.

At an organizational meeting held a few days later on the county courthouse steps, Hamilton found seventy curious men awaiting him. That proved to be the high point of the gathering. Mounting a bench, the would-be general called out the names of several military men. None answered. "Is there a Grand Army man here, then?" Silence. "Well, we must have an officer, men, if we are going to be organized."

The crowd began to tease Hamilton. Someone offered the name of a deputy sheriff who was standing nearby. He declined. "Then we'll get you a game warden," the crowd laughed. Angered and flustered, the hapless general challenged everyone interested in going to Washington to assemble on the sidewalk. He found himself heading an army of seven men and a crop-eared bulldog. "You fellows who think I'm crazy don't know what you are talking about," Hamilton responded to his hecklers. "I've been offered free transportation for everyone with us from here to Washington and you who want to go with us fall in." His ranks swelled to thirteen; the bulldog dropped out.

Hamilton appointed recruiting officers and promised to make captains of them if they did well. One soon claimed to have fifty men ready to march, but a rival trumped him by rounding up a company of sixty hoboes and barflies. The response of the nattily attired general was to refuse any recruit who could not produce a pair of overalls, the badge of a genuine workman.

Incongruity should have been Hamilton's middle name as he bungled along from one crisis to another. He promised his followers that people sympathetic to the crusade would feed them, but added as an afterthought, "If they don't, they will give us all we need to have us move on." When negotiations for a Santa Fe train broke down, he shot back, "I warn you that I will not be responsible for any trouble on Saturday." Only a short time earlier he had assured everyone that his was an army of peace.

On the eve of his proposed departure on April Fools' Day, Hamilton was speaking to his forty-man army when a lawman appeared and asked for him. The general thought he wished to sign up. The visitor modestly declined, then arrested Hamilton for petty larceny, charging him with having stolen a suit of clothes and other articles from his landlady. Hamilton's followers angrily protested that local plutocrats had framed him (it actually turned out to be a case of unrequited love). But before he could rejoin them, a rumor that lawmen were about to corral the whole lot sent the panicked remnant of the Silver Legion scurrying south to Colorado Springs. Two days later they nearly disbanded when Hamilton failed to show up after his release from jail.[1]

A few diehards chose a new general, William Grayson, a man with a Scottish accent who claimed once to have been in the British army. That, at least, was an improvement over Hamilton. He led the remnant back to Denver, where he reorganized it and recruited a new following. "I find many idle working men in Denver who would be willing and glad to enlist if they felt that their leader was in earnest and would stand by them." Unlike Hamilton, he did not try to create false hopes. Grayson's message was that because they all had to die sometime, they might as well die a sudden death in Washington as a lingering one in Denver.

The arrival of Kelley's army in Ogden, which created a great deal more interest in the Coxey movement than when Hamilton first proposed his Silver Legion, aided Grayson's recruitment. Moreover, Governor Davis Waite and Denver authorities now encouraged the growth of the Grayson's contingent so that it could join Kelley's overlanders as they headed east.

When Grayson announced that his men would take a train east, an old sailor from Scotland piped up and said they should raft down the Platte instead: "I will pilot yees safely over the bloomin' sand bars." But the one hundred troops were not yet desperate enough to become mariners. On April 17 they went to the yards of the Burlington and Missouri River Railroad and climbed aboard empty boxcars to begin the journey to Capitol Hill.

The yardmaster played a cruel prank on the freeloaders by having their cars shuttled from track to track for several hours until they realized they were going nowhere. Reluctantly, they climbed out and headed up busy Larimer Street in a blinding snowstorm. Not a dozen of them had overcoats, and none had overshoes. Friendly saloonkeepers took pity on them and invited Grayson and his men in for free drinks and food. After this pause for nourishment, they made their way to the Union Pacific yards, where they spent the night in the roundhouse. The next morning they climbed aboard some empty furniture cars that were supposedly destined for Julesburg in northeastern Colorado, where the Denver branch intersected the Union Pacific main line from Ogden to Omaha. There they hoped to have better luck getting train rides, but meanwhile they waited and waited.

Growing hungry, they sent their financial secretary, Barney Hudson, to buy whatever food he could afford. When he did not return, bricklayer Jack O'Hara set out to learn why. He found Hudson in a saloon in the Haymarket, "indulging in a game of craps which was receiving financial support from the trust funds of the army." The treasurer had gambled away the army's last penny. But the men generously forgave the miscreant and readmitted him into their ranks.

When the train was ready to leave, the yardmaster sprang a surprise: crewmen cut it in two, dropped out the carloads of Coxeyites, reconnected the train, and sent it on its way before the freeloaders realized what had happened. Climbing out of the cars, the unlucky pilgrims ate handfuls of snow to dull their gnawing stomachs and cursed the railroad's dirty tricks. "We are going out on a train and will remain right in this yard until we are hauled out," said Grayson. "We have learned one trick, and I suppose by the time we get to Washington we will all be good railroaders."

It was brave but empty talk. The men milled about the yards all morning. That afternoon they gave up and headed east across the rolling, grassy prairie on foot, outcasts from industrial civilization and strangers in the solitary land once labeled the Great American Desert.[2]

Hard luck continued to dog the Denver Coxeyites. Grayson's men seemed to inch along unless they were given a lift in a farmer's wagon, and they were never certain about meals. They ended up following an arc-shaped course that took them north to Nebraska then southeast across Kansas toward the Missouri River. They hoped to link up with Sanders's men in Leavenworth, build a raft, and float down the Big Muddy.

In their wanderings the men changed leaders three times. They deposed Grayson near Julesburg and elected Barney Hudson, the man who had gambled away their money in Denver. When he got drunk in North Platte, Nebraska, and landed in jail, they elected a new general, Henry Bennett, an unemployed painter and paper-hanger. A soft-spoken native of Virginia, he was well liked by all. Bennett got them to Kansas City but then decamped with their trea-sury, $103 in donations from Kansas Populists. Few Coxeyites suf-fered a greater variety of troubles than the Coloradans, but the worst was yet to come.[3]

When Grayson's pilgrims left the Colorado capital in mid-April, interest in the Coxey crusade remained so strong that a third army soon formed there. This was the largest of the lot, numbering more than a thousand men. Fostering its growth was the local Home Guard unit that organized in late April. Its purpose was to provide moral support and financial aid to Coxeyites on the road and unite the movement's many supporters in Denver.

Home Guards, together with a spin-off organization, the Ladies' Relief Corps, and organized labor, claimed to represent ten thou-sand Coxey sympathizers in the Colorado capital. When leaders of the Commonweal were arrested in Washington, the Home Guards staged a mass meeting and wired a protest to their Populist con-gressman, Lafayette Pence, demanding the prisoners' immediate re-lease. Throughout May their weekly meetings noticeably heightened local interest in the Coxey crusade. Members occasionally marched through the streets of Denver with banners reading "Hurrah for Coxey," "Keep off the Grass," and "Call us when you need us." Dur-ing one of their rallies, they added a banner with the words, "Adam and Eve walked on the Grass and Had Plenty to Eat."[4]

While Denver's Home Guards agitated, hundreds more unem-ployed people arrived in the city every day, nearly three hundred more on the morning of May 28 alone. Some of these were members of still another California contingent; others were part of Henry Carter's army making their way east from Salt Lake City, having al-ready experienced terrible hardships crossing the desert sands of eastern Utah. The Colorado militia loaned them cooking utensils and several hundred tents, and soon a little city sprang up on the banks of the South Platte in Denver's River Front Park. Even when there were no more tents, the unemployed kept arriving, until the population of River Front Park neared fifteen hundred. It became the largest encampment of Coxeyites in the United States.

Even though sentries armed with canes patrolled the campground to maintain law and order and keep out genuine hoboes—defined as those who refused to bathe in the river—Denver's conservatives grew alarmed. To them the "white city" in River Front Park was nothing more than a glorified hobo camp where "unwashed men and women revel in debauchery during the night and scour the city during the day for whatever they can steal or beg." They were angry with Governor Waite for inviting the indigents, particularly when railroads going east refused to haul them out. The Burlington and Missouri even threatened to pull up a few bridges if necessary to stop their eastward movement by rail.

The generous meals provided by the Home Guards nearly proved to be the movement's undoing. "We are in no particular hurry," explained one resident of River Front Park, who had almost forgotten his mission to Washington. And as still more people poured into the tent city, even the Home Guards grew alarmed at the prospect of having to feed all the unemployed of the West. As a consequence, contributions fell off sharply as the number of indigents increased. During the first week of June, the quality and quantity of the rations diminished so noticeably that the residents of River Front Park were reduced to a diet that consisted of little more than bread and coffee. With the railroad yards heavily guarded, there seemed to be no way for the hungry visitors to leave the city.[5]

It was then that someone revived the idea of boating down the Platte. A Montana contingent had proposed to raft down the Missouri River; might not the Denver Coxeyites join them where the rivers met south of Omaha? The Denver Chamber of Commerce agreed to provision them for the voyage, and others promised materials to build the boats. In certain seasons a voyage across Colorado and Nebraska on the unpredictable Platte would have been impossible even in small boats, but recent heavy rains made the trip seem feasible. Scouts sent downstream by the Coxeyites reported that a flotilla of small boats should encounter no trouble.[6]

Three men who claimed to be shipbuilders offered advice and direction, and the Commonwealers pitched in to construct one hundred flat-bottomed boats similar in design to the mud scows of

Kelley's navy. In these they proposed to reach Kansas City, and optimists talked of reaching Pittsburgh. To raise money for their expedition, they charged onlookers fifteen cents and put on a show complete with bicycle races, a tug of war, baseball games, and a tightrope walker. The real attraction, though, was watching the boatbuilders. They worked in assembly-line fashion, some sawing planks, others hammering, and still others caulking the seams. They christened each scow with a name like *Down with the Rothschilds*, *Keep Off the Grass*, and *General Coxey*.

When one officer was questioned about the voyage, he replied with words that soon proved a classic of understatement: "We don't expect to have much of a picnic." He hoped to reach Kansas City in twelve days. A pilot boat would travel ahead to mark dangerous places with red flags, and the others would follow behind in single file. The Coxeyites even planned to take along a small letterpress and publish a daily newspaper. But some who inspected the scows closely had serious reservations. "The boats are not so formidable looking and they do not look any too seaworthy either," worried one reporter. They were built from material that to some seemed altogether too light and flimsy for a trip of any distance.

Men eager to begin the voyage refused to heed the warnings of onlookers that they would crash into hidden snags and fill the river with their lifeless bodies. "You are crazy," corrected a Coxeyite. "Why, I had the bottom of a boat drop out from under me in Lake Michigan and yet I'm here. Why do you suppose we are going to have steersmen?" The man who had survived Lake Michigan could see no reason to fear a river so shallow in places that a person could easily walk across.

The Coxeyites launched the first of their navy on June 4. Two days later an advance guard of 150 men set out for nearby Brighton. There they would wait for General Carter and the main body of troops, who would follow a day later. A few accidents marred the first day on the river, but none was serious. The little boats, however, did seem to have a design problem. In the water they proved as slippery as banana peels—or behaved like "angry curs," in the words of one observer. They had a disconcerting way of lurching out from under the crewmen, and it did not take much for a piling or half-submerged log to stave in their flimsy hulls.

The Platte proved far less placid than many a landlubber expected. Men who fell overboard had to fight to reach shore in the deceptively strong current, and some had to be rescued by the onlookers who had gathered to cheer them on. While many seemed to regard the dunkings as part of the fun, some Commonwealers who watched their comrades founder in the river were not amused, particularly those who could not swim. They protested that the scows were not safe. But their companions belittled their fears, claiming that those men had been planted by detectives who wanted to keep them in town so they could continue to earn money guarding the railway yards.

Carter and the majority of the sailors set out as planned. The current was as strong as the day before, but a very strong crosswind made the boats impossible to steer. The men in River Front Park who were busily launching the scows with shouts of "On to Washington!" did not realize the disaster that overtook the crafts as they passed from view. In narrow places the river resembled a millrace, as the water shot by at fifteen to twenty miles an hour. A boat improperly guided was bound to overturn or smash into a piling.

One scow with five men aboard, none of whom could swim, careened into the pilings of a railroad bridge. The lucky ones screamed for help, while an unconscious companion sank beneath the surface and disappeared. Onlookers rushed to save them, but the swift current dragged the men under and lodged them fast in a thicket of submerged branches and logs. As rescuers tried to chop one man free, the body of another washed up on a sandbar in midstream. Several more bodies were reported at a bridge nearby. Another peril hidden just below the surface was the barbed wire fencing that was used to keep cattle from escaping during low water. These caught and ripped scows apart and ensnared their struggling occupants. Many survivors remained trapped on sandbars, while others clutched the branches of half-submerged trees.

Into Brighton stumbled hundreds of bedraggled men. The townspeople opened their homes, barns, and even their jail to them. At the local post office, survivors bought cards to let loved ones know they were safe. Their messages typically began, "My Dear Wife and Children. . . ." The writers then paused for lack of words to describe the horrors of the Platte. After a hearty breakfast furnished by the towns-people, they began again the work of rescue.

Rumors poured in. Someone reported seeing a man wearing a blue coat with epaulets disappear beneath the water. That could only have been General Carter, and the *Salt Lake Tribune* carried the sad news to his wife and little children. One of the first bodies recovered was that of Charles Duplessis, a fifty-three-year-old carpenter. After placing him in a pine box, the men scoured a nearby field for a bouquet of spring flowers to honor their dead comrade. Two hundred fifty rough and rugged men, many with their clothes still wet from the river, stood around the coffin as a minister conducted the funeral. They followed the body to the gravesite, then returned to camp, expecting that many other funerals would soon follow.

An officer reported that the body of a black man named Roberts had been found. But hardly had the expressions of regret ended than in walked a healthy Roberts. General Carter, too, turned up unhurt. The search for missing comrades went on. Some rumors placed the death toll as high as forty, but in the end only six bodies were ever found. Had the swift current carried others downstream? "Only God," lamented the *Rocky Mountain News*, "will ever know how many of the Coxeyites were drowned in the Platte last night."[7]

Some of the survivors angrily blamed the debacle on the railroads that had forced them onto the river in the first place. Others censured the leader of the advance guard, a General Higginson, for poor planning; some even claimed that he was "too busy guzzling beer" to do his job. He was demoted to quartermaster general. All agreed, however, that the immediate cause of the disaster was the poor design of the boats themselves, which were incapable of carrying many crewmen.

A reporter asked a county official if the Coxeyites would be allowed to continue in the boats. "Allow them?" he snorted. "Why, man, you could not drive them into those boats again with shotguns." Sad as the disaster was, Denver officials were so determined to prevent the survivors from returning there that they threatened to arrest anyone who tried to do so. Members of the Home Guard collected donations of food for those who elected to continue to Washington, and almost four hundred did, though not necessarily by boat.[8]

One hundred fifty very determined crusaders managed to swallow their fears of the "hitherto unnavigable" Platte and prepared to set out once again in their flimsy scows, but with far fewer occupants in each boat than before. As an added precaution, before leaving Brighton they compelled each man to undress while officers minutely examined his clothes for any signs that he was a deputy. Half a dozen suspicious men were drummed out of camp before the rest cast off. Five weeks later, a remnant of twenty-seven men floated into Kansas City. The record of what happened to them after that is blank.

The majority of the survivors at Brighton abandoned the treacherous Platte for the more predictable hazards of the Union Pacific right-of-way. Denver authorities and Home Guards lured them away from the Colorado capital by forwarding a large donation of food to Fort Morgan. When the Coxeyites arrived there, however, they were angered to learn that the carload of provisions had been sent to Julesburg, a hundred miles farther ahead on the Nebraska border.

At Julesburg they got their promised food, but there they also commandeered a locomotive and a string of boxcars. In their haste to get away, they ran the train through an open switch and off the track. Rather than take time to rerail the locomotive and risk capture, most of the pilgrims hastened across the state line into Nebraska. After marching to Ogallala, they decided by majority vote to commandeer another train. The Union Pacific had anticipated this move and had a special train waiting in Omaha to speed a hundred deputy marshals west on orders from Nebraska's federal judge, Elmer S. Dundy. True to form, the autocratic Dundy deputized crewmen on several passenger trains so that they might arrest any Coxeyites who attempted to steal aboard.

Dundy ordered the ringleaders brought to Omaha for a trial; but with permission from Attorney General Richard Olney and the War Department, he directed that the other prisoners be sealed in boxcars and taken west under guard to Fort Sidney, which had been abandoned only days earlier by the United States Army. In that isolated place he held court.

It was a highly unprecedented and heavy-handed move: "Judge Dundy having been given the Union Pacific road has now been handed an army post in which to confine the Coxeys who try to steal his trains," complained the *Omaha World-Herald*. But public opinion never concerned Dundy. The Coxeyites were charged with contempt of court and, as an extra precaution, obstructing the mails. They were found guilty, although some were never quite sure of what. Dundy, however, never formally sentenced the Coxeyites to prison but simply confined them to the fort for several more weeks. Following the example of his Idaho colleague, he released members of the broken and dispirited army during the course of the next month in groups of five, each man being provided with rations enough for two days.[9]

When Montana's federal judge Hiram Knowles freed the rank-and-file of Hogan's army, the city of Helena found itself providing for the contingent, which remained committed to visiting Capitol Hill. After examining several options, including an overland walk to Washington, the Montana capital decided to launch Hogan's men on a mission down the Missouri. The city purchased wood for building scows, hired a master boatwright to oversee construction, and restocked the army's commissary. It also paid the men's rail fare to Fort Benton.[10]

For almost a week several hundred would-be sailors hammered together ten sturdy flatboats under the expert direction of William Sprague, a man wise to the often brutal ways of the Missouri. Besides the flagship *Montana*, the *Hogan*, and the *Free Silver*, vessels were named for seven Montana cities that had befriended the Coxeyites. Following a farewell parade through Fort Benton on June 4, the Hoganites finally launched their vessels on June 5.

A month later the flotilla reached Omaha without the loss of a single life, though the Hoganites had weathered a harrowing journey down the treacherous river. When they finally climbed ashore, they faced a most disappointing welcome. Actually, it was hardly a welcome at all. On the shore a dozen policemen and six or seven sympathizers waved lanterns to guide them to a dubious camping spot circumscribed by a railroad bridge, a garbage dump, and a large sewer. Where were the crowds that had welcomed Kelley? Where were the pies?

Life looked a little rosier the next morning. Omaha's Central Labor Council, which explained that it had not greeted the voyagers at the waterfront because it expected them the next morning, arranged a public rally to demonstrate the city's support. The Central Labor

Council collected gifts of potatoes, crackers, onions, eggs, sugar, coffee, and flour from businessmen. County commissioners contributed $225 worth of supplies, including 100 bars of soap, and individual members of the city council gave $53 in cash. Local merchants provided fresh bunting to spruce up the navy for the Fourth of July. Each man also got a shiny new badge. But it was the last big handout that the protest navy received.

Their Omaha stay taught Hogan's sailors an important lesson in human psychology. As a rule, the first army to visit a community got the apple pie; all others got leftovers—or nothing at all. Little of the movement's novelty value remained after an initial visit. Thus it must have sobered Hogan's men to know that they would be the second, third, or, in some cases, fourth Coxey contingent to visit the remaining cities on their itinerary. In fact, because Kelley's men had already traveled the water route from Saint Louis most of the way to Pittsburgh, Hogan's flotilla would likely attract little press coverage in the Mississippi and Ohio valleys. News accounts of their adventure were already becoming scarce when they left Omaha. By that time the public was far more interested in the gigantic Pullman strike that radiated out from Chicago and caused the greatest railway tie-up that westerners had ever experienced.[11] As the sailors continued down the Missouri, they found donations of food increasingly rare.

When Hogan's navy finally arrived at Saint Louis during the last week of July, the men were half starved and wholly demoralized. The reform crusade had become a battle for survival. About the only group to give them any aid was the tiny Socialist Labor party. Its members held a public rally that netted $11.80, and they collected two dozen loaves of bread and a few bundles of old clothing from businessmen. Though one of the navy's leaders maintained that the men would still reach Washington before the snow flew, most sensed that their once-grand crusade was tottering toward collapse.[12]

Approximately 60 days and 2,670 miles from Fort Benton, life left the movement at Carondelet, on the south side of Saint Louis, but not before the men suffered one last disillusioning blow. After enduring several frustrating and unproductive days at Carondelet, the men convened a council to debate their fate and decided to let the crewmen of each boat decide the future for themselves. Five crews elected to proceed down the Mississippi to Cairo or New Orleans and from there travel overland to Washington. The remainder agreed to sell their boats, divide the proceeds, and separate for individual destinations. The sailors also decided to divide equally the navy's $435 treasury, most of the money being a recent gift from an anonymous Iowa philanthropist.

J. D. Sullivan, their treasurer, and two companions headed for town to get the necessary cash. The sailors waited for the three to return, until it became obvious that their crewmates had betrayed and abandoned them. Penniless and dispirited, Hogan's navy broke up. Singing a bitter version of a song entitled "He Never Came Back," a few men headed down the Mississippi. Others continued east toward Washington, but most apparently returned to Montana in "side-door Pullmans," better known as boxcars.[13]

As for Hogan himself, at about the time of the breakup, Judge Knowles released him from prison to take a job. Now that he had work, quipped Knowles, he hoped Hogan would stay away from railroading, especially the kind that got him in jail. Hogan received many congratulations from local supporters, although the navy that bore his name halfway across the continent was no more.

CHAPTER 14

We are not an agitative body, we
are a living, moving object lesson.
You can look at us and say there
is a condition and not a theory.

Charles T. Kelley, in *Ottumwa
Daily Courier*, May 16, 1894

Soldiers of Misfortune

As July 4 neared and Congress showed no inclination to pass Coxey's
bills, Carl Browne added the final touches to an Independence Day
melodrama that he hoped would draw public attention to the continued presence of the original band of Commonwealers in the
District of Columbia area. The performance was to be an act of
desperation.

To the steady beat of a fife and drum band, 371 Commonwealers
marched to Capitol Hill from their camp in the Maryland suburb
of Bladensburg. Several of them were barefoot; others wore only
ragged stockings to protect their feet from the hot, dusty streets of
Washington. At first glance the scene looked familiar, but first im-
pressions were deceptive; many things had changed since the veterans of Coxey's army had made their first assault on Capitol Hill two
months earlier. The crowds of onlookers had thinned noticeably,
one-third of the paraders were black, and the Commonweal as a
whole looked far more tattered than it had on May Day.

Leading the Commonwealers was the familiar figure of Oklahoma
Sam. Although Browne had planned the day's activities, he was conspicuously missing from the ranks. He was gone before the men
awoke, leaving word that he had business across the Potomac and
would rejoin them later in the day. It must have been important busi-

ness, for the showman was not one to miss any chance to get his name in the news.

No parade staged by Browne was complete without a goddess of some sort, and one rode on a milk-white steed at the head of the column. At first glance she resembled the Commonweal's original goddess in her patriotic costume of red, white, and blue bunting. Long hair of golden hue flowed out from under her liberty cap, but the Goddess of Liberty lacked Mamie Coxey's fine features. Sharp-eyed reporters noticed that her bare arms were muscular and tanned from exposure to the sun (something most women of the time religiously avoided) and that her heavily shrouded face was round and full and vaguely familiar. She was identified only as "Miss Gray."

Creaking along behind the goddess rolled the Car of Liberty, nothing more than the reincarnated panorama wagon decorated with a large American flag and Browne's latest caricatures. The marchers from a number of different regiments carried banners bearing a mixture of familiar slogans and new warnings to keep off the grass. A small detail of police provided an escort.

The procession halted at the white marble Peace monument just below Capitol Hill and a discreet distance from the now infamous grass. Fixing her eyes on the bronze figure of Liberty atop the Capitol dome and raising one hand aloft in a dramatic gesture, the goddess spoke in a hoarse, wheezy voice, invoking the names of Washington, Lafayette, and other heroes of the American Revolution. After "theeing" and "thouing" in a Quaker manner in sentences long and full of exclamations, she closed her rambling oration by raising both hands to heaven and shrieking, "Liberty is dead!" With that cry, she fell from her horse. Oklahoma Sam and two Commonwealers lifted her gently into the panorama wagon and closed the curtain. Moments later she was reincarnated as the familiar figure of Carl Browne, clad in his Buffalo Bill outfit but minus his beard. Inside lay the effigy of the Goddess of Liberty.

The crowd remained as quiet as that at a real funeral. A few onlookers exchanged remarks about Browne's appearance without his whiskers, and scattered catcalls mixed with cheering finally broke the awkward silence. The farce did succeed in returning the Coxey movement to prominence in the local papers, but only briefly and then as an object of ridicule. Except for coverage of their July 4 theatrics, Commonwealers continued to find themselves mostly ignored by the press and thus removed from public attention and concern.[1]

By early July, the Coxey movement as a whole had entered its final phase, a time marked by general public indifference to the men and their cause. Wire services stopped carrying news of Coxeyism. No one knew the exact whereabouts of the last of the big western armies headed for Washington, and except for the Commonwealers themselves and those living along the line of the march, no one really cared.[2]

Some of the Commonwealers, reduced to near starvation in their camp near Washington, continued to hope that a growing number of westerners in their ranks would frighten lawmakers into enacting Coxey's bills. In that hope, though, lay a supreme irony: the steady influx of westerners created intolerable strains within the Coxey camp and led to fights over food and a general breakdown of the spirit of community. Josiah Flynt Willard, whose special interest was the tramp in American life, had noted in late 1893 how migrants from the East and West seldom mixed and seldom got along: "The Easterners think the Western bretheren too rough and wild, while the latter think the former too tame." And Coxeyites, though they prided themselves on being a cut above the average hobo, exhibited the same regional prejudices, especially when the dwindling supply of edibles turned every day into a battle for survival.[3]

The problem of finding a suitable campsite near Capitol Hill had bedeviled the original band of Commonwealers during most of May. When at mid-month public health officials forced them to abandon "Camp Tyranny," the cleaned-up dump near downtown Washington that had been their home since May 1, a sympathizer offered a patch of sandy, tangled woodland in suburban Hyattsville, Maryland. The four hundred Commonweal veterans were unhappy about having to retreat from their hard-won post in the shadow of the Capitol, but they quickly cleared away the undergrowth and made the new site so livable that within a day or two they had time to read or play games.

All was not harmonious in Hyattsville, a tiny bedroom community populated mainly by employees of the federal government in nearby Washington and their families. The absence of male breadwinners during the day left Hyattsville largely in the hands of women, children, and shopkeepers, or so many residents claimed. Fearful that the Coxeyites would cause trouble while the menfolk were away, townspeople angrily condemned District of Columbia officials for exposing them to a reign of terror. Some even threatened to take the law into their own hands. But Browne was not looking for a fight, and scarcely had his men settled into their new home than he ordered them to move on, much to the relief of the civil servants of Hyattsville.

On to Bladensburg the Commonwealers moved, and there they remained while Coxey, Browne, and Jones served their time in jail. Army headquarters was in the venerable George Washington House, where the father of his country once spent a night and ate a meal. The veterans camped in back of the building, in a lot enclosed by a high fence. They rearranged their "He is Alive!" canvas wall into a zigzag line of pup tents, and those who could not be accommodated fashioned huts from grass and tree limbs. In the center of camp was a miniature park posted with a conspicuous warning to "Keep off the Grass." The men also laid out a baseball diamond, where each afternoon they played a spirited game. For some, the chief activity was fishing in a nearby stream to supplement their meager diet. In mid-June their leaders emerged from prison and returned to camp for a heroes' welcome. At this proof of loyalty, Coxey broke down and cried. One of the first things Browne did was to set up a printing press, and on June 28 he cranked out the first issue of *Carl's Camp Courier*.[4]

Suffering from a steadily dwindling supply of food, the camp found it increasingly difficult to accommodate the influx of westerners. Colonel Galvin and his regiment of nearly two hundred men arrived in mid-June, and then Fry and his men straggled into camp for the next two weeks. Every westerner brought with him a hearty appetite, a restless spirit, and numerous tales of hardship to enliven the evening campfires. The Galvinites, for example, reached Pittsburgh on tickets purchased by the trade unionists of Columbus and Wheeling, but they had hardly stepped from the coaches when they learned one of the harsh truths the Coxey movement taught: to the first arrivals belonged the spoils. The city that had taken a holiday to welcome Coxey and his Commonwealers was wholly indifferent to the

Galvin regiment. "I guess you won't get much sympathy in Pittsburgh," said a policeman there. "The best thing you can do is to move right along."[5]

Moving right along and subsisting on meager handouts was the story of Galvin's march across Pennsylvania. And it was much the same for Fry's men, who reached Washington after a three-month journey from Los Angeles. After Galvin's secession in Illinois, Fry's army had fragmented again in Indianapolis when two more regiments split off. Fry and his loyal followers spent much of May tramping through the rolling countryside of southern Indiana, seemingly in no great hurry to get to Cincinnati.

Reaching the Ohio River metropolis in Galvin's wake, Fry's army got only a tepid welcome from everyone but organized labor. When Coxey sent Fry a special commission appointing him commander-in-chief of the entire Commonweal during his stay in jail, union labor in Cincinnati purchased a railway ticket to speed the new leader to Washington. It also raised $400 to hire a towboat and barge to take his 276 followers up the Ohio River to Parkersburg, West Virginia. Breaking into small groups, they boarded Baltimore and Ohio freights to continue their odyssey across the mountains as best as they could.[6]

A majority of them reassembled ten days later in Cumberland, and from there they boated down the Chesapeake and Ohio Canal. On June 23 Fry rejoined his troops outside Washington and was warmly received. But if the 125 new arrivals expected anyone else to welcome them, they were doomed to disappointment. When they finally stumbled into the Commonweal's Bladensburg camp after a long hike across the District of Columbia, they found Browne not as eager to receive them as he professed. Although they were ravenously hungry, he directed them to a nearby camp maintained by the Galvinites, a miserable lot subsisting on little more than bread and water. Relations between the original Coxeyites and the newcomers from the West became so strained that in late June those who had marched across the continent with Galvin and Fry picked up their meager belongings and moved to a fresh campsite on the bank of the Potomac River opposite Washington, near Rosslyn, Virginia.[7]

It would be hard to say who suffered more during the final phase of the Coxey movement: the men encamped near Washington or those still making their way east. For the men in Kelley's navy, troubles multiplied after they reached Saint Louis. Two members drowned when an overloaded scow sank in the Mississippi, and the impetuous colonel from Sacramento, George Speed, sparked another row with Kelley. Speed and a band of about sixty seceders abandoned the main force and hurried east by stealing rides on freight cars. Alas, one of the railroads on their itinerary was in the hands of the federal court, so instead of reaching Washington ahead of Kelley, they were arrested for contempt and sentenced to an Illinois prison for several weeks.[8]

Also leaving Kelley's ranks in Saint Louis was one of the "angels," Edna Harper. She departed to rejoin her husband, but not before sparking a short-lived scandal by complaining to the press about "intimate relations" between Anna Hooten and Kelley. What that meant exactly, neither she nor any of the reporters covering the Kelleyites would say. The Victorian age left such things to the imagination. Perhaps a jealous Harper was only trying to create trouble where none really existed, for a short while later Hooten married Thomas Sutcliffe, a carpenter from San Francisco.[9]

About sixty miles north of its junction with the Ohio River, the water of the Mississippi boiled past a series of rocky obstacles bearing such ominous names as the Devil's Bake Oven, the Devil's Tea Table, the Devil's Backbone, and the Devil's Anvil. But these presented less of a problem to Kelley's navy than the southernmost city in Illinois: Cairo, a manufacturing center of ten thousand inhabitants. Long before the sailors arrived there, rumors circulated up the Mississippi Valley that the townsfolk would not permit them to land.[10]

Situated on a flat tongue of land where the gray waters of the Ohio River poured into the yellow Mississippi, Cairo was of strategic importance to the Kelleyites. There they either had to land and hire a towboat for the thousand-mile voyage up the Ohio Valley to Wheeling or Pittsburgh, or allow the Mississippi's powerful current to carry them south to New Orleans and the Gulf of Mexico. "Well," boasted Kelley when he heard the bad news, "we've been in the habit of landing where we like and if we take a notion to land at Cairo, I have no doubt that we will." Cairo authorities were afraid that if they failed to make a show of force against the Kelleyites, the community would be harassed by several other western armies reported to be following the river route east.

No sooner had Kelley's flotilla put ashore about six miles north of Cairo than city officials quarantined it. Two hundred special guards armed with Winchester rifles and shotguns formed a cordon across the northern limits of town and patrolled the riverbank. They permitted no one to cross their line, including Cairo citizens sympathetic to the pilgrims.

The Kelleyites camped in a cornfield. They had no tents and no food; many were sick. Kelley sent a special plea to sympathizers in Saint Louis: "Quarantined here and held without cause or provocation. Help us." Saint Louis labor promptly responded with a load of supplies. The impasse was finally broken when the Kelleyites dismantled their boats and traded the lumber to farmers in exchange for wagons that could haul them and their supplies across the narrow neck of land to the Ohio River.

Residents of tiny Mound City on the Ohio River side of the peninsula were unhappy about the arrangement and initially tried to checkmate the Kelleyites with a special force of armed guards. Badly outnumbered, they then reversed themselves and agreed to furnish rations and $100 to hire a boat. Five or six Cairo citizens donated another $100, but steamboaters were afraid to haul the Kelleyites, fearful perhaps that the men would commandeer the vessel. Finally one captain agreed to tow them on two open barges, and in this way Kelley and his crusaders sailed up the winding Ohio Valley to Paducah, Evansville, and Owensboro, using donations received in one town to get them to the next.

This unorthodox process of ascending the Ohio incensed Louisville Mayor Henry Tyler, who labeled it blackmail "under the guise of charity." He proposed to bar the Kelleyites from the Kentucky metropolis and to that end ordered out all available policemen. At New Albany and Jeffersonville, on the Indiana side of the Ohio, they were no more welcome. Officials of the three cities that clustered about the falls of the Ohio River proposed to use Cairo's quarantine tactic and sent a spokesman, Alexander Dowling, downriver to warn the Coxeyites away.

"If you come up the river we will quarantine against you," Dowling advised Kelley.

"What disease will you claim we have in the army?"

"Smallpox."

"Well, sir," said Kelley to Dowling, "we can show you certificates from good physicians to the effect that we are free from smallpox or any other disease. You will have to specify some disease before you can quarantine us."

"I know you have some disease and will quarantine you. This is an end of that."

"All right," responded Kelley softly, "if you quarantine us we will not kick. You know the law says that when you quarantine a ship you have to feed the passengers. We will just remain until you see fit to let us go on or stop feeding us."

Dowling capitulated. Kelley and his six hundred men pulled ashore at New Albany and pitched camp. A local streetcar company furnished them a camp and made money taking the curious out to view them. When Kelley and an aide crossed the river to Louisville in defiance of the mayor, they were promptly arrested for vagrancy. A judge set bail at $2,500 each, which local sympathizers paid. The case was dismissed.

The Kelleyites continued upriver by open barge from New Albany to Lawrenceburg, near the Indiana-Ohio line, where officials hired wagons to take them into Ohio. When Kelley appealed to Cincinnati labor organizations for help, trade unionists reluctantly agreed to put on a benefit to raise funds; but city councilmen who had earlier helped Fry now opposed any aid for Kelley. The municipal welcome mat had been worn threadbare by too many Coxeyites.

In the end, Cincinnati and its labor organizations hired a towboat and two barges to take the Kelleyites a hundred miles farther upriver to Portsmouth. Twelve miles short of their destination, they were unceremoniously dumped ashore, the towboat captain explaining that his vessel had been chartered for a hundred miles and he would not haul them a mile farther. City authorities in Portsmouth did not want the visitors and threatened to barge them all back to Cincinnati, but before they could become pawns in a contest between the two communities, Kelley's army disintegrated. Kelley was desperately ill and confined to bed with an apparent case of typhoid fever; he ordered his troops to reach Washington by any means possible and promised to rejoin them later.

In the eyes of his followers he remained a hero, and for good reason: his men seemed helpless without him. Many had only a vague idea of how to get to Washington and at first wandered about the countryside begging food from farmers. Some finally stole aboard the freight trains of the Chesapeake and Ohio Railway, which ran from the Ohio Valley across the mountains of West Virginia to Washington. Others continued up the Ohio River but were unwelcome everywhere. In Wheeling, one band attempted to sustain itself by peddling printed songs for five cents a sheet. One of these was a Kelleyite version of the popular Civil War anthem, "The Battle Cry of Freedom":

> And when our march is over
> And good wages we can earn,
> We'll turn our faces westward
> To our homes we will return,
> For there our loved ones watch and wait
> For us their hearts do yearn—
> While we are marching to Washington."[11]

CHAPTER 15

Suppose they put us in the chain
gang. The government merely dem-
onstrates that it can support the unemployed and the question will
arise: If the government can support us that way, why not have us
employed on public improvements
where the country could benefit?

"General" Edward J. Jeffries, quoted
in the *Alliance Standard Review*,
August 2, 1894

The Rivals; Or, Gambling on Jumbo

A mixture of motives drove the westerners toward Washington. For
some it was idealism; for others the alternatives to life in the ranks
were even worse, as Jack London learned after he left Kelley's ranks
and ran afoul of vagrancy laws near Buffalo. Members of a group
found safety in numbers, as Kelley's steady progress up the Ohio Valley illustrated. Finally, for members of two armies that formed in the
Far West, there was the added impetus of a longstanding urban
rivalry, and for them the trip across the continent became something
of an endurance contest.[1]

The history of the American West is punctuated with tales of urban rivalries, but few were more vigorous than that between Seattle
and Tacoma, two competing ports on Washington's Puget Sound.
Tacoma, nicknamed the "City of Destiny" by the eccentric George
Francis Train, won the contest to become the Pacific terminus of the
first northern transcontinental railroad, the Northern Pacific. Seattle,
however, refused to surrender and in 1893 became the terminus of another transcontinental railroad, James J. Hill's Great Northern.

The rivalry found many modes of expression, as in graffiti scrawled
on the men's room wall of a Seattle railroad station during the
Spanish-American War in 1898:

Remember the Maine
To Hell with Spain
And don't forget
To pull the chain—
Tacoma needs the water!

Tacoma school children and businessmen, too, chanted at luncheon meetings, "Seattle, Seattle! Death rattle, death rattle!" During the Coxey movement, the *Evening Telegram* of Portland poked fun at the adolescent rivals to the north when it claimed that Seattle had begged its Coxeyites *not* to march to Washington: "If the unemployed move out, Tacoma will stand a chance to lead Seattle in the next census."[2]

Large armies formed among the unemployed of both Seattle and Tacoma, and on April 27 they converged temporarily in the tiny railway junction of Puyallup to await a train. The Seattle contingent, nine hundred strong and led by a mild-mannered surveyor, Henry Shepard, arrived first and found shelter from the rain in an unfinished and abandoned hotel.

An hour later someone shouted, "Here comes Jumbo!" In the distance loomed the bulky form of the Tacoma general, Frank T. Cantwell, riding in a buggy. There was an immediate rush to greet him. "Three cheers for Jumbo!" shouted a Seattleite. Jumbo, dressed in a new navy-blue uniform decorated with shiny brass buttons, grinned from ear to ear; he looked like a cross between a railway conductor and a cannibal chief. One of United States marshal James C. Drake's deputies handed him a copy of an injunction issued by federal Judge Cornelius Hanford. Jumbo looked briefly at the document, then laughed, saying he could draw up a paper like that himself. It was not worth a thing, he added.

Cantwell's seven hundred followers arrived a short while later, and though they camped in another part of the village, the two leaders put in a joint appearance before the temporarily united armies. Jumbo energized the troops with his red-hot oratory and simple solutions to complex problems: "The Northern Pacific is in the receivers' hands now. Haven't we got the right to use our property? Are we not the government?"

The big man made quite an impression on Seattle's troops. Shepard, by contrast, seemed ineffective, particularly when his com-

Jumbo Cantwell. Courtesy Historical Photographs
Collection, University of Washington Libraries.

missary wagon did not arrive until late in the evening: "Never was a
commissary so taxed to get through a meal. Another such one and
the Seattle industrials would have mutinied and gone home." Over at

Cantwell's commissary, everything went smoothly. Bread, pretzels, bologna, fish, and other edibles were piled high on the tables, and hungry men enjoyed a feast. "Jumbo declared his men would eat if they got nowhere."

Jumbo was always the center of attention. A crowd of admirers followed him about, and women begged men to introduce them so they might shake his hand. When he spoke, his words carried over the whole town, even though he was a bit hoarse from speaking fourteen consecutive nights in Tacoma. Carlotta Cantwell came to Puyallup, too, and in the eyes of the press she "seemed to enjoy the whole affair as a huge joke. She heard her husband speak in the afternoon and seemed to regard the matter as very amusing."[3]

One thing not very amusing was the continued want of a train. The federal government's use of the army to corral train pirates in Montana and Oregon strengthened the resolve of the Northern Pacific to resist Commonwealers from Puget Sound. "We ain't too good to steal a train," warned Jumbo. "Them fellers in Congress has broke the law, so why can't we." Jumbo's listeners never seemed to tire of his bravado style of haranguing. While Jumbo thundered, Carlotta tried to charm the Northern Pacific out of a train. Handsomely dressed in a spring outfit and diamond jewelry, she marched with four hundred supporters to the Northern Pacific building in Tacoma to see the road's assistant general superintendent, G. W. Dickinson. He was suddenly away on business. After some difficulty, Carlotta located a minor company official and tried to hire enough freight cars to transport her husband's army, but the railroad stood its ground. Commonwealers appealed to the governor of Washington, John Hart McGraw, asking him to intercede with the company; but unlike his Oregon counterpart, he had no sympathy for the movement. There seemed no easy way out for the two industrial armies.[4]

During the first week of May, the press carried yet another story sure to add to the woes of the folk in Puyallup: "Unless supplies are received in forty-eight hours these men will be in a starving condition." Added to that was the problem of drizzling rain. With each passing day the dampness took its toll on the crusaders' morale and contributed to friction within the ranks.[5]

From the time that Seattle marchers had first seen Shepard and Cantwell together, they could not help making invidious comparisons. Shepard was small of stature—he looked like a boy when standing beside the great Jumbo—and he was colorless. The Seattle men spent hours discussing the merits of the two leaders. They hated to give in to their Tacoma rivals, but everyone could see that Jumbo's men were a better-fed and happier lot. Whatever desire the marchers from Seattle had to join the Tacoma army decreased, however, when old urban rivalries resurfaced and Jumbo proclaimed he would not take in any new recruits. He refused to share any provisions with the Seattle men, saying, "That money was raised for the Tacoma boys and they'll get it all."

A few days earlier, the Seattle men had looked upon Jumbo "as a sort of Moses, who would lead them out of the wilderness and bondage." But many had now come to the conclusion that he was frothy, an opinion that grew stronger every day that the armies remained trapped in Puyallup. That, however, did not make Seattle marchers like their own leader any better. They accused Shepard of becoming dictatorial in his imposition of military discipline on the men, of usurping the powers of the executive committee, and of not providing an adequate accounting of their funds.

Flexing the muscles of democracy, the marchers demoted Shepard and elected in his place a young journalist and lawyer, Edward J. Jeffries. To guard against any dictatorial tendencies on the part of the private suddenly elevated to general, they created a supreme council to function as a court of last resort. Jeffries, though quite the opposite of Cantwell, could hold his own against the big man—verbally if not physically. And intellectually there was no comparison: the twenty-eight-year-old Jeffries had attended the University of Michigan Law School after learning the ropes of journalism on several daily papers in his hometown of Detroit. In 1889 he had moved his family to Spokane, where during the next four years he was active in various labor and agrarian reform organizations, most importantly the Populist Party. (Jumbo, by contrast, was a self-appointed bouncer for the Tacoma Democrats.) Jeffries's interest lay in defending the underdog through the reform press or in court. Cantwell was ever the blustering frontier gambler and prizefighter looking out mainly for himself.[6]

For a time it seemed as if Shepard's fall was but a prelude to the general collapse of Coxeyism at Puyallup. After remaining there for ten frustrating days, the crusaders started slipping out of town as individuals or in small groups, leading the press to report that the armies had broken up into an "unemployed band of tramps." In fact, Cantwell and Jeffries had hit upon a new tactic: to send their men across the state in small bands to Spokane, where they would recollect into armies. Each general invoked a sense of honor and the old urban rivalries to spur their troops along in what was at times an undisguised race. "Talk about Jumbo's army breaking up into squads and going east," bragged Jeffries. "Why, we can give 'em two days start and beat 'em in every time."

The four-hundred-mile obstacle course from Puyallup to Spokane wound up the west face of the Cascade Mountains to the long tunnel under Stampede Pass and then descended to Ellensburg, at the edge of the arid side of the state. They would have to pass through the narrow canyon of the Yakima River and cross the wide Columbia near Pasco—where the only bridge was operated by the Northern Pacific and guarded by federal marshals. From there they would have to continue northeast through a sparsely settled desert of sand and sage until they reached Spokane. This they did, encountering trouble all along the way. A large raft built in Ellensburg overturned in the icy waters of the Yakima River and drowned four men. A fight with federal deputies at Yakima led to the arrest and jailing of 120 Coxeyites.

But Commonwealers also had several sources of support, not the least of which was Jumbo himself. As the Tacoma men left Puyallup, Cantwell purchased a railway ticket to avoid trouble with the marshals and rode up and down the line encouraging his men. "Spokane or bust!" he would yell from the rear platform of a passing train. "Come on, boys, I'm wid you." He advised his men to avoid passenger trains, but a number nonetheless climbed aboard when his train pulled out of a station. A short distance down the line it stopped in order for marshals to pull them off. But Cantwell climbed out and boosted his men up to the tops of the cars as fast as marshals could remove them. And railroad employees typically stood around with their hands in their pockets. When the Coxeyites were still stranded in Puyallup, the railroaders invariably greeted Jumbo with cheers as they rolled through town, and he responded with a wave of his hat and a loud, "You're all right, boys; we'll fix these guys."[7]

A Northern Pacific conductor confided to a reporter, "No matter what the men may tell the bosses you can put it down as a fact that they are as a rule in sympathy with the Commonwealers. It would not surprise me much to see one of our men help Jumbo's gang, although I doubt very much there would be more than one or two among all our boys who would lend themselves to bucking the United States government." He added that the Northern Pacific employees disliked having the deputy marshals riding their trains and bossing them around.

"The railroad men are our best friends," Jeffries told a group of sympathizers when he got to Spokane. "Down at Yakima one told us: 'Now when I say "get off all you sons of bitches," just climb on as fast as you can. We've got our orders, but you can ride as far as you want to.'"

"Hooray for the shacks [conductors]!" shouted a listener.[8]

Some of the deputies, too, quietly helped the Commonwealers along. On occasion they fed the men as brothers, which in a sense they were. Marshal Drake and others who recruited them did not realize that some of the newly hired deputies were members of Eugene Debs's American Railway Union. They had signed up as marshals in order to help the Coxeyites cross the state and thus prevent them from succumbing to the temptation to scab on the union during its strike against the Great Northern. Other members of organized labor had quietly signed up as well.

It was no easy game to play. Union men serving as deputies did not like being called "pinheads" and other names by those who did not understand what was happening. Nor was it much fun to ride up and down the railway line in a pelting rain trying to police the trains. Two deputies generally rode in the locomotive and several more scattered among the cars. In general, though, they pulled off only enough of the freeloaders to make a show of force, and let the majority go through, unless railway officials ordered the whole train sidetracked. The press reported that if it became necessary to use extreme force, many marshals would turn in their badges.[9]

After a week of playing a serious game of cat and mouse with the deputies and the railroaders, Coxeyites from Puget Sound collected in Spokane. There they picked up several hundred more members when a local army disintegrated after its general attempted to decamp with the treasury. During the days they remained in Spokane, Jeffries and Cantwell put on benefit performances to raise money for the trip east, explained their mission in public meetings, and proved their patriotism in frequent games of baseball with Spokane teams.

Accompanying Jumbo when he arrived in Spokane were his wife, her little girl (Mabel Morgan), and Jumbo's canine counterpart, a pet Saint Bernard named Colonel. The general's family continued to Chicago, where they were to serve as the army's advance guard. At a large public indignation meeting in Spokane, Cantwell vowed to obtain transportation for his men. "I ain't broke," he said as he flourished a wad of money. "But they won't take us for money. My wife offered them $10,000 to take the boys from Seattle, Tacoma, Spokane, and Butte to Washington, but it didn't go."

With each passing day, it became increasingly clear to the Coxeyites in Spokane that they would never continue east unless they resorted to the proven tactic of riding the trains in small groups. Jeffries was quite proud of the resourcefulness of his troops: "Our boys are artists, every one of them. When we say we are going to meet at a certain time, it is a point of honor with us to get there." His men sang:

> Jeffries, Jeffries, he's all right;
> Seattle boys are out of sight.
> Every time a train goes through
> It takes out a dozen or two.
> Ta-ra-boom-de-aye; ta-ra-boom-de-aye
> We, the Coxey men, will win the day.
> Ta-ra-ra boom de aye.[10]

The rival armies left Spokane in late May and headed toward Montana destinations, where each planned to regroup, hold meetings, collect donations from sympathizers, and continue on. Jumbo proposed to take the high line—the Great Northern route through Montana to Great Falls—and Jeffries the Northern Pacific route through southern Montana to Helena. After crossing some fifteen hundred miles of mountains and prairies, both railway lines met again at the twin cities of Minneapolis and Saint Paul, and which army would win that leg of the race was anyone's guess.

First, though, they had to get through the rugged country of the Idaho panhandle; and waiting there for them were deputy sheriffs, soldiers from the United States Army, and federal marshals armed with rifles and a court injunction. With help from numerous sympathizers among the region's metal miners and a little bit of native wit, most crusaders made it. A marcher named Callahan, who was quite adept at imitating a Swedish accent, displayed his technique when he climbed aboard a train heavily guarded by lawmen. One of them immediately ordered him off.

"Vat?" responded the Irish Swede.

"Get off!"

"I not ond'stand Anglis," said Callahan with a blank look on his face.

"Well ride then, you dumb Swede."[11]

Cantwell and Jeffries both reached Minneapolis during the last half of June. Jumbo arrived first, having suddenly and somewhat mysteriously switched roles with his wife. She went to Great Falls to lead the troops east, and he assumed the role of advance agent. Jumbo arrived in Minnesota claiming that he had organized contingents in Grand Forks and Fargo and that twenty-five hundred men were coming behind him. But with his usually smooth-shaven face wearing a week's growth of beard, he looked more like a fugitive from justice than anything else. In any case, after a stay at one of the finest hotels in Minneapolis, he seemed his old expansive self once again.

Jumbo regaled a Minneapolis audience with tales of his adventures in the Far West and presented a series of bombastic arguments that seemed even more outrageous than usual: "If the Commonwealers had shouldered arms when they left Tacoma they would have had a clear road through to Washington. The tin horn gamblers and pimps and United States marshals would never have troubled us." He mused aloud that it was no more wrong for the Commonwealers to go to Washington and hang a few senators and congressmen than it was to permit the Congress of the United States to steal from the people. The crowd of a thousand people that had gathered in the old Haymarket Square vigorously applauded his three-hour harangue, but the silliness of his arguments earned him the animosity of city officials in both Minneapolis and Saint Paul.

Armed with a letter of introduction from the Spokane Trades Council, Cantwell won the support of organized workmen in the Twin Cities. With the aid of their donations, he soon collected an army of nearly two hundred men. He led them east across Minnesota and Wisconsin, but it was not an easy trip. They were frequently harassed by law officers and near Racine were clubbed by a squad of railroad policemen employed by the Chicago and North-Western.[12]

Cantwell's erstwhile rival, Jeffries, waited in the Twin Cities to collect his men. Crossing the plains of North Dakota in small bands, they had encountered considerable difficulty with federal deputies. From Saint Paul, Jeffries advised his men to head 150 miles due north to Duluth, Minnesota's third-largest city. But why Duluth and why north? Washington lay to the southeast. Jeffries had read about the hostility that Cantwell encountered in Wisconsin and also about the Pullman strike that had tied up railway lines into Chicago. As a native of Michigan, he also knew something about the geography of the Great Lakes country. By going to Duluth and hiring a boat to Cleveland or Buffalo, he could take his men to towns that had as yet had little or no direct contact with the Coxey movement. Furthermore, it beat walking or riding under freight cars. Maybe Cantwell would reach Washington first, but traveling through parts of the Midwest already visited by three or four other armies did not appeal to Jeffries.[13]

Only one problem remained for him to solve: where would he get the money to hire a boat? He had several hundred dollars in contributions from organized labor and wealthy mine owners in Montana, but that was not enough. For starters, Jeffries collected $25 from members of the local branch of the International Typographical Union when he showed them his membership card.

Through public meetings and private contributions, the Seattleite raised enough money to pay his army's way across Lake Superior on a steamer bound for Marquette, in the iron-mining country of Michigan's upper peninsula. Jeffries and about four hundred followers sailed out of Duluth on July 7. From Marquette they traveled by chartered boxcars to the Straits of Mackinac, which they crossed by boat, and then hiked sixteen miles to Cheboygan. From there the Michigan Central Railroad reluctantly hauled them south to the lumber town of Bay City, which proved the most congenial stopping place they had found since leaving Seattle. "The hearts of the people of Bay City were big and their pocketbooks overflowed with wealth," observed a local paper. In Bay City and nearby Saginaw, the friends and enemies of the movement combined to raise a purse of $400 to charter a lumber schooner to take them to Cleveland, with an intermediate stop in Jeffries's hometown of Detroit.[14]

In Detroit, Jeffries was reunited with his recently widowed mother for the first time since he had gone west, but even that tear-jerking story, duly reported in the press, was not enough to make citizens of Michigan's largest city open their purses. Few Detroiters donated food or clothing to the visitors, not even members of organized labor. Because of the disappointing reception, the Coxeyites sailed for Cleveland a day earlier than planned. So little food remained in their commissary that only the seasickness caused by a lake storm kept them from eating it bare.

Cleveland proved even less hospitable than Detroit. Police officers would not permit Jeffries to speak in the public square, nor would they find the army shelter for the night. "Well, this is the meanest place we have struck yet," grumbled one of Jeffries's lieutenants. But Jeffries was clever. He and his men muzzled themselves with handkerchiefs and strips of cloth and paraded silently through downtown streets and around but not on the public square. Their banner read "Free Speech in Cleveland." The unusual demonstration created quite a stir and aided their cause by calling it to public attention. "People are not so dull witted as to fail to see the point the Washingtonians were making against the policy of the city government," observed the *Plain Dealer*.

As the crusaders continued overland from Cleveland to Pittsburgh during the last week of July, Jeffries found opportunities to improvise other forms of passive protest. Fifty of his men aboard a freight train at Ravenna were ordered off at gunpoint and lodged in jail, prompting several hundred comrades to pitch camp on the courthouse lawn and dare police to arrest them, too. They had no food and no money, and every freight train from the West brought in reinforcements.

Jeffries used the occasion to elaborate on his method of operation: "The only way to transport a large body of men over a long distance is to give them orders that they will obey. I always ordered them to ride; I knew they wouldn't walk." He also explained the virtues of passive resistance. "They can't shoot or club a fellow who won't fight back. The authorities may order a fellow away, but they can't kill him for not going." (This was more than a decade before Gandhi began practicing his own version of passive resistance.) "The only force we ever use is the force of numbers," gloated Jeffries. That same tactic, he believed, would win the day in Washington. "If we can get a million men there we can just swarm all over the Capitol grass and everything else. What could they do? Arrest us? Let them arrest. For everyone they could arrest there would be ten to take his place." [15]

Using passive resistance and variety of other tactics, Jeffries and his men managed to remain a step or two ahead of those who would send them to the workhouse or jail. At the entrance to Allegheny City, where Coxey's army had come to grief and nearly disbanded (and where other armies had been turned away), Jeffries refused to be rerouted. He gave police the choice of arresting all 430 of his men and paying the cost of feeding them, or allowing them to proceed. The police stepped aside. Being the seventh or eighth army to reach Pittsburgh meant that his men received a tepid welcome at best, although the *Post* conceded that Jeffries was "the most intelligent and unique commander who has visited this city."

Jeffries's troops walked sixty miles from Pittsburgh to Connellsville, a railway town and coke-producing center nestled in the mountains of western Pennsylvania; but they refused to walk farther. When they clambered aboard a Baltimore and Ohio freight, the railroad that had persuaded Governor McKinley to send out the Ohio National Guard to clear its trains gave battle. The air was filled with clubs, heavy chain links, coupling pins, and scrap iron that flew back and forth between the Coxeyites and railroad crewmen and detectives. Jeffries fought beside his men and received many bruises. Several on both sides were injured seriously and had to be hospitalized. At least a hundred of the soldiers of misfortune were arrested and taken to Uniontown, the county seat, for trial. Sixty-five men were sentenced to pay a five-dollar fine or serve five days in jail. Jeffries realized that the brief confinement was not all that bad. Failing in his legal efforts to get the men released, he and the remainder of his army continued to Washington, where in early August the long journey from Pike Street in Seattle to Pennsylvania Avenue ended. [16]

In the race to reach Capitol Hill, Jumbo won handily, but under very suspicious circumstances and at the cost of leaving embittered members of his original army scattered all the way to Great Falls and beyond. Having apparently traveled east from Chicago by regular coach, Cantwell and a handful of followers recruited from the Midwest reached Washington in time to participate in Browne's July 4 funeral for the Goddess of Liberty. They brought a promise of many more troops to follow. But Jumbo could be thankful that the national wire services were no longer carrying news of the Coxey movement, for he could regale people in Washington with tales of his western adventures without fear of contradiction until his wife or some of his followers from the Pacific Northwest arrived. Then the full story of the mess he had created in Montana would leak out, and the reason for the sudden switch of roles with his wife would become clear.[17]

The circumstances that led to Jumbo's downfall originated in Spokane. True to form, the big man grabbed the headlines as he made his way east from Spokane toward Great Falls, where his army planned to rendezvous. But if the press was correct, the "sporting man" had a rendezvous of another sort in mind, and it was not with his men or his wife. While his devoted followers were beating their way to central Montana by boxcar and stolen train, Jumbo went by coach in the company of Hilda Steen, a teenager he had met in Spokane. Steen, according to witnesses, was a tall, blue-eyed beauty who had been introduced to Jumbo at a Home Guard meeting, found him quite appealing, and indicated a desire to accompany him east.

Spokane papers made the most of the episode, especially the incident in the village of Havre, where the pair was to change trains for Great Falls. In Havre, Jumbo reportedly pulled out a pistol and threatened the young girl if she tried to return home. Responding to reporters who inquired about the altercation, Jumbo provided a plausible explanation for their friendship and the quarrel; but the story grew. One Spokane woman wired ahead to a Methodist minister in Great Falls, saying that friends of the girl "feel it is our duty to do all we can to save them from eternal ruin." But Cantwell had already sent Hilda back from Havre. Upon reaching Great Falls, he denounced reports that he had had "criminal relations" with a teenager, and offered $100 to any who could prove him wrong.[18]

Waiting for Jumbo in Great Falls were hundreds of his half-starved followers, who ever since Spokane had grown increasingly disillusioned with the big man. Also awaiting him in Great Falls was his "advance guard," who had just returned from Chicago. What

Carlotta said to Jumbo about the Spokane teenager went unrecorded, but at this point the two switched roles. Jumbo now traveled ahead to act as the army's advance guard, his steps no doubt quickened by rumors of an arrest warrant following close behind.

Carlotta could have abandoned her husband and the whole depressing enterprise at this point, but instead she summoned up the inner strength to fulfill a prophecy she had made earlier in Puyallup. Jumbo, she had declared, might fall by the wayside, but she was going through. To the men who were experiencing hard times, Carlotta was nothing less than an angel of mercy. "The men were not ashamed to be under her control," reported one, "as it was not a case of petticoat tyranny." She nursed the sick to health, and in towns along the way she spent her fortune renting empty structures to house her followers.

She and her eight-year-old daughter Mabel staged benefit performances to raise money for food. Carlotta sang a lament for poor workingmen called "After the Fall," patterned after a popular song, and Mabel sang too and then passed the hat. Colonel, the Saint Bernard, solicited alms by carrying a little bucket in his mouth. "His large, frank, brown eyes were often suffused with tears at the suffering and helplessness he beheld among the big, husky, hungry men in the army," the *Tacoma News* later recalled. "But woe to anyone who tried to rob his bucket." Stories of Carlotta's kindness reached the Coxeyites camped in Washington, D.C., and they eagerly awaited her arrival. "The men of the army are anxious to see her and admire her for her bravery and self-devotion to the cause," reported the *Washington Post*. When she arrives, "a royal welcome will be extended her by all the members of the industrial army. This will be partly due to the reports of her good deeds which have preceded her and also on account of the fact that she was brave enough to organize an army of unemployed workmen and champion their cause."

On July 15 a telegram reached Washington, stating that Carlotta would arrive two days later, bringing 250 men. Two days passed. A newspaper reported her in the Washington suburb of Georgetown. Another placed her just across the Potomac in Virginia. More days passed and still she did not appear. "Where is General Mrs. Jumbo?" the Washington papers asked.[19]

At the time she was expected to make a triumphal entry, Carlotta was three thousand miles removed from the city on the Potomac.

She was indeed nearing Washington—but it was Washington state. "Mrs. General," as she was called by her followers, had arrived in Great Falls to find her husband's troops languishing along the banks of the Missouri, suffering from a lack of shoes, and near starvation. She immediately set about to rebuild the army's morale and physical strength. "But what uphill work it is for me. Oh, the irony of fate! Twelve hundred men depending on one woman and a child for food, clothes, etc."

She got the men as far as Chicago, where her health gave out. The swelling in her hands and feet became so severe that she could hardly walk. Heeding the advice of a physician, she headed home to Tacoma, though she planned to rejoin her "boys" if her health improved.

A few days after she returned to Tacoma, several hundred Home Guards gathered to hear her story. "Mrs. General" appeared on stage wearing an evening dress of black lace, a red rose corsage, and sparkling diamonds on her ears and fingers. Accompanying her were her daughter Mabel, who sang and recited, and the Saint Bernard, who lent dignity to the proceedings. Being a woman, Carlotta noted during her talk, had enabled her to accomplish more than a man might have done. She found North Dakota the toughest state to cross, while Washington was "a picnic." The audience took up a small collection for the cause.[20]

Harry Holmes, one of the men in her command, returned to Tacoma a few months later. He praised Carlotta, but damned Jumbo for exploiting the men while he went around giving lectures that swelled his "wad." According to Holmes and others, the big man finally stole the army's treasury and fled to South America.[21]

CHAPTER 16

It is move on, move out of Virginia,
move out of the District, move
out of Maryland, move off the earth.

A Coxeyite's lament recorded in the
Baltimore Sun, August 13, 1894

The Disinherited

As the summer of 1894 wore on, the people of Maryland and Virginia found it increasingly hard to tolerate two camps of half-starved Coxeyites in their midst. But no one, including the movement's originators, was certain what course to follow.

After early July neither Coxey nor Browne spent much time with their followers. For the Californian, the idea of languishing out of the public eye while waiting for Congress to act held little appeal. Shortly after his release from prison, Browne proposed a new march, this time to Wall Street, where he would introduce a select number of followers to the very fountainhead of financial evil in America. There he proposed to exhibit his panoramas and gather new material for caricatures of grasping bondholders. From New York City he planned to travel west, stopping in Massillon to aid Coxey—now a local hero and a Populist candidate for Congress in William McKinley's old district—and soliciting contributions to be shipped to a storehouse near the Bladensburg camp. In this way he proposed to feed the hundred thousand men he expected to collect there by December. Whether Browne was serious or only dreaming, no one could say, but at the very least he expected his foray into the heart of New York's financial district to generate the newspaper publicity he craved.[1]

What Browne did not say was that the trip would also provide him a graceful way to bid his original followers farewell and shake the dust of the doleful Bladensburg camp from his boots. In their famished condition, the crusaders grew more unruly by the day. When a Fresno sympathizer sent Browne three barrels of "medicinal" wine, several men broke into his "cellar" and got drunk. "We thought it was the reincarnation communion day," laughed one besotted Coxeyite. Browne blamed the incident on Lewis Fry's men, who had no use for him.

After his Independence Day melodrama failed to renew popular interest in the protest, Browne devoted his time to the assault on Wall Street. On July 7, he and sixty specially selected "apostles," as he labeled them, headed for New York, leaving the thankless task of attempting to lead the men remaining in camp to Oklahoma Sam and later Jesse Coxey. Among the names of the apostles was that of Louis Smith. Was this the patent-medicine fakir who once billed himself as the Great Unknown? Had Browne readmitted his former adversary to the ranks of the faithful? Unfortunately, the record is silent.

To sustain themselves while on the road, Browne and the apostles tried unsucessfully to sell copies of *Carl's Camp Courier* and a portrait of the marshal for five cents each. Inspired by W. T. Stead's observation that Coxey's followers were the "sandwich-men of poverty," they offered themselves as mobile billboards to advertise patent medicine, tobacco, baking powder, and other items on their way to Wall Street. Again there were no takers. Browne was reduced to giving a nightly lecture and hoping for handouts. The men reached Wall Street in late July, but in every respect their mission proved a failure.

At about the same time, Coxey paid a brief final visit to his troops, complaining to them that his recent fund-raising tour of the Midwest had not generated enough money even to cover the cost of his own railway ticket; people all over the country had promised much aid but delivered little. Accompanied by his son Jesse, he returned to Massillon and his campaign for Congress. Those left in "Camp Bastile" complained bitterly that they had been abandoned by their leaders. Coxey denied this, but his suggestion that they get arrested and let the government provide for them was not reassuring. Another alternative was to abandon the Maryland camp and move in with the westerners bivouacked among the willows and blackberry bushes on the Potomac. Many did so.

In fact, life in the Virginia camp was only marginally better. Throughout July a steady stream of new arrivals from the West swelled the number of Coxeyites living near Rosslyn to more than a thousand, and observers expected that number to double or triple in the near future. Leadership became a major problem: Fry was supposed to be in charge, but five subordinate commanders who had overcome all sorts of obstacles during their transcontinental odyssey found themselves unable to overcome their jealousy of one another. They bickered, and some sought excuses to abandon their followers and head elsewhere. Charles T. Kelley, who arrived in mid-July, remained in camp less than two weeks before he returned home to California, claiming that family illness forced his departure. Jumbo Cantwell made a foray of his own into New York City shortly before he turned thief and fled to South America. When fighting broke out between the followers of Fry and Galvin over Fry's system of accounting, a majority deposed Fry and adopted the democratic expedient of choosing a new camp commander each day.[2]

For food the campers at Rosslyn found themselves depending heavily on members of the Public Comfort Committee established by the *Woman's Tribune*. They celebrated Independence Day with a feast of boiled beets, corned beef and cabbage, coffee, and blackberry dumplings, but during the weeks that followed, such lavish meals became only a memory. Tea and a small piece of bread often constituted supper. Though the men found themselves going without food for twenty-four hours at a time, they nonetheless respected the property of their Virginia neighbors. When a chicken from a nearby farm wandered into camp, Galvin cast a longing glance at it, then growled, "You'd better get out of here, pullet. You're treading on dangerous grounds."

Coxeyites resorted to various strategems in the struggle for food. According to an unverifiable story that appeared in the *Richmond Times*, a Rosslyn Coxeyite on a foraging mission approached a southern mansion. The house had a beautifully manicured lawn and a broad front porch, in the shade of which an old woman rocked comfortably. Without saying a word, the Coxeyite opened the gate, fell to his knees, and began nibbling the short grass. The old lady watched the strange behavior and continued rocking for some time. Finally she arose and called out:

"Poor man, are you so hungry as that?"

"Indeed, dear madam, I am so hungry that even this grass is delicious."

"Well, poor man, I pity you, and you can go in the back yard; the grass is much longer out there."

Even less rewarding than nibbling grass was begging on the streets of Washington. A San Franciscan arrested for panhandling told the court, "I never had to beg before and if I could get transportation I would be more than glad to return home." He claimed that a wife and two children awaited him. An unsympathetic judge sent him instead to the local workhouse for thirty days. J. K. Morrison, a lawyer who led a small contingent of men from his hometown of Saint Louis, occasionally tried to defend those arrested for begging, but it was hopeless. The attitude of Washington was clear: "This city is willing to look after its own poor, but it cannot and will not attempt to feed the poor from all over the country."

It became increasingly obvious that the Rosslyn campsite was an unlucky selection, because southerners were generally unsympathetic to the Coxey movement. On several occasions Virginia governor Charles T. O'Ferrall threatened to arrest the campers if they did not leave, but he failed to use force. Fry discounted O'Ferrall's bluster, claiming that the governor had no jurisdiction over them anyway because they were camped on federal property. And when an officer of the Virginia militia threatened to remove the Commonwealers by force of arms, the battle-hardened westerners simply responded that they would pitch him in the Potomac if he tried. "If Governor O'Ferrall sends any of his play soldiers up here we'll take their guns away from 'em an' sell 'em for meat and bread," boasted one Coxeyite. The War Department, on whose property they camped, did nothing.

The Coxeyite remnant struggled to make their bivouac livable. At the entrance they erected a huge floral arch with the word "Welcome" woven in evergreen boughs. It led to Fifth Avenue. The Stars and Stripes floating lazily in the breeze identified the headquarters tent. Men whiled away the hours giving or listening to speeches or watching a boxing match staged by the men of Cantwell's command. Kelley's glee club occasionally provided an evening's entertainment, and until he decamped, Kelley himself often sang solos. Morrison, the Saint Louis lawyer, sometimes entertained the men by practicing aloud one of his defenses of a beggar in police court. The worst day of the week was Sunday, not because the church services and prayer meetings conducted by local preachers were boring (which they may have been), but because blue laws prohibited the men from soliciting donations in Virginia on that day. They had to subsist on Saturday's leftovers.

They sweltered in the summer heat and humidity. "The sun didn't smile when he got up this morning," complained the *Washington Star*, as the temperature climbed toward the hundred-degree mark in late July. "He just simply leered with grim satisfaction at the fun he was going to have with the population in this part of the country today." Thunderstorms occasionally brought relief, but some violent ones roared through camp, battering the crude shelters to pieces and drenching the unfortunate occupants. Most campers had no blankets to protect them from the bare ground. On cool nights they suffered from chills, fevers, and rheumatism. Mosquitoes were a problem every night.

As July turned to August with no prospect of a change except for the worst, the men in the Rosslyn camp grew desperate. Their leaders issued a general appeal for help and warned of mass starvation. Some talked of hiking to Capitol Hill, trampling on the grass, and getting themselves arrested. But the majority opposed this. Many did not like the disgrace of jail; others were afraid of being clubbed, and some feared being corralled into a makeshift prison camp as horrible as the infamous Andersonville of Civil War days. They bolstered their spirits by telling themselves that Congress would ultimately come to their rescue.

"I don't see how they can put off long doing something," maintained one officer. "Here we've walked clear across the country to present our petition and show Congress the state we are really in. We've got our bill in, and I don't see how they can help doing something before long." Another Coxeyite promised to remain until winter even if he had to cook broth out of leaves. Others, however, were tired of waiting. Their hope gone, they wanted only to go home. One man jumped into the Potomac from Aqueduct Bridge in an apparent suicide attempt. Three hundred Kelleyites petitioned Colorado Congressman Lafayette Pence to help them find transportation back to the Rocky Mountain region, where they now believed they could make enough money to survive the winter.

Ninety-one diehards remained encamped near Bladensburg after Coxey and Browne abandoned them. Then, in a swift and almost merciful move, Maryland governor Frank Brown did what no one else had dared to do. For several weeks he had hoped that the Coxeyites remaining in "Camp Bastile" would leave voluntarily. They were, said the governor, the "unfortunate victims of misplaced confidence." But he was done waiting. Just before sunrise on the morning of August 9, forty special policemen from Baltimore, acting on orders from Brown, invaded the camp and arrested everyone for vagrancy. The move surprised the slumbering Coxeyites—including Christopher Columbus Jones, the only well-known figure still in camp—and not one escaped. Many prisoners seemed relieved at the prospect of being fed by the state.

The police marched the prisoners to a justice of the peace in Hyattsville. They had no attorney and no defense witnesses, and within two hours after the raid began, all had been sentenced to three months in the Maryland House of Correction, there to spend their time crushing rock to make good roads. They named the first one "Coxey Avenue."

In their sudden departure, the Coxeyites left their Bladensburg campsite in disarray. A pair of trousers and a coat lay on the ground; eight or nine flags drooped from their poles. George H. Stegmeier, who owned the grounds and a saloon nearby, was furious about the removal. He offered Rosslyn Commonwealers five cents a head—or thirty dollars a day for their commissary—if they would move to his property, but Maryland officers threatened to arrest any newcomers the moment they arrived. Stegmeier also protested the farce that some called a trial. When news of the affair reached Coxey, he hired a District of Columbia attorney to investigate it.[3]

Meanwhile, Brown's summary action strengthened the resolve of his Virginia counterpart. O' Ferrall, a lawyer and onetime Confederate cavalry officer who had been inaugurated governor only the previous January, had been under mounting pressure from various sources to do something about the Coxeyites. In late July the *Richmond*

Times complained that they were "absolutely hungry, and even with fully satisfied stomachs are hardly of a class of folks who would hesitate at petty infringement of the law, and just now they are ripe for more serious offenses."

Only a couple of days before his Maryland counterpart acted, O'Ferrall issued yet another warning to the Commonwealers camped on Virginia soil. "I have no sympathy with these people, and regard them as a lot of common idlers, who would not work if it were offered. The Virginia officers have already been too lenient with them, and the strong arm of the law will not be withheld much longer. Virginia does not intend that she shall become the dumping ground of all the tramps, hoodlums, and cranks of the West." Some left. Eighty men from Fry's army departed Washington for Cincinnati on a railway coach chartered by the District of Columbia commissioners, but their places were immediately filled by new arrivals from the West: on August 6, Seattle commander Edward J. Jeffries walked into camp with forty men and the promise of hundreds more.[4]

The arrival of the feisty little lawyer from the Pacific Northwest injected some life back into the movement. The men at Rosslyn voted to reorganize themselves into a permanent organization, the Cooperative Commonweal of the United States, and Jeffries proposed to lead a new march on Washington the following year. But the "permanent" organization had scarcely been formed before O'Ferrall made good on a month of threats.[5]

So determined was the Virginia governor to keep his plan of action a secret that he dared not trust it to telegraph operators, fearful that if either the District of Columbia authorities or the Coxeyites learned of it in advance, Virginia militiamen would never be able to drive the indigents across the Potomac without heated opposition. From his vacation retreat in the Blue Ridge Mountains, O'Ferrall sent his private secretary to Richmond with orders for Adjutant General Charles J. Anderson. A short while later, two companies of state troops boarded a train and left the Virginia capital in a scene that reminded old-timers of the day Richmond soldiers went to Harper's Ferry to quell John Brown's raid. "The boys are young, but they are Virginians, and should they be ordered to shoot, every man of them would pick his target," emphasized the *Richmond Times*.

At Alexandria, a company of local infantrymen joined the Richmond troops, and together they marched ten miles through the warm night to Rosslyn. The stillness was broken only by the occasional neighing of a horse or a scabbard banging against something. There were several light showers, but barely enough rain fell to settle the dust of the road. The Coxeyites picked up rumors of a major troop movement and dispatched a party of scouts to investigate, but they returned to camp with nothing definite to report, and most men went to bed that night as usual.

At about half-past three on Saturday morning, August 11, the Virginia militiamen reached a high knoll above the Potomac and dropped to the ground exhausted. Below them the fires of the Coxey camp smoldered, and several men slept on the ground with no more covering than pieces of rugs and bits of blankets. Neither the Coxeyites nor the District of Columbia authorities suspected the presence of the Virginians. Quietly they surrounded the camp. At 5:00 A.M. a trumpet sounded in the Coxey bivouac, and the men arose as usual and started breakfast. Just as the first light of the rising sun reflected on the smooth waters of the Potomac, Anderson and his troops walked into camp. The Coxeyites stared in surprise at the militiamen, who wore full military dress, including knapsacks, canteens, and blankets. Each soldier carried a rifle to which a bayonet had been attached and wore a belt containing twenty rounds of ball cartridges.

Anderson, a southerner of great personal charm, was friendly but unyielding as he strode to the headquarters tent and announced, "Well, boys, I'm mighty sorry for you, but you must leave this place by order of the governor of Virginia." They had one hour to get their belongings together. Shortly after seven o'clock, Anderson ordered the militiamen to carry out the enforced exodus. Some Coxeyites who had not yet finished a breakfast of flour and water pancakes had to eat on the run. One man stumbled along with a flapjack in one hand and a cup of coffee in the other; and some hurriedly stuffed bits of food into their pockets, not knowing when they would eat again. Several of the evacuees were clad only in rags and shivered from malaria. Anderson sent three men too sick to move to his hospital surgeon. As a group of Coxeyites carried an American flag past Anderson, he took off his hat and commented, "I'll salute that flag anytime."

Militiamen scouring the bushes for stragglers flushed out two men encumbered with the army's battered pots and kettles, and they, along with everyone else, were forced onto Aqueduct Bridge and barred from reentering Virginia. The three to four hundred soldiers of misfortune trapped on the bridge watched as Anderson ordered his troops to burn their camp. Some Coxeyites yelled in protest as their only worldly possessions went up in flames. One of them complained that he lost two suits of underwear, but another calmly imitated Nero by fiddling while the brush and straw shanties burned.

"The boys seemed to be delighted with this sort of work," observed the *Richmond Times*. Indeed, some of the young militiamen went wild with glee as they stabbed their bayonets into tin cups and bashed pots and kettles. They hacked down the camp flagpole and threw it into the fire, along with an assortment of bedding and clothes. According to one news report, a group of militiamen bayonetted a pet cat left behind and roasted it to death over a campfire. Others spat tobacco juice into sacks of flour to render it unfit for human consumption. (Tobacco juice may have been a polite term, for some papers spoke of fouling the flour by "unspeakable" means.) Anderson returned a few minutes later to halt the wanton destruction.

The Coxeyites remained trapped on Aqueduct Bridge most of the morning, using their flags and insignias to shield themselves from the boiling sun. District of Columbia officials, who blocked them from entering Washington, were in a difficult position. They were furious with Governor O'Ferrall, and they were loath to let the indigents return to the district; but one commissioner conceded, "these men are human beings and must be treated with some sort of consideration. It would be inhuman to keep them out for any length of time without food or shelter, and it was, of course, out of the question to think of leaving them indefinitely on the bridge."

Sympathizers arrived about noon bearing bologna, bread, and buckets of coffee and water to turn the bridge into a soup kitchen. Virginia authorities sought to persuade California Senator George C. Perkins, a steamship magnate, to give his constituents steerage passage home; but Perkins, who did not want them to return to California, favored instead a scheme to send Coxeyites to the lumber camps of the Pacific Northwest by train.[6]

District commissioners finally secured the permission of the assistant secretary of the navy, William McAdoo, to quarter the men on the grounds of the Naval Observatory for three days. Shortly after 1:00 P.M., the indigents marched off the bridge and along the tow-path of the Chesapeake and Ohio Canal as they headed for their new campsite. The next day, Sunday, was miserable. Rain showers were frequent, and those camped on the observatory grounds had only the shelter afforded by trees and shrubs. Between squalls, the ladies of the Women's Christian Temperance Union and local ministers con-ducted special open-air religious services in front of the white ob-servatory building, and sympathizers brought several wagonloads of food.

The campers were not confined as prisoners and eventually found housing in stables on the observatory grounds. Marines guarded only the buildings and a vegetable garden. A dozen campfires blazed in different locations, and one Coxeyite was heard to remark with considerable satisfaction, "Well, we are on Uncle Sam's grass after all." They expected General Mrs. Jumbo Cantwell and her reinforcements to arrive at any time; unaware that she was then on the opposite side of the continent, they sent out search parties to locate her.[7]

Jeffries and several associates used the time to perfect the organi-zation of a permanent industrial army. Its distinctively Populist pro-gram, which called for direct legislation, nationalization of the rail-roads, free coinage of silver, compulsory education of children, and repeal of tramp and vagrancy laws, was far broader than that of the original Commonweal.[8]

District officials talked of shipping the indigents to Cincinnati, as they had done earlier with another group. There was a protest against this, however: "We would rather go to the workhouse here than to be shipped about like a lot of cattle, and having been dumped on some western city, be pinched and jailed out there." A compro-mise of sorts was finally worked out when district commissioners chartered railway coaches to take the Pacific northwesterners to Saint Paul and the Californians to Saint Louis and Kansas City. As the first carload left for Missouri, Jeffries was on hand to wish them good fortune and voice his hope that they would return to participate in next year's march. Some cheered his words, but survivors of the long trek from California were conspicuously silent. District officials pro-vided each group with sandwich makings and coffee enough to last for several days.

The last carload of Coxeyites was scheduled to leave Washington for Saint Paul on Tuesday evening. The men assembled to hear a final speech by Jeffries, and then marched double file to the station singing light-hearted songs. One of these was "Powerful Grover C."

> Grover, Grover, Give us your answer do!
> Think it over before we make trouble for you.
> Just set the day you'll hear us—
> The crowd will be there to cheer us
> And won't we look great when we take a seat
> On the grass that was raised for you.

Perhaps the Coxeyites had grown fond of the president, for when the men of Kelley's command marched by the White House on their way to the station, they gave Cleveland a special fife and drum salute. Perhaps it was just the American way to treat a respected adversary. Or perhaps forgiving and forgetting was in the air.

Certainly the Coxeyites who were serving three-month sentences in the Maryland House of Correction had reason to think so, when the following Saturday night the lights suddenly snapped on and they awoke to see Governor Brown. Earlier he had interviewed each man and offered a pardon to anyone who pledged never to return to Maryland unless he came as a self-supporting and responsible citizen. All but two had agreed. Now Brown announced that he was releasing them and had railway coaches standing by to take the westerners to Cincinnati. The men dressed as quickly as possible, and by 3:00 A.M. they were ready to go. Forming a column with the Maryland governor at the head, they whistled and sang as they marched from prison to Baltimore's Camden Station. The governor thoughtfully furnished the travelers with sandwiches and coffee, and they departed giving three cheers for Brown.[9]

Two hundred crusaders from the Northwest returned to Minneapolis in late August. They were tired but jubilant as they stepped down from the train, and they were especially glad to be out of the East. The mayor of Minneapolis invited them to a soup party, and some of the famished travelers downed several quarts apiece. Afterwards, many headed to North Dakota to harvest wheat; others returned to the Pacific Coast aboard boxcars. "The Washington campaign did not bring much honor to the Industrials," said the *Minneapolis Journal*, "but they retreated in good order and carried their flags with them." One of those weatherbeaten flags adorned the walls of the headquarters of Spokane's Populist Party.[10]

Most people associated with the great crusade disappeared into the obscurity from whence they had come. There were exceptions, however. Journalist Ray Stannard Baker left the *Chicago Record* in 1898 and went on to earn a reputation as America's foremost reporter and Pulitzer Prize–winning biographer of President Woodrow Wilson. The California general, Charles T. Kelley, attempted to repeat the crusade to Washington during the depression year of 1914 but got no farther east than Sacramento. There his men were dispersed by lawmen, and he served a term in jail. The experience convinced him that most radicals were on the wrong track, as he indicated in a 1924 article, "Are Radicals Insane?" The Reverend Kelley ended his days heading a small gospel mission in San Francisco. His onetime associate, George Speed, had no such qualms about militant radicalism; after an odyssey to the Klondike goldfields in 1897, he became a pioneer Socialist soapboxer in Oakland.[11]

Edward J. Jeffries's plans for a new Commonweal never materialized. He returned to Seattle, where he promoted a local self-help scheme called the Industrial Cooperative Society, which sustained 150 men during the winter of 1894/95. They lived communally and pooled whatever wages any member was able to earn. "Self help through cooperation," said a Populist journal that supported the movement, "is at present the only remedy for a plundered and degraded people." Jeffries later returned to his hometown of Detroit, where he campaigned for public office on a variety of tickets. Three times he ran for mayor and twice for governor of Michigan. In 1915 he became a Recorder's Court judge in Detroit, a post he retained until his death in 1939. His years on the bench were often stormy, and he became legendary as a champion of the underdog, the "Knight of the Open Mouth and the Bleeding Heart," some called him. One of his three children, Edward J. Jeffries, Jr., served as mayor of Detroit from 1940 to 1948.[12]

Carl Browne, unwilling to relinquish leadership of the Commonweal to the upstart Jeffries, formed a new organization in Vineland, New Jersey, on August 15, 1894. It was called the Commonweal of the

United States of America, the original reference to Christ having been dropped in response to criticism that it was sacrilegious; its official uniform was a striped outfit like that worn by prisoners. In October Browne made another foray into Wall Street but was arrested for failing to have a parade permit (which police refused to issue him).

The Californian spent the winter at the Coxey home in Massillon, where he perfected plans for a new march on Washington in 1895 and courted Mamie behind her father's back. Whatever hopes Browne had of a repeat of the first march came to grief in mid-June, when journalists leaked the news that the lovers had been secretly married by a justice of the peace. At the wedding the groom was clad in his familiar outfit of buckskin; the bride wore a simple white dress. From Philadelphia, where Coxey had gone on business, came this telegram to his second wife: "I see by the evening papers that Mamie is married, if so, tell her to go with him before I reach home Sunday evening. JSC."

Browne and his new bride made a trip to Washington—counting railway ties at least part of the way—and on July 4, 1895, enacted a quiet exchange of wedding vows on the Capitol steps. Browne prided himself in having at last outsmarted the Capitol police, who had threatened to arrest the couple for holding a public ceremony in violation of the Capitol Grounds Act. Little is recorded of their life together after this. By the turn of the century they were living on Browne's "Commonweal Castle" ranch near Calistoga, where Mamie bore a son, William R. Browne. But sometime afterwards, the family split.

As a soapbox orator in San Francisco, Browne championed the cause of the underdog, at various times supporting both the Socialist party and the radical labor organization, the Industrial Workers of the World, though not necessarily as a regular member. Preferring to work as a free-lancer, the Don Quixote of California turned up at every radical gathering that kept open house. He also devoted his time to building a flying machine that boasted eight engines, no doubt the aviation counterpart to his great panoramic painting of the Battle of Gettysburg. On January 16, 1914, during an extended trip to Washington, where he had gone to promote various causes on Capitol Hill and to demonstrate his "Octo plane," Browne suffered an apparent heart attack and died. Members of the Socialist party, his only real family, conducted the funeral. A few months earlier, he had at least had the satisfaction of speaking legally from the Capitol steps.[13]

Estrangement from his onetime religious mentor, crusade companion, and son-in-law did not diminish Jacob Coxey's interest in reform. He often campaigned for public office—distinguishing himself primarily as an indefatigable monetary reformer—and lost, with the one exception of being elected mayor of Massillon in 1931. He repeated his march on Washington in 1914 and this time spoke legally from the Capitol steps. On May 1, 1944, on the occasion of the fiftieth anniversary of the great march and in the ninetieth year of Coxey's long life, the elder statesman of reform again mounted the Capitol steps and with the permission of Speaker Sam Rayburn and Vice-President Henry Wallace completed the protest speech he had attempted to deliver there once before. His two hundred listeners were mostly federal employees and servicemen. Coxey died on May 18, 1951.[14]

As for the Great Unknown, he committed suicide in Cleveland, about a year after the original march. And little Legal Tender Coxey, the youngest member of the Commonweal's May Day parade down Pennsylvania Avenue, never lived to reach manhood. The Coxey movement, too, suffered a melancholy fate. Whatever its arguable consequences, it represented only a temporary coming together of people, ideas, and circumstances. When it was over, most participants wanted no part of a repeat performance. "Me, I didn't have to join it and if I had to make the tramp over again I wouldn't start," emphasized a member of Kelley's army. "I've got a good home in Virginia City, Nevada, a wife and family." Proposals for federally funded public-works jobs and for marches on Washington by various disaffected groups had surfaced before and would do so again, but none resulted in anything remotely resembling Coxey's remarkable crusade.[15]

Finally, it must be noted that federal authorities could have crushed Coxey's armies with a massive show of force, and in some countries probably would have. President Cleveland and Congress acted with restraint for the same reason that the Coxeyites honored the flag and proclaimed their loyalty to the existing government: even if Coxeyism was a unique manifestation of protest, both sides chose to respond to one another within the framework of America's longstanding values and traditions. "It may not have occurred to us to be proud of Coxey's army, but when we think about it we will see that we have reason to be," a West Coast newspaper observed at the peak of the crusade. "These men who feel themselves wronged do not propose to kill and overthrow—they do not march with guns—they do not threaten—they appeal—they petition—they protest—they reason." If Coxeyism did nothing else, it demonstrated the strength of the nation's values and traditions during a time of severe social and economic stress.[16]

CHAPTER 17

Coxeyism teaches a bad lesson,
the most dangerous lesson indeed
that can be taught to the American
people—the lesson of dependence
on the Federal government.

Tacoma News, April 16, 1894

Coxeyism in Perspective

An earlier age might have found Charles T. Kelley or Edward J.
Jeffries in the role of patient and gentle wagon master, coaxing a
party of Illinois farm families toward the promised land of California
or Oregon, and "Jumbo" Cantwell and Carl Browne as sellers of orchard sites in the Mojave Desert. The Coxey march was, in fact, as
much a chapter in the history of the American West as of reform or
labor. Ostensibly a crusade for jobs and an advocate of what we now
call the modern welfare state, its methods and traditions were largely
those of the classic frontier; and the transcontinental odyssey undertaken by the Kelleyites and other argonauts from the Pacific Slope
was basically a variation on a familiar theme. It was a late nineteenth-
century version of the journey overland by pioneer seekers of El
Dorado or the new Garden of Eden.

In each case, necessity forced the creation of a temporary community on the trail, one that embodied grass-roots democracy at its best
and worst. Observers who expected Coxeyites to be an ill-disciplined
agglomeration of tramps—the "idle, useless dregs of humanity," in
the words of New York City police superintendent Thomas Byrnes—
time and again expressed surprise and wonder at the personal clean-
liness of the troops and the organization that prevailed in their camps.
Each member had an assigned task, whether it be mending shoes,

cutting hair, or policing the campsite; and most armies operated both commissary and medical departments. "If a revolution should start suddenly, Coxey's disciplined crusaders would have the whip hand over the regulars," marveled an Oregon newspaper during the early phase of the movement.

"If we should come to a town which, by any strange cause, had been depopulated, we would be able to take immediate control of all the departments of commerce and conduct the business with experienced men," bragged one of Jeffries's officers to a Detroit reporter.[1]

The boast was basically true. Surveys conducted by B. O. Aylesworth of Drake University, I. A. Hourwich of the University of Chicago, and various journalists all agreed that a wide range of occupations was represented in the ranks of the Coxey movement. The same diversity characterized the marchers' political leanings and most other categories that could be measured: "The soldiers comprise all colors, complexions, sizes, religions and nationalities," observed the *Omaha Bee* of the Kelleyites. "They are a unit, however, in the respect that they are out of work and want to get East." The ranks invariably contained a sprinkling of Odd Fellows, Masons, and other fraternal brothers in addition to trade unionists, and these men received help from fellow members along the way.[2]

It is remarkable that anyone expected to command an ad hoc collection of such diverse individuals, even when the contingent numbered fifty members or less; many officers could not do so. Westerners in particular bore authority only with great difficulty, especially if a leader gave the impression that he preferred not to eat and sleep in camp with his followers. A poor officer was certain to fall from grace, and a gifted one was likely to rise quickly from the ranks, a fact recognized by regular army troops stationed at Fort Snelling (near Minneapolis) when they visited a camp of Coxeyites pitched nearby.

"Its too bad, too bad, but you have come too late to join Coxey's army," one of the campers greeted them with mock seriousness.

"That's so?" a soldier responded with a smile. "I'm sorry. I was thinking of joining Coxey's army because I understood there was a chance in it for rapid promotion."[3]

There was also an opportunity for rapid demotion, as a hapless band of Californians camped near Sacramento illustrated. Captain J. W. Williams told his fifty followers the bad news: "We have only a little bread and coffee and I think we'd better save these for breakfast. What do you say, men?" he asked in a loud voice. "Shall we have our coffee and bread tonight, or shall we go without supper and keep them for breakfast? All in favor of not having any supper say aye." Three-fourths of the men voted aye and the remainder nay. "The ayes have it and that settles it," said Williams. The men uttered not a murmur, but after enduring a few more days of gnawing stomachs, a bewildered leader, and no prospect for improvement, the men deposed Williams and turned to Louis Inman. They knew nothing about his past, but he seemed to be a competent officer.

A few days later, the Sacramento chief of police summoned Inman to his office. "I have an unpleasant duty to perform, Colonel Inman," the chief said when they met. "Please remove your coat and bare your arms."

Turning pale, then flush, Inman stared at the chief with a look of astonishment but did as he was told. Tattooed on his arm was an anchor, just what the police had hoped to find.

"Aren't you just out of the penitentiary, and haven't you served four terms for various crimes?" asked the chief.

The charge was true, Inman admitted, but he explained that twice he had stolen a horse and buggy while drunk. "The last time I was arrested and sentenced for forgery. I served my time and now would like to know what I am here for."

"You are under arrest."

"What for?"

"For vagrancy. You have been in this city some two weeks doing nothing for a livelihood and I understand you joined this so-called army as soon as you got here from Folsom assuming a different name from your right one."

Van R. Carpenter was his real name, and he had served time in Folsom and San Quentin prisons. Carpenter came to Sacramento from Folsom on April 16, joined a Coxey contingent under an assumed name the following day, was appointed its camp correspondent, and four days later was elevated to the rank of colonel. "I conducted myself in a manner that was intended to prove that I had reformed." And his followers agreed, welcoming him back as their leader when the vagrancy charge was soon dropped.[4]

Inman was a thief trying to make good. But in the Coxey movement, the opposite was more often the case: a variety of leaders, both idealists and opportunists, succumbed to temptation and decamped with the army's funds. Thieving officers stunned, betrayed, and disenchanted members of Jumbo Cantwell's band, Hogan's navy, and several other contingents. While Mother Jones made her way down the Missouri Valley from Kansas City working as an advance guard for a hard-luck army from Denver, General Henry Bennett left with the army's treasury to buy a boat, or so he told his followers; he never returned. And in what was the crowning injury to a trusting band of Californians, the several hundred dollars they raised for their trip east by putting on minstrel shows disappeared one day along with their ex-convict colonel, Louis Inman.[5]

Not surprisingly, Coxeyites occasionally ended their participation in the crusade with a profound distrust of leadership. Sixty-one Kelleyites pausing in Saint Louis on their way home to California offered a simple response to a reporter who asked about their leader: "We don't acknowledge any leader." The refrain was similar to the "We're all leaders" attitude of the militant and antiauthoritarian Industrial Workers of the World a decade and a half later. While the continuing cycle of work and idleness in the extractive industries of the West, along with the region's large force of individualistic, migratory labor and its equally individualistic and strong-willed employers, had something to do with the rise of both movements, it is not inconceivable that the West's free-spirited Wobblies might have borrowed at least something from former Coxeyites.

The free speech protests that Wobblies conducted in cities on the Pacific Slope beginning in 1909 resembled the passive resistance tactics that Jeffries used to get his men across Ohio and Pennsylvania. And it is entirely possible that during the off-season when lumberjacks and harvest hands congregated in the missions, soup kitchens, and Wobbly halls of Portland and Seattle, they spent more than one rainy winter afternoon discussing the Coxey movement, perhaps with someone who had tramped across the country with Jeffries. It could be that the Coxey crusade proved to realists among the Wobblies that workers could expect little relief from Congress or from politicians in general.[6]

One thing is certain: the Coxeyites would never have sung a refrain like the Wobbly favorite, "Hallelujah, I'm a Bum!" Whatever their internal strengths and weaknesses, the Coxey communities were populated by members acutely aware that their personal survival, as well as the success of their crusade, depended on cultivating a favorable public impression. Thus they conspicuously distanced themselves from the revolutionaries and hoboes, tramps, and bums with whom a disdainful public often lumped them.

When Fry's troops were camped along the Mississippi River in Saint Louis, a tramp came out of the brush and approached Colonel Galvin. "Say, Colonel," he said talking out one corner of his mouth. "I think I'll join dis gang if yez got no objections. I'm a wire worker [a pickpocket] meself. I've jes got off 'ez de pile [prison], see? and dis business suits me to a T. I'm a pretty good hustler meself, an' I knows all de boss' and some er de workin' men. What 'er yer say? Humn?"

Galvin referred the man to Captain Collins, an unemployed electrician. When the captain informed the would-be recruit that first he had to understand the purpose of the movement, the tramp responded with the same line he gave Galvin. This angered Collins, a former soldier in the United States Army: "You're off the track, my friend. You're not our kind of people. You may know all the hobos, but you don't know us, and we don't want the kind of man you are around. We get rid of them as fast as we find them."[7]

With few exceptions, the crusaders likewise shunned the rhetoric and emblems of socialism and anarchism, as when Coxey chastised the fun-loving crew of journalists on the Chesapeake and Ohio Canal for flying a red flag. And when the Ford Marching Club of South Bend, a Cleveland campaign organization, donated a collection of bright red hats to visiting Coxeyites, one worried recipient told a reporter standing nearby to remind his readers that just because they wore red hats they were not revolutionaries.

In similar fashion, during the Sunday that the men of Deming Smith's California army spent in Salt Lake City, they voted unanimously to attend the services of the Mormon Church in preference to those of the Methodists, Baptists, or Presbyterians. In a community heavily populated by Mormons, it was a prudent decision, many thought, particularly when the *Salt Lake Tribune* reported that Smith seemed to enjoy the speakers and the music. The impulse to sing religious and patriotic anthems, the conspicuous waving of the flag, and even the choice of where to worship no doubt sprang from genuine sentiment and conviction; but it also served a diplomatic purpose. Under the folds of the American flag, the Coxeyites felt safe. "And they are," observed the *Commercial Gazette* of Cincinnati, "so long as they are true to all that it means. Nor is there anything to fear from men who in good faith, follow the flag of the country." Or played baseball or wrote letters home to their wives, sweethearts, and mothers.[8]

An integral part of a favorable public image was adherence to the work ethic. Nothing, not even the wearing of a red hat or failing to attend Sunday services, was more fatal to the cause than being tagged with a reputation for shirking work. Inman, before he took the money and ran, created goodwill for his men in Sacramento by offering their services to clean up city streets and alleys at the daily rate of twelve cents per person and to cut the grass of private citizens. By the same token, when the men of Bennett's Denver army declined to abandon their crusade to take jobs building a railway line in northern Wyoming, they created no end of trouble for themselves. The mayor of Hastings, Nebraska, for example, "upon learning that the army refused to work, ordered the gang to move instantly."[9]

It was difficult for casual observers to understand why Coxeyites would not abandon their mission to Washington to take a job. "Every man of them could have found work en route, if work had been what they were looking for," sneered the *Boston Herald*. In one of several highly publicized incidents used to suggest that Coxeyites were avoiding work, an Iowa farmer turned to a group of Kelleyites riding with him: "I'll give every man in the wagon work for all the summer on my farm and in the neighborhood and guarantee him from $1 to $1.50 a day. Now, what do you say? Shall I drop out of the procession at the gate?" The riders said not a word.

"Well," continued the farmer, "what do you think you are doing anyway?"

"We are going to Washington."

"Yes, but for what?"

"To make Congress do something for the workingman."[10]

As a matter of principle, Coxeyites refused offers to "scab" on striking workers or to take jobs that could be done by local labor. General John Barker and his Californians faced that issue when they were offered $1 a day per person to cut 2,000 cords of wood. Barker replied that he did not want to interfere with the local job market. And the Salt Lake City general, Henry Carter, rejected an offer of work for his troops at $1.50 a day on railway construction, calling it a scheme to break his army: "We have in our ranks men of all trades and many professions, and to ask them to go to the wilds of Montana and work as common laborers is an insult to them." The refusals nonetheless stigmatized the men as work-shirkers.

"What do you think of Fry's army refusing work for $1.50 a day in East St. Louis?" Coxey was asked during a business trip to New York City in late April.

"Why should they accept work and let themselves be sacrificed for the main issue by temporary relief. We believe in work. Don't forget," continued the Ohioan, "that I believe that they who will not work should not be allowed to eat."

"And your army, is it working?"

"Yes, indeed; it represents millions of people and is working in their cause. The army has had no pleasure trip. This march was no junket." [11]

Also related to the Coxey movement's favorable public image was the question of violence. Some saw in it a revolutionary potential, a foreboding of bloodshed: "Wake up! Coxey is the Jeff Davis of 1894. Put down the insurrection!" screamed a western paper invoking memories of the Civil War. Hints of violence could occasionally be heard in the public speeches of Commonwealers and their sympathizers, and Coxey admitted, "I do not mean to say that there is no possibility of danger and trouble. The country today is in a perilous condition, and every thinking person realizes it."

But Coxey's language and that of the crusaders was temperate compared to the storm raised by two widely quoted sympathizers in Kansas. "I think that each state should have an army that would be organized so that if Coxey's army at Washington should meet with resistance, these state armies could rush to the state capitals and take charge of the government," said Populist A. A. Artz, former head of the state's militia and one of the most blatant exploiters of the Coxey movement. Echoing Artz was Russell Osborne, the Kansas secretary of state, who a few days after Coxey's arrest made headlines with his prediction that "there will be no overt act until the next election. Then simultaneously, the flames will shoot up into the air from the

Atlantic to the Pacific, and every palatial residence will be destroyed in this uprising of the people."[12]

Firsthand contact with the Coxeyites invariably proved reassuring to the public, as when Kelley emphasized to his Iowa listeners, "We will not break a civil or moral law at any price." For the most part, the few violent episodes that resulted in bloodshed were precipitated by bystanders or by officers of the law, as in the May Day riot on Capitol Hill or in the shooting of two Billings citizens by a posse of poorly trained deputy marshals. Several more Commonwealers were injured in violent encounters with federal deputies or railroad policemen in Yakima, the Coeur d'Alene mining region of north Idaho, and Connellsville, but these were exceptions to the general restraint exercised by both Coxeyites and the authorities. "I can't stop the Coxeyites without shooting, and I won't do that," emphasized Marshal Sam Vinson in Spokane, voicing a belief apparently shared by most federal lawmen. In each of the several encounters between Coxeyites and the United States Army, the regulars prevailed without having to fire a shot.[13]

During the entire Coxey movement, only one crusader died at the hands of lawmen. He was Colonel William S. Paisley, a handsome young boilermaker in Deming Smith's California army. In an incident involving a captured train near Sacramento, a constable shot him in what was perhaps an accident. Smith, an Englishman of slight build who had once practiced medicine in Oakland, rushed forward to protect the frightened lawman from the wrath of his troops, who took up the cry "Lynch him!" Two thousand people turned out for Paisley's funeral in Oakland, and an indignation meeting passed resolutions condemning the killing. A jury later acquitted the constable.[14]

Among the various forces that made the Coxey crusade possible—such as the misery created by hard times, the boost given Coxeyism by the press, the sympathy of organized labor and the Populist party, and the American tendency to root for the underdog—one of the most important was the intensely local orientation of the nation's communities. At one time villagers had been largely self-sufficient, knowing little about what happened beyond their borders. Although the nation had undergone a noticeable degree of economic centralization during the three decades after the Civil War—"economic cephalization," in the words of Thorstein Veblen—localism remained the focus of Americans when confronting social problems.[15]

"Ladies," an Indianapolis merchant told the sellers of Henry Vincent's *The Story of the Commonweal*, "if it were a worthy cause I would not hesitate in buying one. Your armies are not of the best class. I have already contributed largely for relief work last winter and this spring, and intend to do so in the future if the people need it—that is, for the people of this city. Indianapolis, too, has enough to take care of its own needy and not to look out for outsiders." And similar forms of localism were the rule from San Francisco to Washington, D.C.

The practical implications of localism were made abundantly clear to one young member of Fry's army, who suffered from a severe case of swollen and blistered feet. "Can't you do something for me, officer?" the boy asked an Indianapolis police sergeant.

"You are not a citizen [local resident] so you would not be allowed to be taken to the city hospital. You fellows ought to have a physician along with you. However, don't cry, my boy, and I'll see if we can't fix you out all right." The kindhearted Sergeant La Porte returned a few minutes later with a bottle of liniment.[16]

Because of the pervasive localism, the first industrial army to enter a community could not always predict whether it would be welcomed or shunned. And, in a curious way, the local orientation of the nation's communities actually fostered the mobility of Coxeyites: while sympathizers sustained them on the road, even people unsympathetic to the movement found it easier to feed the marchers and pass them on to the next town rather than have them disband on their doorstep. "If six men should come to town and fasten themselves on the people and refuse to labor for their subsistence they would be treated as common vagrants." But when the number was sixty or six hundred, local authorities thought twice about the cost of jailing so many visitors. What were the alternatives, police and city officials in Cleveland asked one another in an open debate.

"Escort them to the city limits with a large detail of police," said one.

"But if they won't march?"

"Get a special train of streetcars and ride them out."

"But if they won't get on the cars?

"Then arrest them."

"But we don't want to arrest them."

"Then let them alone."

"I guess we'll have to unless we can think of some other scheme." [17]

Occasionally a community arrested the crusaders, then suspended their sentences if they promised to leave town. A more common practice was to provide them a meal and send them on as soon as possible, in some cases by encouraging them to steal trains. This practice prompted railroad magnate James J. Hill to complain to President Cleveland, "There seems to be absolutely no way of enforcing municipal or state authority. Local communities where these men gather are only too glad to connive at anything that will take them away, and even ready to help them." [18]

Even the most generous people resented the idea of providing for Coxeyites on a long-term basis, and there was a limit to the altruism of the home guards. Said the secretary of the Denver unit, "The home reserve was not formed to support men from Utah and California and all the other places, but was to take care of the people of Denver." If the Coxeyites really expected the federal government to shoulder the responsibility for providing work to all Americans who desired it, they would have to educate their fellow citizens to see the problem of unemployment relief from a national perspective. And they could have begun by broadening the horizons of their own locally oriented supporters. [19]

Commentators, especially those who had no personal contact with the Coxeyites, frequently disparaged their intelligence and motivation: "What the army wants is bacon, whiskey, hominy, pie and the like, without working for them." Some members probably did see the crusade as nothing more than a meal ticket, but there were also participants who self-consciously believed they were making history. In every contingent members kept diaries, and some intended to immortalize the great adventure by writing a book about it after they reached Washington. One man, an accomplished stenographer, was seen jotting down extensive notes in shorthand.

Even those crusaders who kept no records often possessed a sense of history. Upon showing his membership book to a reporter, a member of Hogan's navy remarked, "I would not part with that book for anything, for long in the future it will be something for my people to be proud of." Unfortunately, few membership books and diaries survived, and no lengthy recollections were published afterwards. The voluminous newspaper record of the movement, however, makes it abundantly clear that the members endured their hardships because they expected their mission to result in better times for all. If Congress should fail to act upon their petitions in 1894, their protest would nonetheless further the ongoing economic and political education of the common folk and plant seeds of thought that would later bear the fruits of reform, or so the Coxeyites consoled themselves.[20]

Although there was no way to measure accurately the educational impact of the crusade, even hostile onlookers believed it had one: "These men, after their own fashion are building more wisely than they know of," asserted the *Press-Times* of Seattle. They had made an impression on Americans, "and once the national mind agrees upon the fact that a new direction must be given to affairs, there is no telling to what great and good ends it may lead." The *Rocky Mountain News*, a supporter of the movement, added that it would move the country at the polls. "Better, wiser and more humane laws in the near future must be the outcome." And in an effort to treat the movement in its historical perspective, the *National Labor Tribune* reminded readers that the absurdity of today may become the wisdom of tomorrow, an aphorism that must have crossed the mind of many a reformer who suffered a setback.[21]

Coxeyism, in short, was perceived by a variety of contemporaries as part of an ongoing process of education. It chipped away at the popular belief that poverty and unemployment were mainly the result of individual weakness and laziness and promoted the idea that the federal government was responsible for the economic well-being of its citizens.

The Coxey movement contributed to the reform education of Americans through direct contact with individuals who lived along the way and by stimulating debate on a variety of issues by the press, study clubs, lyceums, and other public forums that once functioned as the primary agencies of adult education. Moreover, dozens of colporteurs accompanied the marchers, selling an assortment of reform

"We Demand Nothing but Justice"—Kelley's army in Iowa. Courtesy
Iowa State Historical Department, State Historical Society.

tracts that ranged from Douglas McCallum's eccentric allegory *Dogs
and Fleas, by One of the Dogs* to Edward Bellamy's utopian novel *Looking Backward.* The marchers themselves peddled copies of their songs
and special newspapers such as *Keep off the Grass, The Commonweal,*
and the *Industrial Army News,* the latter printed on cheap butcher
paper and selling for five cents. The most popular item was Vincent's
The Story of the Commonweal, which appeared in late April. Forty
thousand copies of that illustrated tract were consigned to Indianapolis alone, and with Fry's army in town they sold briskly. Many of the
peddlers were women.[22]

Public debate centered mainly on two issues: the complaint of the
disinherited and fears of governmental paternalism. Speaking for
the disinherited were the Coxey movement's numerous unlettered
oracles, such as Henry Carter, who described the voices of the unemployed as joining in a "hoarse swelling chorus, sounding through the
nation a protest against plutocracy and the corporate power that has
ground them into the dust and made them slaves in this land of the
free and home of the brave." His counterpart, Lewis Fry, told five

hundred listeners in Indianapolis, "When Jesus was on earth He said that the earth and the fullness [thereof] belonged to the Lord. If he came to Indianapolis He would find that it belongs to the bond-holders." Furthermore, said Fry, the authorities "would have him in jail as a vagrant." Such sentiments were not unique to Coxeyism, al-though the unprecedented "petition in boots" seemed to give them special urgency.[23]

Edward Jeffries offered one solution to disinheritance. He empha-sized the inflationary potential of Coxeyism when he stated: "The government could end these hard times in a couple of months if it would only issue enough money so that the millionaires would not have it all and there would be some left for the rest of us." But the various Coxeyite proposals for government aid amounted to nothing less than a call for paternalism, warned the *Chicago Record*, one of America's many staunch defenders of the ideal of rugged indi-vidualism. "The country is sick just to the extent that its people try to lean on the government instead of standing upright on their own two feet."

Joining the debate was the *Kansas City Star*, which was certain that the "rage for paternalism which is sweeping the land must neces-sarily be short lived. It will speedily run its course. It is opposed to the spirit of true Americanism, and it is not favored by the mass of the people." But *Munsey's*, one of the new breed of popular maga-zines, was not so sure: once paternalism began its march, the result would be the "subordination of all individual initiative and the de-struction of the very keystone of our social fabric." *Munsey's* pre-dicted correctly that paternalism would become a major issue in the twentieth century.[24]

Some commentators treated paternalism as an exotic import, like the Coxey movement itself. Others argued that it was well rooted in the American past, and they recalled how the Civil War had encour-aged the growth of the federal government. "Laws are now passed by Congress and enforced by federal officials, and acquiesced in and ap-proved by the people, which would have been stoutly resisted by the states prior to 1850." The protective tariff and other subsidies to busi-ness were most frequently identified as the fountainheads of pater-nalism. "Coxey's followers proposed to demand at Washington what has been freely granted to the beneficiaries of the protective tariff, to the receivers of sugar bounties and ship subsidies, to the promoters of land grant railways and tombstone contracts, to all the schemers and adventurers who have for thirty years gorged themselves out of the commonwealth," the *Post-Dispatch* of Saint Louis reminded its readers. A Montana newspaper chimed in that if "a maker of Pennsylvania pig iron is to be supported in luxury at public expense, why not a Coxeyite. The Coxeyite idea is the logical result of protection. It is paternalism run mad." [25]

Some Americans equated paternalism with socialism or subversion: "To change the republic to a paternal form of government is an experiment no patriotic citizen can desire for one moment." Such assertions prompted one observer of the discontent of the 1890s to respond, "All they ask is the society they have always known, with the prosperity they have from time to time enjoyed. This is not socialism." Whatever the merits of the debate, it seemed clear to many that if Coxeyism prevailed, the federal government would have to assume vast new responsibilities for the welfare of its citizens. That worried people like H. L. Stetson, president of Des Moines College, who told his students, "The business of government is not to furnish employment to all at $2.50 per day. The very hour that the United States agrees so to do, that hour it goes out of existence." [26]

In a way, the Coxey movement represented a double-barreled assault on the fundamental beliefs of Americans. Not only did it seek to educate them into accepting a certain amount of federal responsibility for the economic health of the nation; but the very existence of the crusade—and especially its prominence in the West—undermined the popular belief that the fertile agricultural lands of the frontier represented America's most practical form of social security and a wise alternative to governmental paternalism.

The numerous cases of train piracy in Montana, Oregon, and other parts of the West by armies of unemployed men helped to direct public attention to the dwindling supply of free land in America. What did it mean when the nation's supposedly inexhaustible supply of fertile, easily obtainable farmland ran out? A Seattle newspaper succinctly expressed the popular belief when it editorialized in early 1894, "All social problems solve themselves in the presence of a boundless expanse of vacant fertile land." Free land was for Americans their

God-given inheritance, distinguishing them from the less richly endowed inhabitants of Old World nations. Thus they had a right to wonder whether the numerous episodes of train stealing by the unemployed signaled the end of the free-land era. Was the unnerving spectacle of lawlessness a portent of troubled times to come? Many observers thought so.[27]

What was really at stake was the traditional meaning of America, and newspapers in the West were quick to voice the popular concern. The *Seattle Telegraph*, which worried a great deal about the end of free land and the supposed closing of the frontier in 1890, observed, "The Anglo-Saxon race has hitherto gained its triumphs through individual self-reliance. It is something new that from points all along the Pacific Coast between Canada and Mexico organized troops of men have set their faces toward the East to seek from the government what their fathers would have scorned from the hands of the state. Has the Anglo-Saxon race, as represented in this country, passed its meridian?" A North Dakota daily expressed a similar worry: "There is one great and significant feature about this crusade movement, and that is it proceeds from the west. For centuries in all countries the first movements toward relief from oppression, and towards independence, have arisen in the west. Men and women have moved west for greater freedom, and to better their condition. Reforms have originated in the west. But the end of the west has been reached." The various journalists who addressed this theme contributed to the national mood of concern.[28]

Especially during periods of hard times, the West had long been seen as having a special quality, its free land mythologized into a kind of safety valve relieving the discontent that arose among dwellers in the nation's densely populated industrial neighborhoods. Free land was thereby supposed to prevent the kind of massive social disruptions that Americans chauvinistically identified with decadent European social and economic systems.

But historians writing in more recent times have challenged the mythology of the free-land safety valve; some have used statistics to show that more people moved from the country to the city during periods of economic distress than the other way around. The fact remains that a good many nineteenth-century Americans believed in the free-land safety valve and formulated their outlooks and actions accordingly. People, in other words, responded to perceptions of reality as if they were dealing with reality itself. And as long as even a handful of people escaped the industrial city for the free lands of the West, the dream seemed real enough.[29]

Clinging rigidly to the dream without considering reality occasionally produced unhappy consequences, as Coxeyites caught up in violence in Yakima learned. Before federal Judge Cornelius Hanford sentenced them to McNeil Island Penitentiary, he gave them a stern lecture on western opportunity: "The people that came to this Northwest country when my father did, found here no railroads, nor steamboats, nor manufacturing industries to give employment and afford wages . . . and when they met with hard times, instead of going back east making demands on the government for relief, they planted potatoes and peas and cabbage, and preserved themselves and their families from starvation. They set out fruit trees, which bore fruit a good deal quicker than any extraordinary measures by which it is proposed to obtain relief." For some reason, the unemployed in Hanford's court were not inclined to wait three or four years for trees to bear fruit so that they might ease their hunger.[30]

Other westerners remained convinced that free land was an excellent curative for the woes of unemployment but unlike Judge Hanford were willing to admit that times had changed. The spectacle of armies of the unemployed moving across the West caused General Grenville M. Dodge, famous for building the Union Pacific line west from Omaha, to endorse an irrigation plan proposed by members of the western contingents. "The fertile and tillable lands," said Dodge, "are pretty well taken up and there is no doubt but that there is a vast area in the West that might be made into valuable farms by the construction of irrigation ditches."

The idea of building irrigation ditches brought a real gleam of hope to the eyes of unemployed westerners. Kelley explained to a Saint Louis audience how Uncle Sam could help the unemployed realize the western dream of individual opportunity by putting them to work building the vast irrigation systems necessary to bring water to arid lands: "When the ditches are dug and the lands reclaimed we can register homestead claims and be self-supporting ever after." To his listeners in Michigan, Jeffries elaborated on what irrigation of western lands would mean to wageworkers, claiming that if irrigated lands were readily available, "the laboring man who cannot get the price which he considers his work to be worth can become a farmer, be his own master and become independent." Concurring with this proposal, the *Los Angeles Times* editorialized, "If Congress would only get through squabbling over the tariff and the income tax, and spend some weeks devising a plan for irrigating what is now worthless land, they would go a long way toward settling the labor difficulties which now confront us."[31]

In the mythology of the West, pioneer residents were self-reliant, rugged individualists, or at least they publicly aspired to that status. But in reality they were quick to turn to the federal government for help. That should not seem so strange, for Uncle Sam's presence was more visible in the West than in any other region. The government was and is today the most prominent custodian of its natural resources. Legislators sitting in Washington, D.C., voted to create homesteads on lands most would never see, to encourage private development of remote timber and mineral resources, and to grant the land and loans that helped to finance most of the western transcontinental railways. Uncle Sam's army occasionally protected western settlers from Indians (or vice versa). And the treasury department's purchases of silver bullion subsidized the western mining industry for years and gave employment to thousands. Why, then, the Coxeyites asked, should not the federal government put the unemployed to work making the desert bloom? The jobless of 1894 were asking Uncle Sam to lend them a helping hand as he had done earlier for the entrepreneurs who built the Pacific railroads or the homesteaders eager to tackle the problems of farming 160 acres of prairieland. Thus the call for federal sponsorship of irrigation projects to put the unemployed to work building canals in the ultimate hope of resettling them in the new garden marked no real break with the past.[32]

The irrigation scheme was only a way of buying time, and ultimately the mythology of the free-land safety valve proved to be a poor tool to deal with massive unemployment in an urban-industrial society. But it took the hard times of the 1890s and such disorders as the Coxey movement and the Pullman strike to hasten the process of exploding that myth. Only when people discarded the environmental approach to unemployment were they able to recognize that the state might deal directly with the problem without using free land as an intermediary. Eventually the idea voiced by the Coxey crusaders— that the federal government should provide them with public-works jobs— found its way onto the nation's political agenda and was finally accepted by the president and Congress during the hard times of the 1930s. In a 1935 radio speech, President Franklin D. Roosevelt observed: "Today we can no longer escape into virgin territory. . . . We have been compelled by stark necessity to unlearn the too comfortable superstition that the American soil was mystically blessed with every kind of immunity to grave economic maladjustments." In short, the modern welfare state was a response by government to some of the social and economic problems that the free-land safety valve once supposedly addressed.[33]

Although Coxey's proposal for non-interest-bearing bonds was never accepted by Congress, the public-works principle of his crusade was embodied in the New Deal's relief and recovery programs that put the nation's unemployed to work building roads, dams, and a host of other projects during the Great Depression of the 1930s. In the Employment Act of 1946, the federal government finally assumed legal responsibility for full employment.[34]

Historian Henry Steele Commager described the 1890s as a watershed. On one side lay an America predominantly agricultural, self-contained, and self-reliant. On the other side lay modern America, urban and industrial, "experiencing profound changes in population, social institutions, economy, and technology; and trying to accommodate its traditional institutions and habits of thought to conditions new and in part alien." The Coxey movement straddled that great divide. Its origin was a popular belief in the continued viability of grass-roots democracy, and from its many opponents it elicited condemnations firmly grounded in the self-reliant, agrarian tradition of the older America. To many supporters, on the other hand, Coxeyism also underscored the economic and political problems confronting modern America and offered a reasonable solution to one of the worst of these—unemployment. In common with the Populist revolt, Coxeyism was a democratic movement that called into question the underlying values of the new industrial society. In a general sense both movements failed, although ameliorative elements of their protest programs were in time appropriated by Democrats and Republicans and enacted into law. The story of the Coxey movement is ultimately a case study of how ordinary citizens influence—or fail to influence—political and economic issues in modern America.[35]

The primary repository of information on the Coxey movement is the daily and weekly press. In researching this study, I consulted runs of 142 newspapers from 31 states and territories and the District of Columbia. Represented were 98 cities as diverse as Boston and Houston, Marquette and Bakersfield. Political orientation ranged from Republican and Democrat to Populist and labor. The most useful of these papers are cited in individual chapter notes. Heavy reliance upon this source, however, is not without its pitfalls: the pressures of deadlines occasionally led reporters to make factual errors, as when Ray Stannard Baker confused the towns of Brownsville and Uniontown, Pennsylvania. The press also used contemporary terms and concepts that became unfamiliar a generation or two later.

In an effort to double-check the press and to provide necessary background information, I relied on maps, the various state and city guides prepared by the Federal Writers' Project of the Works Progress Administration, and a number of travel documents, most notably four useful reprints:

Frederick E. Shearer, ed., *The Pacific Tourist: Adams and Bishop's Illustrated Trans-Continental Guide of Travel from the Atlantic to the Pacific Ocean*, introduction by James D. Horan (1884; reprint ed., New York: Bounty Books, 1970).

Karl Baedeker, *The United States, with an Excursion into Mexico: A Handbook for Travellers, 1893*, new introduction by Henry Steele Commager (1893; reprint ed., New York: Da Capo Press, 1971).

Moses King, ed., *King's Handbook of the United States, 1896* (1896; reprint ed., New York: Benjamin Blom, 1972).

Travelers' Official Guide of the Railway and Steam Navigation Lines in the United States and Canada, June 1893 (1893; reissue of original ed., New York: National Railway Publication Company, 1972).

Notes to Prologue

1 Unless otherwise noted, the events of May Day are reconstructed from the *Washington Post*, May 1–2, 1894; *Washington Star*, May 1, 1894; *Washington Times*, May 2, 1894; *New York Times*, May 2, 1894; *Ohio State Journal* (Columbus), May 2, 1894; *Chicago Record*, May 2, 1894; Carl Browne, *When Coxey's "Army" Marcht on Washington, 1894,* ed. William McDevitt (San Francisco: n.p., 1944); W. T. Stead, "'Coxeyism': A Character Sketch," *American Review of Reviews* 10 (July 1894): 47–56; Embrey Bernard Howson, "Jacob Sechler Coxey: A Biography of a Monetary Reformer, 1854–1951" (Ph.D. diss., Ohio State University, 1973), pp. 115–18; Ray Stannard Baker, "Coxey's Army: One of the Humors of Modern History," *Nickell Magazine* 7 (February 27, 1897): 67–84; Gerald G. Eggert, *Richard Olney: Evolution of a Statesman* (University Park, Pa.: Pennsylvania State University Press, 1974), pp. 119–21. Also of value were Henry Vincent, *The Story of the Commonweal* (1894; reprint ed., New York: Arno, 1969), and Donald L. McMurry, *Coxey's Army: A Study of the Industrial Army Movement of 1894* (1929; reprint ed., Seattle: University of Washington Press, 1968).
2 *Chicago Herald*, December 10, 1893.
3 Ray Stannard Baker, *Native American: The Book of My Youth* (New York: Charles Scribner's Sons, 1941), p. 249; John E. Semonche, *Ray Stannard Baker, A Quest for Democracy in Modern America, 1870–1918* (Chapel Hill: University of North Carolina Press, 1969), pp. 61–65. See also Robert C. Bannister, Jr., *Ray Stannard Baker: The Mind and Thought of a Progressive* (New Haven: Yale University Press, 1966).
4 Browne, *Coxey's "Army"*, p. 19.
5 U.S., Congress, *Congressional Record*, 53rd Cong., 2d sess., 1894, 26, pt. 5: 4295–307; *Omaha World-Herald*, May 2, 1894; Reports, May 1, 1894, Grover Cleveland Papers, Library of Congress, Washington, D.C.
6 *Daily Iowa Capital* (Des Moines), April 30, 1894.
7 Murray Morgan, *Puget's Sound: A Narrative of Early Tacoma and the Southern Sound* (Seattle: University of Washington Press, 1979), pp. 195–211, 288–89; *Seattle Daily Telegraph*, May 8, 1894; *Chicago Searchlight*, clip-

ping (n.d.) in the Jacob Sechler Coxey Papers, Massillon Museum, Ohio Historical Society microfilm.

8 The Polish contingent originated in April, when organizers of Chicago's main army refused to admit anyone who was unable to speak English. Led by Count Joseph Rybakowski, the 200 members of the Commonweal's "International Branch" left Chicago in early June and made their way through South Bend, Detroit, Toledo, and Cleveland, all centers of Polish settlement. Rybakowski's band came to grief in Buffalo in mid-August when it was attacked by lawmen and dispersed. *Buffalo Evening News*, August 21–25, 1894.

9 Roger A. Bruns, *Knights of the Road: A Hobo History* (New York: Methuen, 1980), pp. 47–60; Richard W. Etulain, ed., *Jack London on the Road: The Tramp Diary and Other Hobo Writings* (Logan: Utah State University Press, 1979).

10 Samuel Gompers, *Seventy Years of Life and Labor; An Autobiography* (New York: Dutton, 1925), vol. 2, p. 11.

11 Walter T. K. Nugent, *From Centennial to World War: American Society, 1876–1917* (Indianapolis: Bobbs-Merrill, 1977); Robert H. Wiebe, *The Search For Order, 1877–1920* (New York: Hill and Wang, 1967); Alan Trachtenberg, *The Incorporation of America: Culture and Society in the Gilded Age* (New York: Hill & Wang, 1982).

12 *Chicago Herald*, August 25, 1893; Samuel Reznick, "Unemployment, Unrest, and Relief in the United States during the Depression of 1893–1897," *Journal of Political Economy* 61 (August 1953): 324–45; Douglas W. Steeples, "The Panic of 1893: Contemporary Reflections and Reactions," *Mid-America* 47 (July 1965): 155–75; Charles Hoffmann, *The Depression of the Nineties, an Economic History* (Westport, Conn.: Greenwood, 1970); H. Roger Grant, *Self-Help in the 1890s Depression* (Ames: Iowa State University Press, 1983), pp. 3–22; Leah Hannah Feder, *Unemployment Relief in Periods of Depression: A Study of Measures Adopted in Certain American Cities, 1857 Through 1922* (New York: Russell Sage Foundation, 1936), pp. 71–188; *Fourth Biennial Report of the Bureau of Labor Statistics of the State of Colorado, 1893–1894* (Denver: Smith-Brooks, 1894), pp. 361–63; *Chicago Inter Ocean*, December 30, 1893; *Tacoma Daily News*, January 2, 1894.

13 *Chicago Inter Ocean*, December 30, 1894.

14 *Chicago Tribune*, August 22, 1893; *Chicago Inter Ocean*, July 27, August 1, 1893; *Chicago Herald*, July 31, 1893; *Tacoma Daily News*, September 13, 1894. See also M. Harvey Brenner, *Mental Illness and the Economy* (Cambridge, Mass.: Harvard University Press, 1973).

15 *Chicago Inter Ocean*, December 17, 1893; *Cleveland Citizen*, March 10, July 21, 1894.

16 W. T. Stead, *If Christ Came to Chicago* (London: n.p., 1894), pp. 158–59; *Chicago Inter Ocean*, December 22, 1893; *Denver Republican*, July 28, 1893, clipping in the Industrial Army File, Union Pacific Collection, Nebraska Historical Society, Lincoln; *Seattle People's Call*, August 3, 1893.

17 *Northwest Magazine* 12 (June 1894): 22; *Popular Science Monthly* 44 (April 1894): 842, 843; ibid., 45 (August 1894): 557; Frank Leonard, "'Helping' the Unemployed in the Nineteenth Century: The Case of the American Tramp," *Social Service Review* 40 (December 1966): 429–34; William Graham Sumner, "The Absurd Effort to Make the World Over," *Forum* 17 (March 1894): 92–102. See also Sidney Fine, *Laissez Faire and the General-Welfare State: A Study of Conflict in American Thought, 1865–1901* (Ann Arbor: University of Michigan Press, 1956), and John A. Garraty, *Unemployment in History: Economic Thought and Public Policy* (New York, Harper & Row, 1978), pp. 103–28.

18 *Denver News*, July 28, 1893, clipping in the Industrial Army File, Union Pacific Collection, Nebraska Historical Society; Richard Erdoes, *Saloons of the Old West* (New York: Knopf, 1979), p. 103; *Butte Miner*, April 6, 1894; *Anaconda Standard*, April 22, 1894; Reznick, "Unemployment, Unrest, and Relief," p. 330; *Tacoma Morning Union*, December 26, 1894; Morgan, *Puget's Sound*, pp. 320–21.

19 Feder, *Unemployment Relief*, pp. 71–188; *Tacoma Morning Union*, January 16, 1894; *Chicago Record*, September 4, 1893; Reznick, "Unemployment, Unrest, and Relief," pp. 330–31.

20 *Omaha Daily Bee*, November 26, 1894; *Tacoma Morning Union*, November 30, December 17, 1893; January 21, 1894; *Chicago Herald*, January 9, 1894.

21 *Indianapolis News*, April 24, 1894; Carter Goodrich and Sol Davison, "The Wage Earner in the Westward Movement, I," *Political Science Quarterly* 50 (June 1935): 161–85; *Seattle Telegraph*, April 26, June 8, 1894; Frederick Jackson Turner, "The Significance of the Frontier in American History," in *The Frontier in American History*, ed. Frederick Jackson Turner (1920; reprint ed., Huntington, N.Y.: Robert E. Krieger, 1976), pp. 1–38; Ray Allen Billington, *Frederick Jackson Turner: Historian, Scholar, Teacher* (New York: Oxford University Press, 1973), pp. 108–26.

22 W. G. Sumner, "Absurd Effort," pp, 92, 94.

23 Lawrence Goodwyn, *Democratic Promise: The Populist Moment in America* (New York: Oxford University Press, 1976); Lyman Abbott, "The Wages System," *Forum* 9 (July 1890): 527; James B. Weaver, "The Commonweal Crusade," *Midland Monthly* 1 (June 1894): 591.

24 *Cleveland Plain Dealer*, April 1, 1894; *Seattle Telegraph*, March 30, 1894; Grover Cleveland, "Fourth Annual Message to Congress, December 3, 1888," in *A Compilation of Messages and Papers of the Presidents*, vol. 8, comp. James D. Richardson (Washington, D.C.: By authority of Congress, 1899), p. 776.

25 *San Francisco Examiner*, as quoted in the *Tacoma Daily News*, March 30, 1894; *Chicago Sentinel*, as quoted in the *Cleveland Citizen*, May 12, 1894; Leopold Vincent, comp., *The Alliance Songster: A Collection of Labor and Comic Songs for the Use of Grange, Alliance and Debating Clubs* (Winfield, Kan.: H. & L. Vincent Printers, 1891).

26 *Washington Post*, June 21, 1894, p. 1; Samuel P. Hayes, *The Response to Industrialism, 1885–1914* (Chicago: University of Chicago Press, 1957), pp. 71–93; Garraty, *The New Commonwealth*, pp. 128–78; Carlos A. Schwantes, "Protest in a Promised Land: Unemployment, Disinheritance, and the Origin of Labor Militancy in the Pacific Northwest, 1885–1886," *Western Historical Quarterly* 13 (October 1982): 373–90.

27 Henry M. Littlefield, "The Wizard of Oz: Parable on Populism," *American Quarterly* 16 (Spring 1964): 47–58. See also Raylun Moore, *Wonderful Wizard, Marvelous Land* (Bowling Green, Ohio: Bowling Green University Popular Press, 1974); L. Frank Baum, *The Wizard of Oz* (Chicago: Rand McNally, 1900).

28 *Tacoma Daily News*, May 2, 1894; *Washington Star*, April 17, 1894.

Notes to Chapter 1

1 David F. Burg, *Chicago's White City of 1893* (Lexington: University of Kentucky Press, 1976); Ray Ginger, *Altgeld's America, 1890–1905: The Lincoln Idea versus Changing Realities* (1958; reprint ed., Chicago: Quadrangle Books, 1965), pp. 20–21; Emmett Dedmon, *Fabulous Chicago*, enlarged ed. (New York: Atheneum Publishers, 1981), p. 234; *Chicago Inter Ocean*, August 2, 1893.

2 Claudius O. Johnson, *Carter Henry Harrison I: Political Leader* (Chicago: University of Chicago Press, 1928); *Chicago Inter Ocean*, August 1–3, 1893; *Public Opinion* 15 (August 12, 1893): 449; *Chicago Tribune*, July 23, 1893; August 2, 1893; Frank Basil Tracy, "Menacing Socialism in the Western States," *Forum* 15 (May 1893): 332–42; Martin Ridge, *Ignatius Donnelly, The Portrait of a Politician* (Chicago: University of Chicago Press, 1962), pp. 265, 322–23.

3 Carl Browne, *When Coxey's "Army" Marcht on Washington, 1894*, ed. William McDevitt (San Francisco: n.p., 1944) p. 4; *Washington Star*,

April 25, April 26, 1894; *Chicago Inter Ocean*, July 31, 1893; *Cactus*, February 11, 1888; *Chicago Tribune*, August 1, 1893.

4 H. Wayne Morgan, *From Hayes to McKinley: National Party Politics, 1877–1896* (Syracuse: Syracuse University Press, 1969), pp. 448–58; Leopold Vincent, comp., *The Alliance Songster, A Collection of Labor and Comic Songs, for the Use of Grange, Alliance and Debating Clubs* (Winfield, Kan.: H. & L. Vincent Printers, 1891), p. 17.

5 *Chicago Tribune*, July 30, August 1, 1893; *Chicago Inter Ocean*, December 15, 1893.

6 Ray Stannard Baker, *Native American: The Book of My Youth* (New York: Charles Scribner's Sons, 1941), pp. 259–62, 288, 321.

7 *Chicago Inter Ocean*, August 16, 1893; *Chicago Herald*, August 27–31, 1893; *Chicago Tribune*, August 22, August 27, 1893; *Chicago Record*, August 30–31, September 4, 1893.

8 Baker, *Native American*, pp. 320, 324; *Chicago Inter Ocean*, December 10, 17, 18, 22, 23, 1893.

9 Baker, *Native American*, p. 325; *Chicago Inter Ocean*, December 4, 9–10, 1893.

10 *Chicago Record*, October 30, November 25, 1893.

11 Ignatius Donnelly, *Caesar's Column: A Story of the Twentieth Century* (Chicago: M. A. Donohue, [1889]).

12 *Public Opinion* 15 (September 22, 1893): 502; *Chicago Herald*, December 22, 1893.

13 *Chicago Herald*, August 1, August 29, 1893; *Chicago Tribune*, August 3, 1893; *Chicago Inter Ocean*, July 31, 1893.

14 Browne, *Coxey's "Army"*, pp. 4, 5; *Coxey Good Roads & Non-Interest Bearing Bond Library* (Massillon) 1 (May 1895): 23; *Chicago Record*, December 16, 1893; *Chicago Inter Ocean*, December 17, 1893; Edward W. Bemis, "The Convention of the American Federation of Labor," *Journal of Political Economy* 2 (March 1894): 298–99; Samuel Gompers, *Seventy Years of Life and Labor; an Autobiography* (New York: E. P. Dutton, 1925), vol. 2, p. 8.

15 *Ohio State Journal*, March 25, 1894; Browne, *Coxey's "Army"*, p. 5; W. T. Stead, "'Coxeyism': A Character Sketch," *American Review of Reviews* 10 (July 1894): 48–49.

Notes to Chapter 2

1 *Chicago Record*, March 17, 1894; Embry Bernard Howson, "Jacob Sechler Coxey: A Biography of a Monetary Reformer, 1854–1951" (Ph.D. diss., Ohio State University, 1973), p. 117; Henry Vincent, *The Story of the Com-*

monweal (1894; reprint ed., New York: Arno, 1969), p. 49.

2 Advertisement for "Cox-e-lax" in Jacob Sechler Coxey Papers, Box 4, Folder 8, Ohio Historical Society microfilm, *Baltimore American*, May 20, 1894; *Philadelphia Inquirer*, March 29, 1894; Howson, "Jacob Sechler Coxey," pp. 4, 5, 7, 15–16, 115, 369n3, 397; *Washington Post*, April 30, 1894; *Chicago Tribune*, May 8, 1894, p. 2. Coxey's first wife, the former Caroline Amerman, was the sister of Pennsylvania Congressman Lemuel Amerman. Howson, "Jacob Sechler Coxey," pp. 115, 117.

3 *Chicago Record*, March 17–19, 1894; *Cleveland Plain Dealer*, March 21, 1894; Carey McWilliams, *Southern California Country: An Island on the Land* (New York: Duell, Sloan and Pearce, 1946), pp. 253, 254.

4 *Washington Post*, April 30, 1894; Ray Stannard Baker, "Coxey and his Commonweal" (Manuscript in the Ray Stannard Baker Papers, Box 72, Library of Congress, Washington, D.C.), p. 117; *Washington Times*, April 28, 1894; *Tacoma News*, July 10, 1894; Donald L. McMurry, *Coxey's Army: A Study of the Industrial Army Movement of 1894* (1929; reprint ed., Seattle: University of Washington Press, 1968), pp. 28–29.

5 Vincent, *Commonweal*, pp. 109–11; *Omaha World-Herald*, May 2, 1894, p. 1; Howson, "Jacob Sechler Coxey," p. 257n12 (quotation); W. T. Stead, "Coxeyism: A Character Sketch," *American Review of Reviews* 10 (July 1894): 52; Carl Browne, *When Coxey's "Army" Marcht on Washington, 1894*, ed. William McDevitt (San Francisco: n.p., 1944), p. 26; *Washington Star*, April 23, 25, and 30, 1894; *St. Louis Post-Dispatch*, April 29, 1894; *Carl Browne's Labor Knight* (Sacramento), June 19, 1911; *Wasp* (San Francisco), March 31, 1894; *American Nonconformist* (Indianapolis), April 19, 1896.

6 Except where noted otherwise, the description of march preparations is derived from *Coxey Good Roads & Non-Interest Bearing Bond Library* (Massillon) 1 (May 1895): 23; Browne, *Coxey's "Army"*, pp. 5–7; *St. Louis Post-Dispatch*, April 8, 1894; *Chicago Record*, March 19–28, 1894; *Washington Star*, April 23, 1894; *Pittsburgh Post*, March 26, 1894; *Ohio State Journal* (Columbus), May 15, 1894; *Cleveland Plain Dealer*, March 21–28, 1894; *Los Angeles Times*, March 24, 1894; *Seattle Daily Telegraph*, March 30, 1894; *Washington Star*, March 24, May 1, 1894; *Pittsburgh Post*, March 25, 1894; *Kansas City Star*, April 29, 1894; McMurry, *Coxey's Army*, pp. 34–48; Henry Vincent, *Commonweal* (1894; reprint ed., New York: Arno, 1969), pp. 119–20.

7 For a compilation of Coxey documents and pictures, see Osman C. Hooper, "The Coxey Movement in Ohio," *Ohio State Archeological and Historical Society* 9 (1901): 155–76.

8 *Woman's Tribune* (Washington, D.C.), May 12, 1894; *St. Louis Post-Dispatch*;

288

Ray Ginger, *Altgeld's America: The Lincoln Ideal Versus Changing Realities* (1958; reprint ed., Chicago: Quadrangle Books, 1965), pp. 35–36.

9 Carl Browne Open Letter in Jacob Sechler Coxey Papers, Box 4, Folder 11, Ohio Historical Society, Columbus; *Cleveland Plain Dealer*, March 18, 1894; *Washington Times*, April 16, 1894.

10 *Chicago Record*, April 4, 1894; *Louisville Courier-Journal*, March 26, 1894.

11 *Chicago Express*, March 31, 1894, clipping in Coxey Papers; *Public Opinion* 16 (March 22, 1894): 595.

12 Except where noted otherwise, the story of the Commonweal's march out of Massillon is derived from the *Chicago Record*, March 26, 1894; *Los Angeles Times*, March 26, 1894; *Chicago Herald*, March 26, 1894; W. T. Stead, "'Coxeyism': A Character Sketch," *American Review of Reviews* 10 (July 1894): 53.

13 *Omaha World-Herald*, March 26, 1894.

14 Stead, "'Coxeyism,'" p. 47.

15 *American Review of Reviews* 9 (June 1894): 649, 650.

16 Burton J. Bledstein, *The Culture of Professionalism: The Middle Class and the Development of Higher Education in America* (New York: Norton, 1976). Advancing the "shake-up period" thesis is Aileen S. Kraditor, *The Radical Persuasion, 1890–1917: Aspects of the Intellectual History and the Historiography of Three American Radical Organizations* (Baton Rouge: Louisiana State University Press, 1981), pp. 55–57, 71–73.

17 Gilman M. Ostrander, *American Civilization in the First Machine Age, 1890–1940* (New York: Harper & Row, 1970), pp. 216–17; Morton Keller, *Affairs of State: Public Life in Late Nineteenth Century America* (Cambridge, Mass.: Belknap Press, 1977), pp. 439–40.

18 Wyn Wachorst, *Thomas Alva Edison, An American Myth* (Cambridge, Mass.: M.I.T. Press, 1981); John Higham, *Strangers in the Land: Patterns of American Nativism, 1860–1925* (New York: Atheneum Publishers, 1963), pp. 283–85.

Notes to Chapter 3

1 The story of the Commonweal's march from Massillon to Pittsburgh is derived from the *Washington Star*, March 26 April 23, 1894; Carl Browne, *When Coxey's "Army" Marcht on Washington, 1894*, ed. William McDevitt (San Francisco: n.p., 1944); Henry Vincent, *The Story of the Commonweal* (1894; reprint ed., New York: Arno, 1969), p. 57; *Ohio State Journal* (Columbus), March 26, 1894; *Chicago Record*, March 16, March 28–April 7, 1894; Donald L. McMurry, *Coxey's Army: A Study of the Industrial Army Movement of 1894* (1929; reprint ed., Seattle: University of Washington

Press, 1968), pp. 63–66; *St. Louis Post-Dispatch*, April 8, 1894; *Omaha World-Herald*, March 26, 1894; *Cleveland Plain Dealer*, March 28, 1894; *Chicago Herald*, March 29, April 1–4, 1894; *Washington Star*, April 23, 1894; W. T. Stead, "'Coxeyism': A Character Sketch," *American Review of Reviews* 10 (July 1894), 51–54; A. Cleveland Hall, "An Observer in Coxey's Camp," *Independent* 46 (May 17, 1894): 615; *Los Angeles Times*, March 28–29, 1894; *Pittsburgh Post*, April 4, 1894.

2 *Washington Star*, July 19, 1894; *St. Louis Post-Dispatch*, May 26, May 29, 1894; *Terre Haute Express*, April 22, 1894; *Des Moines Leader*, May 8, 1894; H. L. Stetson, "The Industrial Army," *Independent* 46 (May 31, 1894): 681; *Portland Evening Telegram*, May 1, 1894.

3 *Snohomish Eye*, May 17, 1894; *Ellensburg Capital*, May 31, 1894; *Nation* 58 (May 17, 1894): 358; *Chicago Inter Ocean*, September 10, 1893; *Washington Star*, July 20, 1894; *Indianapolis Journal*, May 3, 1894; John D. Hicks, *The Populist Revolt: A History of the Farmers' Alliance and the People's Party* (1931; reprint ed., Lincoln: University of Nebraska Press, 1962), pp. 54–95.

4 Leah Hannah Feder, *Unemployment Relief in Periods of Depression: A Study of Measures Adopted in Certain American Cities, 1857 Through 1922* (New York: Russell Sage Foundation, 1936), pp. 71–94; Charles Hoffmann, *The Depression of the Nineties: An Economic History* (Westport, Conn.: Greenwood, 1970) pp. 97–112.

5 *Philadelphia Inquirer*, April 13–15, 1894.

6 *Los Angeles Times*, April 25, 1894; *San Francisco Bulletin*, April 9, 1894; *Review of Reviews* 10 (July 1894): 44; *Ohio State Journal*, May 15, 1894; *Independent* 46 (May 3, 1894): 558; Julian Ralph, *Our Great West; A Study of the Present Conditions and Future Possibilities of the New Commonwealths and Capitals of the United States* (New York: Harper & Brother, 1893), p. 307.

7 Charles S. Gleed, "The True Significance of Western Unrest," *Forum* 16 (October 1893): 251–60; *The New Empire: Oregon, Washington, Idaho* (Portland: Oregon Immigration Board, [1889]), p. 27.

8 John E. Bennett, "Is the West Discontented? Is a Revolution at Hand?" *Arena* 81 (August 1896): 400; *Ogden Standard*, May 30, 1894; *Review of Reviews* 10 (July 1894): 43–44; *Chicago Herald*, August 29, 1893; *Rocky Mountain News*, June 1, 1894; *Public Opinion* 16 (October 1893): 21.

Notes to Chapter 4

1 Details of the Commonweal's stay in the Pittsburgh area are taken from the *Chicago Record*, April 5–6, 1894; *Chicago Herald*, April 5, April 9, 1894; Henry Vincent, *The Story of the Commonweal* (1894; reprint ed., New York: Arno, 1969), pp. 73–82; Donald L. McMurry, *Coxey's Army:*

A Study of the Industrial Army Movement of 1894 (1929; reprint ed., Seattle: University of Washington Press, 1968), pp. 86–92.

2 Frank Morn, *"The Eye that Never Sleeps": A History of the Pinkerton National Detective Agency* (Bloomington: Indiana University Press, 1982), pp. 102–8.

3 Except where noted, the details of the Commonweal march from Homestead to Frostburg are derived from the *Chicago Record*, April 6–16, 1894; *Chicago Herald*, April 8–14, 1894; *Washington Star*, April 26, 1894; *Washington Times*, April 16, 1894; *Cumberland Evening Times*, April 10–16, 1894; *Pittsburgh Post*, April 9–16, 1894; Carl Browne, *When Coxey's "Army" Marcht on Washington, 1894*, ed. William McDevitt (San Francisco: n.p., 1944); Vincent, *Commonweal*, pp. 80–113; McMurry, *Coxey's Army*, p. 93–100.

4 McMurry, *Coxey's Army*, p. 92; Nick Salvatore, *Eugene V. Debs: Citizen and Socialist* (Urbana: University of Illinois Press, 1982), p. 127; Philip Taft, *The A.F.L. in the Time of Gompers* (1957; reprint ed., New York: Octagon Books, 1970), pp. 302–5, 311–12.

5 *National Labor Tribune* (Pittsburgh), April 12, 1894.

6 Pictures of mountaineers in Ray Stannard Baker Collection, Scrapbook, Box 72, Library of Congress, Washington, D.C.

7 *San Francisco Examiner*, April 14–15, 1894; *St. Louis Post-Dispatch*, April 14–16, 1894; *Cumberland Evening Times*, April 16, 1894.

8 *Pittsburgh Post*, April 16, 1894; *St. Louis Post-Dispatch*, April 22, 1894.

Notes to Chapter 5

1 Except where noted, the story of the Commonweal's trip through Maryland is derived from the *Kansas City Star*, April 29, 1894; *Washington Evening Star*, April 16–23, 1894; *Cumberland Evening Times*, April 12–20, 1894; *Chicago Herald*, April 16, 1894; *Chicago Record*, April 17–21, 1894; *American Nonconformist* (Indianapolis), April 19, April 26, 1894; *Chicago Tribune*, April 17, 1894, p. 2; *Ohio State Journal* (Columbus), April 18, 1894.

2 *Chicago Record*, April 16–17, 1894; *Chicago Tribune*, April 17, 1894; *Washington Evening Star*, April 16, April 23, 1894; *Chicago Tribune*, April 17, 1894; *American Nonconformist*, April 19, 1894; Carl Browne, *When Coxey's "Army" Marcht on Washington, 1894*, ed. William McDevitt (San Francisco: n.p., 1944) p. 8; *Pittsburgh Post*, April 16, 1894; *Cumberland Evening Times*, April 16, 1894.

3 *Washington Evening Star*, April 23, 1894; *Kansas City Star*, April 29, 1894.

4 *Tacoma Daily News*, April 28, 1894; *Kansas City Star*, April 29, 1894.

5 *National Labor Tribune*, June 28, 1894; *Washington Evening Star*, April 23, 1894.

6 Archer B. Hulbert, *The Great American Canals* (Cleveland: Arthur H. Clark, 1904), vol. 1, pp. 65–168; Walter S. Sanderlin, *The Great National Project: A History of the Chesapeake and Ohio Canal* (Baltimore: Johns Hopkins University Press, 1946).

7 *Washington Star*, April 18, 1894; Henry Vincent, *The Story of the Commonweal* (1894; reprint ed., New York: Arno, 1969), p. 64.

8 *Cumberland Evening Times*, April 12, 1894; *Baltimore American*, May 20, 1894, clipping in Ray Stannard Baker Papers, Box 72, Library of Congress, Washington, D.C.

9 *Cumberland Evening Times*, April 12, 1894; *Baltimore American*, May 20, 1894, clipping in Ray Stannard Baker Papers; *Washington Star*, April 19, 1894; *American Nonconformist*, April 26, 1894.

10 *American Nonconformist*, April 26, 1894.

11 W. T. Stead, "'Coxeyism': A Character Sketch," *American Review of Reviews* 10 (July 1894): 52; *New York Tribune*, April 27, 1894; Browne, *Coxey's "Army"*, p. 8; *Washington Star*, April 23, 1894; *Baltimore American*, May 20, 1894, clipping in Ray Stannard Baker Papers; A. Cleveland Hall, "An Observer in Coxey's Camp," *Independent* 46 (May 17, 1894): 615.

12 C. H. Dennis to Ray S. Baker, March 20, 1894; C. H. Dennis to Ray S. Baker, March 28, 1894; both in Ray Stannard Baker Papers, Box 23.

13 *Chicago Tribune*, April 17, 1894; *Kansas City Star*, April 17, 1894.

14 *Baltimore American*, May 20, 1894, clipping in Ray Stannard Baker Papers, Box 72.

15 *Washington Star*, April 19, 1894, p. 2.

Notes to Chapter 6

1 Carl Browne, *When Coxey's "Army" Marcht on Washington, 1894*, ed. William McDevitt (San Francisco: n.p., 1944), p. 29; *Sacramento Record-Union*, March 15, 1894; *Los Angeles Times*, March 22, 1894; April 14, 1894; Robert V. Hine, *California Utopianism: Contemplations of Eden* (San Francisco: Boyd and Fraser, 1981).

2 *San Francisco Examiner*, March 16, 1894.

3 W. T. Stead, "'Coxeyism': A Character Sketch," *American Review of Reviews* 10 (July 1894): 49, 55.

4 W. T. Stead, "Incidents of Labour War in America," *Contemporary Review* 46 (July 1894): 73.

5 Lyman Abbott, "The Wages System," *Forum* 9 (July 1890): 525; Walton

Bean, *California: An Interpretive History* (New York, McGraw-Hill, 1968), p. 298.

6 Glenn S. Dumke, *The Boom of the Eighties in Southern California* (San Marino, Calif.: Huntington Library, 1944); Carey McWilliams, *Southern California Country: An Island on the Land* (New York: Duell, Sloan & Pearce, 1946).

7 *San Francisco Examiner*, March 15, 1894; *Los Angeles Times*, March 14, March 23, 1894; *Chicago Tribune*, June 28, 1894.

8 *San Francisco Examiner*, March 13, 1894; *Los Angeles Times*, March 13, 1894.

9 Donald L. McMurry, *Coxey's Army: A Study of the Industrial Army Movement of 1894* (1929; reprint ed., Seattle: University of Washington Press, 1968); *San Francisco Examiner*, March 14, 1894, p. 1; Bernard Baes Diary, p. 1, in the Industrial Army of the United States Collection, University of Washington Library, Seattle. Baes was an officer in Fry's army.

10 *San Francisco Examiner*, March 14, 1894; Henry Frank, "The Crusade of the Unemployed," *Arena* 10 (July 1894): 242.

11 *Los Angeles Times*, March 18, 1894; *Indianapolis Sun*, April 26, 1894; *Indianapolis News*, April 26–27, 1894; *Dallas Morning News*, April 1, April 21, 1894; *San Francisco Examiner*, March 16, 1894; *Washington Star*, May 3, 1894.

12 Fry's journey from Los Angeles to west Texas, except as noted, is taken from the *Los Angeles Times*, March 16–22, 1894; Baes Diary, entries for March 16–25; *San Francisco Examiner*, March 18, 1894; *Arizona Daily Star* (Tucson), March 22, 1894; *Dallas Morning News*, March 23, April 2, 1894; *San Francisco Chronicle*, March 22, 1894; *Houston Daily Post*, March 22, 1894; *San Antonio Express*, March 26–30, 1894.

13 *San Antonio Express*, March 24, 1894; Robert C. Cotner, *James Stephen Hogg: A Biography* (Austin: University of Texas Press, 1959), p. 425.

14 Details of the confrontation between Hogg and the Southern Pacific are derived from the *Dallas Morning News*, March 27–29, 1894; *San Antonio Express*, March 27, 1894; *St. Louis Post-Dispatch*, March 29, 1894; *San Francisco Chronicle*, March 27, 1894; *Washington Star*, March 29, 1894; *Houston Daily Post*, March 28–30, 1894; *Los Angeles Times*, March 31, 1894; Cotner, *James Stephen Hogg*, p. 427.

15 *Indianapolis News*, April 26, 1894; *Dallas Morning News*, March 29, 1894; *St. Louis Post-Dispatch*, April 3, 1894; *San Antonio Express*, March 29, 1894.

16 *Dallas Morning News*, March 31, April 1, 1894; *San Antonio Express*, March 31, 1894.

17 *Dallas Morning News*, March 31, 1894; *Arkansas Gazette* (Little Rock), April 2, 1894; Cotner, *James Stephen Hogg*, p. 426.

18 *Dallas Morning News*, March 31, 1894; *Rocky Mountain News* (Denver), March 30, 1894; *Los Angeles Times*, March 30, 1894.

19 *Dallas Morning News*, March 31, April 1–2, 1894.
20 *San Antonio Express*, March 31, 1891. The Houston army was led by a bricklayer, John R. Patterson. *Houston Daily Post*, May 4–5, May 17, 1894.
21 *Galveston News* as quoted in *San Antonio Express*, March 30, 1894.

Notes to Chapter 7

1 *Los Angeles Times*, March 22, 1894; *Kansas City Star*, June 25, 1894; *Chicago Labor*, July 14, 1894; Henry Winfred Splitter, "Concerning Vinette's Los Angeles Regiment of Coxey's Army," *Pacific Historical Review* 17 (February 1948): 29–36.
2 *San Francisco Bulletin*, April 4–5, 1894; *San Francisco Chronicle*, April 2, 1894; *San Francisco Examiner*, April 4, April 13, 1894; *Salt Lake Tribune*, April 10, 1894; *Ogden Standard*, April 10, 1894; *Omaha World-Herald*, April 23, 1894.
3 Donald L. McMurry, *Coxey's Army: A Study of the Industrial Army Movement of 1894* (1929; reprint ed., Seattle: University of Washington Press, 1968), p. 149; T. B. Veblen, "The Army of the Commonweal," *Journal of Political Economy* 2 (June 1894): 459; *San Francisco Bulletin*, April 6, 1894; *San Francisco Chronicle*, April 4, 1894; *San Francisco Examiner*, April 5, 1894.
4 *San Francisco Bulletin*, April 6–7, 1894; *San Francisco Examiner*, April 6, 1894; *Sacramento Record-Union*, April 7, 1894.
5 *Ogden Standard*, April 10, 1894.
6 *Salt Lake Tribune*, April 9, 1894; *San Francisco Examiner*, April 9–10, 1894; *Sacramento Record-Union*, April 9, 1894; *Rocky Mountain News* (Denver), April 14, 1894.
7 *Commercial and Financial Chronicle* 58 (May 12, 1894): 792; *Railroad Gazette*, May 18, 1894, p. 356; Robert Edgar Riegel, *The Story of the Western Railroads* (New York: Macmillan, 1926), pp. 138–42, 286–88. See also James J. Hill to Grover Cleveland, May 5, 1894, Grover Cleveland Papers, Library of Congress, Washington, D.C.
8 The story of Kelley's army in Ogden is taken from the *Salt Lake Tribune*, April 8–12, 1894; *Ogden Standard*, April 9–12, 1894; *San Francisco Examiner*, April 9–13, 1894; *Sacramento Record-Union*, April 10–12, 1894.
9 *Ogden Standard*, April 11, 1894; *Washington Star*, April 24, 1894.
10 *San Francisco Examiner*, April 13, 1894; *Ogden Standard*, April 13, 1894; *Chicago Record*, April 24, 1894.
11 *Omaha World-Herald*, April 13, 1894; *Denver Times*, April 13, 1894.
12 *Omaha World-Herald*, April 14, 1894; *Cheyenne Daily Leader*, April 14, 1894; *Denver Republican*, April 14, 1894.

13 *Fremont Daily Tribune*, April 16, 1894; *Kearney Daily Hub*, April 14, 1894; *Omaha World-Herald*, April 15–16, 1894; *Omaha Bee*, April 14–15, 1894.

Notes to Chapter 8

1 *Daily Iowa State Register* (Des Moines), April 15, 1894; *Omaha World-Herald*, April 16, 1894.

2 *Omaha World-Herald*, April 16, 1894; *Daily Iowa State Register*, April 15, 1894.

3 Except where noted otherwise, the story of Kelley's army in the Council Bluffs area is derived from the *Omaha World-Herald*, April 14–22, 1894; *Omaha Bee*, April 15–22, 1894; *Council Bluffs Nonpareil*, April 15–22, 1894; *Ogden Standard*, April 19–20, 1894; *Chicago Daily Tribune*, April 16, 1894; *Daily Iowa State Register*, April 17–20, 1894; *Des Moines Leader*, April 24, 1894; *St. Louis Post-Dispatch*, May 13, 1894; *San Francisco Examiner*, April 21, 1894; *Minneapolis Journal*, June 5, 1894; Joseph T. Duryea, "The 'Industrial Army' in Omaha," *Outlook* 49 (May 5, 1894): 781; Richard W. Etulain, ed., *Jack London on the Road: The Tramp Diary and Other Hobo Writings* (Logan: Utah State University Press, 1979). See also Carlos A. Schwantes, "Soldiers of Misfortune, Part I: Iowa Railroads versus Kelley's Army of Unemployed, 1894," *Annals of Iowa* 46 (Winter 1983): 487–509.

4 *Omaha Bee*, April 15–16, 1894; *Daily Iowa State Register*, April 17, 1894; *Chicago Tribune*, April 26, 1894; *San Francisco Chronicle*, April 18, 1894; *Omaha World-Herald*, April 14–15, 1894; *Council Bluffs Nonpareil*, April 17, 1894; *Tacoma Daily Ledger*, May 27, 1894, p. 8.

5 *St. Louis Post-Dispatch*, May 27, 1894; *Omaha Bee*, April 15, 1894.

6 Some of Kelley's men were former Union Pacific employees and had friends among the shopmen. One Kelleyite had been a foreman in the U.P.'s North Platte, Nebraska, shops. *Omaha World-Herald*, April 16, 1894.

7 *Omaha World-Herald*, April 21, 1894; *Omaha Bee*, April 16–18, 1894; *Chicago Daily Tribune*, April 21, 1894; *New York Sun*, April 21, 1894; *Daily Iowa State Register*, April 21, April 26, 1894; *Chicago Tribune*, April 23, 1894.

8 *Omaha World-Herald*, April 22, 1894. Bemis's sympathy for the Kelleyites was not merely a matter of keeping them from disbanding near Omaha. He served as president of the United States Industrials, an organization formed in Des Moines on May 16 to provide an institutional framework to perpetuate the movement as a political force. *Farmers' Tribune* (Des Moines), June 6, 1894.

9 *Omaha World-Herald*, April 16, April 24, April 29, 1894.

10 Ibid., April 24, April 27, 1894; *Des Moines Leader*, April 24, 1894; *Omaha*

Bee, April 16, 1894; *St. Louis Post-Dispatch*, May 29, 1894.

11 *Kansas City Mail*, April 26, 1894.

12 *Chicago Record*, March 19, 1894.

13 *Sacramento Record-Union*, April 3, 1894; *San Francisco Examiner*, April 7, 1894; *Seattle Post-Intelligencer*, April 17, 1894; *Seattle Press-Times*, April 22, 1894; *Des Moines Leader*, May 1, 1894; *Rocky Mountain News*, May 2, 1894.

14 *St. Joseph Daily News*, July 9, 1894.

15 *Salt Lake Tribune*, May 2, May 6, June 28, 1894.

16 *Chicago Record*, April 24, 1894; *Indianapolis Journal*, May 2, 1894; *Denver Republican*, May 3, 1894; *Chicago Tribune*, May 5, 1894; *Rocky Mountain News*, May 15, 1894; Henry Vincent, *The Story of the Commonweal* (1894; reprint ed., New York: Arno, 1969), pp. 183–84, 192–94.

17 *Woman's Tribune*, April 21, April 28, May 5, 1894; *Sacramento Record-Union*, May 7, 1894; *Kansas City Star*, June 10, 1894.

18 *Omaha Bee*, April 16, 1894; *Council Bluffs Nonpareil*, April 22, 1894; *Topeka Daily Capital*, June 26, 1894.

19 *Seattle Telegraph*, April 30, 1894; *San Francisco Examiner*, April 5, April 12, 1894.

20 *Ogden Standard*, May 23, 1894.

21 *San Francisco Bulletin*, April 12, April 17, April 19, May 28, 1894; *Omaha Bee*, April 16, 1894; *San Francisco Examiner*, April 28, April 30, 1894; *San Francisco Chronicle*, May 1, May 31, 1894; *Sacramento Record-Union*, April 30, May 1, May 7, 1894; *Stockton Daily Independent*, May 16–17, 1894; *Bakersfield Daily Californian*, June 2, June 6–7, 1894; California File, in File 4017–1894, Records of the United States Department of Justice, Records Group 60, National Archives, Washington, D.C.; *Los Angeles Times*, June 8, June 13–14, 1894; *Troy* (New York) *Labor*, July 28, 1894; Mari Jo Buhle, *Women and American Socialism, 1870–1920* (Urbana: University of Illinois Press, 1983), pp. 74, 120.

Notes to Chapter 9

1 Jack London's diary is reproduced in Richard W. Etulain, ed., *Jack London on the Road: The Tramp Diary and Other Hobo Writings* (Logan: Utah State University Press, 1979), pp. 30–56; Carl Browne, *When Coxey's "Army" Marcht on Washington, 1894*, ed. William McDevitt (San Francisco: n.p., 1944), pp. 28–29.

2 The story of Kelley's army on the road in Iowa is derived from the *Des Moines Leader*, April 24–May 2, May 11, 1894; *Omaha World-Herald*, April 23–30, 1894; *Atlantic Weekly Telegraph*, May 2, 1894; *Daily Iowa Capital*

(Des Moines), April 25–30, May 8, 1894; *Daily Iowa State Register* (Des Moines), April 26–May 2, 1894; *Chicago Tribune*, April 23–30, 1894; *Farmers' Tribune* (Des Moines), May 2, 1894; Henry Vincent, *The Story of the Commonweal* (1894; reprint ed., New York: Arno, 1969), pp. 146–52; Etulain, *Jack London*, pp. 30–56. See also Carlos A. Schwantes, "Soldiers of Misfortune, Part II: Jack London, Kelley's Army, and the Struggle for Survival in Iowa," *Annals of Iowa* 46 (Spring 1983): 567–92.

3 Except where noted otherwise, details of Coxey's march from Williamsport to Frederick are derived from the *Chicago Record*, April 21–26, 1894; *Washington Post*, April 23–26, 1894; *Washington Star*, April 20–24, 1894; *Cumberland Evening Times*, April 23, 1894; *Frederick News*, April 24, 1894; *Chicago Daily Tribune*, April 24, 1894.

4 Browne, *Coxey's "Army"*; *Los Angeles Times*, March 12, 1894.

5 George Francis Train, *My Life in Many States and in Foreign Lands* (New York: D. Appleton and Company, 1902), pp. 293–99; Don C. Seitz, *Uncommon Americans: Pencil Portraits of Men and Women who Have Broken the Rules* (Indianapolis: Bobbs-Merrill, 1925), p. 180.

6 Train, *My Life*, pp. 301, 324; Seitz, *Uncommon Americans*, p. 180; *Washington Evening Star*, April 26, 1894.

7 *Chicago Record*, April 25, 1894; *Kansas City Star*, April 29, 1894.

8 *Chicago Record*, April 25, 1894; *Washington Post*, April 26, 1894; *Frederick News*, April 26, 1894.

9 *St. Louis Post-Dispatch*, April 22, 1894; *Tacoma Daily News*, April 28, 1894.

10 *Washington Times*, April 28, 1894.

11 *Chicago Record*, April 26, 1894; *Washington Post*, April 26, 1894.

Notes to Chapter 10

1 *Butte Miner*, April 25, 1894; *Anaconda Standard*, April 25–26, 1894.

2 *Helena Independent*, June 29, 1894; *Anaconda Standard*, April 13, 1894; *Third Annual Report of the Bureau of Agriculture, Labor and Industry, Montana, 1895* (Helena: State Publishing Co., 1896), p. 97; Thomas A. Clinch, "Coxey's Army in Montana," *Montana Magazine of Western History* 15 (October 1964): 2–5; Michael P. Malone and Richard B. Roeder, *Montana: A History of Two Centuries* (Seattle: University of Washington Press, 1976), pp. 140–47; Clinch, "Coxey's Army in Montana," p. 5. See also Michael P. Malone, *The Battle for Butte: Mining and Politics on the Northern Frontier, 1864–1906* (Seattle: University of Washington Press, 1981).

3 *Third Annual Report of the Bureau of Agriculture, Labor and Industry,*

p. 95; Clinch, "Coxey's Army in Montana," p. 6; *Anaconda Standard*, April 5–8, April 18, April 21, April 24, May 1, May 16, 1894.

4 *Anaconda Standard*, April 24, 1894; Gerald G. Eggert, *Railroad Labor Disputes: The Beginnings of Federal Strike Policy* (Ann Arbor: University of Michigan Press, 1967), p. 130; idem, *Richard Olney: Evolution of a Statesman* (University Park, Pa.: Pennsylvania State University Press, 1974), p. 120.

5 *Butte Miner*, April 20, 1894; Clinch, "Coxey's Army in Montana," p. 9; William McDermott to the Attorney General, April 21, 1894, in Justice Department, Records Group 60, National Archives, Washington, D.C.; *Anaconda Standard*, April 21–22, 1894.

6 *Anaconda Standard*, April 23–24, 1894; *Helena Independent*, April 24, 1894.

7 Except where noted otherwise, details of Hogan's ride across Montana are derived from the *Butte Miner*, April 25, 1894; *Bozeman Weekly Chronicle*, April 26, 1894; *Helena Independent*, April 25, 1894; *Billings Weekly Gazette*, April 28, 1894; *Bozeman Weekly Chronicle*, April 26, May 3, 1894; *Chicago Record*, April 24, 1894; Clinch, "Coxey's Army in Montana," p. 7; Hiram Knowles to Richard Olney, April 25, 1894, Justice Department, Records Group 60; *Anaconda Standard*, April 25, 1894, p. 4. The single most useful source of information on the episode was the *Anaconda Standard*, April 24–May 4 and May 16, 1894. It was the only newspaper that had a reporter accompanying Hogan's army.

8 *Anaconda Standard*, April 26, 1894; *Billings Weekly Gazette*, April 28, 1894; *Bozeman Weekly Chronicle*, May 3, 1894.

9 *Billings Weekly Gazette*, April 28, 1894; *Butte Bystander*, April 28, 1894.

10 *Anaconda Standard*, May 1, 1894; *New York Times*, April 26, 1894; *Chicago Record*, April 26, 1894.

11 *Anaconda Standard*, April 29, 1894; Clinch, "Coxey's Army in Montana," p. 7.

12 *New York Tribune*, April 26, 1894; *New York Times*, April 26, 1894; Eggert, *Railroad Labor Disputes*, pp. 136–37; Eggert, *Richard Olney*, pp. 115, 138; *San Francisco Call* as quoted in the *Omaha Bee*, May 5, 1894.

13 *Anaconda Standard*, April 26, 1894; *New York Times*, April 26, 1894, p. 1; Eggert, *Railroad Labor Disputes*, p. 142; Jerry M. Cooper, *The Army and Civil Disorder: Federal Military Intervention in Labor Disputes, 1877–1900* (Westport, Conn.: Greenwood, 1980), pp. 106–9.

14 *Anaconda Standard*, April 25–May 1, May 11, 1894.

15 William McDermott to Richard Olney, May 2, 1894, Justice Department, Records Group 60; *Helena Independent*, April 28, 1894.

16 *Omaha World-Herald*, April 25, 1894; *Daily Iowa State Register*, April 26, 1894; Henry Vincent, *The Story of the Commonweal* (1894; reprint ed., New York: Arno, 1969), pp. 151–52, 216–19.

17 *Washington Star*, April 26, 1894.

Notes to Chapter 11

1 Details of the march from Frederick to the District of Columbia are taken from the *Washington Star*, April 26–30, 1894; *Washington Times*, April 28, 1894; *Washington Post*, April 30, 1894; *Frederick News*, April 27, 1894; *Chicago Record*, April 27–30, 1894; *Chicago Herald*, April 30, 1894. On Jones's march, see the *Philadelphia Inquirer*, April 12, April 15, 1894.

2 *Washington Star*, April 23, 1894; *Chicago Record*, April 28, 1894; *New York Tribune*, April 27, 1894; William P. Hazen to John G. Carlisle, April 20, April 26, 1894, Grover Cleveland Papers, Library of Congress, Washington, D.C.; Gerald G. Eggert, *Richard Olney: Evolution of a Statesman* (University Park, Pa.: Pennsylvania State University Press, 1974), p. 119.

3 *New York Tribune*, April 25–27, 1894; *Boston Herald*, April 27, 1894; *Chicago Record*, April 26, 1894.

4 *Washington Star*, April 17, 1894; *New York Sun*, April 18, 1894; *New York Tribune*, April 25–26, 1894.

5 *Tacoma Daily News*, April 28, 1894; *Washington Times*, April 28, 1894; *Washington Star*, April 27, 1894; Carl Browne, *When Coxey's "Army" Marcht to Washington, 1894*, ed. William McDevitt (San Francisco: n.p., 1944), p. 15; A. Cleveland Hall, "An Observer in Coxey's Camp," *Independent* 46 (May 17, 1894): 616.

6 *Washington Star*, March 22, March 28, 1894; *New York Tribune*, April 25, 1894; *Boston Herald*, April 20, 1894, p. 1; Donald L. McMurry, *Coxey's Army: A Study of the Industrial Army Movement of 1894* (1929; reprint ed., Seattle: University of Washington Press, 1968), pp. 106–13.

7 The story of the Commonweal's reception and initial difficulties is taken from the *Chicago Record*, April 26–May 1, 1894; *Washington Post*, April 30–May 1, 1894; *Washington Star*, April 23, April 30, 1894; *Frederick News*, April 30, 1894; *Cleveland Plain Dealer*, April 30, 1894; Browne, *Coxey's "Army"*, pp. 17–19; *Washington Times*, April 30, 1894; *Philadelphia Inquirer*, April 30, 1894; *Chicago Herald*, April 30–May 1, 1894; *New York Tribune*, May 1, 1894; *Ohio State Journal* (Columbus), May 1, 1894.

8 Except where noted otherwise, details of the Commonweal's May Day activities are taken from the *Washington Post*, May 1–2, 1894; *Washington Star*, May 1–2, 1894; *Washington Times*, May 2, 1894; *Newark Evening News*, May 1, 1894; *New York Times*, May 2, 1894; *Chicago Record*, May 2,

1894; *Cleveland Plain Dealer*, May 2, 1894; Browne, *Coxey's "Army"*, pp. 18–21; U.S., Congress, *Congressional Record*, 53rd Cong., 2d sess., 1894, 26, pt. 5 : 4512.

9 *Washington Star*, May 1, 1894; *Washington Times*, May 5, 1894.

10 U.S., Congress, *Congressional Record*, 53rd Cong., 2d sess., 1894, 26, pt. 5 : 4334–35; *Washington Times*, May 2, 1894.

11 *Chicago Tribune*, May 2, 1894; *Washington Post*, May 2, 1894.

12 *Washington Star*, May 2, 1894; *Washington Post*, May 2–3, 1894; *Woman's Tribune* (Washington, D.C.), May 1894, p. 85; *Topeka Daily Capital*, May 2, 1894; *Chicago Record*, May 2, 1894; Hall, "Coxey's Camp," p. 616.

13 *Washington Post*, May 3, May 7, 1894; *Washington Times*, May 10, 1894.

14 Details of the legal troubles of Coxey and Browne are taken from the *Washington Post*, May 3, May 9, 1894; *Washington Times*, May 3–9, 1894; *Washington Star*, May 5–8, 1894; *Chicago Record*, May 3, 1894; McMurry, *Coxey's Army*, p. 123. The text of the law is in U.S., Congress, *Congressional Record*, 53rd Cong., 2d sess., 1894, 26, pt. 5 : 4513.

15 U.S., Congress, *Congressional Record*, 53rd Cong., 2d sess., 1894, 26, pt. 5 : 4569; *Omaha World-Herald*, May 9, 1894; *Anaconda Standard*, May 11, 1894; McMurry, *Coxey's Army*, pp. 124–26.

16 *Boston Herald*, May 22, 1894; *Washington Times*, May 22, 1894.

17 *Indianapolis Journal*, May 3, 1894; *New York Tribune*, May 1, 1894.

18 *Chicago Record* to Ray Stannard Baker, May 2, 1894, in Ray Stannard Baker Papers, Box 23, Library of Congress, Washington, D.C.; Ray Stannard Baker to J. S. Baker, May 3, 1894, Baker Papers, Box 23.

19 *Washington Post*, May 7, 1894.

Notes to Chapter 12

1 *Philadelphia Inquirer*, April 28, 1894; *St. Louis Post-Dispatch*, April 29, 1894; *Spokane Chronicle*, April 30, 1894; Shirley Plumer Austin, "The Downfall of Coxeyism," *Chautauquan* 18 (July 1894): 452.

2 Donald L. McMurry, *Coxey's Army: A Study of the Industrial Army Movement of 1894* (1929; reprint ed., Seattle: University of Washington Press, 1968), pp. 127–28; *Seattle Telegraph*, April 29, 1894.

3 *Tacoma News*, April 20, 1894; *Tacoma Daily Ledger*, May 2, 1894.

4 *Daily Iowa State Register*, May 2, 1894; *Daily Iowa Capital*, May 1, 1894; *Chicago Tribune*, May 3, 1894.

5 Aylesworth's survey shows that of the 763 men questioned about their nationality, 549 claimed to be American born. Of the foreign born, two-fifths came from the British Isles or British Colonies, and more than a fourth came from Germany. Eighty-three trades were represented among

the 425 respondents who claimed to have any, with miners being most numerous. There were 240 Populists, 218 Republicans, 196 Democrats, and 92 who were undecided or independent. As to religion, 358 were Protestants, 280 were Catholics, and 114 claimed no religion. Donald L. McMurry, *Coxey's Army: A Study of the Industrial Army Movement of 1894* (1929; reprint ed., Seattle: University of Washington Press, 1968), pp. 187–88.

6 Except where noted otherwise, details of Kelley's odyssey from Des Moines to Saint Louis are taken from the *Daily Iowa State Register*, May 2–17, 1894; *Daily Iowa Capital*, May 1–12, 1894; *Chicago Tribune*, May 3, 1894; McMurry, *Coxey's Army*, pp. 116–21; Jack London, *The Road* (New York: Macmillan, 1907), pp. 181–85; *Omaha World-Herald*, April 28–May 11, 1894; *Ottumwa Daily Courier*, May 9–17, 1894; *Des Moines Leader*, April 25, May 1–18, 1894; *Rocky Mountain News*, May 12, 1894; *St. Louis Post-Dispatch*, May 13, 1894; Richard W. Etulain, *Jack London on the Road: The Tramp Diary and Other Hobo Writings* (Logan: Utah State University Press, 1979), pp. 51–55; *Burlington Hawk-Eye*, May 15–20, 1894. See also Carlos A. Schwantes, "Soldiers of Misfortune, Part II: Jack London, Kelley's Army, and the Struggle for Survival in Iowa," *Annals of Iowa* 46 (Spring 1983): 578–92.

7 *Daily Gate City* (Keokuk), May 20, 1894; *Daily Iowa State Register*, May 20, 1894; *Des Moines Leader*, May 22, 1894.

8 *St. Louis Post-Dispatch*, May 27–29, 1894.

9 For a sampling of the opinion of trade unionists on the Coxey movement, see the *St. Louis Post-Dispatch*, April 29, 1894.

10 *Butte Miner*, May 20, 1894.

11 *Chicago Herald*, May 10, 1894; *Indianapolis Journal*, April 27, 1894; *Railroad Gazette*, May 18, 1894, p. 356.

12 *Nation* 58 (May 10, 1894): 340; *Weekly Olympian*, May 24, 1894; *United States Investor* 5 (April 28, 1894): 10; *Rocky Mountain News*, May 14, 1894.

13 *Terre Haute Express*, April 17, 1894; *Ohio State Journal*, April 29, 1894 (quotations); Margaret Leech, *In Days of McKinley* (New York: Harper & Brothers, 1959), p. 55.

14 *Portland Telegram*, April 19–20, May 9, 1894; A. J. Borie to E. Dickinson, April 25, 1894, Industrial Army File, Union Pacific Collection, Nebraska Historical Society, Lincoln (cited hereafter as UP Collection); Herman C. Voeltz, "Coxey's Army in Oregon, 1894," *Oregon Historical Quarterly* 65 (September 1964): 263–95.

15 *Portland Telegram*, April 27, 1894; *Oregonian*, April 28–29, 1894; R. W. Baxter to E. Dickinson, May 7, 1894, UP Collection; H. C. Grady to Richard Olney, April 27, 1894, p. 1, File 4017–1894, Justice Department,

Records Group 60, National Archives, Washington, D.C. (cited hereafter as JDR).

16 *Oregonian*, April 27–30, 1894; *Portland Telegram*, April 30–May 1, 1894; The Dalles (Oregon) *Times-Mountaineer*, May 1, 1894, p. 2; R. W. Baxter to E. Dickinson, May 7, 1894, UP Collection; McMurry, *Coxey's Army*, pp. 225–26; Voeltz, "Coxey's Army in Oregon," p. 288.

17 *Oregonian*, April 27, 1894; *Portland Telegram*, May 1, 1894.

18 Details of the Portland army's troubles in Idaho and Wyoming are taken from the *Weiser Signal*, May 17, May 24, 1894; *Idaho Daily Statesman* (Boise), May 12–30, 1894; *Caldwell Tribune*, May 12, 1894; *Pocatello Tribune*, May 18, 1894; Benjamin Fowler to Richard Olney, May 18, 1894, JDR; [Edward B.] Whitney to Joseph Pinkham, May 18, 1894, in "Fees and Expenses of U.S. Marshals," U.S., Congress, *Senate Executive Document 120*, 53rd Cong., 2d sess., 1895, 4:12; Joseph Pinkham to Richard Olney, May 22, 1894, JDR; and the Industrial Army File in the UP Collection. Relevant items from the UP Collection are cited in Carlos A. Schwantes, "Law and Disorder: The Suppression of Coxey's Army in Idaho," *Idaho Yesterdays* 25 (Summer 1981): 10–15, 18–26.

19 *Seattle Daily Telegraph*, May 14, 1894; William McDermott to Richard Olney, June 7, 1894, JDR; *Cheyenne Daily Leader*, May 18, 1894; *Portland Telegram*, Voeltz, "Coxey's Army in Oregon," pp. 290–91.

20 *Tacoma Daily Ledger*, May 14, 1894; Murray Morgan, *Puget's Sound: A Narrative of Early Tacoma and the Southern Sound* (Seattle: University of Washington Press, 1979), pp. 289–90.

21 Gerald G. Eggert, *Richard Olney, Evolution of a Statesman* (University Park, Pa.: Pennsylvania State University Press, 1974), pp. 120–27.

22 *Pueblo Chieftain*, May 6–10, 1894; *Topeka Daily Capital*, May 10–11, July 9, 1894; *Rocky Mountain News*, May 12, 1894; McMurry, *Coxey's Army*, pp. 206–9; "Notes," *American Law Review* 28 (May–June 1894): 420–28.

23 *St. Louis Post-Dispatch*, April 22, 1894; *Topeka Daily Capital*, April 20, 1894; *Rocky Mountain News*, February 26, 1894; O. Gene Clanton, *Kansas Populism: Ideas and Men* (Lawrence: University Press of Kansas, 1969).

24 *Topeka Daily Capital*, May 5, 1894; *New York Post* as quoted in the *Washington Star*, April 21, 1894; McMurry, *Coxey's Army*, pp. 209, 212.

25 Details of the army's sojourn in Kansas are taken from the *Topeka Daily Capital*, May 10–11, July 1, 1894; *Rocky Mountain News*, May 11–12, 1894; *Omaha World-Herald*, May 11, 1894.

26 *Rocky Mountain News*, May 11–12, 1894; *Sacramento Record-Union*, May 15, 1894.

27 *Topeka Daily Capital*, May 11, 1894; *Rocky Mountain News*, May 11, May 12, 1894.

28 W. C. Perry to the Attorney General, June 21, 1894, JDR. The Justice Department file on Coxey's Army contains a wealth of information on the legal tactics used to disrupt the movement. See also Gerald G. Eggert, *Railroad Labor Disputes: The Beginnings of Federal Strike Policy* (Ann Arbor: University of Michigan Press, 1967), pp. 139–51.

29 *Topeka Daily Capital*, May 13–18, 1894; *Kansas City Star*, May 25, 1894.

30 James H. Beatty to Richard Olney, May 23, 1894; and James H. Forney to Richard Olney, May 22, 1894, both in JDR; *Idaho Daily Statesman*, May 24, 1894; Eggert, *Railroad Labor Disputes*, p. 138.

31 *Idaho Daily Statesman*, May 22–June 6, 1894; James H. Beatty to Richard Olney, June 5, 1894, JDR.

32 James H. Beatty to Richard Olney, June 5, 1894, JDR; James H. Beatty to John M. Thurston, June 11, 1894; John M. Thurston to E. Dickinson, June 16, 1894; E. Dickinson to R. W. Baxter, June 19, 1894, all in UP Collection; *Idaho Daily Statesman*, May 22, June 2, June 9–12, 1894; Richard Olney to J. P. Rankin, May 31, 1894, in "Fees and Expenses of U.S. Marshals," p. 13.

33 *Leavenworth Times*, May 30, June 19–20, 1894; W. C. Perry to the Attorney General, June 21, 1894, JDR.

34 *Salt Lake Tribune*, April 16, May 1, May 16, May 29, May 28, 1894; McMurry, *Coxey's Army*, pp. 224–25.

35 U.S., Congress, House, House Executive Documents, *Report of the Secretary of War, 1894*, 53rd Cong., 3d sess., 1894, 1, pt. 2:155; Jerry M. Cooper, *The Army and Civil Disorder: Federal Military Intervention in Labor Disputes, 1877–1900* (Westport, Conn.: Greenwood, 1980), pp. 113–14.

Notes to Chapter 13

1 *Denver Republican*, March 26–31, 1894; *Denver Times*, April 2, 1894; Donald L. McMurry, *Coxey's Army: A Study of the Industrial Army Movement of 1894* (1929; reprint ed., Seattle: University of Washington Press, 1968), pp. 213, 225; Carl Abbott, Stephen J. Leonard, and David McComb, *Colorado: A History of the Centennial State* (Boulder: Colorado Associated University Press, 1982), pp. 233–43; Lyle W. Dorsett, *The Queen City: A History of Denver* (Boulder: Pruett, 1977), pp. 80–83.

2 *Denver Times*, April 4–18, 1894; *Denver Republican*, April 13–18, 1894; *Rocky Mountain News*, April 17–19, 1894; Leon W. Fuller, "Colorado's Revolt Against Capitalism," *Mississippi Valley Historical Review* 21 (December 1934): 343–60.

3 *Denver Times*, April 27, 1894; *Hastings Daily Nebraskan*, May 8, 1894;

Omaha Daily Bee, May 6, May 15, 1894; *Kansas City Star*, June 4, June 23, 1894; *Topeka Daily Capital*, May 24, 1894.

4 *Denver Times*, April 23–24, 1894; *Rocky Mountain News*, May 2, May 13–14, 1894.

5 *San Francisco Chronicle*, May 29, 1894; *Denver Times*, May 28, June 4, 1894; *Rocky Mountain News*, May 25–27, 1894; *Salt Lake Tribune*, May 23, May 29, 1894.

6 The story of the Denver Coxeyites' tragic nautical adventure is taken from the *Rocky Mountain News*, May 25–June 9, 1894; *Denver Republican*, June 4–6, 1894; *Denver Times*, June 4–8, 1894; *Salt Lake Tribune*, May 7, June 9–10, 1894.

7 *Denver Times*, June 8–9, 1894; *Rocky Mountain News*, June 9–11, 1894; *Sidney* (Nebraska) *Telegraph*, June 16, 1894.

8 *Rocky Mountain News*, June 11, 1894; *Denver Times*, June 12, 1894, p. 1; *Sidney Telegraph*, June 16, 1894; *Kansas City Star*, July 19, 1894; *Omaha Bee*, June 23, 1894; *Omaha World-Herald*, June 14–17, June 26, July 27, 1894; Gerald G. Eggert, *Railroad Labor Disputes: The Beginnings of Federal Strike Policy* (Ann Arbor: University of Michigan Press, 1967), p. 85; A. J. Sawyer to the Attorney General, February 5, March 12, 1895, File 4017–1894, Justice Department, Records Group 60, National Archives, Washington, D.C.

9 The story of the Hoganites' voyage down the Missouri is taken from the *Helena Independent*, May 31, June 7–9, 1894; *Fort Benton River Press*, May 9, May 30, June 6, June 13, June 20, 1894; *Butte Bystander*, June 9, June 23, 1894; *Butte Miner*, June 9, 1894; *Bismarck Daily Tribune*, June 15, 1894; *Yankton* (South Dakota) *Press and Dakotan*, June 27–28, 1894; *Sioux City Journal*, June 30, 1894; *Omaha World-Herald*, July 2–3, 1894; *Omaha Bee*, July 4, 1894; *St. Joseph* (Missouri) *Daily News*, July 6, July 9, 1894; *Kansas City Star*, July 13, 1894. For a more detailed account of the voyage undertaken by Montana's jobless, see Carlos A. Schwantes, "Coxey's Montana Navy: A Protest Against Unemployment on the Wageworkers' Frontier," *Pacific Northwest Quarterly* 73 (July 1982): 98–107.

10 McMurry, *Coxey's Army*, pp. 195–96; Almont Lindsey, *The Pullman Strike: The Story of a Unique Experiment and of a Great Labor Upheaval* (Chicago: University of Chicago Press, 1942).

11 *Jefferson City Daily Tribune*, July 21, 1894; *St. Louis Globe-Democrat*, July 29–30, 1894.

12 *Anaconda Standard*, August 8–9, September 2, 1894.

13 *Fort Benton River Press*, May 30, August 15, 1894; *Anaconda Standard*, August 9, 1894; *Yankton Press and Dakotan*, June 28, 1894; *St. Joseph Daily News*, July 9, 1894.

Notes to Chapter 14

1 *Washington Star*, July 4, 1894; *Washington Post*, July 5, 1894; *Washington Times*, July 5, 1894.

2 *American Non-Conformist*, August 16, 1894.

3 Josiah Flynt [Willard], "Tramping with Tramps," *Century* 47 (November 1893): 106; Roger A. Bruns, *Knights of the Road: A Hobo History* (New York: Methuen, 1980).

4 *Washington Star*, May 12, 1894; *Washington Post*, May 12–15, 1894; Joseph V. Tracy, "A Mission to Coxey's Army," *Catholic World* 59 (August 1894): 666–80; *Woman's Tribune*, July 16, 1894, p. 110; *American Review of Reviews* 10 (July 1894): 4–5.

5 *Wheeling Daily Intelligencer*, May 4–5, 1894.

6 *Indianapolis Journal*, May 7, 1894; *Cincinnati Enquirer*, May 24–29, 1894; *Parkersburg Sentinel*, June 4–5, 1894.

7 *Cumberland Evening Times*, June 15–16, 1894; *Washington Post*, June 26–27, 1894; *Washington Star*, June 29, 1894; Donald L. McMurry, *Coxey's Army: A Story of the Industrial Army Movement of 1894* (1929; reprint ed., Seattle: University of Washington Press, 1968), pp. 246–47.

8 *St. Louis Post-Dispatch*, June 2, 1894; Illinois File in File 4017–1894, Justice Department, Records Group 60, National Archives, Washington, D.C.

9 *St. Louis Post-Dispatch*, May 31, 1894; *Des Moines Leader*, June 6, 1894; *Minneapolis Journal*, June 5, 1894; *San Francisco Chronicle*, June 9, 1894.

10 Details of Kelley's odyssey from southern Illinois to West Virginia are from the *St. Louis Post-Dispatch*, May 31–June 9, 1894; *Des Moines Leader*, June 8, 1894; *Evansville Journal*, June 11–12, 1894; *Louisville Courier-Journal*, June 19–24, 1894; *New Albany Daily Ledger*, June 20–25, 1894; *Cincinnati Enquirer*, May 29, June 28–July 2, 1894; *Parkersburg Daily Sentinel*, July 9, 1894; McMurry, *Coxey's Army*, p. 196.

11 *Charleston Evening Mail*, July 9, 1894; *Wheeling Daily Intelligencer*, July 14, July 20, 1894; *Parkersburg Daily Sentinel*, July 14, 1894.

Notes to Chapter 15

1 Jack London, *The Road*, reprinted in *Jack London: Novels and Social Writing* (New York: Literary Classics of the United States, 1982), pp. 230–32.

2 Robert C. Nesbit, *"He Built Seattle": A Biography of Judge Thomas Burke* (Seattle: University of Washington Press, 1961); Murray Morgan, *Puget's Sound: A Narrative of Early Tacoma and the Southern Sound* (Seattle: University of Washington Press, 1979), pp. 271–74; Earl Pomeroy, *The Pacific Slope: A History of California, Oregon, Washington, Idaho, Utah, and Ne-*

vada (New York: Alfred A. Knopf, 1968), pp. 146–51; Harry Ault Papers, Box 6, Part I, Folder 69, University of Washington Library, Seattle; *Portland Evening Telegram*, April 14, 1894.

3 *Seattle Daily Telegraph*, April 8, April 29–30, 1894; *Seattle Post-Intelligencer*, April 29, 1894; *Tacoma Daily News*, April 30–May 1, 1894; Donald L. McMurry, *Coxey's Army: A Story of the Industrial Army Movement of 1894* (1929; reprint ed., Seattle: University of Washington Press, 1968), pp. 216–17.

4 *Tacoma Daily Ledger*, April 26, May 2–3, 1894; *Tacoma Morning Union*, May 5, 1894.

5 *Seattle Daily Telegraph*, April 28–30, 1894; *Tacoma Daily News*, May 1, 1894; *Tacoma Weekly Ledger*, May 4, 1894.

6 *Tacoma Daily News*, April 30–May 1, 1894; *Tacoma Daily Ledger*, May 1–4, 1894; *Tacoma Morning Union*, May 1, 1894; *Seattle Daily Telegraph*, April 21, 1894; *Detroit Free Press*, September 12, 1939.

7 *Tacoma Daily News*, May 3, 1894; *Seattle Daily Telegraph*, May 5, May 30, 1894; *Spokane Review*, May 5–7, 1894; *Tacoma Daily News*, May 1, May 8, 1894; *Tacoma Daily Ledger*, May 4, 1894; *Tacoma Morning Union*, May 4, 1894; *Ellensburg Capital*, May 17, 1894; Morgan, *Puget's Sound*, pp. 281–93.

8 *Tacoma Daily News*, May 1, 1894; *Spokane Review*, May 7, 1894.

9 *Seattle Telegraph*, April 29–30, 1894; *Tacoma Daily News*, April 27, 1894; *Tacoma Daily Ledger*, May 5, May 12, 1894.

10 *Spokane Review*, May 7–12, May 21, 1894; *Spokane Daily Chronicle*, May 8–10, 1894; McMurry, *Coxey's Army*, pp. 220–21; *Seattle Telegraph*, May 30, 1894.

11 *Tacoma Morning Union*, May 20, 1894; *Tacoma Daily News*, May 25, 1894; *Seattle Telegraph*, May 30, 1894; *Anaconda Standard*, June 2, 1894; *Tacoma Daily Ledger*, May 21, 1894.

12 *Fargo Forum*, June 4, 1894; *Minneapolis Journal*, June 14–18, 1894; *St. Paul Pioneer-Press*, June 18, June 26, 1894; *Anaconda Standard*, June 12, 1894; *Tacoma Daily Ledger*, June 23, 1894; *Milwaukee Journal*, June 19–22, 1894; *Chicago Inter Ocean*, June 23, 1894; McMurry, *Coxey's Army*, pp. 222–23.

13 *St. Paul Pioneer-Press*, May 6, 1894; *Jamestown Daily Alert*, June 20, 1894; *Fargo Forum*, June 15, 1894; *Minneapolis Journal*, June 18, 1894; *St. Paul Globe*, July 5, August 25, 1894; *Milwaukee Journal*, June 21, 1894; *Detroit News*, July 22, 1894.

14 Details of Jeffries's journey through the Great Lakes Country are from the *Duluth News-Tribune*, July 1–2, 1894; *Tacoma Daily Ledger*, August 7, 1894; *Tacoma News*, August 2, 1894; *Weekly Mining Journal* (Marquette), July 14, 1894; *Bay City Times-Press*, July 17–18, 1894, p. 5; *Chicago Inter Ocean*, July 22, 1894; *St. Paul Globe*, July 26, 1894; *Detroit Free Press*, July

22, 1894; *Detroit Evening News*, July 24, 1894; *Cleveland Plain Dealer*, July 25–28, 1894.

15 *Pittsburgh Press*, July 28, 1894; *Ohio State Journal*, July 29, 1894; *Alliance Standard Review*, August 2, 1894; *Seattle Telegraph*, August 7, 1894.

16 *Pittsburgh Press*, July 30–August 5, 1894; *Pittsburgh Post*, July 31–August 2, 1894; *Homestead News*, August 2, 1894; *Seattle Telegraph*, August 7, 1894; *Keep off the Grass* (Anaconda, Mont.), June 1, 1894; *New York Times*, August 5, 1894; *Connellsville Courier*, August 10, 1894.

17 *Tacoma Daily News*, July 11, 1894.

18 *Tacoma Daily Ledger*, May 29, 1894; *Spokesman-Review* (Spokane), July 1, 1894; *Anaconda Standard*, May 27–29, 1894; *Helena Independent*, May 29, 1894.

19 *Tacoma Morning Union*, June 2, 1894; *Tacoma News*, June 19, August 2, 1894; *Seattle Daily Telegraph*, April 30, August 13, 1894; *Washington Post*, June 16, July 15–16, August 13, 1894; *St. Paul Globe*, June 23, August 11, 1894; *Fargo Forum*, June 29, 1894.

20 *Tacoma News*, June 19, 1894; *Tacoma Daily Ledger*, August 3, August 7, 1894; *Tacoma News*, August 2, 1894.

21 *Tacoma Morning Union*, November 4, 1894; *Seattle Telegraph*, October 7, 1894; Morgan, *Puget's Sound*, pp. 290–92.

Notes to Chapter 16

1 Details of the Commonweal's final days in Maryland are taken from the *Washington Star*, June 23, July 7, 1894; *Washington Post*, July 2, July 16, July 26–28, 1894; *Baltimore Sun*, July 9–12, July 26–27, 1894.

2 Life in the Virginia camp is described in the *Baltimore Sun*, July 12, 1894; *Washington Post*, July 5–6, July 14–28, August 1, August 8, 1894; *Washington Star*, July 7, July 17–30, August 3, August 10, 1894; *Woman's Tribune*, July 28, August 4, 1894; *Richmond Times*, July 28, August 8, 1894.

3 *Washington Star*, August 9, 1894; *Baltimore American*, August 10, August 15, 1894; *Baltimore Sun*, August 16, 1894; *American Non-Conformist*, August 16, 1894; *Pittsburgh Press*, August 11, 1894.

4 *Richmond Times*, July 28, August 5, 1894; *Chicago Times*, August 12, 1894; *Washington Post*, August 8, August 11, 1894.

5 The story of Governor O'Ferrall versus the Commonwealers is taken from the *Washington Post*, August 9–12, 1894; *Washington Star*, August 11, August 21, 1894; *Richmond Times*, August 11–14, 1894; *Pittsburgh Press*, August 11, 1894; *Ohio State Journal*, August 12, 1894; *Baltimore Sun*, August 13, 1894.

6 *Washington Star*, August 11, 1894; *Washington Post*, August 12, 1894; *Rich-*

mond Times, August 11, 1894.

7 *Richmond Times*, August 12, 1894; *Washington Post*, August 12–13, 1894; *Washington Star*, August 13, 1894.

8 *Washington Star*, August 13, 1894; *Washington Post*, August 14, 1894.

9 *St. Louis Chronicle*, August 13, 1894; *Washington Star*, August 13, 1894; *Washington Post*, August 14–17, 1894; *Baltimore Sun*, August 16–22, 1894; *Baltimore American*, August 20, 1894.

10 *St. Paul Globe*, August 19, 1894; *St. Paul Pioneer-Press*, August 19, 1894; *Minneapolis Journal*, August 18, 1894; *Spokane Spokesman-Review*, August 29, 1894.

11 Carl Browne, *When Coxey's "Army" Marcht on Washington, 1894*, ed. William McDevitt (San Francisco: n.p., 1944), pp. 28–29; Charles T. Kelley, "Are Radicals Insane?" *Current History* 20 (May 1924): 205–10.

12 *Seattle Call*, April 4, 1895; Malcolm W. Bingay, *Detroit is My Hometown* (Indianapolis: Bobbs-Merrill, 1946), pp. 244–50.

13 *Washington Star*, August 20, 1894; *Coxey Good Roads*, May 1895 (Copy in Labadic Collection, University of Michigan, Ann Arbor); *New York Times*, October 22, 1894, June 16, 1895; *Carl's Cactus* in the Ray Stannard Baker Papers, Box 72, Library of Congress; Samuel Gompers, *Seventy Years of Life and Labor* (New York: E. P. Dutton, 1925), vol. 2, p. 12; *San Francisco Chronicle*, January 17, January 24, 1914; Browne, *Coxey's "Army"*, p. 26–27.

14 Embry Bernard Howson, "Jacob S. Coxey: A Biography of a Monetary Reformer, 1854–1951" (Ph.D. diss., Ohio State University, 1973); *New York Times*, May 2, 1944, May 19, 1951.

15 Browne, *Coxey's "Army"*, p. 13; John D. Hicks, Introduction to *Coxey's Army: A Study of the Industrial Army Movement of 1894*, ed. Donald L. McMurry (1929; reprint ed., Seattle: University of Washington Press, 1968), p. xxii; *Daily Iowa Capital*, May 10, 1894.

16 *Tacoma News*, April 14, 1894.

Notes to Chapter 17

1 Thomas Byrnes, "Character and Methods of the Men," *North American Review* 451 (June 1894): 696; *St. Louis Post-Dispatch*, April 4, 1894; *Portland Evening Telegram*, April 16, 1894; *Cincinnati Enquirer*, April 21, 1894; *Minneapolis Journal*, May 12, 1894; *Chicago Tribune*, May 2, 1894; *Detroit News*, July 22, 1894.

2 *Omaha Bee*, April 15, 1894; *American Non-Conformist*, April 26, 1894; *Daily Iowa State Register*, May 1, 1894; *Topeka Daily Capital*, May 5, May 13, 1894; *Chicago Herald*, May 7, 1894; *Chicago Tribune*, May 8, 1894; A. Cleveland Hall, "An Observer in Coxey's Camp," *Independent* 46

(May 17, 1894): 615; Donald L. McMurry, *Coxey's Army: A Study of the Industrial Army Movement of 1894* (1929; reprint ed., Seattle: University of Washington Press, 1968), pp. 232–34.

3 *Chicago Tribune*, May 8, 1894; *South Bend Tribune*, May 12, 1894; *St. Paul Pioneer-Press*, May 14, 1894; *Topeka Daily Capital*, June 25, 1894.

4 *Sacramento Record-Union*, April 17–23, April 30, 1894.

5 *Salt Lake Tribune*, May 9, 1894; *Sacramento Record-Union*, May 11, 1894; *Kansas City Star*, June 14–18, 1894; *Kansas City Mail*, June 18, 1894.

6 *St. Louis Chronicle*, August 13, 1894; Melvyn Dubofsky, "The Origins of Western Working Class Radicalism, 1890–1905," *Labor History* 7 (Spring 1966): 131–54; *St. Louis Labor News*, April 28, 1894; Melvyn Dubofsky, *We Shall Be All: A History of the Industrial Workers of the World* (Chicago: Quadrangle Books, 1969), pp. 173–97.

7 Frank Leonard, "'Helping' the Unemployed in the Nineteenth Century: The Case of the American Tramp," *Social Service Review* 40 (December 1966): 429; *Philadelphia Inquirer*, March 24, 1894; W. T. Stead, "'Coxeyism': A Character Sketch," *Review of Reviews* 10 (July 1894): 51; *Washington Post*, April 23, 1894; E. Hoffer, "The Tramp Problem," *Overland Monthly* 23 (June 1894): 628–32; *St. Louis Post-Dispatch*, April 4, 1894.

8 *Chicago Tribune*, May 2, 1894; *South Bend Tribune*, May 10, 1894; *Salt Lake Tribune*, June 4, 1894; *Commercial Gazette* as quoted in *Literary Digest* 9 (May 5, 1894): 2.

9 *Sacramento Record-Union*, April 25, 1894; *Seattle Daily Telegraph*, May 14, 1894; *Omaha World-Herald*, June 17, 1894; Daniel T. Rodgers, *The Work Ethic in Industrial America, 1850–1920* (Chicago: University of Chicago Press, 1978), pp. 210–32.

10 *Boston Herald*, April 23, 1894; *Chicago Tribune*, April 27, 1894.

11 *Los Angeles Times*, March 24, 1894; *Sacramento Record-Union*, April 25, May 12, 1894; *Seattle Post-Intelligencer*, May 5, 1894; *Salt Lake Tribune*, May 8, 1894; *San Francisco Chronicle*, May 29, 1894; *Terre Haute Express*, April 21, 1894; *St. Louis Post-Dispatch*, April 22, 1894; *Topeka Daily Capital*, April 29, 1894.

12 *Washington Star*, April 14, 1894; *Walla Walla Union*, April 29, 1894; *New York Tribune*, April 27, 1894; *Topeka Daily Capital*, April 25, 1894; *New York Sun*, May 3, 1894.

13 *Des Moines Leader*, May 1, 1894; *Tacoma Morning Union*, May 10, 1894; *Salt Lake Tribune*, May 27, 1894; Carlos A. Schwantes, "Law and Disorder: The Suppression of Coxey's Army in Idaho," *Idaho Yesterdays* 27 (Fall 1983): 14–15.

14 *San Francisco Bulletin*, May 11, 1894; *Sacramento Record-Union*, May 12,

1894; *San Francisco Examiner*, May 14, 1894; *Salt Lake Tribune*, May 21–27, 1894.

15 *Topeka Daily Capital*, April 25, May 13, 1894; *Minneapolis Journal*, May 12, 1894; T. B. Veblen, "The Army of the Commonweal," *Journal of Political Economy* 2 (June 1894): 459; *American Review of Reviews* 10 (July 1894): 4-5.

16 *Indianapolis Journal*, April 28, May 3, 1894.

17 *Kansas City Star*, June 4, 1894; *Los Angeles Times*, March 22, 1894; *Des Moines Leader*, April 24, 1894; *Spectator* (London), April 28, 1894; *Chicago Tribune*, May 5, 1894; *Salt Lake Tribune*, May 23, 1894; *Cleveland Plain Dealer*, July 27, 1894.

18 *Minneapolis Journal*, May 8, 1894; *South Bend Tribune*, May 10, 1894; *American Law Review* 28 (1894): 420–27; James J. Hill to Grover Cleveland, May 5, 1894, Cleveland Papers, Library of Congress.

19 *Denver Times*, June 12, 1894; *St. Paul Pioneer-Press*, April 16, 1894; *Salt Lake Tribune*, May 22, 1894.

20 *St. Louis Post-Dispatch*, April 8, 1894; *Chicago Record*, April 14, 1894; *American Non-Conformist*, April 26, 1894; *Nation* 58 (April 26, 1894): 306; *Keep off the Grass*, June 1, 1894, p. 1; Carlos A. Schwantes, "Coxey's Montana Navy: A Protest Against Unemployment on the Wageworkers' Frontier," *Pacific Northwest Quarterly* 73 (July 1982): 106–7.

21 *Seattle Press-Times*, April 17, 1894; *Rocky Mountain News*, April 27, 1894; *National Labor Tribune* (Pittsburgh), April 5, 1894.

22 *Indianapolis Journal*, May 3, May 6, 1894; *Butte Miner*, June 4, 1894; Carl Browne, *When Coxey's "Army" Marcht on Washington, 1894*, ed. William McDevitt (San Francisco: n.p., 1944), p. 25.

23 *Salt Lake Tribune*, May 4, 1894; *Indianapolis Journal*, April 30, 1894.

24 *Seattle Telegraph*, August 7, 1894; *Chicago Record*, March 30, 1894; *Butte Miner*, April 22, 1894; *St. Louis Post-Dispatch*, April 29, 1894; *Keep off the Grass*, June 1, 1894; *Kansas City Star*, April 23, 1894; *Munsey's Magazine* 11 (May 1894): 221; *Idaho Daily Statesman*, May 18, 1894; Frank Basil Tracy, "Menacing Socialism in the Western States," *Forum* 15 (May 1893): 334, 336.

25 *Denver News* as quoted in the *Omaha World-Herald*, July 8, 1894; *St. Louis Post-Dispatch*, April 22, 1894; *Helena Independent*, April 27, 1894; *Seattle Telegraph*, March 27, 1894; *Tacoma News*, April 16, 1894; *Seattle Post-Intelligencer*, May 8, 1894.

26 *Topeka Daily Capital*, May 13, 1894; Charles S. Gleed, "The True Significance of Western Unrest," *Forum* 16 (October 1893): 260; H. L. Stetson, "The Industrial Army," *Independent* 44 (May 31, 1894): 681; *Daily Iowa State Register*, May 4, 1894; *Nation* 58 (May 3, 1894): 323; Byrnes, "Character and Methods of the Men," p. 699.

27 *Seattle Daily Telegraph*, April 26, May 10, June 8, 1894; *New York Sun*, May 6, 1894; Henry Nash Smith, *Virgin Land: The American West as Myth and Symbol* (New York: Vintage Books, 1950), pp. 234–45; Gilbert C. Fite, *The Farmers' Frontier, 1865–1900* (New York: Holt, Rinehart and Winston, 1966), pp. 215–24.

28 Carter Goodrich and Sol Davison, "The Wage-Earner in the Westward Movement, I," *Political Science Quarterly* 50 (June 1935): 161–85; *Seattle Daily Telegraph*, April 26, 1894; *Jamestown Daily Alert*, June 14, 1894; *Portland Daily Oregonian*, April 6, 1894, p. 4.

29 *Los Angeles Times*, May 22, 1894; *Literary Digest* 9 (May 5, 1894): 2; Carl N. Degler, "The West as a Solution to Urban Unemployment," *New York History* 36 (January 1955): 70–71, 80; Fred A. Shannon, "A Post Mortem on the Labor-Safety-Valve Theory," *Agricultural History* 19 (January 1945): 31–37.

30 *Seattle Post-Intelligencer*, May 23, 1894.

31 *Daily Iowa State Register*, May 4, 1894; *St. Louis Post-Dispatch*, May 27, 1894; *Mining Journal*, July 14, 1894; *San Francisco Examiner*, March 14, 1894; *Los Angeles Times*, May 22, 1894; *St. Louis Globe-Democrat*, August 8, 1894.

32 Earl Pomeroy, *The Pacific Slope: A History of California, Oregon, Washington, Idaho, and Nevada* (New York: Alfred A. Knopf, 1968), pp. 82, 191–214; Fite, *The Farmers' Frontier*, pp. 70–71.

33 Smith, *Virgin Land*, pp. 234, 291n. See also Carlos A. Schwantes, "Blessed are the Mythmakers? Free Land, Unemployment, and Uncle Sam in the American West," *Idaho Yesterdays* 27 (Fall 1983): 2–12.

34 Leonard, "'Helping' the Unemployed," p. 435; John A. Garraty, *Unemployment in History: Economic Thought and Public Policy* (New York: Harper & Row, 1978), pp. 231, 232.

35 Henry Steele Commager, *The American Mind: An Interpretation of American Thought and Character Since the 1880's* (New Haven: Yale University Press, 1950), p. 41; Lawrence Goodwyn, *Democratic Promise: The Populist Moment in America* (New York: Oxford University Press, 1976), pp. 515–55.

Addams, Jane, 31

Allen, Senator William V. (Nebraska), 169, 173

American Federation of Labor, 12, 32

American Nonconformist (Indianapolis), 79–80

American society in the 1890s: decentralization of, 100, 268–70; economic attitudes, 15–21 passim, 56, 278–79; fears of paternalism, 273–74; fears of social cataclysm, 17, 31, 274–75, 277; protests and protest movements, 13, 19–20, 24–25, 27–33 passim; 83–84, 278–79. *See also* Depression of 1893; Railroads; Reform and reform movements

Anderson, Adjutant General Charles J. (Virginia), 252–54

Arizona, Territory of: and Fry's army, 89–90

Artz, A. A. (former adjutant general of Kansas), 203, 267

Atchison, Topeka and Santa Fe Railroad: competition with Southern Pacific, 85; refuses transportation to Fry's army, 86–87; and Smith-Barker army, 130, 132; mentioned, 26–27, 97

Atlanta, Georgia, 13

Atlantic, Iowa: Kelley's army at, 136–37

Austin, Texas: Fry's army at, 96

Aylesworth, B. O.: aids Kelley's army, 140; studies composition of Kelley's army, 188, 262, 299 n.5

Babcock, W. P., of the *New York World*, 79

Baker, George. *See* Kelley's army

Baker, Ray Stannard: biographical sketch, 3, 27, 30, 32, 257; covers Coxey's Army for the *Chicago Record*, 45, 50, 52, 62, 78, 146, 184, 281

Baltimore, Maryland, 56, 256

Baltimore and Ohio Railroad, 196, 242

Barker, John. *See* Smith-Barker army

Baum, L. Frank, 20

Beatty, Judge James H. (Idaho):
conducts trial of Scheffler's
army, 204–5; imprisons and
breaks morale of Coxeyites,
205–7; mentioned, 199, 200
Bellinger, Judge Charles B. (Ore-
gon), 199, 201, 204, 205
Bemis, George P. (Mayor of
Omaha): supports Kelley's army,
119, 125; mentioned, 144, 294n.8
Bennett, Henry. See Denver,
Colorado
Bierce, Ambrose, 19
Bimetallic League, 24
Billings, Montana: Hogan's army
at, 159–60; mentioned, 157, 268
Blacks: life in the ranks, 193; response to industrial army movement, 62, 146, 180
Boston, Massachusetts, 11, 39
Brandeis, Emil, 115, 119
Briggs, Emily Edson, 181
Brown, Governor Frank (Maryland), 251, 256
Browne, Carl: appearance of, 4, 40,
43, 63; arrest and trial of, 179–84
passim; biographical details, 6,
25–26, 28, 29, 31, 37–40, 48, 83,
257–59; on Capitol Hill, 178–80;
and Mamie Coxey, 5–6, 258–59;
originates march on Washington, 32; preparations in Washington, D.C., 173–77; as publicist,
4–5, 12, 46–47, 74–75, 82, 222–
23, 225, 247; relationship with
Coxey, 4, 25, 36–37, 41, 70, 74,
258–59; role in Coxey's army,
44–45, 50, 63, 65, 70, 142, 173;
role in latter phase of the Coxey
movement, 246–47. See also
Coxey's Army

Brough, Charles M. (Mayor of
Ogden, Utah), 109–10
Bryan, William Jennings, 24
Buffalo, New York, 283n.8
Burlington and Missouri River
Railroad, 211, 214
Butte, Montana, 11, 149–50, 152, 164

California: background to Coxey
movement, 38–39, 83, 85;
Kearney movement, 39; miscel-
laneous industrial armies, 130–
32; unemployment in, 57, 84–86.
See also Fry's army; Kelley's army
Canton, Ohio, 49–50, 53, 73
Cantwell's army (Washington,
Idaho, Montana): Carlotta
Cantwell, 187, 234, 238–39,
243–45, 248; Frank T. "Jumbo"
Cantwell, 187, 232, 235–40 passim, 242–45, 264; organized in
Tacoma, Washington, 232; tactics
employed crossing continent,
236–40. See also Jeffries's army
Carlisle, John G. (secretary of the
treasury), 167
Carter's army (Utah and Colorado): General Henry Carter,
215–17 passim, 267, 272; tragedy
in Denver, 214–17; mentioned,
207, 213
Chesapeake and Ohio Canal:
Coxey's army on, 75–82 passim;
mentioned, 141, 226, 255, 265
Chesapeake and Ohio Railway,
230
Cheyenne, Wyoming, 111
Chicago, Illinois: 1893 depression,
29–31; 1893 World's Fair, 23,
26–27; and Kelley's army, 137;
protest by unemployed, 27–29,

33; mentioned, 11, 12, 14, 16, 23–26 passim

Chicago and North-Western Railway: and Cantwell's army, 240; opposes Kelley's army, 113–14, 120–21, 124–25

Chicago, Burlington, and Quincy Railroad, 162

Chicago Great Western Railway, 138, 141

Chicago, Rock Island, and Pacific Railway: opposes Kelley's army, 121–24, 136, 138, 190; precipitates trouble with Kelley's army, 193–94; mentioned, 27

Chinese, 39, 62, 99, 131

Cincinnati, Ohio, 226, 229

Cleveland, Ohio, 241

Cleveland, President Grover: on "communism of combined wealth," 19; and Coxey's army, 167; and Hogan's army, 161–62; mentioned, 1, 3, 12, 106

Cody, William F. "Buffalo Bill," 173

Coke, Senator Richard (Texas), 173

Colby, Clara Bewick (editor of *Woman's Tribune*), 128

Colorado, 14–15, 209–18 passim

Columbian Exposition, 1893: description of, 25–26; and unemployed, 26–27, 30–32; mentioned, 23

Commonweal of Christ. *See* Coxey's army

Congress: and Commonweal, 7, 169; and money question, 26; and unemployed, 15

Cooperative Commonweal of the United States, 252

Council Bluffs, Iowa: Kelley's army at, 113–21 passim

Courts. *See* Judiciary

Coxey, Jacob S.: appearance of, 1–2; arrest and trial of, 181–84; attempts to give speech on Capitol Hill, 178–81; biographical details, 2, 34–35, 74–75, 258–59; family, 6, 36, 41–42, 289 n.2; Good Roads program, 32, 33, 37, 40; origin of non-interest-bearing bond plan, 37; preparations in Washington, D.C., 173–77 passim; reform ideas, 36–37, 40, 147–48, 173–74, 267; relationship with Carl Browne, 4, 25, 36–37, 70, 74, 258–59; role in Coxey's army, 33, 40–41, 44, 50, 69–70, 142, 168. *See also* Coxey's army

Coxey, Jesse, 6, 67–69, 72, 175, 247

Coxey, Legal Tender, 6, 7, 36, 173, 177, 259

Coxey, Mamie, 4–6, 175–78 passim, 183, 258

Coxey's army (Commonweal of Christ): appeal of, 47, 57–59, 61, 71, 73–74; arrest and imprisonment of Coxey and Browne, 180–84; arrest and imprisonment of remaining members, 251; confrontation on Capitol Hill, 9–10, 178–80; crossing Ohio, 49–53 passim; description of, 6, 42–43; difficulties crossing southwestern Pennsylvania, 62–66; in District of Columbia, 1–10 passim, 178–80; early organizational difficulties, 44, 63; final phase of movement, 184–85; formed in Massillon, Ohio, 2, 40–45 passim; from Frederick to the District of Columbia, 166–

Coxey's army (*continued*)
72; life in, 49–53 passim, 63–64,
78, 82, 142, 144, 147, 172, 175–77,
225; origin of idea, 32–33; over-
view of movement, 10–12 passim, 17, 20–21; in Pittsburgh
area, 54–56, 60–61; recruitment, 41, 51; religion in, 142, 173;
schism in, 63, 66–69; search for
suitable campsite in District of
Columbia area, 181–82, 224–25;
sympathizers, 181, 183; in western
Maryland, 66–82 passim, 141–
48 passim. *See also* Browne, Carl;
Coxey, Jacob S.; Industrial
armies
Cranks. *See* Reform and reform
movements
Crisp, Charles F. (speaker, U. S.
House of Representatives), 176
Crocker, C. F., 105
Cumberland, Maryland: Coxey's
army at, 71–76 passim; mentioned, 64

Daly, Marcus, 153
Debs, Eugene V., 56, 62, 189
Denver, Colorado: Henry Bennett
assumes command of local army,
213, 264, 266; Coxeyite disaster
on South Platte, 214–17; William Grayson reorganizes army,
211–13; Bert Hamilton organizes
"Free Silver Legion," 209–11;
home guards, 213–14, 217, 218,
270; as mecca for Coxeyites, 209,
211–12
Depew, Chauncy M.: advice to unemployed, 13–14
Depression of 1893, 13–21 passim,
27–33 passim, 57

Des Moines, Iowa: Kelley's army at,
140–41, 187–91
Detroit, Michigan: and Edward J.
Jeffries, 11, 241, 257; and Ryba-
kowski's army, 283 n.8
Dickinson, E. (general manager,
Union Pacific Railway), 111, 120,
198
Diggs, Annie, 4, 128, 203
Dodge, Grenville M., 276
Dolliver, Representative Jonathan
(Iowa), 173
Dolph, Senator Joseph (Oregon),
173
Donnelly, Ignatius, 25, 31
Dundy, Judge Elmer S. (Nebraska),
218–19

Ellert, L. R. (mayor of San Francisco), 99–100
El Paso, Texas: Fry's army at, 90–
92; mentioned, 86, 87, 95
Ethnicity and Coxeyism, 27, 28,
61–62, 283 n.8

Federal government: response to
Coxeyism, 3, 4, 7, 11–12, 162–65,
167–68, 205–8. *See also* Judiciary; Lawmen; U.S. Army
Fillmore, J. A., 105
Frye, Senator William (Maine),
173
Fry's army (California, Arizona,
New Mexico, Texas, Midwest):
confrontation in Texas, 92–96;
crossing Southwest, 89–91;
Lewis C. Fry, 86–88, 226, 272;
organization of, 86–89; troubles
crossing Midwest, 96, 186, 196,
265, 267, 272–73; in Washington,
D.C., area, 225, 247, 248, 252

Galvin's army (Ohio, Pennsylvania): confrontation with Ohio National Guard, 196–97; Colonel Thomas Galvin, 186, 265; reaches District of Columbia, 225–26, 248; secession from Fry's army, 186, 196

George, Henry, 29

Gompers, Samuel: opinion of Carl Browne, 12; and Coxeyism, 181; and the unemployed, 29, 32

Grayson, William. *See* Denver, Colorado

Great Northern Railway, 151, 231

Great Unknown (Louis Smith): biography, 72, 259; conflict with Browne, 50, 63, 65–69; introduced, 43–44; leads schismatic movement, 69, 78, 81, 169, 170, 174, 247; role in Coxey movement, 44, 50–52, 65; and "Veiled Lady," 51–52

Hagerstown, Maryland, 141–42

Hamilton, Bert. *See* Denver, Colorado

Hanford, Judge Cornelius (state of Washington), 232, 276

Harrison, Carter Henry (mayor of Chicago): assassination of, 30; and monetary reformers, 23–24; response to unemployment protests, 28–29

Hayes, Rutherford B.: Carl Browne and Denis Kearney visit, 39

Haymarket Riot, 1886, 28, 43, 44, 128

Hill, James J., 231, 270

Hillis, Isaac L. (mayor of Des Moines, Iowa), 141

Hogan's army (Montana): William Hogan, 150, 221; imprisonment of, 187, 205; organization of, 150–51; pursued by federal marshals and U.S. Army, 154–65 passim; sources of support, 150–51, 155, 156–57, 160–61; steals a train, 153–54; voyage down Missouri River, 209, 219–21, 264, 270–71

Hogg, Governor James Stephen (Texas): and Coxeyism, 96–97; and Fry's army, 91–96; vs. Southern Pacific officials, 91–95

Homestead, Pennsylvania: Coxey's army at, 61, 63

Houston, Texas, 11, 57, 97, 293 n.20

Hubbard, Nat M., 114, 120–21, 124

Hudson, Representative Thomas Jefferson (Colorado), 183–84

Huntington, Collis P.: and Kelley's army, 105, 106

Idaho: and Scheffler's army, 199–200, 204–6; mentioned, 24, 268

Illinois, 194, 196, 227–28. *See also* Chicago; Randall's army; Rybakowski's army

Indiana: Fry's army at Indianapolis, 96, 186, 226, 269, 273; Kelley's army at Jeffersonville and New Albany, 228–29

Industrial armies (except Coxey's army): composition of, 112, 197, 262, 299 n.5; end of movement, 206–8, 226–27, 249–60 passim, 259; image of, 270–71, 274; life and death in the ranks, 89–90, 102, 119, 135–36, 215–17, 253–54; meaning of the movement, 46, 74–75, 259–60, 264, 270–75, 277–79, organizational structure,

Industrial armies (*continued*)
69–70, 82, 86–87, 116–17, 262–
63; patriotism of, 265–66; recruitment, 96; as reform movement, 271–73, 278; regional
nature of support, 56–57, 184–
86, 195, 225–26; religion, 117–18,
265; sources of support, 104–6,
111–12, 114–15, 119–21, 141, 150–
51; 203–68; strategy and tactics,
84, 159, 220, 228–29, 236–39 passim, 241–42, 269, 270; and work
ethic, 266–67. *See also* Coxey's
army; *names of other individual
armies*
Industrial Workers of the World
("Wobblies"), 264
Iowa. *See* Kelley's army
Irrigation of arid lands. *See* Western
United States

Jackson, Governor Frank T. (Iowa):
confronts Kelley's army, 113–14;
opinion of Kelley's army, 140;
seeks transportation for Kelley's
army, 120
Jaxon, Honoré, 42–43, 45
Jeffries's army (Washington, Idaho,
Montana, Midwest): difficulties
crossing state of Washington,
236–38; in Great Lakes country,
240–41; Edward J. Jeffries, 11, 56,
235, 257, 273, 276–77; Jeffries assumes command of Seattle army,
235; in Pennsylvania, 242; tactics
crossing continent, 238–42 passim; in Washington, D.C., area,
242, 252, 255–56
Johnson, Representative Tom
(Ohio), 180–81
Jones, Christopher Columbus

(leader of Philadelphia army), 7,
57, 171, 178, 181–84 passim, 251
Jones, Mary G. ("Mother"), 129,
264
Journalism: Associated Press and
national wire services, 40, 224;
erroneous information about
Hogan's army, 161; evokes sympathy for Fry's army, 93; news
management, 80–81; newspaper
coverage of Coxey's army, 2, 10,
45–46, 47, 52, 56, 72, 224, 265,
271, 273; newspaper coverage of
Kelley's army 104–5, 112; operations in the field, 77–82; role in
sustaining interest in Coxey
movement, 74–75, 78–79, 80;
role of telegraphers, 77, 81–82.
See also Baker, Ray Stannard
Judiciary: evolution of policy toward Coxeyism, 104–9 passim,
152, 164, 199–208 passim, 219;
and injunctions, 105, 108–9, 132,
197, 203; municipal courts, 182–
84. *See also* Lawmen

Kansas. *See* Lewelling, Governor
Lorenzo; Sanders's army
Kansas City, Missouri, 129, 213, 218,
255, 273
Kearney, Denis, 39
Kelley's army (California, Nevada,
Utah, Wyoming, Nebraska,
Midwest): ascending Ohio
River, 227–29; Colonel George
Baker, 99, 101, 108, 134; crossing
Great Basin desert, 101–2;
Charles T. Kelley assumes command, 100–101; Kelley's biographical sketch, 100, 101, 115–16,
249, 257; Kelley's leadership, 108,

268; life in the ranks, 118–19, 141, 134–37; marchers' wives, 130; in Nebraska, 111–12; organized in San Francisco, 98–99; stranded in Council Bluffs, Iowa, 113–27 passim, 132; stranded in Des Moines, Iowa, 140–41, 187–91; troubles in Utah, 102–10; voyage to St. Louis, 189–95 passim; in Washington, D.C., 248, 250; in western Iowa, 133–40 passim, 266; women in the ranks, 123–25 passim, 127, 129, 190–92 passim, 227; in Wyoming, 110–11. *See also* Industrial armies

Kelly, Florence, 31

Kentucky, 228–29

Kilgore, Representative Constantine B. (Texas), 173

Knights of Labor, 19, 122, 123, 188

Knowles, Judge Hiram (Montana), 152, 154, 164, 201, 205, 219

Kruttschnitt, Julius, 94–95, 97

Kyle, Senator James H. (South Dakota), 169

Labor: Butte Miners' Union, 150, 157, 159; endorsement of Coxey plan, 32; organized labor debates Coxeyism, 56, 300 n.9; railroad workers and Coxeyism, 87, 104–5, 122–23, 156–57, 236–37, 294 n.6; response to industrial armies, 20, 53, 55, 61, 71, 76, 177, 239; support for Fry's army, 97, 186, 226; support for Galvin's army, 225; support for Hogan's army, 219–20; support for Kelley's army, 141, 189, 195, 229; wage slavery issue, 18–19, 27, 28. *See also* Gompers, Samuel

Lamont, Daniel S. (secretary of war), 162

Lawmen: District of Columbia police attack Coxey's army, 178–81, 185; District of Columbia police prepare for Coxey's army, 168, 176–77; in Frederick, Maryland, area, 145–47; and organized labor, 237; popular image of U.S. marshals, 200–201; response of local law enforcement officers to Coxeyism, 3, 7, 45, 55, 61, 66, 169, 241–42, 261; sympathy for Coxeyites, 114, 121, 200, 268; Texas Rangers, 93; U.S. marshals in Montana, 152–65 passim; U.S. marshals in Oregon, 198; U.S. marshals in state of Washington, 237; U.S. Secret Service, 3, 167. *See also* Military; U.S. Army

Lease, Mary Elizabeth, 202

Lewelling, Governor Lorenzo (Kansas), 129, 199, 201–2

London, Jack: and Kelley's army, 12, 132, 136, 141, 188, 192–94, 231

Los Angeles, California: Fry's army organizes in, 86–87; and Vinette's army, 98; mentioned, 11, 25, 85, 132

Louisville, Kentucky, 229

McBride, John, 32

McDermott, Marshal William (Montana), 152, 161

McGraw, Governor John Hart (Washington), 234

McKinley, Governor William (Ohio), 44, 49, 196–97, 242

Manderson, Senator Charles F. (Nebraska), 173

Markham, Governor Henry H. (California), 100

Maryland: Coxey's army in District of Columbia suburbs, 166, 169–72; Coxey's army in western Maryland, 68–82 passim, 141–48 passim; Coxey's army searches for suitable Maryland campsite, 224–25, 247; imprisonment of Coxeyites, 251, 256

Massillon, Ohio: and formation of Coxey's army, 40–47 passim; mentioned, 2, 3, 4, 25, 26, 32, 33, 35, 37, 246, 247, 259. *See also* Coxey's Army

Maybell, Stephen, 83–84

Merritt, Judge S. A. (Utah), 207

Michigan, 14, 240–41

Michigan Central Railroad, 240

Military: militiamen of Iowa, 116, 119, 120; militiamen of Utah, 104–10; militiamen of Virginia, 249, 251–54; Ohio National Guard, 196–97. *See also* U.S. Army

Miner, Judge James A. (Utah), 108–9

Minneapolis, Minnesota, 239, 256

Minnesota, 239–40, 256

Missouri Pacific Railway, 201–2, 204

Money question, 18, 24–26, 28, 31, 32, 150

Montana: Cantwell's army in, 238–39, 243–44; Hogan's army in, 150–65, 219; Jeffries's army in, 238; and silver mining industry, 57, 149–50; mentioned, 13, 57, 148

Morton, J. Sterling (secretary of agriculture), 162, 173

National Labor Tribune (Pittsburgh), 75, 271

National Road, 62, 64–65

Nebraska, 38, 218–20, 266. *See also* Kelley's army

Newlands, Senator Francis G. (Nevada), 24

New York City, 13, 15–16, 142, 246–47

North Dakota, 245, 256, 275

Northern Pacific Railroad: and Cantwell's army, 232, 234; and pursuit of Hogan's army, 154–64 passim; refuses to transport Hogan's army, 151–53; train stolen by Hogan's army, 153–54

O'Ferrall, Governor Charles T. (Virginia): dispatches militia, 251–54; orders Coxeyites to leave state, 249

Ogden, Utah: Kelley's army at, 102–10 passim; mentioned, 86

Ohio, 229, 241–42. *See also* Coxey's army; Massillon, Ohio

Olney, Richard (U.S. attorney general), and Hogan's army, 154, 162; and Sanders's army, 202, 204; and Scheffler's army, 198, 201, 205; mentioned, 20, 218

Omaha, Nebraska: Kelley's army at, 112; support for Kelley's army, 115–23 passim; mentioned, 11, 38, 207

Oregon, 14. *See also* Scheffler's army

Osborne, Governor John E. (Wyoming), 110

Osborne, Russell (Kansas secretary of state), 267

Pardee, George C. (mayor of Oakland, California), 100–101

Parsons, Lucy, 128

Peffer, Senator William A. (Kansas), 32, 169, 173
Pence, Representative Lafayette (Colorado), 250
Pennoyer, Governor Sylvester (Oregon), 198–99
Pennsylvania, 35, 53. *See also* Coxey's army; Galvin's army
Pennsylvania Railroad, 42, 53
Perkins, Senator George C. (California), 254
Pittsburgh, Pennsylvania (including Allegheny City): description, 54–55; reception of Coxey's army, 55–56; reception of Galvin's army, 225–26; reception of Jeffries's army, 242
Populism: and courts, 207; Coxey as a Populist, 246; in Kansas, 201–4; and Kelley's army, 141, 188; and Jeffries's army, 235; Populist journalism, 97, 161; Populist women, 127, 131; response to Coxeyism, 20, 53, 56, 58–59, 169, 182, 194–96, 257; and Sanders's army, 202–4; and Scheffler's army, 198
Portland, Oregon, 11, 187, 197–99
Prendergast, Patrick Eugene, 30, 41
Pullman strike, 220, 240, 277

Railroads: anti-railroad sentiment, 163–64, 193–96 passim; and the courts, 105–9 passim, 151–52, 197–200 passim, 204–5; power of, 58, 84–85, 162; response to Coxeyism, 124–25; and stealing of trains by Coxeyites, 123–24, 149–65 passim, 195–96; and the unemployed, 14–15, 26–27,

84–85; in the West, 103–4. *See also names of individual railroad companies*
Randall's army (Chicago): J. H. Randall, 187; Mrs. J. H. Randall, 128
Rayburn, Representative Sam (Texas), 259
Redstone, A. E., 143–44, 177
Reform and reform movements, 17–20, 47–48, 271–72, 277–79. *See also* Populism
Reno, Nevada, 11, 101, 135
Rickards, Governor John E. (Montana), 151, 161, 195
Rio Grande Western Railway, 102, 106
Roosevelt, Franklin D., 278
Rybakowski's army (Chicago), 11, 283 n.8

Sacramento, California, 39, 101, 134, 262–63
Saint Louis, Missouri: Hogan's army at, 220–21; Kelley's army at, 194–95, 227; mentioned, 11, 255, 265
Saint Paul, Minnesota: Jumbo Cantwell at, 239; Jeffries's army at, 240; mentioned, 14, 255–56, 264
Salt Lake City, Utah, 11, 109, 127, 128, 213, 265
San Antonio, Texas: Fry's army at, 95–96
Sanders's army (Colorado and Kansas): John Sherman Sanders, 201, 204; sympathizers in Kansas, 202–4; train stealing, 201–2; trial and imprisonment of, 206; mentioned, 129, 212

San Francisco, California: organization of Kelley's army, 98–100; unemployment in, 13, 58; mentioned, 11, 25, 82, 130

Scheffler's army (Oregon, Idaho, and Wyoming): composition of, 197; organization of, 197; S. L. Scheffler, 197; steals train in Idaho, 199–200; steals train in Oregon, 198–99; trial and imprisonment of, 200–206

Schofield, J. M. (commanding general, U.S. Army), 162, 167

Seattle, Washington: industrial army organized in, 232; rivalry with Tacoma, 231–32, 235; mentioned, 11, 16, 127

Shepard, Henry, 232–35 passim. See also Jeffries's army

Smith, Anna Ferry: organizes and leads an industrial army, 130–32. See also Smith-Barker army

Smith, Deming, 265, 268

Smith, Judge H. W. (Utah), 207

Smith, Louis. See Great Unknown

Smith-Barker army (California), 130–32, 266

Socialist Labor Party, 132, 220

South Bend, Indiana, 265, 283n.8

Southern Pacific system: and Fry's army, 89, 91–95; and Kelley's army, 100–102, 104–9; and tramps, 85–86, 92; mentioned, 87, 97, 99

Sovereign, James R.: rallies Knights of Labor support for Kelley's army, 188

Speed, George: and Kelley's army, 135, 227, 257

Spokane, Washington: industrial armies at, 237–38, 243, 257; mentioned, 239, 268

Stead, W. T., 31, 46, 84, 247

Stevenson, Vice-President Adlai, 176

Sumner, William Graham, 18

Tacoma, Washington: and Cantwell's army, 187, 245; rivalry with Seattle, 231–32, 235; mentioned, 11, 16

Terre Haute, Indiana, 56

Texas, 90–97 passim

Topeka, Kansas, 127, 129–30, 203–4

Train, George Francis, 144–45, 168, 231

Tramps: Governor Hogg's view of, 94; Governor Lewelling's view of, 202; mentioned, 12, 56, 224, 261, 264–65

Turner, Frederick Jackson, 17

Unemployment: attitudes toward, 15, 278; responses to, 13–19 passim; 27–33 passim, 149–50; statistics for, 1893, 13

Union Pacific Railway: and Kelley's army in Utah, 102; and Scheffler's army, 197–200, 205–6; transports Kelley's army, 110–14, 120; mentioned, 144, 151, 152

U.S. Army: captures Hogan's army, 152–65; captures Scheffler's army, 198, 200; preparations for Coxey's army in Washington, D.C., 167–68; mentioned, 161, 208, 212, 218, 268. See also Military

U.S. Department of Justice. See Lawmen

U.S. Secret Service. See Lawmen

Utah, Territory of, 13, 128, 207. *See also* Kelley's army

Van Vleck, W. G., 92
Veblen, Thorstein, 100, 269
Vincent, Henry: historian of the Commonweal, 42, 148, 272
Vinette, Arthur: organizes regiment in Los Angeles, 98
Violence: in California, 268; on Capitol Hill, 178–81; Coxeyism awakens memories of Civil War, 65, 78–79, 141, 145–46, 168, 252, 267; fears of raised by Coxeyism, 3, 4, 10, 46, 65, 66, 165, 176–77, 267; in Iowa, 193–94; in Montana, 154, 158–61 passim; in Ohio, 196–97; in Pennsylvania, 242; in state of Washington, 201, 236, 238; threats made by Coxeyites, 86, 148, 151, 153, 165, 173; in Wisconsin, 240
Virginia: establishment of Coxeyite camp at Rosslyn, 226, 246, 248–51; and expulsion of Coxeyites, 251–54

Waite, Governor Davis (Colorado), 24, 108, 129, 199, 214
Wallace, Vice-President Henry A., 259
Washington, D.C.: and end of the Coxey movement, 254–56; preparations for Coxey's army, 143–44, 165, 167–68, 172; reception of Coxey's army, 1–10 passim, 172–74, 176–85 passim
Washington (state), 10–11, 231–32, 236–38, 245
Weaver, James B., 19, 140–41
West, Governor Caleb (Utah), 104–10 passim
Western United States: and Coxeyism, 11, 17, 57–59 passim, 151, 184–85, 261, 274; irrigation of arid lands, 57, 276–77; promotion of settlement in, 58, 85; in transition, 274–77; vs. East, 18, 20–21, 24–26, 58–59
West Virginia, 7, 81–82, 186, 230
Willard, Josiah Flint, 224
Wisconsin, 14, 240
Woman's Tribune: rallies support for Coxey movement, 128–29
Women: Edna Harper and Anna Hooten ("Kelley's Angels"), 123–27 passim, 129, 190–92 passim, 227; in industrial army ranks, 125–32; response to Coxeyism, 125, 128, 132, 255; role in Coxey movement, 7, 51, 127, 129, 244. *See also* Cantwell's Army (Carlotta Cantwell); Smith, Anna
Working class. *See* Labor
Wyoming, 110–11